STUDIES IN
LUKE-ACTS

STUDIES IN LUKE-ACTS

Edited by
Leander E. Keck
J. Louis Martyn

FORTRESS PRESS   PHILADELPHIA

Eduard Schweizer's "Concerning the Speeches in Acts" was first published in *Theologische Zeitschrift* XIII (1957) and is reprinted by permission. Hans Conzelmann's "The Address of Paul on the Areopagus" was first published in *Gymnasium Helveticum* XII (1958). The English translation of Philipp Vielhauer's "On the Paulinism of Acts" was first published in *The Perkins School of Theology Journal.* The article is reprinted by permission of the *Perkins Journal* and *Evangelische Theologie.*

Biblical quotations from the Revised Standard Version of the Bible, copyright 1946, 1952, by the Division of Christian Education of the National Council of Churches of Christ in the U.S.A., are used by permission.

First Fortress Press edition 1980

Library of Congress Cataloging in Publication Data

Keck, Leander E   ed.
  Studies in Luke-Acts.

  Essays presented in honor of P. Schubert.
  Includes bibliographies.
    1. Bible. N. T. Luke and Acts—Addresses, essays, lectures. 2. Schubert, Paul, 1900- —Addresses, essays, lectures. I. Schubert, Paul, 1900-
II. Martyn, James Louis, 1925-   joint ed.
III. Title.
BS2589.K42 1980   226'.4'06   79-8886
ISBN 0-8006-1379-1

8022I79   Printed in the United States of America   1-1379

INTRODUCTION

That Luke–Acts occupies a central place in New Testament research is even clearer today than it was when the essays in the present volume were produced. In the first place, the more keenly aware students become of the remarkable diversity within early Christianity, the more intriguing becomes Luke's achievement in bringing the diversity under control so as to write a coherent, unilinear narrative of the church's story. A case could now be made for the thesis that a century and a half of painstaking historical research has done no more than bring us abreast of Luke, as regards awareness of the multiple forms of life and thought among the earliest churches. When, then, we glance into the latter part of the second century and note the gradual emergence of the largely unified Great Church, we are compelled to ask ourselves whether with his two-volume work Luke did not prove to be the most influential author in the New Testament. An affirmative answer to this question can be either celebrated or lamented; it cannot be ignored. Hence precisely because of the integrated panorama provided by Luke, his work remains what van Unnik dubbed it in the opening essay: "A Storm Center in Contemporary Scholarship."

In the second place, Luke's portrait of Paul continues to be discussed, not only with respect to the question of its historical accuracy, but also as a key factor in the interpretation of the apostle during the decades following his death. Several of the present essays directed to aspects of the Pauline question continue to be widely cited, suggesting that they are still playing important roles in our study of the apostle and his earliest interpreters.

Moreover, Lucan theology remains an area as fruitful to exploration today as it was when the contributors dealt with its various aspects. The remarkable dominance during the 1960's of the portrait and the assessment of Luke's theology accomplished by Hans Conzelmann and Ernst Haenchen has been significantly eroded since the appearance of the present collection of essays; indeed, knowledgeable readers will not fail to notice that the collection has played its own role in that development. At the same time, much more than erosion is involved; several of the authors planted potent seeds of a reconceived evaluation of Luke the theologian.

Three aspects of Lucan studies are currently forging beyond the areas marked out in this volume: (1) the Lucan portrait of Jesus; (2) the location of Luke's community and of Luke himself in the socioeconomic map of early Christianity, and the resulting interpretation of socioeconomic factors in the narrative; (3) the literary artistry evident in Luke–Acts. The reader who wishes to proceed through the present essays to such issues as these is referred to *Perspectives on Luke–Acts*, edited by Charles H. Talbert (Danville, Va.: Association of Baptist Professors of Religion, 1978).

The original edition of the present book was a Festschrift gathered in honor of Paul Schubert, professor at Yale and lover of Luke–Acts. Like a number of the contributors, he is no longer among us. We believe that these essays on Luke–Acts continue his influence by stimulating a new generation of students to turn their own attention to the text of Luke's two-volume work, and thus to risk falling in love with it themselves.

LEANDER E. KECK
J. LOUIS MARTYN

CONTENTS

Part III

ABBREVIATIONS

AnLov	Analecta Lovaniensia Biblica et Orientalia
ASNU	Acta Seminarii Neotestamentici Upsaliensis
AThR	Anglican Theological Review
BBB	Bonner Biblische Beiträge
BC	The Beginnings of Christianity, ed. by Lake and Cadbury, 5 vols.
BEvTh	Beiträge zur Evangelischen Theologie
BFTh	Beiträge zur Förderung christlicher Theologie
Bh ZNW	Beiheft, Zeitschrift für neutestamentliche Wissenschaft
BWANT	Beiträge zur Wissenschaft vom Alten und Neuen Testament
BZ	Biblische Zeitschrift
CBQ	Catholic Biblical Quarterly
ChW	Christliche Welt
ConAp	Constitutiones Apostolorum
ConNT	Coniectanea Neotestamentica
ErThSt	Erfurter Theologische Studien
EvTh	Evangelische Theologie
ExpT	Expository Times
FGrHist	Fragmenta der griechischen Historiker
FRLANT NF	Forschungen zur Religion und Literatur des Alten und Neuen Testaments, Neue Folge
HNT	Handbuch zum Neuen Testament
HSCPh	Harvard Studies in Classical Philology
HThR	Harvard Theological Review
HThS	Harvard Theological Studies
HUCA	Hebrew Union College Annual
ICC	International Critical Commentary
IDB	The Interpreter's Dictionary of the Bible
Int	Interpretation
JAOS	Journal of the American Oriental Society
JBL	Journal of Biblical Literature
JJS	Journal of Jewish Studies
JRomSt	Journal of Roman Studies
JSS	Journal of Semitic Studies
JThS	Journal of Theological Studies
JW	Jüdische Wissenschaft
KiZ	Kirche in der Zeit
KuD	Kerygma und Dogma
MThZ	Münchener Theologische Zeitschrift

NovTest	Novum Testamentum
NTS	New Testament Studies
NTTS	New Testament Tools and Studies
OCA	Orientalia Christiana Analecta
RB	Revue Biblique
RechSR	Recherches de Science Religieuse
RGG	Religion in Geschichte und Gegenwart
RHPhR	Revue d'Histoire et de Philosophie Religieuses
RScPhTh	Revue de Sciences de Philosophie et de Theologie
SBHA	Sitzungsberichte der Heidelberger Akademie
SBTh	Studies in Biblical Theology
SBU	Symbolae Biblicae Upsaliensis
SNTS	Studiorum Novi Testamenti Societas
StCath	Studia Catholica
StTh	Studia Theologica
ThB	Theologische Blätter
ThF	Theologische Forschung
ThHKNT	Theologischer Hand-Kommentar zum Neuen Testament
ThLZ	Theologische Literatur-Zeitung
ThR	Theologische Rundschau
ThStKr	Theologische Studien und Kritiken
ThT	Theologisch Tijdschrift, Leiden
ThWB	Theologisches Wörterbuch, Kittel
ThZ	Theologische Zeitschrift
TSt	Texts and Studies
TU	Texte und Untersuchungen
UNT	Untersuchungen zum Neuen Testament
VT	Vetus Testamentum
VuF	Verkündigung und Forschung
WMANT	Wissenschaftliche Monographien zum Alten und Neuen Testament
WUNT	Wissenschaftliche Untersuchungen zum Neuen Testament
ZKG	Zeitschrift für Kirchengeschichte
ZSTh	Zeitschrift für systematische Theologie
ZThK	Zeitschrift für Theologie und Kirche
ZwTh	Zeitschrift für wissenschaftliche Theologie

STUDIES IN
LUKE-ACTS

PART I

Luke–Acts, A Storm Center in Contemporary Scholarship

W. C. VAN UNNIK

I

During my visit to the United States in 1964, a B.D. student came to consult me about his future plans for graduate work in New Testament. He said it would be extremely helpful to him if I could tell him what would be the burning issues by the time he would have finished his studies. My only answer to this embarrassing question was that, because a professor is not a prophet—at least I for one am not—it was impossible to give a prediction. Everyone who has followed the trend of New Testament studies during some decades or read surveys of the history of our discipline knows that a sudden shift may take place quite unexpectedly by which the whole picture gets changed. In the 1930's, who would have been so daring as to prophesy the great discoveries of Qumran and Nag Hammadi, with their immense consequences for the study of early Christianity? We have seen so far only the very beginnings of the materials from these finds. Who knows what is still in store? So I said to my young friend that the proper thing for him to do was to acquire the tools of New Testament scholarship, the languages, and knowledge of the *Umwelt* as well as to study some of the major problems of the moment. In this way he would acquire the capacities to labor in the field as a scholar and not as a parrot.

The theme of this book—studies in Luke–Acts—could also serve as an example of this kind of unpredictability. The editors chose the subject not only because they knew of the special predeliction which their teacher and friend, Dr. Schubert, has for the problems involved and to which he himself has devoted much of his scholarly interest, but also because they were quite well aware that at the present moment Luke–Acts holds a key position in the New Testament field, far more than it did a generation ago. Of course, both for its subject matter and length this two-volume work has

15

never been neglected; on the contrary, one has only to glance through the bibliographies to learn that much attention has always been bestowed upon it, and rightly so. Is there another single New Testament book that has been honored in this century by the monumental and almost all-comprising elucidation of *The Beginnings of Christianity?* And yet in 1950 no one could have foretold that in the next decade Luke–Acts would become one of the great storm centers of New Testament scholarship, second only to that of the "historical Jesus."

For many years Paul had dominated the New Testament field: his relation to Jesus, to Hellenistic religiosity and culture, to Judaism; his own contribution to Christian life and thought stood in the center. Then, after Bultmann's commentary on John and Dodd's *Interpretation of the Fourth Gospel* it might have seemed as though the emphasis would shift to the Johannine problem. All of a sudden, however, Luke–Acts came to the fore. In 1960 Käsemann wrote that the Lucan problem had suddenly become a burning issue.[1] Was this a whim of scholars who, like the Athenians of old (Acts 17:21), were always after something new? I hope to make it clear in this introductory essay that this was not the case, that there were other causes behind it. At any rate, the Rev. Mr. Luke—we keep this traditional name for the author of Luke–Acts without any prejudice—became one of the heroes or, perhaps in some cases, more or less the villain of the play on the New Testament stage.

Even though this development could not have been foreseen some fifteen years ago, the success of Conzelmann's book on the theology of Luke[2] and of Haenchen's critical commentary on Acts[3]—to mention only these two high-water marks in the rising flood—is striking and significant. It should not be misunderstood. It is mainly in Germany that Lucan studies have taken on a new look, and increasingly so. As far as I can see, the impact of these studies on the Anglo-Saxon side is not yet very great, in spite of an interesting survey by Barrett in 1962 and, in a different way, by Fuller in the same year.[4] There is a marked difference, I feel, between this area of studies and the problems connected with the "historical Jesus" and "hermeneutics," which also started in Germany but are now discussed vigorously in America and England too. By setting the Luke–Acts discussion against a wider horizon, the danger of provincialism may be overcome, and New Testament scholarship may develop more and more its international character. Hence I greatly welcomed the plan set up by the editors of this volume, designed with care, to discuss a number of points in the study of Luke–Acts which may appear in a new light today.

This introductory essay tries to outline the main problems involved. In the present state of affairs it is hard to speak about a "debate," because that presupposes that points have been raised and tested, criticized, accepted, or rejected; but this second stage, I feel, has not yet been reached. The real debate has hardly started. I would be very rash if I were to draw up something like a balance sheet; I am well aware of the fact that I am more or less like the man who tells people what game they will see, without knowing exactly how the playing will be, because I do not know the opinions expressed and solutions proposed by the other contributors. I cannot solemnly declare: "Here stands New Testament scholarship in the matters of Luke–Acts," because the present book itself may pass that mark. Still another proviso must be put in. Sometimes one is requested to say whether definite results have been reached and at what points. In the world of sports it is easy to give the answer: stopwatch in hand, one can see progress and, with a scorecard, decide who is the winning party. In scientific research, especially in the humanities and in theology, it is often much harder to reach a clear decision because much seems to depend on personal experience and judgment. Of course, when new material becomes available real progress can be demonstrated easily and previous theories shown to have been false by the new facts. But if that is not the case and one has to work with the same material as before—and this is so with Luke–Acts, since unfortunately no new book by this author or works describing the same history have turned up (perhaps an exception must be made for the Qumran material; see the essay by Fr. Fitzmyer in this volume)—then it is hard to find out if *real* progress has been made. What one scholar finds a valid solution is considered by his colleague as a rather improbable guess. Much depends here not only on certain observations, but also on general working hypotheses which, in the course of their existence, have the tendency to lose their hypothetical character because they are repeated so often. The danger of circular reasoning is real. Besides, it must be said that the number of problems connected with Luke–Acts is so immense that, while on certain details progress has been made, the same cannot be said of the total picture.

In this introduction we shall sketch the questions that have been raised in the present phase of the Luke–Acts debate, the reasons why they are asked, and their interrelation, and show why this part of the New Testament has become such a storm center. In this way a sort of vantage point may be gained from which the following essays can be seen in the right perspective. The object in view is not a survey of recent literature such as was given a few years ago for Acts by E. Grässer.[5] Hence the number of bibliographical references in this article is strictly limited; the danger of needless repetition has also to be avoided, and the present writer did not want to anticipate what his fellow contributors might say. (The contributions to this volume were not written after previous consultation or from one point of view; therefore conflicting statements may be expected.) In any case, those who are interested in titles will find an excellent selection in the recent "Introduction" by Werner G. Kümmel;[6] the rapid growth of relevant studies may be followed in the bibliographies of *Biblica* and *New Testament Abstracts.*

II

What gave this ascendancy to the study of Luke–Acts in the last decade and a half?

It will have been noticed that the present book is devoted to "Luke–Acts," and that we speak of it as a unit. To a certain extent this fact itself is characteristic for the present situation. It is generally accepted that both books have a common author; the possibility that the Gospel and the Acts, contrary to Acts 1:1, do not belong together is not seriously discussed. By almost unanimous consent[7] they are considered to be two volumes of a single work. Though this unity seems so self-evident, it has some far-reaching consequences. In previous generations in only a few exceptional cases, such as Harnack's studies or Cadbury's *Making of Luke–Acts,* was Luke treated as an author in his own right, though he wrote a major part of the New Testament. In the history of early Christianity Paul and John were outstanding figures, whose literary output was dealt with as units even if some of the writings under their names were disputed. But in the case of Luke it was usual to treat his Gospel and his Acts under separate headings. Of course there was a good reason for that procedure; because the Gospel had so many problems in common with Mark and Matthew, it was natural to bring it under the umbrella of the famous "Synoptic Problem." The description of the apostolic age in Acts fell into such a different category, stood so apart, that if it had to be related to anything it had to go with the Pauline letters. So the student of Luke's writings usually had to look in different directions to study the same author.

Broadly speaking it may be said that in the period before 1950 Luke was almost exclusively viewed as a historian. There is a fairly strong consensus that he wrote after the fall of Jerusalem to which he refers in Luke 21:20 ff.; this dates his work between A.D. 75 and 90.[8] (The dating by Harnack in the early sixties, remarkable because of the great scholar's authority, did not find much following.) But on the whole, the question of the date had no particular significance because attention was concentrated not so much on the time in which Luke wrote as on the historical credit that could be given to his testimony. Was he trustworthy in what he told about Jesus, the church in Jerusalem, and the life of Paul? In other words, what "sources" —written and unwritten—had he at his disposal, and what value can be attached to them?

As far as the Gospel was concerned, the main emphasis was laid on the synoptic analysis. The peculiar stamp of the Third Gospel, its universalism, its attention to the poor and the sinners, etc., was not overlooked, but research tried to unravel the mysteries "behind the Third Gospel," as expressed by the title of a well-known book by Vincent Taylor. That Luke had used Mark was beyond reasonable doubt, but that accounts for only part of his material. What about the rest? Why does he have a framework different from that of Mark and Matthew? Did he have good sources at his disposal for the infancy narratives with their particular Semitic characteristics?[9] Did he follow a special source in the passion story? Next to Mark there was the famous source Q. Or is this a hoax of which we have to dispose, as Farrer maintained?[10] In England the views set forth in Streeter's *The Four Gospels* dominated the field for a long time. This type of analysis, with various modifications and reactions, still goes on; as a result there remained a solid core of good tradition about Jesus. In the meantime research in Germany developed predominantly along the lines of form criticism. The usual solution of the synoptic question, the theory of the two sources Mark and Q, was taken for granted, but what was behind all this? In what way did these words and stories of Jesus take shape? Both their wording and setting were often quite different. The Gospels were not written as historical records but as witnesses of the faith. The material they contained was handed down for the benefit of the Christian church, was formulated with the needs of the church in view. By means of minute literary comparison and critical analysis of the wording of the separate units, their framework was unmasked as completely secondary, and the origin of these little particles was sought in Jewish-Christian or in Hellenistic-Christian communities. Besides, the "laws" regulating the growth and preservation of traditions were traced. To many scholars, direct relation with Jesus of Nazareth seemed rather thin in the sources. For our present purposes it is needless to enter further into these questions. What has been said may be sufficient to indicate the direction in which the studies moved.

In investigating the books of Acts, scholarship had to follow other lines because materials for a synoptic study were missing; in many places Acts offers information that cannot be checked, other sources having vanished. Against the view, dominant in many circles during the nineteenth century, that Luke gave a late and rather biased picture of the apostolic times, effacing all differences and difficulties so that his information had to be met with great suspicion, the studies of Harnack and the archaeological evidence brought to light by William Ramsay threw their weight into the balance in strong favor of Luke's reliability. The so-called "we-sections" in the second part of the book seemed to offer a clue to the solution of the riddle: they pointed to some companion of Paul. Since the language throughout the book showed the same character, one man—presumably this companion— must have written all of Acts. In places he showed a very accurate knowl- edge of local usage; so by extrapolation it could be assumed that in other passages, where he could not be checked, he was likewise trustworthy. Differences with Paul, such as the famous description of the Apostolic Council (Acts 15 as compared with Gal. 2), had to be explained by the fact that Luke was not in the heat of the fight itself but wrote more as an objective onlooker. One also tried to discover written sources in the ma- terial of the first half of Acts, and Torrey hoped to demonstrate that behind Acts 1–15 there lies an ancient document which by its language betrays Aramaic origin. Though his argument did not persuade the majority, there was a tendency to accept the view that there were good traditions here, the more so because traces of ancient christological conceptions seemed to be present. Dodd's influential book, *The Apostolic Preaching and Its Develop- ments,* found in the speeches of Acts a common pattern which reflected the apostolic kerygma. But on the other hand, doubts were not so easily settled, as may be seen from Windisch's contribution to *The Beginnings of Christianity* (Vol. I) and from many observations in Lake-Cadbury's commentary of the same series (Vol. IV). Where Luke could be checked more or less, namely in his picture of Paul, he showed a different man from the vigorous apostle of the fight against the "false brethren." So on the one hand there was good faith in Luke's trustworthiness as far as information went, while on the other hand a certain skepticism still prevailed. But the decisive issues were about his historical reliability.[11] An excellent survey of the course of studies is given by Haenchen in the introduction to his commentary, and for the decade between 1940 and 1950 by J. Dupont.[12] It may be added that form criticism was not applied to Acts in the same way as it was to the Gospels. The article by Martin Dibelius in 1923 was a first venture,[13] but for many years he left it there, his great contributions to the study of Acts appearing a few years before his death in 1947 and becoming really influential after his passing away. The situation here was completely different from that in the Gospels. Apart from the inability of scholars to make a synopsis, Luke was not bound by a given form, the "gospel," and had a much freer hand in ordering his materials. For the early Christians the reasons for preserving traditions—or what was thought to be tradition—about Jesus did not apply in the case of the apostles. Not the criteria of form but of style had to be applied, and Dibelius broke new ground by analyzing various parts of Acts, giving special attention to the speeches. The idea that the writer had used the diary of a companion of Paul was rejected; perhaps he had used an itinerary. It was generally held that Luke wrote his second volume because he wanted to show the expansion of the church from Jerusalem to Rome, the capital of the empire; many scholars accepted also an additional motive: the defense of Christianity in the eyes of the Roman officials.

Thus it cannot be said that the Lucan writings, Acts in particular, have suffered from neglect. The fact that our information about the early development of the church is so scanty, and that much of it is furnished by Luke and Luke alone, makes students always turn to his writings to assess their value. But it could not be said that in the period before 1950 Luke's literary achievement was a real storm center of New Testament studies.

It goes without saying—but it may be said nonetheless before we turn to the new look Lucan studies have taken—that the questions raised and discussed by previous generations have not been swept away with one or two strokes since the fifties. They are still being pursued and will continue to be because they are real questions. Let us mention only two examples: the special problem of the text,[14] and the question of the language (Semitisms in this Hellenistic writer [15]) and the style.[16] But since the change of which we are going to speak set in, they must be viewed in a different context. New questions have been thrown into the debate, and hence old questions must be studied from a different angle.

When the deadly threat of nazism had been crushed and German New Testament scholarship could resume its course, it took up a question that had been left out of sight, more or less, by form-critical research, namely that of the final redaction of the Gospels. Form criticism had dissolved the Gospel accounts into small separate units and investigated their origin and transmission, that is, their stages of development before their present state. But what did it mean for these units to be collected and arranged in their present settings? It may safely be assumed that the evangelists were not just playing with scissors and paste, but had a definite purpose in mind. Differences and changes in structure were presumably not made as a pastime. What can be discovered about this redactional activity, and what was the situation which the evangelists had to face in composing their books? [17]

In the case of Luke another factor was decisive in bringing his writings into the center of interest. As often in scientific research, it was basically a very simple question that started the whole change. The unique fact that Luke wrote a sequel to his Gospel was already mentioned. Now the question arose: Why did he do so? The other evangelists wrote Gospels, describing the life and message of Jesus, ending at his resurrection. Luke added another story, this one about some apostles and the development of Christianity as a continuous history, though this story, on closer scrutiny, reveals many gaps. Nevertheless, Acts was not an afterthought or a second, independent work on another topic; Luke–Acts was well planned as one work in two volumes. Does that have a special meaning? Does this deviation from the pattern set by Mark and followed by Matthew witness to a change in attitude and outlook, all the more significant since Luke implicitly criticizes his predecessors (Luke 1:1 ff.)?

As far as I can see, it was Ernst Käsemann who for the first time clearly formulated this question. In his famous paper of 1953, "Das Problem des historischen Jesus." [18] which evoked a revolution in New Testament scholarship by starting the "new quest of the historical Jesus," he made also some remarks about Luke–Acts, contending that the addition of Acts meant that a great change had indeed taken place. In 1954 Hans Conzelmann devoted his book, *Die Mitte der Zeit*,[19] to the theology of Luke in its totality, dealing with both books, not in the form of a "handbook of dogmatics" but describing what he thought to be Luke's theological conception. In this major contribution to postwar New Testament studies, Conzelmann investigated with meticulous care Luke's arrangement of the material and asked, What is behind all this? His book marked a turning point. As far as Acts alone was concerned, the collected essays of Dibelius (1951) stimulated new interest and a new approach. In this field, deep impression was also made by the article of Philipp Vielhauer, "Zum Paulinismus der Apostelgeschichte." [20] Another landmark was the monumental commentary on Acts by Ernest Haenchen (See note 3). In a very characteristic way the author combined great attention for details with an overall view of the whole work; in applying consistently the style-critical method he is always on his guard, asking what was Luke' intention when he formulated his material in such and such a way.[21] The successive editions of the books by Conzelmann and Haenchen clarified a number of points and showed the reactions of their respective authors to the progress of studies, but they did not change their basic conceptions.

The books and articles mentioned also provoked new discussions. One may have serious doubts and criticisms of various points in them, but one cannot deny that they forced New Testament scholarship to look at the problems of Luke–Acts afresh. Hence the questions connected with this two-volume work became burning issues, for they were not just incidental but belonged to a wider whole which, since the Lucan writings cover such a great deal of the apostolic times, is of vital importance for our understanding of the beginnings of Christianity as a whole.[22]

In these studies Luke appeared no longer as a somewhat shadowy figure who assembled stray pieces of more or less reliable information, but as a theologian of no mean stature who very consciously and deliberately planned and executed his work. Luke the theologian differs not only from Mark and Matthew and John but also from Paul, whom he admired but misrepresented. The picture drawn by Luke of the life of Jesus and of the early church had an enormous influence on succeeding ages. But Luke was not primarily a historian who wanted to give a record of the past for its own sake, but a theologian who, by way of historical writing, wanted to serve the church of his own day amid the questions and perils that beset her. This "discovery" of Luke the theologian seems to me the great gain of the present phase of Luke–Acts study, whatever may be the final judgment about the character and importance of that theology.

What kind of theology was it? What were the difficulties with which Luke had to cope, according to this new approach to Luke–Acts? [23] The addition of Acts to the Gospel is, according to Käsemann, an indication of a great change in outlook among the early Christians, because it shows that the church became important and became interested in its own history. "One does not write the history of the church if one daily expects the end of the world." [24] Therefore the addition of Acts signals that the writer does not expect the return of the Lord at any moment. Luke has changed the eschatological message into a historical development. The clearest example is found in Luke 21:20 where the general prophecy has been replaced by a reference to the historical fact of the fall of Jerusalem. The same decline of the belief in the immediate coming of God's kingdom can be seen also in other texts.[25] The eschatological hope is still living and is a part of the Christian message, but the time is postponed; the final judgment lies ahead in a more or less indefinite future and is not the motivating power any more. To be sure, Luke transmits sayings of a strong eschatological character, but they are embedded in material he took over. The place of the primitive Christian eschatology as a decisive power, as a message of momentous decision, has been taken by a "history of salvation," connected by certain links, such as Luke 2:1; 3:1, with the history of the world. He brings a kind of order into the tradition about Jesus. The life and work of Jesus is the beginning of Christianity, and Acts shows the picture of the Christian life in the present work in which the church becomes all important as a guarantee for the Word of God. Within the history of salvation the church is the institution of salvation. This history of salvation has been described by Conzelmann in great detail and with great acumen. It has three phases: the time until John the Baptist (Luke 16:16), the time of Jesus, the time of the church. The difference in outlook was aptly illustrated by Conzelmann in comparing Paul's word, "Now is the day of salvation" (II Cor. 6:2)—where it is present—with Luke 4:21, "Today this scripture has been fulfilled in your hearing"—where this word of Jesus is for Luke a thing in the past, in the life of Jesus many years ago.

Why did this change come about? The answer is found in the delay of the second coming (*Parousieverzögerung*).[26] By the time Luke wrote, the expectation of an imminent return of Christ had been proven wrong by the course of events. The world continued day after day and did not come to a catastrophic end. Was not the whole message completely wrong? The church had to face a crisis and, if it were to continue, had to adapt itself to this new situation of a continuing existence in this world. Luke's answer was the writing of his Gospel and Acts. By the way in which he rearranged the traditional material about Jesus and wrote about the apostles and the spread of Christianity he historicized the message; in short, by his theology in which the life of Christ after his death is continued by the life of the church under the Holy Spirit, by his concept of a "history of salvation" which reckons with history, Luke helped his fellow Christian through this crisis. Barrett also saw a second threat, the coming of the gnostic flood (Acts 20:29).[27]

Haenchen did not stress so much the idea of the *Heilsgeschichte,* which may also be found in other writers such as Paul; rather, he emphasized the "Word of God" as the connecting link between the Gospel and the Acts. The message of Jesus brought about forgiveness of sins and salvation in the judgment; this was given in the time of salvation during Jesus' life[28] but must be preached to all men; the history of this course of events itself awakens faith.[29] In Luke's day the mission to the Gentiles was an established fact, no longer a problem. But by this fact itself a problem was posed, because the Jews had rejected salvation in Jesus and the Gentiles had accepted it. What, then, was the role of Jesus? Was this not a break in the history of salvation? Luke wanted to show that all this went according to the plan of God, that Christianity without the Jewish law was intended by the Lord. And though Luke no longer hopes for the repentance of Israel, as Paul did, he underscores the relation between Christianity and Judaism to prevent Roman authorities from looking upon Christianity as a new and dangerous religion. The way in which he wrote also served to edify his readers, for he handled his material freely in order to create a lively and penetrating picture of the way in which salvation unfolded according to the plan of God.

This last element, the plan of God as the leading idea of Luke's theology, was especially elaborated in Schulz's inaugural address.[30] Accepting Conzelmann's threefold division of the history of salvation in Luke–Acts, he develops the thesis that "for Luke, salvation is there and only there where this *providentia Dei* becomes an event." [31] He sees a link here with the

Roman idea of *fatum,* which in Virgil was the motivation of Rome's destination; Luke had brought this into a Christian context. By various means, some of which he found in earlier tradition (historiography, miracles, doctrine of the Spirit, exegesis of Old Testament texts, and preaching, he tried to demonstrate that this and only this was the will of God.

Luke is a theologian of the second generation which was confronted with totally different problems from those of its predecessors. Therefore, it is said, his theology is so distinct from that of Paul. He admires Paul and devotes half of the Acts to this great apostle. But though he shares with him the conception of the gospel for all men, without the Jewish law, he does not understand him, and he neglects Paul's bitter fight for that freedom. Luke has no understanding of the doctrine of justification by faith as the center of Pauline thought. The speech in Athens (Acts 17:22 ff.) reveals a natural theology [32] of a completely un-Pauline character.[33] In general the picture of Paul in Acts does not resemble that of his letters, which Luke neglects.[34] His speeches are similar to those of Peter and therefore are not Pauline but Lucan. This relation between Paul himself and his portrait in Acts is an old question which has been discussed by New Testament scholars since the Tübingen school of F. C. Baur. But in the present context it takes a very acute form and must be discussed afresh.[35] Does this difference reveal a change in Christian theology and a break away from its original message?

A special area in which we get to know Luke's theology are the many speeches which are interspersed in Acts. They show a great similarity in structure.[36] Dodd and Dibelius considered them reproductions of the apostolic preaching. Wilckens devoted a monograph to these in *Die Missionsreden der Apostelgeschichte,* and concluded that they did not embody traditional material but were formulated by Luke and were closely connected with the structure of the accounts in which they are found. This leads also to a different and much later dating of the Christology in these discourses than was commonly maintained; the Christology is not primitive, the expression of the faith of the Jerusalem church, but that of Luke's own time. The articles in the present volume show that the discussion of the Christology in Acts is going forward in more than one direction.[37]

Because these topics—the discourses and their teaching, the image of Paul—which together cover so much ground in Acts are again thrown into the testing fire of debate, the question of sources arises again.[38] Did Luke have at his disposal written sources, or was he dependent on good, or bad, oral traditions which he changed at will? If he is giving a theology for his own time in historical garb, does there lie behind it real knowledge about the events he describes? To characterize the situation, Barrett uses the comparison of "a screen upon which two pictures are being projected at the same time—a picture of the church at the first period, and, super-imposed upon it, a picture of his own times." [39] Can these pictures be clearly distinguished or are they completely mixed? His treatment of Mark can be controlled. Is this his usual procedure? What is the value of the peculiar material (the *Sonderstoff*) in the Gospel for the life of Jesus? Does the picture of the church in Jerusalem offer features that can be compared with those of the Qumran community,[40] and is his description perhaps less idealized than it seemed at first? Must we make a decision in each separate case? [41] But if so, by what standard? Or is it possible to get a more general estimate of Luke's value for the history of Jesus and the early church?

This leads us to another point that has not received sufficient attention in the present phase of the Luke–Acts debate. Luke is often dismissed as a historian but treated as a theologian. Is this valid? Ehrhardt strongly stressed the fact that Luke was a historian,[42] and Barrett too did not neglect this aspect which he expressed even in the title of his book.[43] In the latter's opinion, Luke would not have understood the distinction be-tween "historian" and "preacher"; Barrett, however, tends to underscore the preaching activity. A decision can be reached here only if the relations, if there are any, between Luke and historiography in antiquity, both in its theory and its practice, have been investigated properly. Far too little study has been given to this aspect of the case. Of course, the statement is often repeated that Luke was a historian not in modern times but in antiquity and therefore could allow himself certain liberties. But a thorough study comparing him to well known historians of his own times is missing. It may be that such an investigation would reveal aspects that have been overlooked so far and which might be important for a proper understanding of his undertaking.

What judgment has to be passed on the result of the theological work attributed to Luke by the current discussion? Eduard Lohse in his inaugural address [44] was rather positive, but in the eyes of Käsemann (and Conzel-mann) the change away from eschatology, with its call to decision and the present relation to the *Kyrios,* to the "history of salvation" was a grave misunderstanding of the true Christian message and therefore harmful. Wilckens, in turn has criticized Käsemann, for in Wilckens' opinion Luke discovered history as "the horizon of revelation." [45] He writes, "In faith's looking back to the history of Jesus Christians now are therefore just as 'saved' . . . as they will ever be οἱ σωζόμενοι in the eschaton." [46] According to Wilckens, however, the defect of Luke's theology is that the death of Christ has no soteriological meaning, that sin, repentance, and Christian life get a much more superficial treatment than in Paul's theology. Here again Lucan theology has become a storm center, because here the issues are part of the struggle of theology as a whole which concentrates itself in this area.[47] The extent to which the theology of Luke may be called a specimen of primitive catholicism (*Frühkatholizismus*) is also a point of dispute which, however, largely turns on the difficult and often widely divergent definitions of what constitutes "early catholicism."

In this brief introduction we could only sketch the frame of reference in which the present study of Luke-Acts moves. The chapters which follow will help clarify and illustrate a number of specific points on which one's judgment must be based. But even after this book the debate will continue because much work is still ahead of us, particularly in the field of exegesis; I cannot help confessing that the exegetical basis for many statements in the modern approach to Luke–Acts is often far from convincing, at least highly dubious in my judgment. Besides, some general conceptions do need testing by means of closer investigation. Let me conclude by mentioning a few items, some in the form of questions, that merit exploration. (1) Has the delay of the *parousia* really wrought that havoc that it is somtimes supposed to have done, or did the early Christians react differently from the way modern scholars would have done? In the light of the history of early Christianity this effect of the *Parousieverzögerung* is highly overrated. The faith of the early Christians did not rest on a date but on the work of Christ. (2) What is the real meaning of *Heilsgeschichte?* Often it is used, so it seems, in a fairly depreciatory way. Is the background an unspoken reaction against certain forms of German pietism? I must confess that I cannot see why "history of salvation" is such a bad thing. Is not Luke often measured by a onesided conception of Paulinism? Or, to put the question differently, was for the early Christians the relation between eschatology, salvation, and history different from that held by many modern interpreters? I am inclined to give a positive answer here.[48] (3) What is the relation of Luke to the Old Testament and to the Jewish picture of the history of that people? [49] (4) It is often held that Luke wrote his second volume as a beginning of *church* history or as history of Christian missions. Are these convenient terms a true description of his purpose? We must not go by our impressions but by the indications the writer himself gives. In the great commission (Acts 1:8) the disciples are not merely sent out but are called "witnesses." From this point of view the whole problem of the relation between the two books comes into a different focus.[50] (5) Would it not be wise to be somewhat more moderate in the questions we ask of Luke? Because he was not omniscient on all events of the apostolic age, it does not follow that he was unreliable in what he does tell us, or that he is a pious but untrustworthy preacher. We must grant him the liberty of not being interested in all matters that interest us. I am sure that if the same tests to which Luke has often been subjected were applied to historians of our own time, e.g. about World War II, they would not stand the test. It would be very wholesome to many a New Testament scholar to read a good many sources of secular history—and not only theological books. Then it would appear that sometimes a single story may be really significant for a great development, and that summaries as such are not a sign of lack of information. (6) Much work is still to be done with regard to the relation of Luke to later writers such as I Clement and Justin Martyr. The book by O'Neill [51] is much overdone and far from convincing in my estimation, but it opens a line that needs to be pursued. (7) The problem of Luke–Acts is also inseparably linked with the wider problem of the "Hellenization" of Christianity. The transition from the Jewish to the Greek world is often seen in simple terms of opposition to the Hellenistic synagogues seen as Christianity's rather questionable and suspect forerunners. It is more suggested than clearly expressed that this transition was betrayal of the real message, the beginning of the great apostasy. But is this true to fact? What would have been the alternative?

The longer we study Luke–Acts the more we are impressed by the highly complex and many-sided problems that confront us. The new approach, by which Luke's writings have become a storm center and will remain so for a long time, has greatly stimulated a critical sifting of the material and opened our eyes for many questions that cannot be passed over in a certain naïveté, though they cannot be resolved by some modern slogans either. What we really do need is a very close and attentive listening to Luke and at the same time a severe criticism of our own unexamined presuppositions.

To the continuing study of this fascinating double volume by Luke, the present book hopes to make a contribution worthy of the subject, and at the same time a tribute to a scholar and friend who has devoted much of his work to this area of New Testament studies.

NOTES

1. Ernst Käsemann, *Exegetische Versuche und Besinnungen* (Göttingen, 1960), Vol. I, 8.
2. Hans Conzelmann, *Die Mitte der Zeit* (5th ed. Tübingen, 1964). Within a decade this book was published in five editions together with an English translation, *The Theology of St. Luke*, tr. by G. Buswell (New York, 1960).
3. Ernst Haenchen, *Die Apostelgeschichte* (Meyers Kommentar, [13th ed. Göttingen, 1961]). Between 1956 and 1961 this commentary went through four editions. See also the articles that went with it.
4. C. K. Barrett, *Luke, the Historian in Recent Study* (London, 1961); R. H. Fuller, *The New Testament in Current Study* (New York, 1962).
5. E. Grässer, "Die Apostelgeschichte in der Forschung der Gegenwart," *ThR* XXVI (1960), 93 ff.
6. P. Feine, J. Behm, W. G. Kümmel, *Introduction to the New Testament*, tr. by A. J. Mattill (Nashville, 1966).
7. Some scholars hold that Luke–Acts originally formed *one* book which was divided in two when it was incorporated into the canon; Kümmel, *op. cit.*, p. 110, rejects this opinion on what seems to me good grounds.
8. See the various Introductions.
9. Cf. R. McL. Wilson, "Some Recent Studies in the Lucan Infancy Narratives," *Studia Evangelica, TU* LXXIII (Berlin, 1959), 235 ff.
10. A. M. Farrer, "On Dispensing with Q," in D. E. Nineham, ed., *Studies in the Gospels*, R. H. Lightfoot Festschrift (Oxford, 1955), pp. 55 ff.
11. The persistence of this question can be seen in E. R. Goodenough's essay in this volume, "The Perspective of Acts."
12. J. Dupont, *Les Problèmes du livre des Actes d'après les travaux récents* (Louvain, 1950).
13. Martin Dibelius, "Stilkritisches zur Apostelgeschichte," reprinted in his *Aufsätze zur Apostelgeschichte*, H. Greeven, ed. (Göttingen, 1951). This essay appears in English as "Style Criticism of the Book of Acts" in *Studies in the Acts of the Apostles*, tr. by Mary Ling (New York, 1956).
14. See the article by A. F. J. Klijn in this volume, "In Search of the Original Texts of Acts."
15. See the recent book of M. Wilcox, *The Semitisms of Acts* (Oxford, 1965).
16. See the article by Henry J. Cadbury in this volume, "Four Features of Lucan Style."
17. See, for example, how this question functions when applied to the birth narratives in Paul Minear's contribution to this volume, "Luke's Use of the Birth Stories."

18. Published in *ZThK* LI (1954), reprinted in his *Exegetische Versuche und Besinnungen* I, 187 ff. The article appears in English as "The Problem of the Historical Jesus," *Essays on New Testament Themes, SBTh* XLI (1964).

19. See note 2; see also his commentary on Acts, *Die Apostelgeschichte* (Tübingen, 1963).

20. This article is included in the present volume as "On the 'Paulinism' of Acts."

21. This approach is well illustrated in Haenchen's contribution to this volume, "The Book of Acts as Source Material for the History of Early Christianity."

22. The interrelatedness of critical questions is clearly evident in Hans Conzelmann's essay in this volume, "Luke's Place in the Development of Early Christianity."

23. The impact of new questions on the post-Pauline interpretation of the church in the world is discussed by Ernst Käsemann's "Ephesians and Acts" in this volume.

24. E. Käsemann, *Exegetische Versuche und Besinnungen,* I, 198.

25. No parallel to Mark 1:15; Luke 21:9 f.; Acts 1:7.

26. See E. Grässer, *Das Problem der Parousieverzögerung in den synoptischen Evangelien und in der Apostelgeschichte,* Bh. XXII ZNW (Berlin, 1957).

27. Barrett, *op. cit.,* p. 62.

28. On this theme, see the article in this volume by William C. Robinson, Jr., "On Preaching the Word of God (Luke 8:4-21)."

29. See Haenchen, *Apostelgeschichte,* pp. 87 f.

30. S. Schulz, "Gottes Vorsehung bei Lukas," *ZNW* LIV (1963), 104 ff.

31. *Ibid.,* p. 105.

32. See the article in this volume by Hans Conzelmann, "The Address of Paul on the Areopagus."

33. This view was critically examined by Bertil Gärtner in *The Areopagus Speech and Natural Revelation* (Uppsala, 1955); he affirms the Pauline character of the speech, though in terminology and literary form Lucan influence is unmistakable (p. 250). See the survey of the discussion in Conzelmann, *Apostelgeschichte,* pp. 102 ff. (as well as his own contribution to it in this book).

34. The problem of Acts and the Letters of Paul is treated in this volume by John Knox, "Acts and the Pauline Letter Corpus."

35. Such a new look is taken in this book by the articles by Vielhauer and Bornkamm.

36. The structural similarity of the speeches is graphically shown by Eduard Schweizer's article in this volume, "The Speeches in Acts."

37. See the essay by C. F. D. Moule, "The Christology of Acts" and that by Eduard Schweizer, "The Concept of the Davidic Son of God in Acts."

38. See J. Dupont, *Les sources du Livre des Actes* (Bruges, 1960).

39. Barrett, *op. cit.,* p. 52.

40. For the many questions involved in this issue, see the article by Fr. Fitzmyer in this volume, "Jewish Christianity in Acts in Light of the Qumran Scrolls."

41. As was said by G. Stählin, *Die Apostelgeschichte* (Göttingen, 1962), p. 8.

42. A. Ehrhardt, "The Construction and Purpose of the Acts of the Apostles" reprinted in *The Framework of the New Testament Stories* (Manchester, 1964), pp. 64 ff.

43. See note 4.

44. E. Lohse, "Lukas als Theologe der Heilsgeschichte," *EvTh* IV (1954), 256 ff.

45. An expression taken over from the systematic theologian W. Pannenberg, whose work marks a new phase in German theology. See *Offenbarung als Geschichte* (2d. ed., Göttingen, 1963), which expresses the starting point of the "Pannenberg circle." To this group belongs also Ulrich Wilckens, whose contribution to the aforementioned volume is "Das Offenbarungsverständnis in der Geschichte des Urchistentums."

46. Wilckens, *Die Missionsreden der Apostelgeschichte,* p. 216.

47. See Wilckens' contribution to this volume, "Interpreting Luke-Acts in a Period of Existentialist Theology."

48. See the discussion with Conzelmann by William C. Robinson, Jr., in *The Way of the Lord, a Study of History and Eschatology in the Gospel of Luke* (privately published). German translation: *Der Weg des Herrn, Studien Zur Geschichte u. Eschatologie im Lukas-Evangelium,* tr. by Gisela and Georg Strecker, ThF XXXVI (Hamburg-Bergstedt, 1954). O. Cullmann's new book restates his views on the subject, and develops the *heilsgeschichtliche* perspective in much more detail: *Heil als Geschichte* (Tübingen, 1965).
49. An important aspect of this question is treated in this volume by the essay of N. A. Dahl, "The Story of Abraham in Luke–Acts."
50. I here refer to my article, "The 'Book of Acts,' the Confirmation of the Gospel," *NovTest* IV (1960), 26 ff.
51. J. C. O'Neill, *The Theology of Acts in its Historical Setting* (London, 1961). See also the evaluation of this book by Conzelmann in this volume, p. 309.

On the "Paulinism" of Acts*

PHILIPP VIELHAUER

The following discussion poses the question whether and to what extent
the author of Acts took over and passed on theological ideas of Paul, whether
and to what extent he modified them. (I refer to the author of Acts as Luke,
for the sake of brevity and in order to identify him with the author of the
Third Gospel. I do not thereby equate him with the physician and companion of Paul whom tradition has identified as the author of the two-volume work, Luke and Acts.) Although one would hardly expect from Acts
a compendium of Pauline theology, the question which we put is nonetheless justified, for the author portrays Paul as a missionary and thereby also
as a theologian, at least in his speeches, which are generally acknowledged
to be compositions of the author and which, according to ancient literary
custom, had deliberate and paradigmatic significance.[1] The way in which
the author presents Paul's theology will not only disclose his own understanding of Paul, but will also indicate whether or not he and Paul belong
together theologically. The question as to the Paulinism of Acts is at the
same time the question as to a possible theology of Luke himself. Acts is
a richer field for such an inquiry than the Gospel, because in the composition of Acts Luke had to master material which was much less formed and
arranged than was the Gospel material; in Acts therefore he was more
deeply involved as an author than in the composition of his Gospel. And
in Acts it was precisely the Pauline section to which he was most required
to give form, for apart from the so-called itinerary, which provides the
skeleton for 13:1–14:28; 15:35–21:6, it does not seem possible to demonstrate
a source (although in the portrayal of the earliest congregation there are

*Translated by Wm. C. Robinson, Jr., and Victor P. Furnish from the article "Zum 'Paulinis-
mus' der Apostelgeschichte," *EvTh* X (1950-51), 1-15, published in the *Perkins School
of Theology Journal* XVII (Fall, 1963); used by permission.

already formed individual accounts, in which one may recognize narrative cycles of the pre-Pauline mission[2] or even a source document.[3])

Since this discussion is focused upon the theology involved, we leave aside the question whether Acts gives an accurate portrayal of the person and history of Paul and of his relationship to the earliest congregation, and also the question (which dominated the work of the Tübingen School) as to the party conflicts within the church which lay behind the discrepancy between the Pauline and Lucan accounts of the same historical events and conditions. We restrict ourselves to the elements of the Lucan portrayal of Paul which characterize him as a theologian; that is, we limit ourselves primarily if not exclusively to his speeches and group the theological statements of the Paul of Acts under four headings: natural theology, law, Christology, and eschatology, and compare them with statements on these themes from the letters of Paul.

I

At the high point of his book Luke lets Paul make a speech at the Areopagus in Athens before Stoic and Epicurean philosophers, the only sermon to Gentiles by the missionary to the Gentiles to be found in Acts. In the formal opening of his address the speaker takes his point of departure from an altar inscription, "To an unknown God," and says to his hearers: "What therefore you worship as unknown, this I proclaim to you." (Acts 17:22-23.) Then he speaks of God, the creator and Lord of the world, who needs no temple to honor him because he is without need (vss. 24 f.), of the divine providence which so determines men that they should seek God (vss. 26 f.), and of their kinship to God which excludes the veneration of images (vss. 28 f.). At the conclusion he gives a call to repentance in view of the impending day of judgment "on which God will judge the world in righteousness by a man whom he has appointed, and of this he has given assurance to all men by raising him from the dead" (vss. 30 f.).

In his study "Paul on the Areopagus"[4] Martin Dibelius has carefully analyzed the Areopagus speech as a whole and in its individual motifs, and has come to the convincing conclusions (1) that the speech was conceived as an example of a sermon to Gentiles, (2) that it comes from Luke and not from Paul, and (3) that the speech, looked at from the viewpoint of the comparative study of religion, is a "Hellenistic speech about the true knowledge of God,"[5] which becomes a Christian speech only at its conclusion.[6]

The speech presupposes on the part of its Gentile hearers a presentiment of the true God and seeks by enlightenment to advance this presentiment to a monotheistic idea of God and to a worship of God without images. It describes God as the creator and Lord of the world (vss. 24 f.); yet the Old Testament idea is hellenized both by the concept "cosmos" and by the motif of God's having no needs, both of which are foreign to the Old Testament and are of Hellenistic, specifically Stoic, origin.[7]

Dibelius' work also made probable a Stoic origin of vss. 26 f.:[8] "And he made from one every nation of men to live on all the face of the earth, having determined allotted periods and the boundaries of their habitation, that they should seek God." This sentence states that men were created as inhabitants of the earth in order that they might seek God;[9] they are inclined thereto by God's providence, which determines for them "times" and "boundaries." Dibelius preferred to understand these terms not "historically," that is, of the nations, their epochs, and their national boundaries, but rather "philosophically," of "the ordered times of the year and the fixed zones of habitation." In opposition to this M. Pohlenz has attempted to support the "historical" understanding, that it is here a question of the differentiation of peoples—their temporal and spatial development, peoples who are here contrasted with the unified origin of the human race expressed in the term "from one" (vs. 26), and he has shown that this concept has a Stoic background.[10] Thus the meaning would be: "from the common origin of mankind, regardless of their national differentiations, God has equally implanted the quest for God in the hearts of men who are scattered over the entire face of the globe."[11] This is an element of the Stoic teleological proof of God. This quest for God is a quest for knowledge, and it is understood in Hellenistic terms as an act of thought rather than in Old Testament terms as an act of the will.[12]

In vss. 28 f. the Areopagus speaker bases the possibility of this seeking and finding in humanity's common kinship to God, also a Stoic motif.[13] Quoting from one or two Greek poets,[14] he interprets this kinship as "living, moving, and being in God" and as being "indeed his offspring." And from this divine nature which is man's the speaker deduces the demand for an appropriate knowledge and worship of God, that is, the rejection of the worship of images. The tone of this demand, however, is not of accusation but rather that of enlightenment,[15] for in continuing he refers to the period of image worship emphatically as "times of ignorance" which "God overlooked" (vs. 30), as he also does in the speech at Lystra (14:16) and with reference to the Jews (3:17; 13:27). The emphasis upon "ignorance" as an excuse is a constant motif of the missionary preaching in Acts.[16]

The conclusion of the speech presents judgment as the motivation to repentance, mentions Jesus (without naming him) and his resurrection as proof of his election (vss. 30 f.), but does not mention the saving significance of his death. Indeed, due to the natural kinship to God and the fact that the knowledge of God is vitiated only through ignorance, this is not necessary. The repentance which is called for consists entirely in the self-consciousness of one's natural kinship to God.[17]

Paul also speaks of the pagan's natural knowledge of God: "for what can be known about God is plain to them, because God has shown it to them. Ever since the creation of the world his invisible nature, namely, his eternal power and deity, has been clearly perceived in the things that have been made" (Rom. 1:19 f.). It has long been recognized and acknowledged that this terminology and viewpoint came from Stoic natural theology. Both for Stoicism and for Paul to know God from nature as creator is at the same time to know oneself, insofar as in this knowledge man understands himself in his relationship to God and in his orientation within the cosmos which is ordered and determined by the divine logos.[18] However in Paul the assertion of the natural knowledge of God is surrounded by statements about God's wrath and human guilt; this knowledge of God has led neither to honoring nor to thanking God (vs. 21), but to "ungodliness" and "wickedness" in "suppressing the truth" (vs. 18) and therefore has called forth the "wrath of God" (vs. 18). Paul states the result of this natural knowledge of God unequivocally: "they are without excuse" (vs. 20).

In the Areopagus speech the worship of images was an indication of "ignorance," but was by no means inexcusable; "you worship as unknown," says Paul on the Areopagus (Acts 17:23), "although they knew God they did not honor him as God," says Paul in Romans (1:21), and that is "ungodliness" and "wickedness." But this means that the natural theology has an utterly different function in Rom. 1 and in Acts 17; in the former passage it functions as an aid to the demonstration of human responsibility and is thereafter immediately dropped; in the latter passage it is evaluated positively and employed in missionary pedagogy as a forerunner of faith: the natural knowledge of God needs only to be purified, corrected, and enlarged, but its basic significance is not questioned. "Grace does not destroy nature but presupposes and completes it."

In Paul there is no parallel to the motif of man's kinship to God. Dibelius rightly points out that the Pauline analogue to this is man's nearness to Christ; Paul speaks of fellowship with Christ, not of fellowship with God, and the man who participates in this fellowship is not the natural man but rather the redeemed man.[19] By sin the natural man is essentially separated from God and hostile to God. The connection with God is only established through Christ, through his death on the cross, whereby God judges and pardons the world (II Cor. 5:20 f.; Rom. 3:25 f.). Only "in Christ" is man united with God.   It is no accident that in the Areopagus speech the concepts "sin" and "grace' are lacking, not only the words, but also the ideas. Due to its kinship to God the human race is capable of a natural knowledge of God and of ethics (Acts 10:35) and has immediate access to God. The "word of the cross" has no place in the Areopagus speech because it would make no sense there; it would be "folly." The author of this speech has eliminated Christology from Paul's sermon to the Gentiles.

To be sure this speech functions only as preliminary instruction, but at this place in Acts and in the function which the author intends it to fulfill it is a self-contained whole.[20] The basic difference from the Pauline view of Christian and pre-Christian existence cannot be ignored. When the Areopagus speaker refers to the unity of the human race in its natural kinship to God and to its natural knowledge of God, and when he refers to the altar inscription and to the statements of pagan poets to make this point, he thereby lays claim to pagan history, culture, and religion as the prehistory of Christianity. His distance from Paul is just as clear as his nearness to the apologists. Justin, for example, counted the Greek philosophers and the righteous men among the barbarians just as much the forefathers of Christianity as were the patriarchs; however he gave this thesis a christological basis, in that he maintained that these men partook of the logos which is identical with Christ.[21]

II

Acts depicts Paul's attitude toward the ancient religion of the Jews just as positively as the Areopagus speech presents his attitude toward the ancient religion of the Greeks. His attitude toward the law is reflected in Acts less in basic discussions in his speeches than in his practical attitude toward Judaism and Jewish Christianity. This attitude is characterized by the following aspects (of which only those of basic significance will be discussed here):

1. By his missionary method: beginning at the synagogue; only after a formal rejection by the Jews does he turn directly to the Gentiles;

2. By his submission to the Jerusalem authorities;

3. By the circumcision of Timothy (16:3);

4. By spreading the apostolic decree (16:4) (nonhistorical);

5. By assuming a vow (18:18);

6. By trips to Jerusalem to participate in Jewish religious festivals (18:21; 20:16). In Rom. 15:25 Paul gives as the reason for his last trip to Jerusalem the collection for the congregation, whereas Acts 24:17 combines both reasons: "to bring my nation alms and offerings." But the account in Acts, having said nothing previously about the collection, thus places the major emphasis upon participation in Jewish worship;

7. By participating, on the advice of James, in a Nazirite vow with four members of the Jerusalem congregation (21:18-28);

8. By stressing when on trial that he is a Pharisee (23:6; 26:5) and that he stands for nothing other than the "hope" of the Jews in the resurrection of the dead.

Acts portrays the Gentile missionary Paul as a Jewish Christian who is utterly loyal to the law. Or more precisely said, it pictures him as a true Jew, since he believes in Jesus as the Messiah in contrast to the Jews who have been hardened, who do not share this faith. This portrayal of Paul in Acts is vigorously challenged as well as untiringly defended. According to Paul's letters, however, the Acts' portrayal of his attitude seems to be quite possible with one or two exceptions; whether it is also historical is another question. [Bornkamm explores this theme in the present volume.]

The agreement reached at the Apostolic Council does not contradict Paul's missionary practice of beginning at the synagogue, for the statement (Gal. 2:9) "we should go to the Gentiles and they to the circumcised" marks off mission areas, not religions. Furthermore the synagogues, with their coterie of proselytes and God-fearers, especially women, provided an advantageous basis for the Christian mission. Finally, according to II Cor. 11:24, Paul submitted five times to the synagogue punishment of the lash. In other words, as a Christian he acknowledged the synagogue's jurisdiction over himself. Also as a missionary to Gentiles, in the diaspora he obviously lived as a Jew and, as long as his task permitted, maintained his connection with the synagogue.

This was for him, of course, not a law but one possibility—even though the one lying nearest to hand—among others which he could make use of according to the demand of the hour, as is clear from his statements about his freedom to become as a Jew to the Jews and as one outside the law to those outside the law (I Cor. 9:19-23). As a missionary Paul entered into the "various particular natural and historical situations of the people with whom he dealt," surrendered his own "national and religious ties" [22] and, without regard for his own preferences, participated in the varying limitations and freedoms of the people with whom he dealt.[23] This was not an accommodation of kerygma to the varieties of religious knowledge or attitudes among Jews or pagans, but an accommodation of practical attitude,[24] and was based in the freedom which Christ had given from Jewish law as well as from every law. This freedom was limited by the tie to Christ expressed in the words "under the law of Christ" (I Cor. 9:21), for whom he must "win" Jews and Gentiles and by the principle of "for the sake of the gospel." Where the substance of the gospel is threatened, there is a situation of witness-bearing to one's faith, a situation in which there can be no accommodation (Gal. 2) and in which those who teach something else are anathematized (Gal. 1:8 f.).

In view of Paul's understanding of freedom one must consider as possible not only his participation in the worship of the synagogue, but also his participation in temple worship, in the observation of Jewish festivals, his assumption of private vows, and his participation in the vows of others as portrayed in Acts 21.

To be sure the motivation of this last episode is highly suspect. This ostentatious participation was intended to disprove the accusations of Jews and Jewish Christians, who charged that Paul was teaching apostasy from Moses to all the Jews of the diaspora, that is, that he was teaching them that they should not circumcise their children and that they should not live according to Jewish customs; on the contrary, Paul's participation in the vow was intended to show "that you yourself live in observance of the law" (21:24). True enough, the Jewish accusations are formulated as biased distortions of Paul's teachings; but it was Pauline doctrine that the Mosaic law was not the way of salvation, that circumcision was not a condition of salvation, and that Jewish "customs" were without significance with regard to salvation. To this extent the charge of "apostasy from Moses" was entirely appropriate. To convince the Jew that the charge was unjust would have been extremely difficult for the pioneer of the Gentile church and the author of Galatians and II Corinthians. For Paul Moses was not a prototype but an antitype of the Messiah and a personification of "the dispensation of death" and "of condemnation" (II Cor. 3:4-18); for him the acknowledgment of circumcision meant a nullification of the redemptive act of Christ on the cross (Gal. 5:1-12). Had Paul undertaken to show that such a charge was unjust, he would hardly have succeeded by performing a cultic work of supererogation. Had Paul followed the advice of James, he would not only have been hiding in ambiguity, but he would have been unambiguously denying his actual practice and his gospel; that is, this would have been a denial that the cross of Christ alone was of saving significance for Gentiles *and* Jews. It is extremely unlikely that Paul participated in this episode for the reasons given in Acts. It is also difficult to assume that James, who knew Paul, his gospel, and his mission, could have suggested such a deception to Paul.

Now it is clear, on the one hand, that Acts wishes to portray James' advice and Paul's conduct as subjectively honorable and objectively correct and, on the other hand, that Acts looks upon the Jewish charges as slander. This last corresponds with the fact that Acts ascribes the motivation for the Jews' hostility toward Paul primarily to their jealous rivalry or to their disbelief in the messiahship of Jesus, but never to Paul's doctrine of the freedom from law (and thereby also from circumcision). But it was precisely this doctrine which was the reason for the Jewish hostility, because it nullified the absolute significance of the Jewish people.[25] If the portrayal in Acts is not a biased distortion of the facts, then it represents the author's own theory of the circumstances, which he sets forth in good faith. Whether or not the action here attributed to Paul is historical, the motivation to which Acts ascribes it is due to the author of Acts and "simply shows that the author wished to represent matters in such a way as if in all his preaching on the subject of the law the Apostle had never said anything affecting Judaism in the very least."[26]

It appears to me that this is also the meaning of the remark about the circumcision of Timothy. In my opinion it is wrong to cite I Cor. 9:19-23 to demonstrate the historicity of this episode. If this passage is not intended to circumscribe the wide area of matters of indifference, but rather has its point in "for the sake of the gospel," then it in no sense negates the basic character of the statements in Galatians on circumcision and its relation to the cross and the sacraments (Gal. 5:2-6; 3:27). Circumcision is never a matter of indifference, but rather is confession and acknowledgment of the saving significance of the law, is a denial of baptism, and therefore splits the church: "Now I, Paul, say to you that if you receive circumcision, Christ will be of no advantage to you." The statement about the circumcision of Timothy stands in direct contradiction to the theology of Paul, but it fits Luke's view that the law retains its full validity for Jewish Christians and that Paul acknowledged this in a conciliatory concession to the Jews.

Paul's statements about his teaching, when on trial, are apologetically formed and reduce his teaching to the Jewish "hope" of the resurrection of the dead—and indeed in the sense of a general resurrection (Acts 23:6; 24:15, 21; 26:8); only Acts 26:23 designates Jesus as "the first to rise from the dead," and at 28:20 it is perhaps the messianic hope which is meant. These statements obscure the essential difference from Judaism, its law and its hope, which went with belief in Jesus as the Messiah. Paul also understands his Christian faith to be in agreement with the law and the prophets and to that extent as true Judaism. This is evident from the Abraham-typology (Gal. 3; Rom. 4) and from the parable of the olive tree (Rom. 11). But in Acts the accent is different; the place and function of the "law which came in beside" (Rom. 5:20) in the Pauline conception of redemptive history is not seen, but rather there is an uninterrupted continuity of redemptive history and the simple identification of the Jewish and Christian hope—precisely analogous to the views of the Areopagus speaker on natural and Christian knowledge of God.

Acts permits Paul to express himself thematically on the significance of the law at only one place; at the conclusion of his speech in the synagogue of Pisidian Antioch after a long scripture proof for Jesus' messiahship, suffering, and resurrection, Paul says: "Let it be known to you therefore, brethren, that through this man forgiveness of sins is proclaimed to you, and by him everyone that believes is freed from everything from which you could not be freed by the law of Moses" (Acts 13:38 f.). Clearly Acts intends to let Paul speak in his own terms; one must however point out striking differences from the statements of the letters of Paul.[27] First of all, justification is equated with the forgiveness of sins and thus is conceived entirely negatively, which Paul never does; again, "forgiveness of sins" does not occur in his major letters, but rather in Col. 1:14 and in Eph. 1:7, and is used in Acts 13:38 in the same sense as in the speeches of Peter (Acts 2:38; 3:19; 5:31; 10:43). Furthermore, the forgiveness of sins is tied to the messiahship of Jesus which is based on the resurrection (vs. 37), and also "nothing is said in this connection about the particular significance of his death." [28] Finally, it is here a question only a partial justification, one which is not by faith alone, but *also* by faith. Harnack was right in saying: "According to Paul the law has absolutely no saving significance, and thus also none for the one who was born a Jew; according to Luke . . . justification by faith is so to speak only complementary for Jewish Christians. It is necessary for them because and to the extent that they fall short of the fulfillment of the law or because the law provides no complete justification." [29]

The same concept of law and justification was behind Peter's words, when he pled before the Jerusalem council for the Gentiles' freedom from circumcision, that one should not put upon them a yoke "which neither our fathers nor we have been able to bear" (Acts 15:10). Also according to Paul men do not fulfill the law, but it has been done away with not for this reason but rather because Christ has put an end to the law. "It is thus the theology of Luke that we have here." [30]

Luke did know that Paul proclaimed justification by faith, but he did not know its central significance and absolute importance; he thought it was valid primarily for the Gentiles. This understanding of justification is a product of his understanding of the law. In Acts the law, together with the prophets, is sometimes the sacred book of divine prophecies of the Messiah and in this capacity is common possession of Jews and Christians. Sometimes, however, it is a collection of cultic and ritual commands and as such is property of the Jewish people and of the Christians who stemmed from them, but is not obligatory for Gentile Christians, who indeed possess an analogue to the law and the prophets in their natural knowledge of God, and because of their immediacy to God do not need to make the detour by way of Judaism. As a Greek and Gentile Christian Luke had never experienced the law as a way to salvation and therefore did not understand the Pauline antithesis law—Christ. Paul's question regarding the law as a way of salvation, regarding good works as the condition of salvation,—the whole problem of the law—was entirely foreign to Luke. Paul's biographer was no longer troubled by a question which of necessity confronted Paul: "Is the law sin?" Either Luke no longer knew the basic nature of the battle over the law, or else he did not wish to acknowledge it because this battle had long ago been fought out. Luke speaks of the inadequacy of the law, whereas Paul speaks of the end of the law, which is Christ (Rom. 10:4). In the doctrine of the law which is in Acts, the "word of the cross" has no place because in Acts it would make no sense. The distinction between Luke and Paul was in Christology.

III

In Acts the contents of Paul's message was in general terms first of all the "kingdom" or "the kingdom of God" (19:8; 20:25; 28:23, 31); then Jesus (19:13; 22:18), "Jesus, whom Paul asserted to be alive" (25:19), "the things concerning me" (23:11), "Jesus and the resurrection" (17:18). In Acts Paul describes the content of the preaching as "the whole counsel of God" (20:27), the gospel of God's grace (20:24), repentance and conversion (26:20; cf. 20:21), and, when on trial, as has already been mentioned, the prediction of the law and the prophets and the hope of the fathers in a resurrection of the dead (23:6; 24:14 f., 26:6 ff.; 28:20).

In Acts the only Pauline statements on Christology of any length are made before Jews, in the synagogue in Antioch (13:13-43) and before Agrippa (26:22 f.). They consist primarily in the assertion that Jesus is the Messiah who was promised in the Old Testament and expected by the Jews, and in the scriptural proof that his suffering and resurrection were according to the scripture: ". . . saying nothing but what the prophets and Moses said would come to pass: that the Christ must suffer, and that, by being the first to rise from the dead, he would proclaim light both to the people and to the Gentiles" (26:22 f.). Thus both the Messiah's suffering and resurrection and the justification of the world mission are shown to be according to scripture. The same motifs occur in Acts 13: the suffering and resurrection of Jesus are the fulfillment of "all that was written of him" (vs. 29). The resurrection receives a detailed scripture proof in vss. 34-37 (Ps. 16:10 is the main proof text, and the mode of argument is the same as that in Acts 2:27-31); the Christian mission is also connected to the resurrection (vs. 32). In addition to these parallels Jesus is referred to by name, is designated a descendant of David, is called "Savior" and, according to Ps. 2:7, Son of God (vss. 23, 33).

In Paul's letters there are parallels to these passages at Rom. 1:3 f. and I Cor. 15:3 f.: Jesus is descended from David and installed as Son of God (Rom. 1:3 f.), his appearing is in fulfillment of prophetic writings (vs. 2). In I Cor. 15:3 f. both death and resurrection are described as according to the Scriptures, and also the burial is mentioned. But according to Paul's own statement this passage is an element of tradition from the earliest congregation,[31] and Rom. 1:3 f. is also acknowledged as a pre-Pauline formulation which Paul inserted.[32] Thus it appears that the christological statements of Paul in Acts 13:16-37 and 26:22 f. are neither specifically Pauline nor Lucan but are property of the earliest congregation.

This conclusion is supported by two observations. (1) Some apparent echoes of Pauline passages which are to be found in Acts 13 and 26 are actually not true parallels. Thus the title "Savior" is employed in Acts 13:23 for the earthly Jesus, but is used by Paul in Phil. 3:20 with reference to the returning Lord (cf. Eph. 5:23, with reference to the exalted Lord). In Acts 13:33 Jesus' divine sonship is understood "adoptionistically" whereas Paul understood it metaphysically and never based it on Ps. 2:7. The descriptive phrase "first to rise from the dead" is a strong reminder of Col. 1:18 and I Cor. 15:20, but means something quite different. In Col. 1:18 the resurrection of the firstborn establishes his dominion over the world, and in I Cor. 15:20 it introduces the final drama of the general resurrection of the dead. But in Acts 26:23 it inaugurates the era of the world mission; that is, Acts 26:23 is not a parallel to the cited Pauline passages but rather to Acts 13:31 f.

(2) The structure and content of Paul's speech in Acts 13 is most closely akin to the Petrine speeches in the first part of Acts (the same constitutive elements—kerygma in the form of a brief *vita Jesu,* a scripture proof, and a call to repentance—the same mode of argument, and the same adoptionistic Christology). The introductory part, which is a brief resumé of Israel's history (vss. 16-20), has a parallel in Stephen's speech, and only vss. 38 f. reproduces "Pauline" ideas about justification. Since Luke in composing his speeches made use of preformed material, as Dibelius has shown,[33] the similarity with the speeches of Peter suggests that the Christology of Acts 13 is also that of the earliest congregation, rather than that of Paul.

This Christology is adoptionistic, not a Christology of preexistence. But it is not this difference in the concept of the person of Christ which separates Acts from Paul, but rather the different concept of his "work," the understanding of the cross. For Paul the "cross" is judgment upon all mankind and at the same time reconciliation (Rom. 5:6-11; II Cor. 5:14-21). With the cross, which Paul understood to involve also the resurrection of Christ, has come the turn of the aeons, the eschaton. In "the word of the cross" it encounters the individual and qualifies his present as "the last hour": "behold, now is the acceptable time; behold, now is the day of salvation!" (II

Cor. 6:2). He who believes this proclamation exists "in Christ," belongs to the new world, is "a new creation." This is possible only in the mode of existence in the church, membership in the body of Christ. But in the cross of Christ *salvation is wholly realized*.

According to Acts, specifically in chap. 13, the crucifixion of Jesus is an error of justice and a sin of the Jews, who despite knowledge of holy Scripture did not recognize Jesus' messiahship; but the suffering and death of the Messiah were prophesied, and the Jews unconsciously did their part toward fulfillment of this prophecy. Nothing is said of the saving significance of the cross of Christ; and consequently also nothing of the reality of "in Christ" and of the presence of the whole of salvation. The exalted Messiah demonstrates his power in the mission of the church by directing the mission through the intervention of his Spirit (13:2; 16:6 f.) and the miraculous effects of his "name." But his power as Messiah is not yet complete; his full messianic dignity will be established only at the parousia (3:19 ff.).[34]

Luke himself is closer to the Christology of the earliest congregation, which is set forth in the speeches of Peter, than he is to the Christology of Paul, which is indicated only in hints. To what extent his own viewpoint accords with the concepts of "the servant of God" and "the author of life/ leader" (Acts 3:13, 26; 4:27, 30; 3:15; 5:31) cannot be determined with certainty. He reproduces them but does not expound them.

IV

After what has already been said about the speeches of Paul the question as to the eschatology of the Paul of Acts has in a large measure been answered. The eschatology disappears. It leads a modest existence on the periphery of his speeches as a hope in the resurrection and as faith in the return of Christ as the judge of the world (17:30 f.), and in this aspect as a motivation of the exhortation to repentance. Eschatology has been removed from the center of Pauline faith to the end and has become a "section on the last things." [35]

But that is Lucan theology. He distinguishes himself thereby not only from Paul but also from the earliest congregation which expected the return of Christ, the resurrection of the dead, and the end of the world in the immediate future, and understood the parousia as the beginning of the new aeon. Paul also lived in the expectation of the imminent parousia—it motivated his mission and determined his relationship to the world as that of the "as if not" (I Cor. 7:29 ff.)—but the turning point of the world's history has already occurred, the new aeon is already there with the saving act of God in Christ (Gal. 4:4). Paul still awaits the conversion of Israel (Rom. 9-11), the redemption of the "creation" (Rom. 8:19 ff.), and a final cosmic drama with the conquest of hell and of death (I Cor. 15), and speaks of "this present evil age" (Gal. 1:4); but he never speaks of the "age to come," because the "fullness of time" is already fulfilled. Characteristically, the Pauline "already" and "not yet" are not thought of quantitatively, and their relationship is not understood as a temporal process of gradual realization. It is a question of the paradoxical contemporaneity of the presence and the futurity of salvation, not a question of a temporal but of an ontological dualism. Instructive for this eschatological understanding of history which is Paul's are his statements in I Cor. 15:20, 23 f., which define the present as the time of the resurrection of the dead, which began with the resurrection of Christ: "Christ the first fruits, then at his coming those who belong to Christ, then the end." With this "then" all of world history between Easter and the parousia is majestically ignored; during this interval nothing more of significance can happen, especially no redemptive *history;* the time between resurrection and return is simply a parenthesis in the life of Christ. With Paul eschatology has become a structural element of Christology.

Luke also held that the new aeon had broken in (Acts 2:16-35; cf. Luke 16:16); that joins Luke to Paul and separates him from the earliest congregation. But the essential has not yet occurred and will take place only at the parousia, which brings the "restoration" (Acts 3:19 ff.); that joins Luke with the earliest congregation and separates him from Paul. The Lucan "already" and "not yet" are understood quantitatively and are conceived in the categories of a temporal dualism which finds its resolution in a temporal process. The time between Pentecost and the parousia is the time of the Spirit and of the progressive evangelization of the world, which is thus an ascending redemptive history.

Pre-Christian time is already characterized in this fashion. In Acts 13:16-22 Paul gives a brief sketch of the history of Israel to David. It is organized under the viewpoint of the steadily enlarging saving acts of God which are continued in the appearance of the Son of David and the Savior, Jesus, "according to promise" (vs. 23). Then follows a report of the gospel history from John the Baptist to the appearances of the risen Christ and the beginning of the mission. Its content is "the good news that what God *promised* to the fathers, this he has *fulfilled* to us their children by causing Jesus to appear" (Acts 13:32 f.).

Here Luke's conception of history as a continuous redemptive historical process is clear. The new aeon is here not because God has set an end to the old aeon in the cross of Christ and has brought forth the new; but rather it has *broken in* because and since God has begun to fulfill his promises, and it becomes actualized further up to the fulfillment. The old and the new aeon are related to each other as are promise and fulfillment, that is, as historical processes. The expectation of the imminent end has disappeared and the failure of the parousia is no longer a problem; Luke replaces the apocalyptic expectation of the earliest congregation and the christological eschatology of Paul by a redemptive historical pattern of promise and fulfillment in which then eschatology *also* receives its appropriate place.

How uneschatologically Luke thinks is apparent not only from the content, but especially from the fact of Acts. The earliest Christian congregations, which expected the imminent end of the world, had no interest in leaving behind to posterity reports on their origin and development. Such an undertaking was possible only for one who expected the world to continue.[36] Collecting, arranging, and chronologically connecting the material in Acts was basically different from the collection of the traditions about Jesus, because the former, in contrast to the latter, did not serve missionary, cultic, and didactic purposes; the establishment of congregations was never the subject of sermons or of catechetical instruction. The purpose of Acts was also not *only* to edify by means of the stories about the faithful, but was primarily to give the historical report—regardless of how far the result was from the examples of antiquity and the claims of modern historiography.[37] Luke thought of himself as a historian also in composing the Third Gospel; according to the prologue he was led by historical interest and was historiographically concerned. For him it was a matter of "certainty" (Luke 1:4), the historical reliability of his report. He was led by the same intention also in his portrayal of the apostolic age under the viewpoint of the mission and spread of Christianity. This undertaking was an enormous prolepsis, which antiquated the apologetically intentioned portrayals of church history in the second century even before they appeared, and which drew the author of Acts intellectually closer to Eusebius than to Paul.[38] However, this can be understood only against the background and as a symptom of an uneschatological Christianity which has become secular.

More essential for recognizing the theology of the historian Luke is the fact that he presented his history of the mission as a sequel and second part of the "first book," the Gospel. Without realizing it he thereby called down upon himself the stern reprimand of Overbeck: "Luke took as his subject the one tactlessness of world historical dimensions, the supreme excess of a false viewpoint. . . . Luke treated historiographically what was not history and what was also not handed down as such." [39] Despite its heated tone, this critical judgment cannot be set aside; Overbeck rightly saw that the congregation's traditions of Jesus were something different from the stories about the apostles, missionaries, and congregations, and that Luke coordinated each to the other in that he made them the objects of historical portrayal. In any case, Acts is not intended as kerygma or as "witness," but as a historically reliable account of the "witnesses of Jesus" and their "witness to Jesus" which they set forth in the power of the Holy Spirit from Jerusalem even to the ends of the earth (Acts 1:8); and by means of this historical reliability Acts intends *also* to make a missionary appeal. When the history of Jesus' "witnesses" gives the continuation of the sacred history of Jesus, then the Lucan conception of redemptive history as history is clearly visible.

To summarize: the author of Acts is in his Christology pre-Pauline, in his natural theology, concept of the law, and eschatology, post-Pauline. He presents no specifically Pauline idea. His "Paulinism" consists in his zeal for the worldwide Gentile mission and in his veneration for the greatest missionary to the Gentiles. The obvious material distance from Paul raises the question whether this distance is not also temporal distance, and whether one may really consider Luke, the physician and travel companion of Paul, as the author of Acts. But of greater importance than the question of authorship is that of the author's distinctive theological viewpoint and his place in the history of theology.

His own theological position seems to me to lie in the theology of history which has been sketched, and which determines his attitude toward Jews and Gentiles and his portrayal of their being united into a church. It is a theology of history which combines the Old Testament belief in the action of God with his people and the Hellenistic idea of all men's kinship to God in such a fashion that though the former provided the basis it was essentially modified by the latter. The absolute claim of the Jews to be the people of

Philipp Vielhauer

God was replaced by the idea of natural man's immediacy to God, and the significance of Judaism was relativized to that of a venerable *antiqua religio.* The unity of the church composed of Jews and Gentiles is not based in the "body of Christ," but in the given unity of the human race, and this is first actualized in the church. The object of the divine action is the entire human race, and this action is understood as a redemptive history whose beginning is creation, whose end is the "restoration," and whose center is the gospel history as a *stage* along the way of salvation. From this viewpoint the author of the Third Gospel and of the Acts writes an episode of history as redemptive history and therefore also redemptive history as an episode of history.

With the presuppositions of his historiography he no longer stands within earliest Christianity, but in the nascent early catholic church. His concept of history and his view of earliest Christianity are the same as theirs; whether he gave these views to them or received from them is a question whose answer could be attempted only on the broad basis of a New Testament and patristic investigation.[40]

NOTES

1. See M. Dibelius, "The Speeches in Acts and Ancient Historiography" (1949) in *Studies in the Acts of the Apostles* (New York, 1956). Unless otherwise designated, all subsequent references to Dibelius will be to this volume of collected essays, although in each case the original publication date will be indicated.
2. Dibelius, "Style Criticism of the Book of Acts" (1923), pp. 3 ff.
3. Cf. Jeremias, "Untersuchungen zum Quellenproblem der Apostelgeschichte," *ZNW*, XXXVI (1937), 205-21; on this point compare now E. Haenchen, *Die Apostelgeschichte* (13th ed., Göttingen, 1961), pp. 22-32; 72-80.
4. *Op. cit.*, pp. 26-77.
5. *Ibid.*, p. 57.
6. *Ibid.*, pp. 27, 56.
7. *Ibid.*, pp. 38-46.
8. *Ibid.*, pp. 28, 35.
9. Pohlenz, "Paulus und die Stoa," *ZNW*, XLII (1949), 83 ff.
10. *Ibid.*, pp. 85-88.
11. *Ibid.*, p. 88.
12. Dibelius, p. 32; Pohlenz, p. 85, n. 35.
13. Dibelius, pp. 47 ff.
14. *Ibid.*, pp. 48 ff.; but cf. Pohlenz, pp. 101 ff.
15. Dibelius, pp. 55 f.
16. *Ibid.*, Cf. Dibelius' comment on I Tim. 1:13 in *HNT* XIII and Bultmann, *Theology of the New Testament* (1951), I, 66.
17. Dibelius, p. 58.

18. Bultmann, "Anknüpfung und Widerspruch," *ThZ* II (1946), 401 f.; see also his *Primitive Christianity* (1955), pp. 135 ff.
19. Dibelius, p. 60.
20. This was not noticed by W. Schmid, *Philologus*, 1942, pp. 79-120, esp. pp. 115 f.
21. *Apology* I, 5.4; II, 10; 13.4. Cf. B. Seeberg, *ZKG*, LVIII (1939), 1-81, esp. 53-69; 76-81.
22. Schlier, *ThWB* II, 497, 11. 37 ff.
23. V. Soden, "Sakrament und Ethik bei Paulus," in *Marburger Theologische Studien* (Rudolf Otto Festschrift), (Gotha, 1931), p. 7.
24. Schlier, *op. cit.*, n. 19.
25. F. Chr. Baur, *Paul* (German: 1866; English: 1876), I, 197.
26. *Ibid.*, p. 199.
27. Bauernfeind warns against putting this sentence "under the theological microscope," and wants Luke to say only: "Paul preached about justification by faith" (*Die Apostelgeschichte, ThHKNT*, 1939, p. 177). But then the decisive question to ask with respect to the noteworthy performance in vss. 16-37 is how "righteousness" has been understood.
28. de Wette-Overbeck, *Apostelgeschichte*, 1870, p. 205.
29. Harnack, *Neue Untersuchungen zur Apostelgeschichte*, 1911, p. 48.
30. Dibelius, "The Apostolic Council" (1947), p. 95.
31. Lietzmann, *An die Korinther*, HNT IX, 1931, pp. 76-77; J. Jeremias, *The Eucharistic Words of Jesus* (1955), pp. 127 ff.
32. Bultmann, *Theology of the New Testament*, I, 49.
33. *From Tradition to Gospel* (German: 1933; English: 1934)), pp. 15 ff.
34. Harnack, *op. cit.*, p. 75.
35. Cf. Dibelius, "Paul on the Areopagus" (1939), p. 58.
36. Cf. Dibelius, *A Fresh Approach to the New Testament and Early Christian Literature* (1936), p. 257.
37. W. Nigg fails to recognize this purpose of Luke when he states: "The intention to transmit history to posterity is, however, not present in the author of Acts" (*Die Kirchengeschichtsschreibung*, 1934, p. 2). Ed. Meyer, who approaches Acts with the presuppositions of a historian of antiquity and treats it with the greatest confidence, misunderstands the nature of its accounts and the way in which they are connected (*Ursprung und Anfänge des Christentums*, I, 1921, pp. 1 ff.; III, 1923, pp. 3-208).
38. Although Luke ought by no means to be characterized as a forerunner of Eusebius in the writing of church history.
39. *Christentum und Kultur*, 1919, pp. 78 f.
40. Overbeck has said some things relevant to this question in an instructive but evidently little noticed essay, "Ueber das Verhältnis Justins des Märtyrers zur Apostelgeschichte," *ZwTh*, 1872, pp. 305-49.

The Perspective of Acts*

ERWIN R. GOODENOUGH

Many years ago Kirsopp Lake said to a class that if Acts is not a basically sound historical document we know nothing of the origin of Christianity. The loss of Acts would indeed be a crippling blow, but it is just as devastating to use Acts as literally sound history. We know, or have some evidence, of much in early Christianity that Acts would never have led us to suspect. A historian who writes without a thesis is a chronicler, not a historian at all. "This is written that" lies behind all ancient history, whether Greek or Jewish. I believe we shall not know how to use Acts until we have some inkling of the author's purpose in writing.

The book presents many acute problems. For example, the Gospel of Luke, presumably written by the same man, paints an amazingly different picture of the importance of Jesus from that in Acts. Luke's Gospel gives us our most vivid picture of Jesus the "rabbi," as Bultmann called him, the teacher of new law and parables. In Acts not a trace of this Jesus appears. Peter says at Pentecost that the Jews had crucified Jesus although he had been attested before them by his miracles (Acts 2:22), but not a single passage connects the Jesus of whom he says, "God has made him both Lord and Christ" (Acts 2:36) with the great teacher of parables and ethics in the Gospel. To say the least, here is a new approach. It seems that, like Paul, the author of Acts will know Christ after the flesh no more.

Again, what has become of the Eucharist? Luke tells the story of the institution at the Last Supper, and while he presumably had the Marcan account before him, he is in some details closer to the wording of Paul for that event than to Mark (Luke 22:17-19; Mark 14:22-24; I Cor. 11:23-25).

*With all the best wishes to my honored colleague of many years at Yale.

Paul not only tells of the institution but shows that the sacrament had the deepest significance in his life. "The cup of blessing which we bless, is it not a participation in the blood of Christ? The bread which we break, is it not a participation in the body of Christ?" (I Cor. 10:16.) The sixth chapter of the Gospel of John, which I think also reflects early Christian thinking as does Pual, is like Paul in showing great concern for the necessity and power of the Eucharist. I agree entirely with Catholic tradition which makes the early church deeply eucharistic. But Acts gives not a single instance of its celebration, or of any sacramental idea connected with bread and wine. The allusions to common meals, "breaking of bread," in Acts 2:42, 46 make no suggestion of sacramental value, and indeed such value seems definitely impossible in the account of the trouble with the "Hellenists." For at that time the "Twelve" said that their business was to pray and preach, not to act as waiters at table (Acts 6:1-2). A man who felt himself a priest administering a sacrament could hardly have referred to the sacrament with such contempt. The "breaking of bread" on the first day of the week at Troas may have been a celebration, but Luke's casual allusion to it gives no hint of anything but a weekly communal meal (Acts 20:7). Bread, Luke tells us (Acts 27:33-36), was blessed and eaten aboard the ship that was wrecked on the way to Rome, but here it is specifically said that the company ate to get strength to swim ashore from the ship before it broke up completely. I can suppose only that Acts deliberately omits reference to current celebration, although to judge from Paul, John, the synoptic accounts of the institution, and the developments in the early second century, they must have played an important part in the life of the early church. I can further suppose only that Luke omitted reference to the Eucharist because for some reason he did not like the way it had developed.

The persons qualified to celebrate had by the end of the first century begun clearly to distinguish themselves as what later came to be the priesthood from those not so qualified, but this distinction, or its beginning, does not appear in Acts. Matthias was simply "counted in" as one of the Twelve (Acts 1:26). The apostles did, indeed, "pray and lay their hands upon" the Hellenists chosen to "wait at tables"; but that this gave the new waiters more than a general blessing is not suggested. The incident is told much like Peter's and John's laying on of hands which gave the Spirit to all Samaritan converts without distinction (Acts 8:14-16). It may have been an ordination, and I rather suspect it was; but in that case the text deliberately belittles it. Acts tells how Paul established "elders" whenever he got a nucleus of converts at a single place (Acts 14:23), and he went to Jerusalem to confer with the "apostles and elders" there (Acts 15:2, 4, 23), but Acts gives no suggestion that they had special sacramental function. I see no reason to deny the Catholic claim that these officials reflect the beginning of a sacramental priesthood; I only say that the text would give no hint of such an interpretation to a non-Christian contemporary reading Acts for the first time. Actually I cannot believe that such a priesthood was not taking form during those years, just as the blessing of bread and wine was reserved for special officials in the Qumran groups.[1] With these groups it was "priests," *kohens,* who could bless the bread and wine, men who would seem to be definitely identified as "sons of Zadok." That this meant literally members of the high priestly families I have long doubted, without any but an a priori incredulity that one in ten of covenanters at Qumran had such an elite ancestry. Jewish inscriptions seem to suggest that a priest was rather an official than always the son of a priest.[2] Similarly "elder" was a title in the synagogues, whose meaning there is quite varied. In one bilingual inscription "presbyter," elder, is used to correspond to the Hebrew *kohen,* priest,[3] but the word is used in the feminine form for women in four Jewish inscriptions.[4] The Letter of Aristeas speaks of "priests and elders of the Jewish community,"[5] a completely undefined usage. We are reminded of the apostles and elders already mentioned in Acts. All we can say of the elders of Acts is that they may have been priests in the new Christian sense, but that there is no evidence that the author of Acts recognized them as such. The apostles had the great gift of conferring the Spirit upon people by laying their hands upon them, as Simon Magus saw with envy, but nothing suggests that this, done properly to all converts, conveyed or implied a special priestly office.

Baptism presents a similar problem. Acts lays great emphasis upon baptism in the Name, followed by the reception of the Spirit for all Christians. But except that it was given now in the "Name of Jesus" the rite itself seems to be the one formerly preached and administered by John the Baptist. He too preached a baptism of "repentance for the forgiveness of sins" (Mark 1:4), exactly what Acts describes as a "blotting out" of sins (2:38; 3:19). A person thus "freed" (Acts 13:38-39) would be ready for the great judgment at the founding of the new kingdom. This is exactly the sort of forgiveness Jews have always prayed for, especially in the great rituals of the high holy days. Paul opens an entirely new conception of baptism when he says that the rite removes one's sinful "nature," that one is baptized into Christ's death in order to walk in a newness of life, now dead to sin and alive to God in Christ Jesus, become a new creature in Christ Jesus. This the Fourth Gospel expressed in terms of a new "birth" of water and the Spirit, a figure that created the great sacramental conception of baptismal regeneration. Even if the figure of birth in the Fourth Gospel is "later" (which, as is well known, I do not think likely),[6] still the new sacramental idea is expressed so clearly by Paul himself in his letters that he must have been preaching it long before Acts was written, since he is the famous hero of Acts. That is, theological and sacramental thinking about baptism was fully alive at the stage of Christianity Acts describes, but Acts does not describe such thinking. Here is another deeply important part of the Christianity of Paul which the author of Acts strips away.

Such misrepresentation of Paul's theology goes, as Vielhauer has pointed out,[7] properly with Acts' rejection of the sacramental, hierachical, and mystical developments of the early church. Vielhauer sees the author as reacting from this to return to a Jewish Christianity. To me, Acts seems to be a piece of deliberate propaganda designed to assure Theophilus that Paul also had preached this faith in a call to men everywhere to repent, be baptized, believe that Jesus had risen from the dead, and await the great Return.

For this the author not only minimized or denied Paul's real gospel, but anchored him in Judaism by making him a trained rabbi. In Philippians (3:2-7) Paul indignantly answers some "dogs" who had demanded that the new Christians be circumcised, apparently on the ground that Christianity was the fulfillment of Judaism, and that they spoke with a Jewish authority Paul could not offer. For Paul goes on to make the most of his right to speak as a valid Jew. He lists his qualifications: born of the tribe of Benjamin, circumcised on the eighth day, he had followed Pharisaic interpretation of the law with blameless zeal. This is apparently the best Paul can do for himself. But Acts (22:3; 23:6) has him claim to have been a Pharisee, son of a Pharisee (that is, presumably both were formal and full members of the Pharisaic party) and a pupil of Gamaliel. No one is in a position to say that Paul had or had not been a pupil of Gamaliel, but I cannot believe that he would not have claimed such authority against the "dogs" if he had had such a distinction. And although Gamaliel was a famous liberal in rabbinic circles, he certainly taught his pupils the law in Hebrew, while

Paul's fluent Septuagint allusions suggest someone steeped from childhood in the Septuagint as John Bunyan was in the King James Version. But Acts has Paul say not simply that he had studied with Gamaliel, but that he had been brought up at Gamaliel's feet. The statements in Acts can very well be only a part of what seems increasingly to be the author's creation of a largely fictional Paul. Paul may have been a pupil of Gamaliel, but we cannot, as is usually done, take Paul's "rabbinical training" as a known fact in terms of which we must interpret his letters. The test will be not the straining out of occasional gnats of rabbinical parallels, but similarity or contrast between the basic *Denkweise* of Paul and that of the Tannaim. Even in so cursory a review as I am giving here, it is still in point to recall that talmudists have uniformally hated Paul's attitude toward the law, and have seen nothing in common between themselves and Paul whatever.

Paul the Roman citizen seems to me in all probability still another part of Luke's fiction. Paul gives no suggestion of Roman citizenship in his letters, but in Acts he claims not only to be a citizen, but to have been one by birth (22:25-29), which would mean that Paul's father had been not only a Pharisee, but a Roman citizen as well. If this were true, the father may himself have inherited the citizenship, but if he was given it personally before Paul was born, he must have got it under Augustus or Tiberius. The situation is possible but so unlikely as to be incredible. For such a distinguished honor in the relatively provincial city of Tarsus, which Acts makes Paul's birthplace, was possible in those years only for a few of the great benefactors of the new regime. Caesar and Pompey had granted citizenship somewhat freely to such people and to soldiers in their armies, but Augustus and Tiberius stopped doing so almost entirely.[8] It is of course possible that Paul's grandfather was a soldier in Caesar's legions, but it is hard to believe. In Paul's own day even an officer of the Roman army with a rank roughly corresponding to our colonel, the tribune who commanded the regiment at Jerusalem and who had Paul arrested, said to Paul that he had had to pay a great sum of money for his citizenship (Acts 22:28). If Paul had been born a citizen, then it would mean that he whom Acts itself calls a tentmaker by trade was from one of the greatest families in the East.

Silas, Acts says, was also a Roman citizen. But he and Paul, according to Acts endured being beaten with rods at Philippi and being put into prison by Roman magistrates. Only the next morning did he terrify the magistrates by sending word that they had done this to uncondemned Roman citizens. The magistrates hurried down to apologize and led Paul and Silas publicly and in honor out of the city. (Acts 16:19-29). Silas is first heard of at Jerusalem as one high in the confidence of the Christian "apostles and elders" there. Paul told the Corinthians that the Jews had given him their thirty-nine lashes five times, and that he had been beaten with rods (apparently at Roman hands) three times (II Cor. 11:23-25). According to Acts it was to stop such a beating at Jerusalem that Paul told the centurian that he was a Roman citizen (22:24-25). I believe Paul's own words that he had been beaten three times with rods by the Romans; but from that we are probably to deduce that he failed to stop the torture by announcing he was a citizen because in point of fact, he was not. That Silas was also a Roman citizen, and that he and Paul had submitted to the Roman beating at Philippi and then demanded an apology the next day, seems a bit of quite unlikely historionics.

We can therefore discuss the problem of Paul's Roman citizenship from only two points of view: first, its inherent probability in terms of what we know of Roman citizenship at the time; and second, in terms of the general reliability of the source, in this case Acts, which alone reports it. It seems to me that we have little reason to accept Paul's citizenship on either count. But we must face the consequences of this fairly, since Paul's arrest by the Romans in Jerusalem and his being sent on to Rome—that is, nearly the whole last quarter of Acts—can then have no claim to historicity inasmuch as it all hangs upon Paul's claim of citizenship and his appeal to Caesar. One detail in that section does sound genuine, namely that he was accused of having taught everywhere against the law and the temple (Acts 21:21, 28). It is the only passage in Acts which recognizes such an aspect in Paul's teaching, but the author implies that such an accusation was pure slander. Yet it is at the core of Paul's letters that keeping the law, even circumcision, is not only misleading but quite wrong for one who has died to the old law and been saved in the new law of the Spirit in Christ Jesus. The text shows, at least, that the author knew very well what Paul was actually teaching.

Just as the author of the Fourth Gospel seems deliberately to have invented a whole new body of teaching for Jesus, and written a romance in which Jesus teaches it, so the author of Acts seems to have invented a Paul who was the great Roman-Pharisee pupil of Gamaliel, one who taught that Christianity fulfilled the scheme of salvation in Jewish history. We have no way of testing the stories of the earlier days of Peter's preaching and the first community, but this early part of Acts sounds to me quite as credible as the nonsacramental Jewish Christianity, of which Acts makes Paul the great exemplar, sounds incredible. Why, then, and when would such a romance have been written?

Vielhauer says he will not discuss the date of Acts in his small study, but he implies that it was quite late. On the contrary, its ending—if, as I think, we have the original ending—would in itself imply that it was written while Paul was still preaching in Rome, although this would require that the Gospels were written still earlier, in the late forties or fifties. To this I see no objection, even if in thinking so I stand rather alone. In neither the Gospels nor Acts do the narratives suggest that the authors are talking of a lost temple and civilization at Jerusalem. Even the warning in Luke that armies will surround Jerusalem and destroy it need not at all have been a *post eventum* reference (19:43-44), any more than are the many vivid portrayals now current of man's destruction by the atom bomb. The possibility of such besieging and destruction of Jerusalem must have stood out sharply in the minds of great numbers of people in that city under the Romans. Siege and destruction were everywhere understood to be the price of revolt.

Dating these books has usually been based upon an assumption that Christianity advanced from stage to stage as a block, that is, that it began with ardent hopes of eschatology (a fact which cannot be challenged) and then turned in solid phalanx to theology and sacraments only as the early hopes of Christ's immediate return proved false. Vielhauer is excellent in showing how eschatology in Paul already by the forties and fifties was becoming integrated with theology, and how in Paul's later thinking it lost its central position altogether, that is, presumably by A.D. 60 or 65. Similarly eschatology was integrated with sacramental mysticism in the Fourth Gospel and in the Letter to the Hebrews. Hebrews, indeed, calls the earlier doctrine only elementary milk for children, and lists in excellent outline the essential features of the Christianity of Acts: repentance and faith (for forgiveness), baptism, laying on of hands (for giving the Spirit), the resurrection, and the judgment (5:12-6:2). The author of the letter wants something more mature in Christianity, he says, and so gives us the great High Priest. He is clearly speaking to early churchmen, or people with their point of view, men who still live on the elementary milk, as does Luke. The difficulty is that simplicity of ideas does not indicate with finality an early date. Many Christians must have clung to the early eschatological hope long after others had practically, at least abandoned it. Indeed, many persons of our own time still hold to it; I myself was brought up in ardent and daily expectation of the Return. But such hopes do not endure with most people: five years, ten years, twenty years—at each milestone those who could live in this tension would be fewer, and men who had deeper values to offer in Christianity would increasingly come into favor. Luke is also retreating from the more ardent expectation, but his solution, as Vielhauer has pointed out, is that of Jewish Christianity. For he sees Christianity not as a new covenant, which superseded the old by offering a mystic and sacramental union with the body of Christ, but as the fulfillment of the old covenant itself.

My own guess, accordingly, is that the author wrote Acts in the early sixties to assure Theophilus that, even though he might have heard disturbing rumors of Paul's teaching, Paul was actually a very great man who preached and lived for what he, like the author of the Letter to the Hebrews, considered the childish milk of the gospel (I Cor. 3:1-2).

Such a fiction could, indeed, have been written at almost any time, but I should guess that Acts is a very early production, written before Paul had died and while the issue was still an acute one.

One wonders if it was someone thinking like the author of Acts whom Paul had in mind when he wrote to the Galatians: "Even if we, or an angel from heaven, should preach to you a gospel contrary to that which we preached to you, let him be accursed" (Gal. 1:8). For no one in the Galatian or Corinthian churches would have recognized in the pages of Acts the Paul they had heard preach or had read in his letters.

NOTES

1. *Manual of Discipline*, 6:1-8; see my *Jewish Symbols*, VI, 135 f.
2. *Jewish Symbols*, I, 179 f.
3. J.-B. Frey, *Corpus Inscriptionum Iudaicarum* (Vatican 1952), Vol. II nos. 828 f.
4. *Ibid.*, I (1936) nos. 581, 590, 597, from Venosa, Italy; no. 692 from Thrace.

5. Aristeas, 310; cf. the "elders and priests" in Matt. 16:21; 27:12, 20, 41; 28:11 f.; Mark 8:31; 15:1.

6. "John a Primitive Gospel," *JBL*, LXV (1945), 145-82.

7. Philipp Vielhauer, "On the Paulinism of Acts," in this volume.

8. See Kornemann, "Civitas," Pauly-Wissowa, *Real-Encyclopädie der klassischen Altertumswissenschaft,* Suppl. Bd. I, 300-317, esp. 313-15.

Interpreting Luke-Acts in a Period
of Existentialist Theology

ULRICH WILCKENS

In contemporary German research on the book of Acts[1] considerable attention is being focused on the meaning and relative value of Luke's theology.
In this discussion exegetical observations and theological persuasions are
intertwined. The following essay undertakes the task of freeing them from
each other, in order to inquire whether the low opinion of Lucan theology
held by a number of contemporary interpreters is exegetically defensible.
This is certainly not to deny a just place for theological reflection in the
historical interpretation of biblical texts; nor do I mean that such reflection
should always be eliminated as though it were the subjective prejudice of
the interpreter. That is neither possible nor desirable. For not only is every
interpretation conditioned by the viewpoint of the interpreter, but, since
the primary function of the biblical texts in the history of Christianity is
to utter compellingly what is essentially Christian, biblical exegesis in fact
always presupposes a theological viewpoint. Nevertheless, the critical element
essential to all scientific exegesis consists of asking whether certain definite
theological thoughts, motifs, intentions, and decisions are appropriate to
the exegetical task. This question is to be pursued in constantly renewed
self-criticism. Before it can be raised in connection with the contemporary
view of Lucan theology, however, developments in research on the book
of Acts must be briefly sketched.

I

Ernst Haenchen[2] rightly sees a decisive turning point in the work of
Martin Dibelius.[3] Before him, the book of Acts had been of interest primarily as a historical work from which we were to glean information about
the otherwise largely unattested history of early Christianity; therefore,

critics were mainly concerned with the question about the sources and their historical worth. Dibelius pointed to Acts as a book, to its literary peculiarity, and to the skill of its author. Of course, Dibelius was one of the most important initiators of the form-critical method in the analysis of the Synoptic Gospels. He taught us to watch for the laws which govern the passing-on of oral tradition. He himself proved the Gospels to be editorial collections of multistratified traditional material. But putting the form-critical question to the book of Acts led Dibelius to see that it is a work whose author gave immense care to the literary task, so that in studying it, literary analysis is of even greater importance.

The important gain resulting from this move becomes clear when one compares the picture of Lucan writings which has gradually emerged since the work of Dibelius and others[4] with those nineteenth-century pictures drawn by the so-called Tendenzkritik.[5] To be sure, scholars who tried to determine Luke's bias (Tendenz) were nearer to being on the right track than were those who merely pursued the sources of Acts, for the former were at least seeking to define the peculiar character of the literary work and its significance in its own historical setting. But the Tendenz critics— at least those of F. C. Baur's time—defined the "tendency" of Acts far too much in line with their own preconceived ideas of the course of early Christian history. They failed to grant priority to the task of deducing from the literary design of the book itself the intentions of its author.[6] For only after that task has been accomplished can the author's intentions be correctly related to the course of early Christian history as deducible from other sources. Here modern literary analysis has created a more solid foundation. It located the source material used by Luke, described its pre-Lucan characteristics, and was thereby able to determine more exactly which portions Luke himself created and how he revised his sources. Through painstaking work it also illuminated the composition of the book as such. Since from a form-critical point of view Acts is without parallel, such work is obviously an important factor in the definition of Luke's "Tendenz." There were no other *Acta Apostolorum* prior to Luke's second volume. The literary subject is his own invention. Literary analysis, therefore, leads us to handle this work with greater fairness and to grasp more precisely the author's aim within his own historical situation.[7]

The same holds true for the Third Gospel. In the first years of form-critical work the editorial material in the Gospels was generally regarded merely as a kind of neutral background from which the pieces of tradition were to be separated and studied. Viewed in this way, Luke's composition of the Third Gospel, for example, was said to show only a certain refinement of literary technique.[8] However, a more careful examination of the literary composition soon showed that it is built upon definite theological opinions of the author, and the same thing can be detected by analyzing the book of Acts. Research thus hit upon the phenomenon of a characteristic Lucan theology.

The initial step was taken in 1950 by Ph. Vielhauer,[9] who critically compared the picture of Pauline theology which appears in Acts with that of the Pauline letters. He did this in order to gain a methodologically sound starting point for his "quest for a possible theology of Luke."[10] In four areas Vielhauer finds irreconcilable differences between the Lucan Paul and the historical Paul.

1. In the Areopagus speech which he put in Paul's mouth, Luke made the Stoic idea of natural theology into an enlightened missionary tactic. As a result, Christian faith in God amounts to the true form of mankind's general religion, and Greco-Roman culture emerges as the true preparation for Christianity. The historical Paul, on the other hand, used the Stoic idea of natural theology as the basis for his scorching condemnation of the sinner (particularly Rom. 1:18 ff.).[11]

2. The historical Paul waged an anti-Jewish polemic against the law, but the Lucan Paul does no such thing. On the contrary, it is as the true representative of Israel that he confronts the hardened officials of Judaism. This shows the distance between Luke's theological situation and that of Paul. To Paul, the former Pharisee, the alternative between Christ and the Torah became a sharp, relentless partition between belief and unbelief. Luke, removed as he was from Judaism, was personally untouched by this problem. In harmony with his theory of the church as the realization of the religious unity of all mankind, he was able to reduce the importance of Judaism "to that of a venerable *antiqua religio.*"[12]

3. The Christology of Acts is adoptionistic and pre-Pauline. All traces of the Christology of preexistence, so decisive for Paul, are lacking. And what is more, salvation rests solely upon the resurrection of Jesus. "Nothing is said of the saving significance of the cross of Christ."[13]

4. "Eschatology has been removed from the center of Pauline faith to the end and has become a 'section on the last things.'"[14] Paul sees the death

of Christ for our sins, and his resurrection, as the advent of the new aeon terminating the old one. Salvation is by the redemptive event (Heils*geschehen*) here and now, rather than by redemptive history (Heils*geschichte*). In Acts, on the other hand, the resurrection of Jesus initiates a history of salvation which finds its extension in the history of the church. One finds in Luke's thought neither the early Christian expectation of an imminent final salvation, nor the Pauline paradox of a salvation simultaneously present and future. Luke replaces both of these alternatives by "a redemptive historical pattern of promise and fulfillment in which then eschatology *also* receives its appropriate place." [15] In this regard, it is theologically significant that Luke wrote his Gospel as the first part of a double volume; the second part is the continuation of the first.[16] Thus, "with the pre-suppositions of his historiography he no longer stands within earliest Christianity, but in the nascent early catholic church." [17]

The catchword "early Catholicism" (Frühkatholizismus) was then energetically applied to Luke–Acts by Ernst Käsemann.[18] In addition to the points made by Vielhauer, Käsemann emphasizes the theological interest of Acts in the process by which the apostles, as eyewitnesses, passed on to the postapostolic period information of the story of Jesus.[19] "The Lucan writings as a whole cannot be understood until we realize that for Luke it is only within the stream of apostolic tradition that one belongs to the *Una Sancta* as the earthly place of salvation." [20] Käsemann, too, regards it as fundamental and decisive that Luke replaces early Christian eschatology with the theory that salvation is realized in a history planned and guided by God.[21]

In 1954 this line of thought was advanced, simultaneously and independently, by Eduard Lohse[22] and Hans Conzelmann. Conzelmann's book[23] received immediate and influential recognition.[24] He explored Luke's redaction of his Gospel materials and found a number of leading principles which converge in a definite scheme: in the initial phase of the history of salvation, God gave to Israel, through the prophets, the promise of future salvation. The second period is the central one: the promise of salvation is fulfilled in the story of Jesus. In Jesus, God's salvation was completely present and effective on earth.[25] His ascension then introduced the third period: the history of the church as the time in which the Spirit is at work. According to God's plan, this third period is characterized by the fact that now the message of salvation, which found its fulfillment in Jesus, spreads from

Jerusalem, the place of its realization, to all nations in order to convert all devout and good people to belief in the name of Jesus.[26] Each of these three periods is a closed entity: the time of expectancy ends with John the Baptist's coming upon the scene;[27] the time of Jesus closes with his ascension; and the time of the church will end with the parousia of Jesus.[28] However, the conclusion of each period does not mean a break in the scheme: Each succeeding period is the continuation of the preceding one, directly building upon its fulfillment. Thus, the story of Jesus takes place in Israel,[29] and the history of the church is founded upon the message of the apostles as the legitimate eyewitnesses of the entire story of Jesus.[30] The history of salvation is one continuous movement in which God's plan of salvation is historically realized.

Conzelmann was also the first to point out that this scheme in Luke's two-volume work is of primary theological importance in light of the historical situation of its author: it gave Luke the means for decisively solving the problem of the delayed parousia.[31] To be sure, he did not entirely eliminate the decisive element in that traditional eschatology: the expectation of the immediate end. Christians of the first generation had expected the end in the immediate future. They had not the slightest notion, therefore, that between the life of Jesus and the advent of the end there would lie a historical period whose theological significance arises simply from the fact that it separates these two key points in time. In the days of Luke, however, it had become a matter of universal experience that "the Christians must take into account the continuation of this world."[32] Luke saw theological significance in this experience and drew two conclusions: (a) the history of Jesus definitely belongs to the past, and (b) Christians must reckon with the possibility of a long period of time before the end. Therefore he molded his Gospel into a *historia Jesu,* and in the book of Acts he put this *historia Jesu* into the mouth of the apostles as the central content of their preaching of salvation.[33] At the same time he saw that the period after Jesus' ascension had its own positive meaning: It was the period in which ecumenical preaching showed the story of Jesus to be salvation for all mankind. Luke's literary decision to write Acts as a continuation of his Gospel can thus indeed be taken to be a theological achievement of the first order. The history of Christianity has its meaning in the world mission, which is not only connected with the salvation of Jesus' history but indeed demanded by it.[34] This understanding of "Christianity as an entity of world history"[35] theologically eliminated the disturbing contemporary problem of the delay of the parousia and gave to the whole of early Christian eschatology a subordinate place in a comprehensive history of salvation. Ernst Käsemann's formulation is caustic but not unjustified in its aim: "If, in the other Gospels, the problem of history is a special form of the problem of eschatology, in Luke eschatology has become a special form of the problem of history." [36]

II

Given these developments, a report on the state of Lucan research in the last two decades could enumerate a multitude of significant observations. However, an essay concerning the contemporary discussion of Lucan theology must focus upon one problem: how Luke understands the structure of the history of salvation. For that problem is the center of contemporary discussion. We ask, therefore (a) whether contemporary research is exegetically accurate in its description of the Lucan picture of redemptive history, and (b) whether it is fair when it evaluates the relevance of that picture for our own contemporary theological concerns and intentions.

Considering first of all the question of exegetical accuracy, the basic assumption proves to be correct: In the Lucan writings eschatology is no longer the decisive, all-inclusive force permeating the whole of the tradition, but merely one topic among others. [37] In its place steps the concept of a continuous historical realization of God's plan of salvation. Various passages unmistakably show Luke criticizing the traditional eschatology, which he considers to be a misunderstanding. [38] However, although it is clearly Luke's theological reflections which one finds in such literary reworking, we must still explore the extent of his originality. At the present time the method called redaction-criticism is luring us into a one-sided concentration on the work of editors. It does not ask with sufficient rigor where their personal achievements fit into the early Christian history of tradition, of which those achievements are certainly one part. [39] We should admit that we do not yet know exactly how extensive a part Luke personally played in forming the theological scheme of his two-volume work. Not everything characteristic of Luke's writings is originally Lucan!

One cannot say, for example, that Luke received a tradition entirely oriented toward imminent eschatology and then, being faced with the delay of the parousia, reinterpreted it in an original way by means of his view of redemptive history. The traditions which he worked into his writings are obviously far more varied than such a simple picture would lead us to believe. Above all, it is very questionable whether his concept of the history of salvation originated as a theological reaction to the problem of the delayed parousia.[40] If one allows Luke himself to speak, then it is obvious that the center of his scheme is the idea that in Jesus the fullness of God's salvation was truly present and was for all time established by the resurrection.[41]

However, this tendency to concentrate all soteriological weight upon the earthly appearance of Jesus was already a very early and influential factor in the Jesus-tradition. It was especially clearly developed in the Son of man Christology, obviously a favorite topic of Luke's.[42] The entire Palestinian tradition concerning the earthly Jesus traced all teachings of the Christian community to teachings of *Jesus*. Similarly all testimonies to salvation were narrated as stories about *Jesus'* deeds. This peculiar pattern is unintelligible unless one recognizes the determination behind it: God's salvation proclaimed by Jesus must be seen only in relation to him. Indeed, it must be tightly bound to Jesus' own person.[43] At the same time, however, a strong expectation of the imminent end determined both the tradition and the life of the first Christians. Characteristically these two aspects became intertwined: The expectation of the end presupposed that the *future* judge and mediator of salvation is *Jesus,* in whom God had *already* made the final decision about the fate of his followers. Thus the primitive church, while thoroughly steeped in apocalyptic traditions, did not usually cast its eschatological expectation into the traditional form of an apocalypse. On the contrary, it passed on its tradition in the form of sayings and stories bound to the person of Jesus. In this way, individual pieces of tradition gradually grew into large complexes, and these in turn became the "Gospel," the appropriate form for the Jesus-tradition. In connection with this form, it is interesting to note that the Gospel does not close with an eschatological vision, but rather with the Easter stories. Despite the important and emphatic place the evangelist Mark has given to eschatology within his Gospel (chap. 13), the determining feature for the total aspect is not Jesus' eschatological message, but he himself and his fate. In *him* the kingdom of God is at hand and the time fulfilled (Mark 1:15); his suffering and resurrection are the goal of the Gospel of Mark. Marcan Christology, in spite of its emphasis upon Jesus' parousia (cf. Mark 13:24-37 with 14:62), is on the whole determined by "realized eschatology" (Dodd). This can probably be partially explained by Hellenistic religiosity, which saw in Jesus a divine being, a Θεῖος ἀνήρ. As the Son of God, he showed forth divine power among mankind on earth. However, the Hellenization of the Jesus-tradition is not the real reason for the strong tendency to focus one's faith so centrally upon the earthly, pre-Easter Jesus. This tendency was peculiar to the body of Jesus-tradition from the beginning.

When we turn back to Luke, we realize that he found this whole rich complex of the traditions about Jesus in a late stage of development. The Gospel form had long since been developed. (Luke 1:1-4).[44] This late stage was the essential basis upon which he thought through the various traditions and traditional tendencies which he found in such a way as to make the story of Jesus the "center of time" (Conzelmann). This fact explains why Luke, while reinterpreting the expectation of the imminent end, never found the delayed parousia to be in any way a disturbing problem. To overstate the matter for emphasis: an essential fact about the Jesus-tradition which Luke received was that it had already basically solved the problem of the delayed parousia by concentrating salvation in Jesus himself and by affirming that his followers participate in salvation now.[45] Only when we recognize that the Lucan theology of redemptive history fits into the history of the Jesus-tradition in this manner can we properly evaluate Luke's personal theological achievement and its significance in the light of his contemporary situation.

It is, therefore, apparent that Lucan theology must not be directly compared with Pauline theology. For with respect to the history of tradition, Luke and Paul stand on different ground. The bulk of the Jesus-tradition was not yet accessible to Paul. One of the most immediately evident and basic differences between Luke and Paul is the fact that Paul makes almost no use of the Jesus-tradition of the Gospels, but rather relates nearly all of his christological references to the preexistent, crucified, and exalted Son of God. To be sure, Paul knows isolated instructions of Jesus (cf. I Cor. 7:10, 12, 25; 9:14; 11:23; I Thess. 4:15), but the complex of the tradition of Jesus' words and deeds obviously did not belong to the stock of his εὐαγγέλιον (cf. I Cor. 15:1 ff.).[46] That becomes quite clear when one observes that some expressions in Paul's parenetic passages are more or less distinctly reminiscent of those which the Gospels transmit as words of Jesus.[47] From this, some have concluded that Paul considered the pre-Easter Jesus with all his words and deeds of no consequence for the faith held by the post-Easter church. Such a conclusion is incorrect, in spite of II Cor. 5:16.[48]

The striking lack of Jesus-tradition in the Pauline letters (as well as generally in the materials we have from the area of the Hellenistic-Christian mission[49]) must rather be explained by referring to the history of tradition. The Gospels on the one hand and the rest of the New Testament writings on the other obviously represent two different realms of tradition. Not until post-Pauline times were the two gradually brought together. When we compare Paul and Luke, we must keep these facts in mind. Paul had no possibility at all of making the history of Jesus the dominating center of his theology. By the same token, Luke could not possibly have built upon Pauline theology since his foundation was firmly laid out for him in the Jesus-tradition. Besides, the two men stood at different points in the history of the church: Luke knew neither Judaism nor Gnosticism from personal experience.[50] And the way in which he consistently shows the Christians to be on friendly terms with the Roman authorities presupposes a political context different from the one found in Paul.

In light of the two historical situations, therefore, we must simply not expect theological agreement between Luke and Paul.[51] This should be borne in mind when one considers those theological differences that have been stressed again and again since Vielhauer started the discussion. True enough, with the natural theology of his Areopagus speech Luke is an apologist who makes Christianity appear to be the final stage of all true religion.[52] Furthermore, he recommends the Christians as model citizens to the Roman authorities. And he is keenly interested in a continuity between the history of Jesus and that of the church, between the apostolic and the postapostolic eras. It was because of this interest that he developed his special notion about the apostolate.[53] In other words, Luke takes very seriously the historicity of the church in the world, and his doing so causes his concepts to be different from those of Paul. Luke takes into account the actual situation of Christianity in his time.

That Luke, in formulating his theology, took seriously the facts of the historical development of Christianity is generally unchallenged insofar as it is a matter of historical description. But because Luke was a theological representative of early Catholicism, he has been subjected to radical theological criticism. Ernst Käsemann has rendered the verdict that Luke, in contrast to Paul and, indeed, to the primitive church as a whole, pursues a *theologia gloriae*.[54] And Götz Harbsmeier has driven Vielhauer's conclusion quite far to form the thesis that the church will always be faced with the canonically fixed alternative between Pauline and Lucan theology.[55] The foundation of such verdict must now be investigated.

III

The reproach lodged against Luke finds its center in the accusation that in his concept of redemptive history the eschatological views of the primitive church were substantially lost. He is thereby held responsible for having severely compromised the very essence of early Christian belief. Early Catholicism, with Luke as its responsible representative, is then seen as the cause of defection from the spirit of early Christianity. This view is shared by numerous German exegetes. Indeed, that it is almost taken for granted is reflected by a remark of Ernst Haenchen to whom "the great surprise" in the latest phase of the discussion is the fact that Lucan theology finds "convinced defenders on the contemporary scene."[56]

The interpretation of early Christian eschatology is, therefore, the crucial area of such criticism. But it is equally important to notice that the discussion of eschatology is also the point at which the previously mentioned interweaving of exegetical description and theological reflection creates its greatest difficulties.[57]

Following Wilhelm Wrede and Albert Schweitzer, Rudolf Bultmann emphatically pointed to a development in the history of religion which is significant for the understanding of early Christian theology: In early Christian tradition the forms of Jewish apocalyptic were taken over, but they were also radically transformed. The nerve of Jewish apocalyptic thought is the expectation of the coming divine judgment in which the ultimate decision concerning man's salvation or damnation will be made. Early Christianity believed this divine decision already to have been made in the death and resurrection of Christ, so that the believers in Christ constitute the eschatological community of those who are justified (Rom. 5:8-11). To be sure, the final judgment as such still lies in the future, but it is a very near future (Rom. 2:3 ff.; I Cor. 4:5), and salvation in Christ has already begun (II Cor. 5:17). The Spirit of God already dwells in the believers (Rom. 8:9-11), determining their daily lives (Rom. 6:4) and their hope (Rom. 5:1-5; 8:24-25). Sin, as the power of the old age, belongs to the past for the Christians (Rom. 6:6 ff.). Although they still live in the old age, they recognize that it is dead (II Cor. 10:3). Because as believers they already are what they ultimately will be (Phil. 3:9-10; 20-21; II Cor. 13:4), it is not the reality of the old age (the world, the flesh), but rather the reality of the new age (the Spirit) that determines their present lives (Rom. 8:12 ff.; Gal. 5:16).

From such data Bultmann drew the conclusion that Christ's being called "the end of the law" (Rom. 10:4) really meant that he was seen as the end of history.[58] In Christ the new age has already begun, freeing his believers from the powers of the old age (sin, law, and death). Thus, the observable reality of world history, which in apocalyptic thought will have run its course by the time of the judgment, is altogether done away with, having lost its meaning in view of the all-important salvation (Rom. 8:35 ff.). Inasmuch as man lives by faith, he learns constantly that the reality of the world in which he lives is "passing away." He therefore deals with the world as though he were not under its power (I Cor. 7:29-31). In such a constant practice of distancing himself from the world (Entweltlichung),[59] the Christian knows salvation to be always potentially present (II Cor. 6:2). For him, indeed, everything depends on experiencing the presence of salvation again and again. It is his future. In it he has a future, whereas the worldly present is merely something which is not yet past and which has no power to bestow a future, since the future of the world is judgment. The Christian, then, lives "between the times," [60] basically removed from the history of the world although still living in it. He belongs to God's future, even though its reality cannot be experienced in a single tangible fact, but only as a future which is realized again and again through preaching and believing. Judging from its own experience, the world, therefore, considers Christian existence to be paradoxical.[61] It comes about as a constantly renewed decision of the believer,[62] just as the presence of salvation in the Spirit occurs in the "here and now," i.e., in the proclaimed word which calls forth faith. The whole salvation event is concentrated in the occurrence of proclamation; the whole of man's salvation is concentrated in the occurrence of faith as response to the proclamation.[63] Thus the horizon of all theology is a definite kind of anthropology whose presupposition is a paradoxical eschatology.[64] From all this, Bultmann draws the conclusion that traditional apocalyptic eschatology, which itself had a historical horizon of "cosmic" dimensions, was basically discarded by early Christian faith. For the pure self-understanding of faith such apocalyptic eschatology was superfluous.[65] In the work of the Fourth Evangelist the consequences of this move were fully drawn. Going beyond Paul, John transposed the traditional futuristic eschatology into a thoroughly paradoxical one, in which "the hour is coming" because it "already is." [66]

Now, if one grants validity to this picture of early Christian theology and then proceeds to compare with it Luke's major motif (that God's redemption is realized historically: that the histories of Jesus and of the church are in fact phenomena in world history), there can be little wonder when Luke's work is considered a catastrophic departure from the earlier faith.

In order to understand such an interpretation of early Christian eschatology, it is necessary to recognize that this interpretation itself has its own place within the history of theology. It stands within the context set by the so-called dialectical theology (also called theology of crisis or, more often, theology of the Word of God).[67] A theological school of thought arose in the 1920's whose point of departure was: God cannot in truth be experienced; he chooses to reveal himself ever anew. God cannot in truth be made the object of our thinking and speaking; he himself chooses to speak first in his Word. And God, by revealing himself in his Word, at the same time makes man—along with everything that is human, worldly, factual, and historical—null and void. Only in radical contrast with the world and man does God reveal himself as *totaliter aliter;* only in God's "No" can God's "Yes" be heard; only in death can life be experienced.[68] Therefore revelation and history are irreconcilable antitheses. In 1920 Karl Barth wrote, "Biblical history in the Old and New Testaments is not really history at all. Seen from above, it is a series of free, divine acts; seen from below, it is a series of fruitless attempts to undertake something in itself impossible." [69] That is a programmatically intended, polemically aimed statement which was certainly not formulated as a result of historical-critical exegesis of the New Testament. It sprang, rather, from reflection on contemporary experience.

When in the writings of Bultmann and many of his New Testament pupils we find similar statements presented as the opinions of Paul and John, while by contrast Luke's concept of the history of salvation appears as a blind alley, it becomes clear that the "theology of the Word" is a basic source for such exegetical judgment. In his 1924 articles, "Liberal Theology and the Most Recent Theological Movement," [70] Bultmann, having accepted the fundamental thesis of dialectical theology, summarized it as follows: "The object of theology is God. . . . God is the radical negation and annulment of man. For this reason, the content of a theology which has God as

71

its object can only be the λόγος τοῦ σταυροῦ; this is for man, however, a σκάνδαλον."[71] From this position Bultmann charged Troeltsch with the very same thing with which Luke is currently being charged: "Christianity is here [i.e., in Troeltsch's writings] conceived of as an innerworldly phenomenon subject to the laws of social psychology; such a view is diametrically opposed to the Christian one. . . . What is even more remarkable is that this view could be considered theological! That results from the fact that Liberalism not only inserted the person of Jesus into the general context of historical relatedness, without qualms, but also believed it could perceive the revelation of God in this historical relatedness."[72] Further criticizing Troeltsch, Bultmann quoted Barth: "The judgment of God is the end of history, not the beginning of a new, second history."[73] And he concluded by saying, "Everywhere [in Liberalism], Christianity has been deprived of its σκάνδαλον; that is, the fact is not recognized that the Otherness of God, his Beyondness, means the annulment of man as a whole, his entire history. The attempt is made to provide a basis for faith, and by this very attempt the essence of faith is destroyed."[74] Thirty years later we find Ernst Käsemann formulating the same argument, but this time it is directed not against Troeltsch, but against the Lucan history of salvation: "Revelation ceases to be God's revelation once it has been brought within a causal nexus. It is what it is only when it is seen as an unconditioned happening."[75]

At this point we must return to the question mentioned at the outset:[76] To what extent do such theological formulations correctly describe the self-understanding of early Christianity and especially of Paul?[77]

Among Bultmann and his students the thesis is commonplace that in Rom. 10:4 ("Christ is the end of the law") Paul implicitly declares Christ to be the end of history. This thesis stands in need of critical examination. First, in support of this thesis, it is quite true that early Christianity, in Palestine as well as in the Hellenistic mission communities, was convinced that in the resurrection of Jesus the beginning of the *eschaton* had broken in. Furthermore, this was an event in which Christians already shared by virtue of the Spirit (cf. II Cor. 5:5; Rom. 8:23-24; II Cor. 3:18; 4:6). Since they belonged to Christ, they also belonged to the complete salvation of the future; they already felt themselves definitely separated from sin and its reality. Christ, dying for our sins and rising from the dead, ushered in the end. To that extent, one may indeed say that Christian existence already has the end of the old aeon behind it. Paul, especially, emphasized this point.

The gift of eschatological, actual righteousness *already* belongs to the believers (Rom. 3:21-22) insofar as they have taken part in the life and death of Christ (Rom. 6:3-11). They are therefore separated from sin, law, and death, being removed from the threat of these powers. This "no longer" is valid "now" (cf. Gal. 4:7; Rom. 7:5-6; 8:1). To be sure, Christians are still vulnerable to the constant attempt of sin to re-enslave them (cf. Rom. 6:12 ff.; I Cor. 10:12-13). There is still the possibility of relapsing into the belief that the way of salvation is offered by keeping the law (Gal. 5:3-4). Suffering, transitoriness, and death are still at work on the earthly body (Rom. 8:18 ff.), but the believer must realize that ἐν Χριστῷ both his life and his destiny are freed from the power of these powers. He must live according to the Spirit and not according to the flesh: ἐν καινότητι πνεύματος καὶ οὐ παλαιότητι γράμματος (Rom. 7:6).

However, what must not be overlooked is this: the Christian theology of Paul, however harshly antagonistic against the Jewish one it may be, agrees entirely with the latter in regard to this scheme of eschatological dualism. The so-called apocalyptic theology, which is the background of Paul's thinking,[78] also presupposed a sharp separation between the just and the unjust. The small group of the just was viewed as surrounded and harassed by the mass of evildoers. On the surface, it seems that the evildoers are the masters of world history. However, in reality, i.e., seen from the viewpoint of God who leads history toward its end, they are approaching final perdition. The just, on the other hand, await final salvation which God has prepared as their destiny. Thus for Jewish apocalyptic as for Paul, the present world and the reality of evil coincide. "This age" is an age of evil (cf. Gal. 1:4) which will be brought to its end. Both for Paul and for the Jewish apocalyptic the just are already separated from evil and evildoers. Indeed, they are separated just as sharply as the final judgment of God will draw the line between both groups. Until then the just, to be sure, are being harassed, maligned, and persecuted; until then they are being tempted again and again into apostasy and sin, and are marked by suffering and death. But in spite of all this, these just ones of apocalyptic Judaism know that they are and will be ultimately justified, whereas the evildoers are and will be ultimately judged. They know that their community is and will be the heir of salvation, whereas the other one is the *massa perditionis*. The final judgment will complete both the evil of the evildoers and the righteousness of the just ones. The end, then, does not represent a demolition of history but rather its sum and completion.[79] To be sure, the end event is expected as an act of God which will largely overturn currently existing circumstances: the proud, prosperous, reveling evildoers will be changed into the poor, tormented, eternally lost and dead ones; the poor, tormented, just ones who suffer unto death will be changed into the eternally living who are endowed with the riches of the glory of God in perfect happiness. But the New which will come about in this great change is not entirely new. In God's eyes it is the realization of his will which from the beginning planned for the fulfillment of his election and the complete annihilation of evil.

Thus, with regard to the scheme of eschatological dualism, Paul and Jewish apocalypticism are in essential agreement. To be sure, there is also a sharp and radical contrast, but the contrast cannot be correctly understood unless it is seen within the context of this agreement. The contrast rests in the fact that, according to Paul, it is not the righteous but the sinner whom God will ultimately and definitively justify. All men, especially the Jews boasting of righteousness, have proved themselves by their works to be evildoers. Thus all deserve ultimate perdition. But God has brought about salvation for all; he caused his Son to die vicariously, and he raised the Crucified One by his power. The righteousness of those who are justified finds its basis, therefore, in the Christ-event, not in the law. It is righteousness by faith and not by works. The separation between righteousness and evil, then, is measured by the gospel of Christ and not by the law. Paul speaks of devout Jews who consider themselves ultimately righteous by virtue of their alleged fulfillment of the law through works. According to him, they are in fact replaced by the believing Christians who know themselves to be the truly righteous and sole recipients of final salvation by virtue of the Christ-event. For in the Christ-event God denied to the law all redemptive power and made belief in Christ the sole criterion of eschatological participation in salvation. To those who are under the law (ἐν νόμῳ) this decision on the part of God appears to be something wholly new: a καινὴ διαθήκη (II Cor. 3:6 ff.). To the believing Christian, however, God's decision of love in Christ is the actualization of his electing the patriarchs of ancient Israel. Abraham is the father of present-day believing Christians.[80] In Christ, God has justified sinners, so that the Gentiles now share his salvation on an equal footing with the Jews. And he will ultimately bring the "hardened" Israelites back home into the realm of his election (Rom. 11:25 ff.).

This means that Paul in behalf of the Christian kerygma endorses the Jewish belief concerning God's act of salvation in election and final fulfillment. The kerygma proclaims the ultimate wondrous realization of election through the resurrection of Jesus who died for the salvation of sinners. *Christ as the end of the law is the consummation of God's history of election-salvation.* Where Christ is preached and accepted, God is the God of Jewish tradition, the God of Abraham, Isaac, and Jacob, the God of election whose faithfulness does not waver, the God of Scripture and its promises. The frame of redemptive history which the early Christian kerygma used is in fact essential to that kerygma.[81] In this respect, Luke with his concept of redemptive history stands indeed within a broad early Christian tradition. So the question seems justified, whether a critical comparison of Luke with Paul should not find this profound theological agreement between them of greater importance than is generally assumed.[82]

One may pursue this question by asking to what extent Luke abandons the earliest kerygma by presenting the life of Jesus and the development of Christianity as historical phenomena.

Paul was still convinced, to be sure, that the final events were very close at hand. He viewed the resurrection of Christ and his expected parousia as a single eschatological unit of events. It did not occur to him to attempt a careful definition of the place occupied by the Christian between the poles of the resurrection and the parousia. Even Paul notices, however, that the passing of time indicates the progressing advancement toward final participation in salvation (Rom. 13:11). And still more important, he understands the Gentiles to be significant precisely in connection with the history of salvation. Thus, for him as for Luke, the period between Easter and the parousia is important in view of the end of the history of salvation. From the time he was called as apostle to the Gentiles he knew himself to be confronted with a tremendous task: In a huge geographical circle which centers in Jerusalem and, progressing from west to east, includes the whole world of antiquity, he is to bring the gospel to its completion (Rom. 15:19). His work, then, follows a very precise, historically concrete plan, regardless of how near its eschatological horizon may be. And it is God himself who has given Paul this plan (II Cor. 10:12 ff.). Nowhere is it clearer than here how inaccurate it is to speak of Pauline eschatology as if it were concentrated in the here and now, how inaccurate to say that for Paul the gospel is "fulfilled" when it is heard and accepted here and there by an individual.

On the contrary, Paul understands its fulfillment to be a thoroughly historical process which includes as highly significant elements the growth of faith in the newly founded churches and, more important, the systematic founding of more and more churches throughout the known world. To be sure, the urgency with which Paul pursues his missionary work reflects his expectation of the imminent end. And this kind of urgency is missing in Luke's history of missions. But does that mean that a basic change lies before us in Luke's understanding of missions? How clearly the book of Acts presents the Christian mission as playing a divine and important role in the history of salvation! With what emphasis does it show that Paul's missionary activities are carried out according to divine plan! And how thoroughly does Luke show the redemptive meaning of all church history as a worldwide mission movement! In these respects Luke is entirely in harmony with Paul's view, even if he does not employ the same concepts.

The way in which early Christian thinking about eschatology and history is currently understood under the influence of dialectic theology seems woefully inadequate. We are told that this understanding is characteristic of Paul, and we hear Luke being castigated as the theologian of early Catholicism who surrendered this understanding. But it is most assuredly not the opinion of the historical Paul that "history means the perpetually new decision of the individual." [83] It must be granted that in Paul's understanding the gospel of Christ must be accepted by the individual, and that Christian living is the responsibility of every individual. But just as Christian living is not really an accumulation of momentary "decisions" in which the gospel must perpetually be accepted anew, so the individual believer does not really determine the horizon of the Pauline understanding of Christianity. On the contrary, this horizon is the "history of salvation." The question asked by Ernst Fuchs, "But does salvation have a history?" [84] must be answered in the affirmative both for Paul and for Luke, however different the details may be. For the thinking of both rests upon Old Testament and Jewish belief according to which God realizes his salvation in historical events. Regardless of how deeply it concerns the individual, it goes much further, since it is concerned with the nations, the world. Regardless of how much it has its "here and now," it truly makes all history its field of operations.

This, then, is not the area in which to differentiate between Paul and Luke.[85] The fact that at the present time it is being done anyway can be traced to the exegesis not of Luke's writings but of Paul's. It is Paul, interpreted existentially, who is so sharply set against Luke as the great but dangerous corrupter of the Pauline gospel. But the existentially interpreted Paul is not the historical Paul. And the essential points of theological criticism leveled against Luke are gained not so much from early Christian tradition itself as from the motifs of a certain modern school of theology which disregards or misinterprets essential aspects of early Christian thought. Recognition of these errors may well enliven the discussion of Luke's theology; for Luke, thus freed, is given the possibility of greatly stimulating our own thinking without compelling us to choose between himself and Paul.

NOTES

1. The following essay confines itself to this research. It therefore does not consider non-German literature except for items which belong in the specifically German theological discussion of Luke. Cf. the reports on recent research by J. Dupont, "Les problèmes du livre des Actes d'après les travaux recents" (An. Lov. II, 17) Louvain 1950; W. G. Kümmel, "Das Urchristentum," *ThR* (NF), XXII (1954), 191 ff.; E. Grässer, "Die Apostelgeschichte in der Forschung der Gegenwart," *ThR* (NF), XXVI (1960), 93-167.
2. *Die Apostelgeschichte* (Meyers Kommentar [13th ed. Göttingen, 1961]). Somewhat differently, the short survey by E. Trocmé, "Le 'Livre des Actes' et l'Histoire" (Paris, 1957), pp. 1-19.
3. Cf. the collection of his essays in *Studies in Acts*. In this context, I must also refer to the book by H. J. Cadbury, *The Making of Luke–Acts* (1st ed. 1927). Parallel to the labors of M. Dibelius, Cadbury's work considered the literary problem of Acts and greatly influenced German research on Acts.
4. Besides Dibelius, the commentary on Acts by O. Bauernfeind in *ThHKNT*, V (Leipzig, 1939) should be named first of all; also the commentaries by E. Haenchen (cf. n. 2 above) and H. Conzelmann in *HNT*, VII (1963).
5. Cf. Haenchen, *op. cit.*, pp. 14 ff.
6. This does not hold quite true of F. Overbeck's works on Acts; cf. Ph. Vielhauer, "Franz Overbeck und die neutestamentliche Wissenschaft," *EvTh*, X (1950-51), 193-207.
7. I am not at all arguing that Acts should not be consulted also in regard to the historical value of its text. On the contrary, a detailed literary analysis allows us to define historical questions ever so much more exactly. It must be granted, though, that in contemporary German research the historical questions are sadly neglected in favor of the theological ones.
8. K. L. Schmidt, *Der Rahmen der Geschichte Jesu* (Berlin, 1919). On pp. 316-17 he acknowledges certain "literary aspirations" of the author of the Third Gospel. However, since he was mainly concerned with source criticism for the sake of historical reliability—and in his opinion Luke's Gospel proved of little worth in this regard—he found these literary aspirations quite uninteresting. Also Bultmann in *History of the Synoptic Tradition*. On pp. 358-367 he merely points out certain literary-technical features and otherwise is of the opinion that "[Luke] does not permit his dogmatic conceptions to exercise any essential influence on his work" (366). "We can speak of any leading ideas in Luke's presentation only to a very limited extent" (366). Dibelius even expressed similar judgments about Luke's personal involvement in the Third Gospel; cf.—besides his *From Tradition to Gospel*

(New York Scribner's 1935, *passim*)—his "Geschichte der urchristlichen Literatur" (Sammlung Goeschen, I, 45 ff.; II, 98 ff.).

9. "On the Paulinism of Acts" in the present vol.

10. *Ibid.*, p. 33.

11. *Ibid.*, p. 36.

12. *Ibid.*, p. 49.

13. *Ibid.*, p. 45. Cf. also Conzelmann, *The Theology of St. Luke*, pp. 213 f.; *Die Mitte der Zeit* (5th ed. Tübingen, 1964), pp. 187-88; Haenchen, *op. cit.*, p. 82; Wilckens, *Die Missionsreden der Apostelgeschichte* (2nd ed. Neukirchen, 1963), pp. 77, 184-85, 216-17. The only passages in the whole two-volume work in which one hears about the redemptive significance of Jesus' death in the sense of atonement for sins are Luke 22:19-20, the tradition about the Eucharist, and Acts 20:28, a saying which is equally traditional. These certainly do not provide a basis for attacking Vielhauer's affirmation; cf. F. Dreyfus, *RScPhTh*, XLVIII (1964), 321 ff. Nor do they provide adequate support for the suggestion of J. Dupont, "Les discours missionaries des Apotres," *RB* LXIX (1962), 50, n. 27, that Luke mentioned the atoning death only in Acts 20:28 (a speech directed to Christians) because (a) the atoning death motif found its place only in inner-churchly tradition, not in the missionary kerygma, while (b) Luke is interested only in the church's mission (except for 20:28, etc.).

14. "On the Paulinism of Acts," p. 45.

15. *Ibid.*, p. 47.

16. *Ibid.*, p. 48.

17. *Ibid.*, p. 49.

18. "Aus der neutestamentlichen Arbeit der letzten Jahre," *VuF* (1947-48), p. 221. Also in his essay, "Probleme neutestamentlicher Arbeit in Deutschland," in *Die Freiheit des Evangeliums und die Ordnung der Gesellschaft*, BEvTh, XV (1952), 141-42. [See also Käsemann's essay in this volume.] On the other side note the authors cited by Kümmel in his revision of Feine-Behm, *Introduction to the New Testament*, trans. by A. J. Mattill (Nashville, 1966) pp. 122-23.

19. "Ministry and Community in the New Testament," pp. 63-94 in *Essays on New Testament Themes* (*SCM*, 1964), see esp. pp. 88-92. This theme has now been pursued in a thorough manner with respect to the Lucan understanding of the apostolate: G. Klein, *Die Zwölf Apostel, Ursprung und Gestalt einer Idee* (Göttingen, 1961), esp. pp. 178 ff. and 202 ff.

20. E. Käsemann, "Paulus und der Frühkatholizismus," *ZThK*, LX (1963), 85.

21. Käsemann, "The Problem of the Historical Jesus," pp. 15-47 in *Essays*, esp. pp. 17-18; "Neutestamentliche Fragen von heute," *ZThK*, LIV (1957), 1-21; esp. 20-21.

22. "Lukas als Theologe der "Heilsgeschichte," *EvTh*, XIV (1954), 256-75; cf. also G. W. Lampe, "The Lucan Portrait of Christ," *NTS*, II (1955-56), 160-75.

23. *The Theology of St. Luke* (New York, 1961).

24. See esp. Bultmann, *Theology of the New Testament*, II, 116-18. Also E. Dinkler, "Earliest Christianity," in *The Idea of History in the Ancient Near East*, ed. R. Denton (New Haven, 1955), pp. 195-97; Haenchen, *op. cit.*, pp. 81-88; Grässer, *Das Problem der Parousieverzögerung in den Synoptischen Evangelien und in der Apostelgeschchte* (2nd ed. Berlin, 1960), pp. 178-215.

25. In this regard Conzelmann grasped Luke's evaluation of Jesus' life better than did Vielhauer. The latter credited Luke with seeing in Jesus' life merely the advent of a salvation whose actualization takes place in the historical process of the church's mission, and whose completion does not come until the eschaton. That is the way Paul thinks, not Luke! With regard to Paul, see Käsemann, "Paulus und der Frühkatholizismus," p. 80; also J. Munck, *Paul and the Salvation of Mankind* (1954), *passim*, and Wilckens, *Gottes Offenbarung, Ein Weg durch das Neue Testament* (Hamburg, 1963), pp. 70-78. Luke, on the other hand, takes as his basis the fullness of redemption in the past history of Jesus. The

church's mission mediates participation in this redemption until the end comes in the parousia of Jesus, when redemption will once again be immediately present on earth. For a discussion of this see Wilckens, *Die Missionsreden*, pp. 193 ff. and 205-16.

26. Cf. Conzelmann, *The Theology of St. Luke*, pp. 149 ff., 189, and his *Die Apostelgeschichte*, pp. 9-10.

27. In Luke's view the Baptist belongs to the pre-Christian epoch; cf. Conzelmann, *The Theology of St. Luke*, pp. 22-7, and for Acts, Wilckens, *Die Missionsreden*, pp. 101-6.

28. Cf. esp. Acts 1:9-11, and Conzelmann's comments on this passage, *The Theology of St. Luke*, pp. 150, 195; also Wilckens, *Die Missionsreden*, pp. 215-16.

29. Cf. Conzelmann, *op. cit.*, p. 185.

30. Cf. *ibid.*, pp. 215-18; Klein, *Die Zwölf Apostel*, and Klein's article, "Lukas 1, 1-4 als theologisches Programm," pp. 193-216 in *Zeit und Geschichte, Dankesgabe an Rudolf Bultmann zum 80. Geburtstag* (Tübingen, 1964).

31. Cf. particularly Grässer, *op. cit.*

32. Haenchen, *op. cit.*, p. 86.

33. Cf. Wilckens, "Kerygma und Evangelium. Beobachtungen zu Acta 10:34-43," *ZNW*, XLIX (1958), 223-37; *Missionsreden*, pp. 92-100.

34. To this degree Käsemann's judgment is false when he says, "Luke takes as his essential theme the hour of the church as the mid-point of time" (*Neutestamentliche Fragen von heute*," see n. 21 above). On the other hand, Conzelmann is right that for Luke *Jesus* is the mid-point of time. The redemptive-historical significance of the church lies wholly in its witnessing to the history of Jesus as the completed redemption of God. Cf. n. 25 above.

35. Bultmann, *Theology of the New Testament*, II, p. 116.

36. "The Problem of the Historical Jesus," *Essays*, p. 29.

37. This is the thesis advanced by the authors whose works we have just summarized. They do not say that Luke eliminated eschatology; Cadbury wrongly criticizes Conzelmann in this regard, "Acts and Eschatology," pp. 300-21 (see esp. p. 321) in *The Background of the New Testament and its Eschatology*, Festschrift C. H. Dodd (Cambridge, 1956). It is right, of course, that the eschatological parts of the older tradition are present amid Luke's redemptive-historical editing. The question is, however, to what extent the old imminent expectation is the determining factor for the whole picture; in the Lucan writings, this factor simply does not dominate. Luke says as much in various places and even directly, as in Acts 1:6-7. To this extent one ought also to modify W. C. van Unnik's criticism of Käsemann in his article, "The Book of Acts, the Confirmation of the Gospel," *NovTest*, IV (1960), 26 ff. and esp. 43-46.

38. See passages such as Luke 17:20-21; 19:11; 21:7; Acts 1:6 ff. For detailed discussion of these passages see Conzelmann, *The Theology of St. Luke*, pp. 120 ff., and Grässer, *op. cit.*, pp. 178 ff. True, Luke did not eliminate the materials which affirmed the imminent expectation. He preserved them. But one must pay close attention to the manner in which he handled them. In Luke 21:34-36, for example, the unexpected suddenness of the end is sharply presented. But that is done in order to accent the urgency of the exhortation, and the exhortation is expressly tailored for a pre-eschatological period of some duration (ἐν παντὶ καιρῷ, vs. 36!). Thus, when H.-W. Bartsch's criticism of Conzelmann is carefully scrutinized, it is clear that it supports Conzelmann's thesis; "Die urchristliche Eschatologie und die Verzögerung der Parousie," *KiZ*, XII (1958), 366. Cf. also Grässer, *op. cit.*, p. 167. Kümmel (*ThR*, XXII [1954], 208-10) criticizes Vielhauer on the grounds that in Acts 3:20, 26, and 17:30-31 it is the imminent expectation which serves as the motive for the call to repentance. But Acts 3:20-21 is an old piece of tradition that Luke worked into the speech which he put in Peter's mouth and which thoroughly reflects his interest in redemptive history (cf. 3:22-26!). Cf. Wilckens, *Misionsreden*, pp. 42-43, 153-56. Acts 17:30-31, on the other hand, speaks not of the nearness of redemption, but rather of the fixing of the future day of judgment in God's plan of salvation. In vs. 30 the preacher

considers the fulfillment of the worldwide mission (πάντας πανταχοῦ) to be a presupposition of the final judgment spoken of in vs. 31! See Conzelmann, p. 228 n. 2.

39. The expression "redaction-criticism," coined by W. Marxsen in *Der Evangelist Markus* 2nd ed. Göttingen 1959), p. 11, n. 1, was originally intended in this sense. But a certain one-sidedness is to be noticed in the way in which the redaction-critical method has been employed thus far.

40. So, for example, Conzelmann, *Theology,* pp. 131-32, and Haenchen *op. cit.* p. 85. Also Grässer, *op. cit.,* who emphasizes, however (p. 224), "It has never been my opinion that the delay of the parousia single-handedly created the thought of redemptive history."

41. For Luke the resurrection of Jesus belongs to the period of Jesus' earthly existence. That period does not come to its end without including the communing of the resurrected Lord with his disciples. It closes, therefore, not with the resurrection, but with the ascension, and the communing of the resurrected Lord with his disciples forms the literary seam between the two volumes. In Luke's scheme of redemptive history the meaning of the resurrection is a thoroughly inner-historical one: God, who was "with Jesus" (Acts 2:22; 10:37-38) from the beginning of his life, powerfully canceled the evil deed which the Jews did to him and thus decreed that Jesus—precisely as the suffering one—is the Christ of God. See Luke 17:25; 24:7, 19-27, and Paul Schubert's article, "The Structure and Significance of Luke 24," pp. 165-86 in *Neutestamentliche Studien für Rudolf Bultmann zum 70. Geburtstag* (2nd ed. Berlin, 1957). In Acts one discovers the plan of the Jesus-kerygma in the apostolic speeches in which what is said about the deed of the Jews corresponds to what is said about God's raising Jesus from the dead (cf. Wilckens, *Missionsreden,* pp. 109 ff.). Luke's strong emphasis on the bodily existence of the resurrected Jesus (Luke 24:36 ff.; Acts 1:3) is also closely related to his redemptive-historical view of Jesus' earthly life: Jesus' bodily resurrection documents the real presence of God's salvation in Jesus' earthly existence and thus the complete actualization of the divine plan of redemption. To this also corresponds the emphasis on the apostles as the chosen eyewitnesses whose task it is to witness to later Christendom about the whole of Jesus' earthly way, including the days after his resurrection (Luke 24:48-49; Acts 1:8; 10:40-42; 13:31-33).

42. Cf. H. E. Tödt, *Der Menchensohn in der synoptischen Überlieferung* (2nd ed. Gütersloh, 1963)), *passim,* esp. the summary on pp. 256-57; also Wilckens, *Missionsreden,* pp. 111 ff.

43. The gospel tradition distinguishes itself quite fundamentally from the missionary-kerygmatic tradition characteristic of the Pauline orb precisely by being tradition about Jesus. This fact probably indicates that the two orbs (Paul's and that of the gospel tradition) possessed traditions which were differently structured. In any case an interpreter of the synoptic materials cannot take too seriously the character of these materials as Jesus-tradition. For it was by no means a ubiquitous Christian assumption to be taken for granted that all Christian tradition should be handed on in the form of Jesus-tradition! Cf. Wilckens, *Missionsreden,* pp. 197-98 and "Hellenistisch-christliche Missionstradition und Jesusüberlieferung," *ThLZ,* LXXXIX (1964), 517-20.

44. The term "Gospel" is being used here not in its early Christian sense, but with the meaning developed by form criticism.

45. Developments in christological thinking correspond to this quite closely. As time passed, more emphasis was given to the present sovereignty of the exalted Lord, and, correspondingly, his functions properly reserved for the end time became more peripheral. The centrality of the exaltation was able to serve as the seedbed either for the Hellenization of the portrait of Jesus or for the development of the doctrine of preexistence in the Hellenistic mission churches. Cf. F. Hahn, *Christologische Hoheitstitel* (Göttingen, 1963).

46. This must be said in criticism of the beginning of the form-critical method by Dibelius. Cf. Wilckens, *ThLZ,* LXXXVI (1961), 272-76 and n. 43 above.

47. For example, Rom. 12:14; 13:9; Gal. 5:14; I Cor. 13:2. Further instances may be found

in an article by J. Pairman Brown, "Synoptic Parallels in the Epistles and Form History," *NTS,* X (1963), 27-48.

48. I have in mind Haenchen's statements (*op. cit.,* pp. 687-88) which are directed against the solution of the problem which I proposed on the basis of the history of tradition (cf. n. 43 above). See the important contribution of Bultmann, "Die Bedeutung des geschichtlichen Jesus für die Theologie des Paulus," *Glauben und Verstehen,* I, 188-213.

49. W. Schmithals, in "Paulus und der historische Jesus," *ZNW,* LIII (1962), 145-60, has rightly pointed out that the teachings and deeds of Jesus are absent not only in Paul's writings but generally in the literature of Hellenistic Christianity.

50. This has to be said against Klein, *op. cit.,* pp. 213 ff. On the striking passage Acts 20:29-30 see pp. 111-23 in H. Schürmann, "Das Testament des Paulus für die Kirche," pp. 108-46 in *Unio Christianorum, Festschrift für Erzbischof Lorenz Jaeger* (Paderborn, 1962).

51. Regarding the related question whether Luke knew the letters of Paul, it must be said that Acts gives reason to very much doubt that he did. The opinion of Klein (*op. cit.,* pp. 189 ff.) that Luke "didn't want to use them" is thus to be questioned.

52. But one must not give too much weight to the Areopagus speech, allowing it to overshadow the whole of the Lucan scheme. Cf. esp. the summary of Conzelmann, *Die Apostelgeschichte,* pp. 102-4.

53. Klein has convincingly shown this in the course of his work on the twelve apostles. Aside from Luke, every other early Christian author who mentions Paul considers him to be an apostle. Luke, on the contrary, denies him apostolic status (except for Acts 14:4, 14), making him appear as a missionary commissioned by the church (Acts 13:1 ff.), and subordinated to the twelve apostles. Luke did this, as Klein shows, because of his concern for the carefully ordered continuity of the apostolic testimony to Jesus—a testimony guaranteed by eyewitnesses. Cf. Klein, *op. cit.,* pp. 213 ff., but also my remark above in n. 50.

54. "Neutestamentliche Fragen von heute," p. 21 (see n. 21 above).

55. "Unsere Predigt im Spiegel der Apostelgeschichte," *EvTh,* X (1950-51), 352-68, esp. 365. Vielhauer expressly endorsed G. Harbsmeier's thesis, *EvTh,* XII (1952-53), 481-84.

56. Haenchen, *op. cit.,* p. 671. On pp. 682-89 he critically discusses my book *Missionsreden,* with an eye also to the symposium *Offenbarung als Geschichte,* ed. W. Pannenberg, *KuD Bh,* I (2nd ed., 1963). Theological sympathy with Luke is, incidentally, not so new. See E. Lohse "Lukas als Theologe der Heilsgeschichte," *EvTh* XIV (1954), 256-75, and esp. O. Cullmann, *Christ and Time,* pp. 19-23. It is surprising, to be sure, that the critical responses to Vielhauer's thesis have not concerned themselves essentially with Luke's theology as such, but rather with the question of the canon. Cf. H. Diem, "Die Einheit der Schrift," *EvTh* XIII (1953), 385-405; W. Andersen, "Die Autorität der apostolischen Zeugnisse," *EvTh* XII (1952-53), 467-81. Even Bauernfeind did not turn his attention definitively to Luke's theology as such, "Vom historischen zum lukanischen Paulus," *EvTh,* XIII (1953), 347-53 and "Zur Frage nach der Entscheidung zwischen Paulus and Lukas," *ZST,* XXIII (1954), 59-88.

57. This has been shown by J. Körnrer, *Eschatologie und Geschichte, Eine Untersuchung des Eschatologischen in der Theologie Rudolf Bultmanns* (Hamburg, 1957). See esp. p. 15.

58. Cf. Bultmann's review of Cullmann's *Christ and Time,* pp. 226-40 in *Existence and Faith,* trans, and ed. by S. Ogden. Also E. Fuchs, *Zur Frage nach dem historischen Jesus* (1960), pp. 77-79 (against Kümmel), and Dinkler, "Earliest Christianity" (*op. cit.,* n. 24 above), pp. 182-83.

59. On this concept see Bultmann, "The New Testament and Mythology," in *Kerygma and Myth,* I, 20.

60. Bultmann, "Man Between the Times According to the New Testament," in *Existence and Faith,* pp. 248-66. Similarly in "History and Eschatology in the NT," *NTS,* I (1954), 5-16.

61. This line of thought is summarized in Bultmann, "Man Between the Times According to the New Testament," in *Existence and Faith*, pp. 248-266.

62. Bultmann, *Theology of the NT*, I, 301-2 *et passim*.

63. *Ibid.*, pp. 303 ff., 329 ff.

64. *Ibid.*, pp. 190-91; and *History and Eschatology* (Edinburgh, 1957), pp. 41 ff.

65. Cf. *History and Eschatology*, pp. 41 ff.: "Paul interpreted the historical picture of Apocalypticism on the basis of his anthropology." But that means that he "decisively modified the eschatology of apocalypticism. . . . But although the history of the nation and the world had lost interest for Paul, he brings to light another phenomenon, the historicity of man, the true historical life of the human being, the history which everyone experiences for himself and by which he gains his real essence." *History and Eschatology*, p. 43 [Germ. ed., p. 49 diverges slightly: "Indem Paulus Geschichte und Eschatologie vom Menschen aus interpretiert, ist die Geschichte des Volkes Israel und die Geschichte der Welt seinem Blick entschwunden, und dafür ist etwas anderes entdeckt worden: die Geschichtlichkeit des menschlichen Seins, d.h. die Geschichte, die jeder Mensch erfährt oder erfahren kann und in der er erst sein Wesen gewinnt."]

66. *Ibid.*, pp. 47 ff. (53 ff.).

67. Cf. Pannenberg's article on "Dialektische Theologie" in the 3rd ed. of *RGG*, II, 168 ff.

68. K. Barth, *The Word of God and the Word of Man*, trans. D. Horton (New York, 1957), e.g., p. 80.

69. *Ibid.*, p. 72. During the 1920's this antithesis between revelation and history was taken for granted among dialectical theologians. Cf., for example, F. Gogarten, "Vom heiligen Egoismus des Christen," *ChW*, XXXIV (1920), 548: "One will have a certain relationship to history if one considers the whole breadth of historical development to be the revelation of God. One will have quite another relationship to history if one sees revelation in the original (ursprünglich) deed of God, which does not issue into its results, being modified by them, but which must always be grasped in its pure originality, beyond its historical results and forms, however important these may be." Access to this revelation of God is therefore granted only via " 'the leap' out of the unending mediations of history" (549). Also E. Brunner, "Die Offenbarung als Grund und Gegenstand der Theologie," in *Philosophie und Offenbarung* (Tübingen, 1925), pp. 20-21: The revelation of God is "not something which takes place in continuity with world events and historical existence; it is rather broken continuity, the breaking in of the Entirely Other. In a word, it is the miracle. What happens in revelation is not related to other happenings as a larger to a smaller, as a maximum or optimum, but rather as antithesis in the strongest sense of that word: Anti-thesis, for which the antitheses of the natural world, like light and darkness, death and life, salvation and corruption, are only weak comparisons."

70. *Glauben und Verstehen*, I, 1-25.

71. *Ibid.*, p. 2.

72. *Ibid.*, p. 5.

73. *Ibid.*, p. 9, quoted from Barth, *Romans*, p. 77.

74. *Ibid.*, p. 13.

75. "The Problem of the Historical Jesus," *Essays*, p. 31. Cf. also Conzelmann, *RGG* 3rd ed., 650: "Revelation is no settled fact; it appears—today—in the Word."

76. This question can be handled here only in a sketchy and suggestive manner. A full-scale treatment would require us to consider the whole of the contemporary hermeneutical discussion of Bultmann's work. I am well aware that what I say here is a bit precipitous.

77. In 1919 Barth was of the opinion: "As a man of his own time Paul spoke to his contemporaries. But much more important than this truth is another: as prophet and apostle of God's Kingdom he speaks to all men of all times." For this reason the exegete has as his task "to look through that which is historical in order to see beyond it" (*Romans*, Preface to the 1st ed.). Barth's words earned the censure of the historical-critical exegete A. Jülicher in an article entitled, "Ein moderner Paulusausleger," *ChW*, XXXIV (1920),

453-57; 466-69. At the close of his article, Jülicher wrote: "Whoever is contemptuous of the past, assuming that only the living are correct, can gain nothing from the past. Whoever, being in a state of holy egoism, is interested only in his own questions, despising those who cannot answer them for him, should scarcely demand that a product of the past—which the Epistle to the Romans certainly is—come alive for him." The first duty of the exegete, Jülicher continued, is carefully to listen to "the questions which the men of the past direct toward me," and then to answer them. "And since I am what I am only because those who preceded me were what they were; since I would long ago have famished had I not been able to nourish myself on that which they proffered me, I act in my own interest when I seek to draw still closer to them and to elicit from them even finer nourishment." Consequently Barth was compelled to outline his hermeneutic in the preface to the second edition (1922) and to concede that his understanding of God prior to interpreting Paul might not turn out to be Paul's, even in the course of the exegesis. Nevertheless, he insisted that the subject matter itself (die Sache) which Paul communicated in his own language to his own contemporaries, and the subject matter which the modern exegete must master in his own language for his own time *"cannot* differ from one another." That has remained the central point of his hermeneutic. Bultmann, in his review of Barth's commentary (*ChW*, XXXIV [1922], 320-23; 330-34; 358-61; 369-73, see esp. 371 ff.), not only conceded this point in full, but also sharpened it into a call for a "Sachkritik" of the New Testament texts. This is the hermeneutical presupposition of the theological critique of Luke in contemporary discussion.

78. See H. J. Schoeps, *Paul: The Theology of the Apostle in the Light of Jewish Religious History* (Philadelphia, 1961); Wilckens, "Die Bekehrung des Paulus als religionsgeschichtliches Problem," *ZThK*, LVI (1959), 273-93. On apocalyptic theology see esp. D. Rössler, *Gesetz und Geschichte* (2nd ed. Neukirchen, 1962), pp. 43 ff.

79. Contra Bultmann, *History and Eschatology*, pp. 23-24.

80. Cf. Wilckens, "Die Rechtfertigung Abrahams nach Römer 4," pp. 111-27 in *Studien zur Theologie der alttestamentlichen Überlieferungn,* von Rad Festschrift (Neukirchen, 1961). A contrary opinion is developed by Klein, "Römer 4 und die Idee der Heilsgeschichte und Weltgeschichte," *EvTh,* XXIII (1963), 424-47, and "Individualgeschichte und Weltgeschichte bei Paulus," *EvTh,* XXIV (1964), 126-65. I have continued the debate with another article in *EvTh,* XXIV (1964), 586-610, "Zu Römer 3:2–4:25. Antwort an G. Klein." See Klein's response, *ibid.,* 676-83.

81. Haenchen, *op. cit.,* pp. 686-87, is entirely right to say, "Paul is also a theologian of redemptive history."

82. Just here lies the value of the exegetical position which Cullmann has steadily represented against Bultmann—however questionable in part and even on the whole Cullmann's view may be.

83. Dinkler, "Earliest Christianity," p. 190 (see n. 24 above).

84. *Zur Frage nach dem historischen Jesus,* p. 77.

85. I do not mean to say that there are no areas of grave weakness in Luke's theology. See *Missionsreden,* pp. 216-18.

PART II

Four Features of Lucan Style

HENRY J. CADBURY

The language of the Bible has long been the object of intensive scrutiny. Usually that scrutiny has had as incentive some preconceived answers or at least some a priori problem. Less often observations have been suggested by the wording itself—a by-product of more direct attention to other features. These areas of attention have varied over the centuries—from the days of rabbinic exegesis based on the minor phenomena of language up to the modern times of literary and historical criticism. They were supposed to be contributory to religious, legalistic, allegorical, or numerological understanding of divine revelation. Recently biblical theology has led to theological dictionaries and commentaries. The text itself often yields scanty and unsatisfactory answers to such scrutiny and questioning, in part because verbal expression is subject to less conscious and less meaningful factors. The more these factors are a controlling influence, the more fruitless is the search for subtle evidence in the language used with which to answer other questions. Yet they are easily overlooked. They belong largely to the unconscious or habitual process of expression, whether of the author individually or of the wider linguistic community.

Luke–Acts, the two-volume work of "Luke," has shared this neglect. Of course, it has received its share of more objective treatment. Its relation to contemporary idiom has been indicated by the old "observations" literature, and by modern commentaries and dictionaries. It is one of the most varied writings, but also one with the closest parallelism to secular writing, whether popular or literary. It represents within the canonical books certain advantages for the kind of analysis that I have suggested as being too much neglected.

It is in size the most extensive contribution by any single author to the New Testament. Paul is second in extent, but the Pauline corpus includes smaller units, some of uncertain genuineness and all of uncertain order of date. Luke–Acts has its disadvantages in its relatively greater amount of textual uncertainty created by the existence alongside of the usual readings of several early so-called "western" variants. Its existing order can also be challenged, as is done by those who think Acts was written before Luke,[1] or the preface of Luke after the whole work was finished, which in any case is a minor and not unlikely hypothesis, or by those who espouse, as in Proto-Luke theories, a double stage in the author's own composition.[2] Whatever the underlying sources and development—the present text is compatible with authorship by a single editor.[3] And for long stretches, as for the career of Paul with its assumption of both geographical and chronological sequence, the writing almost certainly was ultimately compiled in the present order and with a wording not often varying from that of a modern critical text.

With good courage, therefore, we may venture to raise with Luke–Acts some of the questions I have mentioned as neglected, or rather we may see whether the work itself offers us almost on its own initiative some noticeable features of style. We shall not be disappointed if they contribute nothing to the successively dominant interests of biblical study. If they are relevant to nothing else, they may at least suggest something of the psychology of the author, the working of his mind in the medium of language.

It is more than fifty years since I began to notice and classify some such phenomena as I shall mention below. Very likely this interest began with a brief article by my former preceptor, James Hardy Ropes, published in 1901.[4] Unless there is something that I have missed in the burgeoning literature which surrounds all our tasks, I know of no further discussion of these phenomena, and without waiting longer for a better opportunity or a better exponent, I attempt here to summarize certain linguistic features in Luke–Acts.[5]

They fall into two pairs of somewhat opposite usages of words or phrases. The first pair is repetition and variation; the second is concentration and distribution. From a more complete collection of examples a few may be given as we discuss each of these two pairs.

I. Repetition and Variation

The cases of longer repetition are more conspicuous in Acts than in Luke, and they amount to whole episodes. They begin in Acts 1:2-12, the farewell scene between Jesus and his disciples, where Luke 24:36-49, with the promise of the Spirit and the command to preach beginning from Jerusalem to which the disciples then return, is retold. Perhaps this repetition is to give an overlap and also an appropriate ending and beginning, respectively, of the two separate books. Later in Acts 1 the list of disciples in Luke 6:13-16 is repeated without the name of Judas Iscariot. Other instances are those where, in the Homeric manner, the content of the objective narrative is repeated later on the lips of a speaker. Familiar here are the account of Paul's conversion in Acts 9 and his own rehearsal of it with its sequel not once but twice thereafter: Acts 22 to a Jewish mob as he stood on the steps between the temple and the Roman barracks in Jerusalem, and Acts 26 at a hearing in Caesarea especially arranged by Festus, the Roman prefect, for consultation with Herod Agrippa. Similarly the narrative of Peter with Cornelius at Caesarea (Acts 10) is repeated, when Peter is made to report the same event at Jerusalem to those who challenged him about it (Acts 11; cf. 15:7-9). Another case of verbal summary of earlier narrative is the letter by Claudius Lysias in Acts 23:26-30, when Paul was transferred from Jerusalem to Caesarea for the direct jurisdiction of the prefect Felix.

In contrast to this prolixity in Acts, the apparent tendency in Luke to avoid parallel scenes must be mentioned. The Gospel, if we may assume that it used Mark, not only omits the second of Mark's accounts of feeding the multitude, but appears to cancel his account of Jesus in his home town (Mark 6:1-6), and of his anointing by a woman (Mark 14:3-9), and perhaps other sayings or scenes in Mark by introducing, before he comes to these scenes, independent versions (Luke 4:16-30; 7:36-50, etc.) Matthew on the contrary appears to repeat passages from Mark a second time.

Shorter instances of repetition occur in both Luke and Acts. First of all may be mentioned here what are commonly called summaries: (a) of the growth of a child in Luke 1:80; 2:40; 2:52; (b) of the extension of Jesus' ministry in Luke 4:14; 4:37; 7:17; (c) of the practice of communism and the life of the early church in Acts 2:41-47; 4:32-35; 5:11-16; (d) of the spread of the gospel and the increased number of believers in Acts 6:7; 9:31; 12:24; 16:5; 19:20; 28:30-31. For these I refer to my fuller discussion in *The Beginnings of Christianity.*[6]

Further instances of repetition in Luke–Acts are in the still shorter phenomena of single words or brief phrases. The identity of expression within the writings of Luke has perhaps never been studied completely, and unfortunately never for just its own sake. Such a study would be a long but fascinating task. But from a great variety of special points of view the evidence has been used to prove the distinctness of the author's vocabulary from that of other New Testament writings and the identity of author for various parts of his works. A large list of words and phrases peculiar to Luke and Acts, or especially frequent in them, may be compiled.[7] Certain nouns and adjectives, certain verbs with their compounds, certain conjunctions and even certain grammatical constructions are peculiar, or nearly peculiar, to these two books among those in the New Testament. Of course, this criterion leaves much to be desired as a basis for general placing of Luke's language. As I wrote long ago,

It must be confessed that in all lexical study of the New Testament such facts ["occurs in the New Testament only in the Lukan writings," etc.] have played an important part; but it seems to the present writer that their significance has been greatly overestimated. It must be remembered that the New Testament is, linguistically at least, a merely accidental collection of a very limited number of books on a considerable variety of subjects. As a result the words peculiar to any New Testament writer (as may be seen from the lists in the Appendix to Thayer's *Lexicon*) are many of them words common in all periods of Greek writing, and typical neither of the vocabulary nor even of the grade of culture of the author. The words *characteristic* of a New Testament writer are a very different kind of list and cannot be determined without reference to the LXX and profane Greek as well as to the other writers in the New Testament.[8]

Nevertheless, these "peculiarities" do bind together the several parts of Luke and Acts, as defenders of their common authorship or editorship are not slow to point out. Thus the two separate volumes are connected not only by many words found in both of them, though in no other books of the New Testament,[9] but by a great variety of longer expressions and more delicate points of stylistic unity.[10] And various parts of each volume are similarly connected with the rest of the two-volume work. In the Gospel, the preface, the two chapters on the infancy including especially the canticles,[11] the passages derived either from Mark[12] or from some sources used also by Matthew,[13] and the words and events of Jesus' life reported only by this Evangelist[14]—each have marked resemblances to the other parts of his writings. Similarly in Acts characteristic phrases occur both in 1–12 and in 13–28,[15] in the "we" passages,[16] and in the various speeches.[17]

In his tables on pp. 15-29 Hawkins indicated the distribution of over 180 "words and phrases characteristic of St. Luke's gospel" both in Luke (chaps. 1–2; other peculiar parts; common parts) and in Acts (chaps. 1–12; chaps. 13–28; the "we" sections).

The opposite and complementary trait of Luke's style has been briefly noticed and illustrated in the article by Ropes already mentioned. As that paper is not widely known, especially two generations later, and since the same subject has not been presented by others, I may quote from it at some length.

I would call attention to a single point in Luke's use of language. The uniformity of his style is one of its striking characteristics. The similar phrases and identical words found at remote points in his great history have overwhelming force when massed in an argument for unity of authorship. . . . But this uniformity, to which hitherto attention has been chiefly directed, is not stereotyped and mechanical. It is accompanied by great variety within the similar phrases, by a manifest fondness for change of expression, and by a notable copiousness of vocabulary in the terms used for things and actions often mentioned.

This could be illustrated from every chapter: . . .

(1) The writer likes to vary his word in the same context. . . .

(2) Similar expressions in distant contexts so often show variation that the habit must be deemed a trait of the writer's style. . . . We have here a mental trait of the writer, a mark of his taste. He likes to vary, and his variation shows a literary feeling and gives his writing a certain elegance.

(3) If this is true it is perhaps not going too far to connect with this trait certain more substantial variations. Luke is fond of repeating his material. . . . [After listing passages like those already mentioned above] all these instances testify to his fondness for repetition, and nearly all to his tendecy to vary even facts of some importance when rehearsing a story for the second time.

Now the bearing of my observation is this. If this tendency to vary is a trait of Luke, these variations must not be used as some of them often have been, as marks of written sources slavishly followed and worked up into a patchwork like the Hexateuch in the Old Testament. For instance, the shifting use of Ἰερουσαλήμ and Ἱεροσόλυμα in Acts has been observed, and attempts made to use it as a criterion for the analysis into sources. In this particular case the attempts have failed, and probably the two forms owe their adoption to the changing fancy of the writer in each several instance. So of the two accounts of the "communism," and the three of Paul's conversion. . . . The point I have tried to make in this article, if well taken, makes the work of analysis [into sources] somewhat less hopeful. Variation of expression in *Luke* and *Acts,* at any rate when of a certain kind, indicates rather unity than diversity of authorship. Nor, it may be added, do such discrepancies show the untrustworthiness of the statements of the writer. They have neither the one significance nor the other, but are merely a part of his mode of writing history, introduced in order to avoid a monotonous uniformity.[18]

Variety, then, almost studied variation of phrase and exchange of synonyms, is a distinct feature of the style of this author and exists alongside of a striking identity of style and diction. To what extent these features were consciously aimed at by the author, and how far they were inspired by the conventions of contemporary rhetoric, are interesting questions, though difficult ones to answer. Peculiar and repeated mannerisms of speech are probably often unconscious and are found in authors of both high and low degrees of culture.

Variety of expression is also often natural and spontaneous, though here art is more likely to imitate nature deliberately. Paraphrase was a well-known exercise of rhetorical training, and even "self-paraphrase" was recommended to writers not merely for practice but in their final composition. An illustration of self-paraphrase may be found in comparing the parallel passages in Josephus' *Jewish War* and his *Antiquities of the Jews.* As in Luke's twice-told narratives, there is evidently no difference of underlying source, oral or written, but merely the same writer repeating from memory or even with his own earlier work before him. Josephus' use of the Greek Old Testament, including I Maccabees,[19] illustrates his paraphrase of a written source. The habit of studied avoidance of an earlier phraseology, whether one's own or another's, would give great facility in variation.

It may be worthwhile to mention two other elements in the literary methods to which Luke was heir, that would increase his skill with synonymous paraphrase. One is the habit of combining synonyms in pairs which he shares with the Greek writers; the other is the Jewish habit of *parallelismus membrorum.*

As for the former, certain combinations in Luke–Acts are standard Greek clichés, while others apparently chosen by him are created *ad hoc* much as is done in other languages or writers.

As for the latter, whether this author was acquainted with Semitic languages or not, their use of synonyms in parallelism was known to him at least from the Septuagint, for the Greek translators had been compelled, in reproducing literally the poetic form of the Hebrew, to search for suitable pairs of words,—a fact which has some interesting effects on the semantics of biblical Greek. Usually this search was not difficult. The Greek language is mostly richer than the original. Indeed, there are prose passages where the Septuagint inclines to variation of phrase when the Hebrew repeats the same word. Possibly the Greek translators would defend this as a deliberate custom much as those of the King James English Version did in a famous passage in their "Translators to the Reader." In any case, Luke's Greek Bible familiarized him with a style not averse to synonyms.

That Luke deliberately avoided repetition seems almost demonstrated by his use of Mark. Mark did not feel the same objection to repetition, but when a word, even the name of an object, occurs too often in his narrative, Luke either by omission or by the use of a synonym secures variety of phrase. Thus in one passage (Luke 5:17 ff.), a bed is called both κλίνη and κλινίδιον and also ἐφ' ὃ κατέκειτο; in another (7:25), clothing is indifferently ἱμάτια and ἱματισμός; in a third (22:50-51), the ear is both οὖς and ὠτίον.[20]

The peculiar stylistic combination of similarity and variation in phrase and vocabulary[21] can be illustrated in great profusion. The likeness is most striking when found in widely sundered passages without any inner connection; the variation is most noteworthy when it occurs in passages adjacent in position and closely connected in thought.

As a good illustration of the latter, Acts 5:1-11 will serve. The incident of Ananias and Sapphira presents opportunity for parallelism. There is of course Luke's usual repetition. The following unusual expressions occur twice each: νοσφίζομαι (each time with ἀπὸ τῆς τιμῆς), and ἐκψύχω, τί ὅτι, and each half of the incident ends with the refrain, verbatim in part, "And great fear came upon the whole church, and upon all who heard of these things." On the other hand, the property is called both κτῆμα and χωρίον; for "sell," the verbs ἐπώλησεν, πραθέν, ἀπέδοσθε are used; the young men are first οἱ νεώτεροι, then οἱ νεανίσκοι; the Holy Spirit is both τὸ πνεῦμα τὸ ἅγιον and τὸ πνεῦμα τοῦ κυρίου; ψεύδομαι is construed in one sentence with the accusative, in another with the dative; collusion is expressed alternately by συνειδυίης and by συνεφωνήθη, etc.

A few examples in related or adjacent passages from many that could be quoted are as follows:

Luke 1:12 ἐταράχθη   29 διεταράχθη

Luke 1:22 ἦν διανεύων   62 ἐνένευον

Luke 1:32 υἱὸς ὑψίστου κληθήσεται   35 κληθήσεται υἱὸς θεοῦ

Luke 1:57 ἐπλήσθη ὁ χρόνος τοῦ τέκειν αὐτήν   2:6 ἐπλήσθησαν αἱ ἡμέραι τοῦ τεκεῖν αὐτήν

Luke 1:58 οἱ περίοικοι καὶ οἱ συγγενεῖς   65 τοὺς περιοικοῦντας

Luke 1:58 οἱ περίοικοι καὶ οἱ συγγενεῖς   2:44 ἐν τοῖς συγγενεῦσιν καὶ τοῖς γνωστοῖς

Luke 2:18 ἐθαύμασαν περὶ τῶν λαληθέντων   33 θαυμάζοντες ἐπὶ τοῖς λαλουμένοις

Luke 4:24 ἀμὴν λέγω ὑμῖν   25 ἐπ' ἀληθείας δὲ λέγω ὑμῖν

Luke 5: 7 τοῖς μετόχοις   10 κοινωνοί

Luke 7: 2 δοῦλος   3 δοῦλον   7 παῖς   10 δοῦλον (Matt. 8:6, 8, 13 παῖς)

Luke 8: 7 ἀπέπνιξαν   14 συμπνίγονται (Mark 4:7, 19 συμπνίγω *bis*)

Luke 8:42 συνέπνιγον   45 συνέχουσι καὶ ἀποθλίβουσι (Mark 5:24, 31 συνθλίβω *bis*)

Luke 9: 5 τὸν κονιορτὸν ἀπὸ τῶν ποδῶν ἀποτινάσσετε   10:11 καὶ τὸν κονιορτὸν τὸν κολληθέντα . . . εἰς τοὺς πόδας ἀπομασσόμεθα

Luke 9:10 κατ' ἰδίαν   18 κατὰ μόνας

Certain words in Greek appear to have the habit of exchanging declension, or gender, or number. For the change of declension phenomenon, the grammarians' term is heteroclisis. The author of Luke–Acts shows an extension of this freedom. It is another example of his tendency to slight variation. Here are some examples:

Luke 16:22 εἰς τὸν κόλπον   23 ἐν τοῖς κόλποις

Luke 23: 4, 14, 22 αἴτιον   Acts 13:28; 28:18, *et passim:* αἰτία

Acts 9:32, 35 Λύδδα (indecl. or acc. plur.)   38 Λύδδας (gen. sing.)

Acts 14: 6, 21; 16:1 Λύστραν (acc. sing.)   14:8; 16:2 Λύστροις (dat. plur.)

Acts 19:27 τῆς θεᾶς   37 τὴν θεόν

Acts 23:34 ποίας ἐπαρχείας   25:1 τῇ ἐπαρχείῳ

Acts 24:27 χάριτα   25:9 χάριν[22]

Acts 27:17 τὸ σκεῦος   19 τὴν σκευήν

Only a shade different are the cases of exchanging in context different derivatives of the same root.

Luke 13: 8 κόπρια (acc. plur.)   14 κοπρίαν (acc. sing.)

Luke 23:53 μνήματι   55 μνημεῖον   24:1 μνῆμα   2 μνημείου (cf. Mark 15:46; 5:2, 3, 5)

Acts   7:43 σκηνήν   44 σκηνή   46 σκήνωμα (3 passages from LXX)

Acts 15: 2 ζητήσεως   ζητήματος

Acts 25:19 ζητήματα   20 ζήτησις

Acts 27:42 βουλή   43 βουλήματος

The variant spellings of Jerusalem have already been noted. Other proper names show like variation. The land of Judah may be described by the patriarch's name Ἰούδας (Luke 1:39), or by the feminine place name Ἰουδαία (Luke 1:5, 65; 2:4, *et passim*). The apostle Peter, besides that simple name, has Simon Peter in Luke 5:8 (cf. 6:14), and Simon who is surnamed Peter (ὃς ἐπικαλεῖται) Acts 10:5; 10, 32), or, surnamed Peter (ὁ ἐπικαλούμενος Acts 10:18; 11:13) twice each, but only in the Cornelius episode and its report. He is simply Simon in Luke 4:38 (*bis*); 5:3, 4, 5, 10 (*bis*), another set of adjacent verses, and in Luke 24:34. Jesus addresses him as Simon, Simon (Luke 22:31)—a characteristic Lucan repetition of the vocative, like 10:41, Martha, Martha—as well as by the vocative Peter only three verses later. James refers to him in the more Semitic-looking spelling Symeon in Acts 15:14. The apostle Paul is addressed by Jesus also in Semitic and double vocative Saoul, Saoul (Acts 9:2; 22:7; and 26:14 "in the Hebrew dialect") and by Ananias as brother Saoul (Acts 9:17; 22:13). And of course there is the striking and permanent change before and after, the idiomatic expression "Saul, *alias* Paul" (Acts 13:9), namely the exclusive use in narrative before that of Saul (declinable Σαῦλος) and after that of Paulus, a good Roman and Greek name. There are of course other persons called Simon, Symeon, Saoul, and Paulus in Luke or Acts. That Sergius Paulus is mentioned just at the point of the writer's transfer from Saul to Paul, and that soon thereafter (Acts 13:21) another Saul is mentioned, is more an indication of the writer's psychology than of any historical considerations. Perhaps the same may be said of the mention in juxtaposition of the town of Gaza and of the treasure (γάζα) of Candace of Ethiopia (Acts 8:26, 27). At Acts 7:16 the mention of Hamor suggests that the author, like scribes after him, has associated Shechem, the place, with Shechem, the Old Testament person.

Examples of repetition (with variation) at widely separate and unrelated passages are very numerous in Luke–Acts:

Luke	1:2	αὐτόπται καὶ ὑπηρέται	Acts 26:16	ὑπηρέτην καὶ μάρτυρα
Luke	1:13	εἰσηκούσθη ἡ δέησίς σου	Acts 10:31	εἰσηκούσθη σου ἡ δέησις
Luke	1:66	χεὶρ κυρίου ἦν μετ' αὐτοῦ	Acts 11:21	χεὶρ κυρίου μετ' αὐτῶν
Luke	1:70	ἐλάλησεν διὰ στόματος τῶν ἁγίων ἀπ' αἰῶνος προφητῶν αὐτοῦ	Acts 3:21	ἐλάλησεν ὁ θεὸς διὰ στόματος τῶν ἁγίων ἀπ' αἰῶνος αὐτοῦ προφητῶν
Luke	2:14	δόξα ἐν ὑψίστοις καὶ ἐπὶ γῆς εἰρήνη	Luke 19:38	ἐν οὐρανῷ εἰρήνη καὶ δόξα ἐν ὑψίστοις
Luke	2:37	λατρεύουσα νύκτα καὶ ἡμέραν	Acts 26: 7	νύκτα καὶ ἡμέραν λατρεῦον
Luke	4:13	ἄχρι καιροῦ	Acts 13:11	ἄχρι καιροῦ
Luke	8:14	μεριμνῶν καὶ πλούτου καὶ ἡδονῶν τοῦ βίου	Luke 21:34	μερίμναις βιωτικαῖς
Luke	10:40	κατέλειπεν διακονεῖν	Acts 6: 2	καταλείψαντας . . . διακονεῖν
Luke	11:27	μακαρία ἡ κοιλία ἡ βαστάσασά σε καὶ οἱ μαστοὶ οὓς ἐθήλασα	Luke 23:29	μακάριαι . . . αἱ κοιλίαι αἳ οὐκ ἐγέννησαν καὶ οἱ μαστοὶ οἳ οὐκ ἔθρεψαν
Luke	15:20	ἐπέπεσεν ἐπὶ τὸν τράχηλον αὐτοῦ καὶ κατεφίλησεν αὐτόν	Acts 20:37	ἐπιπεσόντες ἐπὶ τὸν τράχηλον τοῦ Παύλου κατεφίλουν αὐτόν
Luke	17:13	ἦραν φωνήν	Acts 4:24	ἦραν φωνήν
Luke	21:18	καὶ θρὶξ ἐκ τῆς κεφαλῆς ὑμῶν οὐ μὴ ἀπόληται	Acts 27:35	οὐδενὸς γὰρ ὑμῶν θρὶξ ἀπὸ τῆς κεφαλῆς ἀπολεῖται
Luke	23: 5	διδάσκων καθ' ὅλης τῆς Ἰουδαίας καὶ ἀρξάμενος ἀπὸ τῆς Γαλιλάιας	Acts 10:37	τὸ γενόμενον ῥῆμα καθ' ὅλης τῆς Ἰουδαίας ἀρξάμενος ἀπὸ τῆς Γαλιλαίας
Luke	21:35	ἐπὶ πρόσωπον πάσης τῆς γῆς	Acts 17:26	ἐπὶ παντὸς προσώπου τῆς γῆς
Acts	19:40	στάσεως . . . συστροφῆς	Acts 23:10	στάσεως . . . συστροφήν

Sometimes the passages showing likeness are obviously related in subject matter, as in the thrice-told account of Paul's conversion, and the twice-told account of Cornelius' (or rather Peter's) conversion, or of early communism, or of the two parables of persistence in prayer. Besides less unique expressions, one notes in the first περιαστράπτω in Acts 9:3; 22:6; in the second μηδαμῶς in 10:14; 11:8, and διακρίνω in Acts 10:20; 11:2-12; 15:9; in the

Henry J. Cadbury

third καθότι ἄν τις χρείαν εἶχε in Acts 2:45; 4:35; in the fourth παρέχω κόπον in Luke 11:7; 18:5, and εἰ καὶ . . . οὐ . . . διά γε in 11:8; 18:4. In Luke two passages on renunciation 9:61-62 and 14:33-35 use the words ἀποτάσσομαι (also in Acts) and εὔθετος. The two addresses of Paul to Gentile audiences are tied together not so much by identical words but by similar ones, like Acts 14:11 ὁμοιόω, 15 ὁμοιοπαθής, 17:29 ὅμοιος; and 14:17 καίτοι, 17:27 καίγε. The two last use a participle, and after it comes an instance of litotes. διϊσχυρίζομαι is used twice, Luke 22:59, Acts 12:15, and in both cases of a servant affirming the identity of Peter. κατὰ τὸ εἰωθός is used in Luke 4:16; Acts 17:2, with the dative in each case, and in reference to entering the synagogue (Jesus at Nazareth, Paul at Thessalonica).

Other passages in the Lucan work are bound together verbally in the same way but without the similarity of subject matter. The preface of Luke is associated with Acts 18:23-25 by the recurrence of καθεξῆς, κατηχέω and ἀκριβῶς, and with Acts 26:24-25 by the use of ἀπ᾿ ἀρχῆς . . . ἄνωθεν. The incident of the travelers to Emmaus (Luke 24:13-35) is associated with Paul's Macedonian ministry (Acts 16:11–17:15) by their common use of παραβιάζω, διανοίγω (five times in the figurative sense), γραφαί (plural five times which is also in Acts 18:24, 28), and παθεῖν τὸν χριστὸν (three times, cf. Acts 3:18 and 26:23).

II. Distribution and Concentration

Of the second pair of opposites—the distribution and concentration of terms—examples of the former have been sufficiently given in the preceding section of this paper. But over against this, one notices in Luke–Acts, as often in other writers, a tendency to bunch the use of a term in closely adjacent passages and then to use it rarely, if at all, elsewhere. There are two sorts of close collocation of instances which are intelligible for other reasons, and they should be excluded from the present observations. (1) Their repetition in one paragraph alone is due to the special subject matter. They naturally recur in that context. Thus, the word μνᾶ occurs seven times in the parable of pounds (Luke 19:12-27), στρατηγοί five times in the passage of the colony Philippi (Acts 16:20-38), πολιτάρχαι twice in the report about Thessolonica (Acts 17:6, 8), χιλίαρχος sixteen times in the narrative of the period when Paul was in custody of the tribune Claudius Lysias (between Acts 21:31 and Acts 24:22), etc. (2) Their proximity of recurrence is due to the tendency, especially in the sayings of Jesus, from memory to accumulate

97

terms or words by mere association (*Stichwort*). This was one of the determining factors in the order of Gospel writing. Thus:

Luke 11:33 οὐδεὶς λύχνον ἅψας κτλ.   11:34-36 ὁ λύχνος τοῦ σώματος . . . ὁ λύχνος τῇ ἀστραπῇ φωτίζῃ σε.

Luke 16: 9-13 ἐκ τοῦ μαμωνᾶ τῆς ἀδικίας . . . ἐν τῷ ἀδίκῳ μαμωνᾷ . . . οὐ δύνασθε θεῷ δουλεύειν καὶ μαμωνᾷ

Luke 20:46 τὰς οἰκίας τῶν χηρῶν   21:2 εἶδεν δέ τινα χήραν κτλ. (with Mark 12:40, 42)

Probably even numerals are means of association:

Luke 8:42 about twelve years of age   43 for twelve years (in Mark 5:42, 25 the same data, but more separated)

Luke 13: 4 eighteen persons   11 for eighteen years

Perhaps the nautical subject matter of Acts 27 accounts for the quick recurrence of such terms as shown below:

27: 8, 13 παραλέγομαι

27:18 ἐκβολή   22 ἀποβολή

27:15 ἐφερόμεθα   17 ἐφέροντο in the sense "to sail"

27:17, 26, 29, 32 ἐκπίπτω=run aground (contrast Acts 12:7)

27:43, 44; 28:1, 4 διασώζω in sense "save from the sea," but nautical subject matter does not account for the recurrence here, and only here except as noted, of

27: 1, 42 δεσμώτης, elsewhere δέσμιος

27: 3, 17 χράομαι

27: 7, 8, 16 μόλις, elsewhere Luke 9:39; Acts 14:18

27: 9, 22 παραίνεω

27:20, 40; 28:13 (*si vera lectio*) περιαιρέω

27:22, 25 εὐθυμέω, 36 εὔθυμος, also Acts 24:10 εὐθύμως

27:21 ἀσιτία   33 ἄσιτοι

The recurrence of the same preposition with compound verbs in one sentence is illustrated in the following passages:

Luke 21:15 (3 verbs) ἀντι-

Luke 1:22; 1:29; Acts 2:12-13; 10:17, 19 (3 verbs) δια-

Acts 15:36 ἐπι-

Acts 24:27 κατα-

Luke 2:19; Acts 9:22; 19:32-33 (3 verbs) συν-

Acts 24:24-25 (4 verbs) μετα-

From many examples of locutions repeated in close proximity in Luke and Acts and found rarely, if ever, elsewhere, a few are presented below:

Luke   1:39, 65 ἡ ὀρεινή

Luke   1:68; 2:38 λύτρωσις

Luke   2:15, 17 γνωρίζω, and from LXX in Acts 2:28; 7:13 (*v.l.*)

Luke   2:23, 24, 39 (ὁ) νόμος κυρίου

Luke   11:21-22, 34 ὅταν ... ἐπὰν δέ

Luke   12:51, 13:2-3, 4-5 δοκεῖτε ὅτι ... ; οὐχί, λέγω ὑμῖν, ἀλλ'

Luke   21:36; 23:23 κατισχύω (cf. 23:5 ἐπισχύω)

Luke   22: 6, 35 ἄτερ

Luke   23:47; 24:34 ὄντως

Acts   1:15; 2:1, 44, 47; 4:26 (LXX), also at Luke 17:35 ἐπὶ τὸ αὐτό

Acts   6:11, 14 ἀκηκόαμεν. This perfect for ἠκούσαμεν does not occur again in Luke–Acts, even at Acts 22:15 where it might be expected.

Acts   7: 5, 45 κατάσχεσις

Acts   9:13, 32, 41 οἱ ἅγιοι (also 26:10 parallel to 9:13)

Acts   10: 2, 7 εὐσεβής

Acts   10:20; 11:26 χρηματίζω, elsewhere Luke 2:26

Acts   13:50; 14:2 ἐπεγείρω (but with different objects)

Acts   14:32; 15:32, 41 ἐπιστηρίζω

Acts   15: 2, 4, 6, 22, 23; 16:4 οἱ ἀπόστολοι καὶ (οἱ) πρεσβύτεροι

Acts   16:16, 19, 30 κύριοι, elsewhere only the singular

Acts   17:10 ἀπῄεσαν   15 ἐξῄεσαν   21:18, 26 εἰσῄει (Except in these pairs of adjacent cases, the imperfect of εἰμι does not occur.)

Acts   19:35, 36 καταστέλλω

Acts   19:35 διοπετής   36 προπετής

Acts   20:20, 27 οὐ(οὐδὲν) ὑπεστειλάμην

Acts   20:30; 21:1 ἀποσπάω   also Luke 22:41

Acts   21: 3; 22:5 ἐκεῖσε

Acts   22: 1; 24:13 νυνί

Acts   22:24, 29 ἀνετάζω

Acts   22:28 πολιτεία   23:1 πεπολίτευμαι

Acts   22:24; 24:22; 27:35 εἴπας for εἰπών   also Acts 7:37

Acts   23:15, 22; 24:1; 25:2, 15 ἐμφανίζω

Acts   23: 1; 24:16 συνείδησις

Acts   24: 9; 25:19 φάσκω

Acts 25:15, 20 αὐτοὶ οὗτοι
Acts 24:27; 25:9 κατατίθημι
Acts 25:15, 18, 24, 26 περὶ οὗ   also Acts 19:40
Acts 25:26; 26:3 μάλιστα   also Acts 20:38
Acts 26:22 ἐκτός   29 παρεκτός
For the chapter Acts 27 see above p. 98.

The features of style of Luke–Acts here presented are not intended to prove any subtle hypothesis. I hope the time has not come when linguistic data are of no interest unless they are relevant to edifying, instructive, or controversial matters. If we may suppose that they show the native and unpremeditated working of an author's mind, that in itself is worth our knowing. They are more likely to refute subtle theories than to prove alternative ones. I believe they are of the kind that does not lend itself to the modern computer. They have to be experienced and felt rather than counted. I have no intention of reducing them to statistics.[23] And, as has been said, they fall into supplementary or even contradictory pairs.

Earlier scholars have observed such features sporadically, or at least now one and now another. They are not unique to this writer[24] even among the writers of the New Testament, whether those writers are extensive or limited in scope. And they have not always been appraised as I have done here. Of variation, it has been noticed that in the Gospel of John, when a saying of Jesus is repeated by himself or his interlocutors, it is rarely in the identical words of the verse quoted. Of the repetition of words by the author of II Peter, it has been said:[25]

A special feature of his manner, suggestive of deficient literary feeling, is the repetition of words in close contiguity (see: i:3,4 δεδωρημένος, δεδώρηται; i:10,15 σπουδάσατε, σπουδάσω; i:17,18 φωνῆς ἐνεχθείσης; φωνὴν ἐνεχθεῖσαν; i:20,21 προφη-τεία (bis); ii:1 ἀπωλείας, ἀπώλειαν; ii:13,15 μισθὸν ἀδικίας (bis); ii:14,18 δελεά-ζοντες, δελεάζουσι; ii:18,20 ἀποφεύγοντες, ἀποφυγόντες; iii:10,12 στοιχεῖα καυσού-μενα (bis) etc.

The tendency to use a word and then use it again soon afterward can be found in many writers. W. C. Allen gives examples in Matthew.[26] He calls it "a tendency to repeat a phrase or construction two or three times at short intervals." Vogel thought the habit prominent in John and "in störender Weise" in James.

If the apostle Paul is the next most extensive writer in the New Testament, his writings may be compared to those of Luke–Acts. In his own way he shows sporadically some similar features. There are the same tricks of mind, and perhaps more conspicuously so than in his biographer. The same or similar phrases occur in quite separate places in his correspondence, suggesting common authorship (or, as some would have it, literary dependence). On the other hand, he also, as the older commentators recognized, had the habit we have called "concentration." Zahn called it "a peculiarity of Paul's style, that having once employed a significant word he is apt soon to repeat it, or to make use of a related word."[27] J. H. Bernard even labeled it, when he wrote of "St. Paul's habit of dwelling on a word and coming back to it again and again (an artifice which the Latin rhetoricians called *traductio*)."[28] He was commenting on II Cor. 3:5, and I must confess that in my own experience the phenomenon is particularly marked in that letter— words of limited distribution, or cases of resumption of a phrase, or words used adjacently in different senses. Unhappily they do not often bind the larger parts of the letter together. But what I have said about Paul is perhaps sufficient to indicate that the features of Luke–Acts are to be regarded as characteristic of that work, but not distinctive or unique.

NOTES

1. C. S. C. Williams, *ExpT*, LXIV (1953) 283 ff.; *A Commentary on the Acts of the Apostles* (1957), 12-13, *et al.*; H. G. Russell, *HThR* XLVIII (1956), 167 ff.
2. The same may be said of the view revived by John Knox, *Marcion and the New Testament* (1942), that our Gospel of Luke is not as original as Marcion's. Besides Streeter's hypothetical Proto-Luke, a similar prior stage, Proto-Acts, is conjectured for Acts by A. Q. Morton in *The Structure of Luke and Acts* (1964).
3. The principal modern denier is A. C. Clark, who believes Luke and Acts written by different persons. See his *Acts of the Apostles* (1933).
4. *HSCPh* XII, pp. 299-305, "An Observation on the Style of St. Luke."
5. Compare the notices of these phenomena which I published in 1933 in volumes being reprinted only now in 1965-66, e.g., *The Beginnings of Christianity*, Part I, Vol. 4, note on Acts 5:15, and Vol. 5, p. 380, note 6, where I said, "I hope to publish fuller collections." This essay may be regarded as a partial fulfillment of that hope.
6. Part I, Vol. V ed. by Lake and Cadbury (1933), pp. 392-402.
7. As for example in Hawkins, *Horae Synopticae* (2nd ed. 1909), pp. 15-23, 27-29.
8. *The Style and Literary Method of Luke*, *HThS*, VI (1920), 62, n. 78.
9. Hawkins, *op. cit.*, p. 175.
10. J. Friedrich, *Das Lukasevangelium und die Apostelgeschichte Werke desselben Verfassers* (Halle, 1890).

11. Harnack, *Luke the Physician* (Engl. trans. 1907), pp. 199-218.
12. V. H. Stanton, *The Gospels as Historical Documents,* II (1909), 278-90.
13. Harnack, *The Sayings of Jesus* (Engl. trans. 1908), *passim.*
14. Stanton, *op. cit.,* II, 291-312.
15. Hawkins, *op. cit.,* pp. 181-82 and references there.
16. *Ibid.,* pp. 182 ff.; Harnack, *Luke the Physician,* pp. 40-105.
17. A. Klostermann, *Vindiciae Lucanae* (1866).
18. Ropes, *op. cit.,* pp. 300-304.
19. Cf. my *Making of Luke–Acts* (1927, 1958), pp. 169-78.
20. For fuller illustration see *The Style and Literary Method of Luke,* pp. 83-90.
21. Stanton, *op. cit.,* II, 300 speaks of "the combination of variety with repetition" in Luke 10:31-32; and II, 319 of "the skillful combination of repetition with variation" in Acts 20:9.
22. The passages, except for order, have identical clauses, θέλων χάριτα (χάριν) καταθέσθαι τοῖς Ἰουδαίοις.
23. As in G. Herdan's elaborate and amazing book, *Language as Choice and Chance* (Groningen: Noordhoff, 1956).
24. The unconscious tendency of modern novelists to repeat themselves at separate passages has been frequently ridiculed by *The New Yorker,* under the caption: "Infatuation with the Sound of Own Words Dept."
25. G. W. Wade, *New Testament History* (1923), p. 336.
26. *St. Matthew, ICC* (1907), pp. lxxxvi-lxxxvii.
27. Th. Zahn, *Einleitung in das Neue Testament,* 3rd. ed., cf. 29 note 7 (ET [1909], I, 500 and note pp. 516-17).
28. *Expositor's Greek Testament* (1903), III, 53.

In Search of the Original Text of Acts

A. F. J. KLIJN

The discovery of the original text is the primary aim of New Testament textual criticism. Textual criticism takes into account external evidence (the date, the geographical distribution, and genealogical relationship of manuscripts) and internal evidence (transcriptional probability or intrinsic probability).[1] At present the significance of internal evidence for restoring the original text is emphasized. The name given to this approach is "the eclectic method."[2] The preference for this method ultimately goes back to the development of textual criticism after Westcott and Hort.

Studying the manuscripts, Westcott and Hort arrived at four well-known types of text: The Syrian, the Western, the Alexandrian, and the Neutral text. Intrinsic probability led them to the conclusion that the first three types of text are secondary to the Neutral text. Westcott and Hort's results were generally accepted, but their method was just as generally suspected. The reason was that Westcott and Hort came to their conclusions without going into the historical problems with regard to these secondary texts and without explaining the origin of the Neutral text. This explains later investigations into the history of the types of texts.

Critical study then entered into the era of the so-called local texts[3] which resulted in the discovery of the Caesarean text.[4] The influence of Marcion[5] and Tatian[6] on the Western text was pointed out. It was not long before the Caesarean text was split up into the Caesarean text proper and the pre-Caesarean text. But the more these types of texts were distinguished, the more it became evident that only in a very limited sense is it possible to speak of groups of manuscripts with a definite character. Types of texts appeared to be products of a slow development aiming at standardization and starting in a period in which no types of texts were available. At the beginning each manuscript showed its own character, and it was only after a long time in which manuscripts were compared and corrected that a type of text was born.[7] This means that original readings are found from place to place in all available manuscripts, and that each variant reading has to be considered on its own merits.

Now we direct our attention to the Acts of the Apostles. In comparison with other books of the New Testament we discern in the Acts only two well-known types of text: B and D. These types are different to such an extent that Blass was able to suppose two editions, both from the hand of Luke.[8] That is why it was possible for Ropes to choose B[9] and for Clark to choose D as the original text.[10] Investigations into the text of D made clear that a whole group of variant readings had either to be rejected or accepted.[11] At the moment there is a tendency to consider D secondary to B, because D shows some marked theological trends which can only be explained as elements introduced into a text like B.[12]

This does not mean that it is impossible or unnecessary to apply the eclectic method to Acts.[13] The eclectic method takes into consideration the style, language, and theology of both the original author and the rewriter. In Acts the original author and the rewriter can easily be distinguished. But this does not mean that D has to be rejected as a whole, because it is possible that the text of D was based upon a text which showed original readings in places where they are no longer available in B.

Nevertheless it appears that textual criticism is in a favorable position to deal with the text of Acts. Yet those who, by way of the eclectic method, try to restore the original text have reached markedly disparate results. The eclectic method seems to be the only adequate method to regain the original text, but it also appears to lead us into complete chaos. The individual insights and preferences of investigators appear to vary to such an extent that they arrive at different texts. The following is a survey of the text of Acts 2:16-21 as it is given in some editions[14] and investigations[15] based on the eclectic method. It will show that unanimity seems to be impossible. Starting from the text of Nestle we find the following variant readings:

	C	K	NEB	J
2:16 om. Ιωηλ D h Ir Aug Hil Rebapt	idem	idem	idem	idem
:17 om. και¹ D sa copt syᵖ Ir Hil Aug Rebapt	?	?	και	idem
μετα ταυτα 1. εν ταις εσχαταις ημεραις B sa (LXX)	εν...ημ	εν...ημ	εν...ημ	εν...ημ
κυριος 1. ο θεος D E vg Ir Hil Rebapt	idem	?	ο θεος	idem
πασας σαρκας 1. πασα σαρκα D	...σα...κα ?	?	...σα...κα ?	...κα ?
υιοι αυτων 1. υιοι υμων D Hil Rebapt	idem	idem	υμων	idem
θυγατερες αυτων 1. θυγ υμων D Hil Rebapt	idem	idem	υμων	idem
om. υμων³ D Rebapt	idem	idem	υμων	idem
om. υμων⁴ D Rebapt	idem	idem	υμων	idem
om. ενυπνιοις Dᵍʳ	idem	?	ενυπνιοις	?
om. μου¹ Prisc Rebapt	?	?	μου	μου
om. μου² Rebapt (LXX)	?	?	μου	μου
:18 om. εν ταις ημεραις εκειναις D Rebapt	idem	idem	idem	idem
om. και προφητησουσιν D	idem	κ.προφ.	κ.προφ.	idem
:19 om. αιμα...καπνου D	idem	α...κ...	α...κ...	idem
η ελθειν 1. ελθειν B K	?	?	ελθειν	?
την ημεραν 1. ημεραν A C	?	?	ημεραν	?
:20 om. και επιφανη D gig	idem	και επ.	και επ.	idem

The variant readings deviating from the LXX have been generally accepted.[16] The table clearly shows that there is ample reason for discussing the different variant readings:

1) om. Ιωηλ. The word has been rejected as a later addition. Kilpatrick writes: "There was no occasion for omitting it, if it was in the original text,"[17] and Ropes: "It is probably a later addition."[18]

There is a tendency to add the name of the prophet in such passages:

Matt. 1:22 δια Ησαιου του προφητου in D pc it sy^sc

2: 5 δια του προφητου Μιχαιου λεγοντος in 4, per Eseiam prophetam dicentem in OL a

13:35 δια Ησαιου του προφητου in ℵ* Θ *al*

21: 4 δια του προφητου Ζαχαριου in 42 Chr Hil, Zachariam prophetam dicentem in a c h, ... Ησαιου ... in M aeth

We are, however, not allowed to accept the addition as a rule, since we do meet passages where the name of the prophet has been omitted:

Matt. 2: 7 om. Ιερεμιου in vg^codd

12:17 om. Ησαιου in 1

13:14 om. Ησαιου in 126 al Chr, sermon propheta in OL b

27: 9 om. Ιερεμιου in Φ 33 157 a l sy

2) om. και. The NEB and J disagree. One can understand J's preference for a reading which is not in agreement with the LXX. But here we have to choose between a passage deviating from the LXX and one showing the Hebrew influence on the Greek text.

3) μετα ταυτα 1. εν ταις εσχαταις ημεραις. Everyone chooses the reading deviating from the LXX. Haenchen, however, defends μετα ταυτα ("Er [Luke] ist keineswegs der Meinung, das mit Pfingsten und der Kirche die Endzeit angebrochen ist")[19] Cerfaux, on the contrary, writes: "Les temps eschatologiques chrétiens commencent à la Pentecôte."[20] Conzelmann thinks that the term has no theological significance.[21] Ropes takes this reading together with the variant reading in 18: εν ταις ημεραις εκειναις. According to him εν ταις εκειναις ημεραις was drawn from εν ταις ημεραις εκειναις in 18 which is therefore consistently omitted by D etc.[22] Apart from this εν ταις εκειναις ημεραις may have been introduced by Luke to make the quotation in agreement with the situation.

4) κυριος for ο θεος. Cerfaux and Kilpatrick accept κυριος and explain ο θεος from an attempt to show that God is the author of the quotation. Kilpatrick writes: "The tendency may have been to change κυριος to θεος, as

κυριος is ambiguous and may mean God or Christ." [23] This tendency, however, is by no means to be taken for granted. Manuscripts show very little consistency, as appears from the following list. Starting from Nestle one finds in D (J's choice has been added) : [24]

κυριος for θεος in		θεος for κυριος in	
6: 7	(J. K)	8:24	(J. K)
13: 5	(J. Θ)	10:33	(J. Θ)
13:44	(J. Θ)	12:24	(J. Θ)
16:10	(J. Θ)	15:17	(J. K)
16:32	(J. K)	16:15	(J. K)
20:28	(J. Θ)	19:20	(J. K)
21:20	(J. Θ)	20:32	(J. Θ)
		21:14	(J. K)

5. πασας σαρκας 1. πασα σαρκα. This reading is generally rejected. Cerfaux writes: "C'est d'ailleurs une leçon propre à D (contre Tert. et Ir.)" [25] This is rather weak, since he accepts other readings which can also only be found in D. Ropes and Haenchen believe that this reading is theologically important because it shows a tendency to consider the Holy Spirit as something for the world as a whole. [26]

6) θυγατερες αυτων 1. θυγατερες υμων and other readings in which υμων has been avoided. Apart from the NEB the readings which disagree with the LXX have been accepted. Haenchen takes these readings with πασας σαρκας because in all cases D etc. avoid confining the gift of the Holy Spirit to Israel. [27] We are probably not only dealing with a universalistic trend in D, but also with an anti-Judaic tendency. We draw attention to a number of other passages in Peter's speech where the same phenomenon can be found:

2: 5 om. Ιουδαιοι in ℵ (also in J.)
2:22 ημας 1. υμας in D* al Eus
2:38 εις αφεσιν τ. αμαρτιων 1. εις αφεσιν τ. α. υμων in K D pl gig r Aug Rebapt Ir (J.: ses péchés)
2:39 ημιν 1. υμιν in D Aug
ημων 1. υμων in D Aug

7) om. ενυπνιοις. Cerfaux omits the word. [28] It is, however, possible that D avoids a clear Hebraism. Haenchen takes the word with και επιφανη and speaks about a stylistic correction. [29]

8) om. μου [1 and 2]. One seems to accept the words though μου [1] in disagreement with the LXX.

9) om. εν εκειναις ταις ημεραις. The words are general; omitted. Ropes' ideas have already been mentioned above.

10. om. και προφητησουσιν. This is a peculiar reading because here D agrees with the LXX. Therefore, there must be good reasons for rejecting the words. Cerfaux believes that B adds the words "pour l'emphase."[30] Kilpatrick, however, thinks that D follows the LXX.[31] Ropes speaks of a "Western-non-interpolation" and is following D.[32]

11. om. αιμα . . . καπνου. Kilpatrick deviates from his method of following the text against the LXX, because he attempts to explain the omission as a scribal error. For the same reason he also accepts και επιφανη.[33]

12) The variant readings η ελθειν 1. ελθειν and την ημεραν 1. ημεραν can be left out of consideration, since no one has mentioned them.

From this discussion we see that variant readings have been judged upon totally different grounds. This does not happen in articles written for a few people interested in textual criticism, but in translations meant for the general public. If textual critics are themselves uncertain about the reason why one reading is rejected and another accepted, we hardly need to say that those who have to rely upon translations are left completely in the dark about the differences between the modern translations of the New Testament.

It is evident that textual criticism should not be a playground for the individual textual critic. For this reason it would be wise to register readings deviating from Nestle, so that those interested can make up their minds about them. But above all it appears necessary to work as a team. Then the individual preference of some textual critic can be corrected by those who are of a different opinion.

In conclusion we may say that with the acceptance of the eclectic method there has never been so little agreement about the nature of the original text as at the moment.

NOTES

1. See B. M. Metzger, *The Text of the New Testament* (Oxford, 1964), pp. 209-11.
2. See G. D. Kilpatrick, "Western Text and Original Text in the Gospels and Acts," *JThS*, XLIV (1943), 24-36, and K. W. Clark, "The Effect of Recent Textual Criticism Upon New Testament Studies," in W. D. Davies and D. Daube, *The Background of the New Testament, in Honour of C. H. Dodd* (Cambridge, 1951), pp. 21-51.

3. Cf. B. H. Streeter, *The Four Gospels, a Study of Origins* (2nd ed. London, 1926).
4. See B. M. Metzger, "The Caesarean Text of the Gospels," in *Chapters in the History of New Testament Textual Criticism* (Leiden, 1963), pp. 42-72).
5. Cf. A. Harnack, *Marcion* (2nd ed. Leipzig, 1924), and E. C. Blackmann, *Marcion and His Influence* (London, 1948).
6. Cf. the work of D. Plooy and the useful book of C. Peters, *Das Diatessaron Tatians, OCA,* CXIII (Rome, 1939).
7. See J. N. Birdsall, *The Bodmer Papyrus of the Gospel of John* (London, 1960).
8. F. Blass, *Acta Apostolorum secundum formam, quae videtur romanam* (Leipzig, 1896).
9. J. H. Ropes, *The Text of Acts, BC,* III (London, 1926).
10. A. C. Clark, *The Acts of the Apostles* (Oxford, 1933).
11. See E. Haenchen, "Zum Text der Apostelgeschichte," *ZThK,* LIV (1957), 22-25.
12. P. H. Menoud, "The Western Text and the Theology of Acts," *Bulletin of the Stud. Novi Test. Soc.,* Nos. I-III (Cambridge, 1963), II, 19-32; E. J. Epp, "The 'Ignorance Motif' in Acts and Anti-Judaic Tendencies in Codex Bezae," *HThR,* LV (1962), 51-62; E. J. Epp, *Theological Tendency in the Textual Variants of Codex Bezae Cantabrigiensis: Anti-Judaic Tendencies in Acts* (Ph.D. diss., Harvard Univ., 1961 [typewritten]).
13. Haenchen, "Zum Text . . . ," 55: "Wir sind hier [in D] also gar nicht auf die Untersuchung einzelner Lesarten beschränkt, sondern von vornherein auf einen übergreifenden Textzusammenhang gewiesen."
14. See *La Sainte Bible; traduite en français sous la direction de l'École Biblique de Jérusalem* (Paris, 1956), p. 1436: "Mais plus qu'ailleurs, celles qui relèvent du texte dit 'occidental' (Codex Bezae, anciennes versions latine et syriaque, anciens écrivains ecclésiastiques) méritent de retenir l'attention." *The Greek New Testament; Being the Text Translated by the New English Bible 1961,* ed. R. V G. Tasker (Oxford-Cambridge, 1964), p. vii: "The fluid state of textual criticism today makes the adoption of the eclectic method not only desirable but all but inevitable." The editions are quoted as J (Jerusalem) and NEB (New English Bible).
15. L. Cerfaux, "Citations scripturaires et tradition textuelle dans le Livre des Acts," *Aux Sources de la Tradition Chrétienne,* Goguel Festschrift (Neuchâtel-Paris, 1950), pp. 43-51; G. D. Kilpatrick, "An Eclectic Study of the Text of Acts," *Biblical and Patristic Studies in Memory of R. P. Casey* (Freiburg, 1963), pp. 64-77. These articles are quoted as C and K.
16. *Bible de Jerusalem,* p. 1439 n.c.: "Pour la citation des vv. 17-21, texte occ.; le texte alexandrin tend à revenir aux LXX." Kilpatrick, "An Eclectic Study," p. 65: "the reading which departs from the LXX is more likely to be right than the reading that agrees with it."
17. Kilpatrick, *op. cit.,* p. 65.
18. Ropes, *op. cit.,* p. 16.
19. Haenchen, "Schriftzitate und Textüberlieferung in der Apostelgeschichte," *ZThK,* LI (1954), 162.
20. Cerfaux, *op. cit.,* p. 16.
21. H. Conzelmann, *Die Apostelgeschichte* (Tübingen, 1963), p. 29.
22. Ropes, *op. cit.,* p. 16.
23. Kilpatrick, *op. cit.,* p. 66.
24. With help of J. D. Yoder, *Concordance of the Distinctive Greek Text of Codex Bezae,* NTTS, II (Leiden, 1961).
25. Cerfaux, *op. cit.,* p. 47.
26. Ropes, *op. cit.,* p. ccxxxiii; Haenchen, "Schriftiztate," p. 162.
27. Haenchen, "Schriftzitate . . . ," p. 162.
28. Cerfaux, *op. cit.,* p. 47, n. 1.

29. Haenchen, "Schriftzitate . . . ," p. 167.
30. Cerfaux, *op. cit.*, p. 47.
31. Kilpatrick, *op. cit.*, p. 66.
32. Ropes, *op. cit.*, p. 17.
33. Kilpatrick, *op. cit.*, p. 66.

Luke's Use of the Birth Stories

PAUL S. MINEAR

Nothing has been more characteristic of New Testament scholarship during the past decade than a steadily increasing concentration upon the Lucan corpus as a whole. During the same period, the output of essays dealing with the first two chapters of the corpus has been almost phenomenal, especially among Roman Catholic exegetes. It requires almost the full time of a scholar to examine the essays and monographs which treat of the infancy narratives. Neither of these facts is in itself surprising. But what is curious is the fact that so many recent studies of the Lucan corpus virtually ignore the infancy narratives, and the twin fact that so many studies of those narratives ignore the rest of the corpus. This mutual tendency may not surprise those who deny the homogeneity of the two chapters within the corpus as a whole. A rather casual reading of Luke–Acts may, to be sure, give the impression that the opening chapters form an alien bloc of material which has been assimilated with little change into an eclectic amalgam. But careful, thorough study tends to destroy this impression. If there is cumulative evidence of a basic homogeneity, it is difficult to justify such separate treatment. And there exists, in fact, a massive body of evidence supporting the homogeneity of these chapters within Luke–Acts, so massive, in fact, that no single essay can do more than summarize its extent and character. The objective of this essay is to provide that summary, and then to suggest various implications for those who are interested either in Luke's theology or in the interpretation of the birth narratives.

The scholar in whose honor these essays are prepared is one who fully recognizes the multiple connections between the opening chapters and the rest of the corpus, as reference to his research will show.[1] Professor Schubert indicates why it is so difficult to separate neatly and surely the Lucan sources from their redaction. The editor was especially facile in combining the conventional and the original, everywhere using traditional materials to serve his own "structural-literary propensities" (p. 165). He was able "to fit larger units of tradition . . . as well as little bits of information . . . into his account, and to make them subservient to his over-all literary intentions and theological purposes" (p. 170). Thus, although Luke confesses the use of many sources and is the only synoptist who does so explicitly (1:1-4), he thoroughly assimilates them into his own authorship. As a consequence, analysts are quite unable to sunder sources from redaction except where other writers have preserved the same sources. Scholars' inability to agree on the sources underlying Acts is a reminder of how difficult it would be to recover the sources of the Gospel if Mark and Matthew had not been preserved. Luke is so able an editor that many, if not most, of the marks of his pen are irrecoverable except where we have access to Mark and Q.

We may, of course, be convinced, as I am, that there are sources, both written and oral, behind the birth stories. But that conviction does not entitle us to treat them in their present location as blocs of pre-Lucan tradition, relatively free of editorial revision. We may also be convinced, as I am, that the stories are thoroughly Lucan and are fully congenial in mood and motivation to his perspective as a whole. But this does not entitle us to treat them as an *ad hoc* composition, first produced by Luke to introduce the two volumes. Luke's typical fusion of tradition and redaction is of such an order that neither of the above conclusions is tenable. As a result, to be sure, the scholar's task becomes more complex, his methods must become more supple and subtle, and his conclusions more tentative; but he should be willing to allow the character of the material to condition his own procedures and results.

I. The Integrity of Luke–Acts

Our initial task is to review the evidence for the homogeneity of the infancy stories within Luke's two-volume work. One of the early studies which still has value is the treatment of vocabulary and integrity in Alfred Plummer's commentary.[2] In a detailed study of the seven verses of Luke 2:41-47, for example, Plummer locates four expressions which are found elsewhere in Luke–Acts but nowhere else in the New Testament, and eighteen expressions which appear more times in Luke–Acts than in the rest of the New Testament (p. lxx). Among the significant words or phrases which appear both in the birth narratives and in the rest of Luke–Acts, and which are found more often in these two books than in the rest of the New Testament, are the following (I have added a few items to Plummer's list as given on pp. lix, lx):

ἀγαλλίασις	ἰδοὺ γάρ
ἄγγελος κυρίου	καθαιρεῖν
αἰνεῖν	πᾶς ὁ λαός
ἀμφότεροι	μεγαλύνειν
ἀνάγειν	μήν
ἀνιστάναι	νομίζειν
ἀντιλέγειν	ἀπὸ τοῦ νῦν
ἀνθ'ὧν	οἶκος
καὶ αὐτός	οἰκουμένη
ἄφεσις ἁμαρτιῶν	ὀνόματι
ἀφιστάναι	ὀπτασία
βρέφος	παῖς
διαλογισμοὶ καρδιῶν	παραχρῆμα
διανοίγειν	πλῆθος
διέρχεσθαι	πόλις
δοῦναι	πορεύεσθαι
ἔθος	προέρχεσθαι
εἰσάγειν	προσδέχεσθαι
ἐμπιμπλάναι	προσδοκᾶν
ἐξαίφνης	σήμερον
ἐξαποστέλλειν	σκιπτᾶν
ἐξιστάναι	σπεύδειν
ἐπέρχεσθαι	διὰ στόματος
ἐπιπίπτειν	συλλαμβάνειν
ἐπισκέπτεσθαι	συνβάλλειν
ἔτος	ὑποστρέφειν
εὐαγγελίζεσθαι (with accus.)	ὕψιστος
εὐλογεῖν τὸν θεόν	

Such a list is, of course, vulnerable to various criticisms. An author's distinctive vocabulary cannot be judged simply by a list of expressions which he uses more frequently than do other writers. Nevertheless, to ignore statistical calculations of word frequency is quite hazardous.

Plummer supplemented his word study with acute observations of syntactical phenomena, and other scholars have concurred in his identification of such distinctively Lucan traits as the following: the construction of compound verbs, frequently with two prepositions; the use of periphrastic tenses; the reliance on the articular infinitive; the frequency of πρός and the accusative with verbs of speaking; the optative mood used in indirect questions, the idiomatic attraction of the relative pronoun, a characteristic use of ἐγένετο and αὐτός (pp. li ff.). The conclusion of Plummer's analysis is succinctly stated: "The peculiarities of Luke's style and diction . . . run through our Gospel from end to end. . . . In the first two chapters they are perhaps somewhat more frequent than elsewhere" (p. lxix).

More recent studies of the various linguistic phenomena have been carried through by Robert Morgenthaler, who subjects to minute analysis the 310 words of Luke 2:1-20.[3] Conceding that statistical counting cannot by itself establish or destroy the authenticity of a passage, he concludes that "eine geradezu erdrückende Übermacht von Tatsachen hier für die Echtheit dieses Abschnittes spricht" (p. 63). The evidence is even stronger for the first two chapters as a whole, where no fewer than forty-six of the sixty-two favorite words of Luke appear. An analysis of such stylistic tests as the use of αὐτός, the conjunctions, articular infinitive, the prepositions, the article, Latinisms, reveals a remarkable presence in the birth stories of Lucan elements and an equally remarkable absence of un-Lucan traits.

These results are impressively supported by Morgenthaler's earlier and much more extensive analysis of Luke–Acts.[4] In this study, he examined "das Zweiheitsgesetz" as a distinctive element in the Lucan style. He located various forms of "Zweigliedrigkeit," such as the doubling of words, sentences, and sections; the matching of two persons and their witnesses to revelation; and the organization of the *two*-volume work as a whole. In the following types of parallelism, the birth stories reflect the same stylistic phenomena as the entire corpus.

1. the doubling of cognate words for emphasis
    e.g., ὀνομάσθη τὸ ὄνομα (2:21, pp. 18-19)
2. the matching of sounds and forms of alliteration
    e.g., σκότει καὶ σκιᾷ (1:79, p. 20)
3. tautologies (many instructive examples)
    e.g., πνεῦμα καὶ δύναμις (1:35, pp. 22-29)
4. antitheses, such as God and man, heaven and earth, husband and wife,

kinsmen and friends, day and night, falling and rising, seeing and hearing (pp. 30-31)

5. chiastic structures

e.g., (a) glory (b) highest (b) earth (a) peace (2:14, p. 42)

6. parallel sentences

e.g, 1:80 and 2:40; 2:19 and 2:51 (p. 48)

7. double citation formulas

e.g., 2:23, 24 (p. 70)

8. parallel sections arranged in architectonic fashion (pp. 97-98)

—two annunciations of Gabriel and two hymns of praise in chap. 1

—two birth narratives 1:57-66; 2:1-20

—two temple scenes in chap. 2 with two angelic messages and two meetings with Simeon and Anna

9. Chiastic structure of sections (p. 142)

a—the annunciation to Zechariah

b—the annunciation to Mary

b—the hymn of Mary

a—the hymn of Zechariah

10. The continuation of the parallel structure of the birth stories into the stories of the preaching of John and Jesus and their organization as a single block 1:5-4:13 (pp. 154-55, 167-68)

11. Parallel construction of large sections, with common traits

Luke 1:5-4:13 and Luke 19:45-22:53 (p. 167)

Luke 1:5-3:22 and Acts 1:8-4:13 (pp. 179-80)

In his views of the overall pattern of the corpus, Morgenthaler may be vulnerable to the charge of unjustified schematization, but this charge should not become an excuse for ignoring his observations regarding the phenomena themselves. Quite apart from the validity of his various deductions, we must take seriously the probability that many stylistic and architectonic features which permeate the birth stories link those stories to the entire corpus. They cannot easily be explained solely by reference to the sources on which Luke drew.

Many scholars have found even more impressive evidence of homogeneity in certain pervasive interests and themes. In summarizing their work, with some arbitrariness, which may oversimplify the rich pluralism of Lucan motifs, we can group these observations under eight headings:

1. The historiographical style. This is reflected in the stereotyped intro-

ductory formulas, with their use of such phrases as ἐγένετο δέ and the interest in times, places, and names (1:5; 2:1; 3:1, 19).[5] There is a distinctive conception of Judea (cf. J. M. Creed, *Commentary on St. Luke* [Macmillan 1930] p. 8), and a notable concentration on Jerusalem, on cities, on journeys, and on the temple.

2. The use of speeches, citations, and hymns to serve as "programmatic entrances" (Bultmann). They serve as advance summaries, as proleptic anticipations of what is to follow. There is an observable kinship between the Canticles in the opening chapters, the opening "keynote addresses" of John and Jesus (chaps. 3, 4), and the sermons of Acts.[6] In fact, there is a surprising degree of correlation between the hymns in Luke 1–2, and elements in those summaries of the kerygma which C. H. Dodd and others have culled from Acts. Other links can be noted between the Canticles and the citation from Joel in Acts 2, between the use of Isaiah in the prologue and in the epilogue of Acts 28. Luke's thought gravitates toward and is oriented around strategic speeches, citations, and hymns.

3. Common ecclesiological conceptions. Here may be mentioned the Lucan use of such terms as Israel, πᾶς ὁ λαός, οἱ ἅγιοι, οἱ δίκαιοι. Attention is drawn also to the typological character of individual episodes and characters, whether grounded in the patriarchs (Abraham, the Twelve, Simeon, Asher), or in the prophets (Elijah, Elisha, Moses), or in priestly figures (Aaron, Levi). Moreover, the prologue clearly anticipates both the conflict within Israel occasioned by the Messiah, and the inclusion within this people of both Israel and the Gentiles.[7] From the first to the last chapters of the corpus it is "the hope of Israel" which is at stake. This hope is seen as especially relevant to the poor, to women and especially to widows, to those who walk in darkness, to lepers and outcasts, to sinners who repent, and to the righteous who wait in patient expectancy.

4. The liturgical character of the life of this people. The prevalence of such words as δοξάζειν and εὐλογεῖν is significant, as is the frequency of worship in the temple, of fasting and prayer, of joy and peace.[8] What Bultmann has observed about ἀγαλλίασις (Kittel *ThWB* I) is true of many of these terms: God's help is always the theme; the reality of God's manifestation of vindication is presupposed; the community is empowered by the Spirit to make jubilant, grateful celebration of salvation. Cadbury has observed the extent to which the characters are models of piety and of observance of laws and customs. Especially is this true in the descriptions of

worship, whether in the prologue or in Acts (Cadbury, *Making of Luke-Acts,* pp. 306-7. In this respect there is a measure of affinity with Pirke Aboth 1:2 with its picture of the world sustained by three things: Torah, temple, and acts of piety.)

5. The reliance upon epiphany and angels. The entire corpus gives many examples of complicated and interrelated sets of visions (e.g., to Elizabeth and Mary, to Peter and Cornelius, to Paul and Ananias). The witness of men is made to echo the prior witness of angels. It is the reaction of men to the intervention of angels which determines mood and movement. The mood is marked by fear and fearlessness, by θαυμάζειν and λαλεῖν. The movement is marked by symbolic gestures and actions, by the provision of signs, by visitations which carry forward the divine plan. Gifts of the Spirit produce both consent and denial. Everywhere each sign of God's design serves as "more than mere divine credential for use at the moment. It looks forward to a future destiny." [9]

6. The accent upon the fulfillment of God's promise. Angels, prophets, apostles,—all characters are in one way or another witnesses to the stupendous things which God has determined to accomplish. Every epiphany is related to ὁ λόγος τοῦ θεοῦ or to τὸ ῥῆμα τοῦ θεοῦ. Prominent and distinctive is Luke's use of the verbs εὐαγγελίζεσθαι and ἀποστέλλειν (cf. 1:19; 7:20, 27; Acts 28:28). Even those who reject the gospel become unwitting pointers to it.

7. The pictures of response to God's inaugurated fulfillment. There is a typical Lucan syndrome descriptive of the true response to God's redemption. It includes hearing, turning, repenting, praying, being forgiven, rejoicing, deeds appropriate to repentance, the gift of the Spirit, a people prepared and witnessing. There are many "eye-witnesses and servants of the Word" to be encountered *within* Luke–Acts, beginning with Zechariah in Luke 1 and ending with Paul in Acts 28. All have been given by the Spirit their endowment for future witnessing. (Cadbury, *Making of Luke-Acts,* p. 305.) Very frequently their testimonies are arranged in complementary pairs, in keeping with the Deuteronomic requirements. (Morgenthaler, Vol. II, pp. 8-9.) They all bear witness not alone to their immediate neighbors but also to the readers of the two volumes.

8. The christological shape of the witness. In dogmatic terms, Luke does not think or write in terms of precise discrimination among the various christological titles and images. It would seem that debate over the *right*

titles was not as important to him as to many of his modern interpreters. Characteristic of him is the variety of motifs. He speaks of the prophetic work of Christ; of his links to Abraham, to Moses, to Elijah, to David; of his priestly intercession; of his kingship and kingdom. He shows little awareness of contradiction among these, and little desire to argue the superiority of one over the others. His use of ὁ χριστός to refer to "the Messiah" is quite unaffected and distinctive. He seems to be concerned from first to last with the consolation of Jerusalem, with the Messiah's rule over the house of Jacob, a redemption which comes to "our fathers" and to their "posterity forever" (1:55). The work of God's servant (the Messiah) is seen as inseparable from God's help to "his servant Israel" (1:54). As observed above, this includes rather than excludes God's promise of "light to the Gentiles" (2:32; 28:28).

Our intention in the above summary has been to include only those observable features which link together the birth stories and the entire corpus. For a complete and impartial appraisal we would need, of course, to review the evidence for the other side of the issue but such a task must await another occasion. Sufficient evidence has been offered to enable us to ask whether typical current studies have given adequate weight to it.

II. Consequences for Treatments of Luke's Theology

In this section we shall comment upon the work of two scholars, whose central objective has been the recovery of the theology of Luke. We begin with the work of Professor Schubert as an example of an exegete who recognizes the homogeneity which we have pictured. How might a more thorough recognition of that homogeneity qualify or supplement his position?

Schubert insists that the nativity stories are part and parcel of the "proof-from-prophecy theology" which dominates Luke–Acts. In these stories he observes that no fewer than eight prophets speak successively concerning the redemption of Jerusalem ("The Structure," pp. 178-79). Each of the eight speaks under the power of the Holy Spirit, a central motif in Lucan eschatology. They appear not only to herald the fulfillment of earlier prophecies, but also to serve as "full-fledged messianic prophets themselves." Their stories are so poetic and liturgical in character as to discourage treatments of Luke as a rationalistic historian.

We welcome this scholar's recognition of the nativity stories as a significant prologue not only to the opening messages of John and Jesus but to the whole corpus. (Some scholars limit the term *prologue* to 1:1-4, but I apply it to the first two chapters.) We ask, however, whether we cannot learn even more from the prologue concerning Luke's conception of "proof from prophecy."

Do these stories support the strongly *apologetic* accent upon the word *proof?* I have elsewhere defended the nonapologetic setting for the stories.[10] Here I may issue a warning against use of the word *proof* in this connection. The concept of proof is not characteristically biblical; even less is it Lucan. Proof suggests an appeal to external evidence as a means of appealing to the reason of an unbeliever. It suggests a debating forum or a propaganda leaflet. A term more congenial to the Lucan mood and context would be witness, or testimony. Even these words must be interpreted in a context of joy, penitence, humility, fear—that is, in a situation of communal exultation over long-awaited salvation. In this situation, testimony takes on its most intimate, informal, internal, and evocative character, as an element in the divine-human encounter and in the movement of the Spirit. The scenes in Luke–Acts exert their own "atmospheric pressures" under which the testimonies spring from and seek to elicit shouts of joy and hymns of praise on the part of a devout community, which knows itself dependent on God's saving power. The term *proof* is alien to that milieu.

Similar hesitations accompany the word *prophecy.* Although this is a good biblical word, frequently found in Luke–Acts, its modern connotation focuses upon the separate and specific Old Testament predictions. In Luke–Acts we are dealing with an outburst of the gift of prophecy, in which each interpreter of the Scriptures is himself a prophet for his own day, and for the church of Luke's day. Prophecy often calls to mind the individual messenger and his explicit prediction. It often is associated with the response of formal and rational credence (or rejection). In Luke, all the prophetic figures are servants of the same word, glad recipients of the same promise, linked together into one community by the same Spirit, giving testimonies to a single divine action. The individual prophets, who appear seriatim, have as close a kinship to one another as do those whose tongues were touched at Pentecost. All speak of the same salvation. It is God's fulfillment of his promise to which they all point. And they do more than point to the fact of fulfillment; they illustrate the communal response evoked by that fact; faith, hope, endurance, joy, expectation, exultation. Luke does not argue that the event of consummation is vindicated by its correspondence to specific predictions; rather, he joins in the full spectrum of response to the Good News, with the resurgence of the prophetic gift as one of the phenomena of the new age. The caption "proof from prophecy" does not cover all of the actors, either in the prologue or in the entire corpus. Schubert counts eight prophets in the prologue, but three of these are angels. Moreover, Luke explicitly names only two—Zechariah and Anna—as prophets. A more inclusive label for his theology would be "theology of the time of fulfillment."

The caption "proof" invites the question, Proof of what? Schubert answers: "that Jesus is the Christ and that God has raised him from the dead" (*"The Structure,"* p. 174). This answer seems obvious when one is dealing, as is Schubert, with Luke 24. But it is less germane to the birth stories and to various testimonies in Acts. That answer is not wrong for the two volumes, but it is not entirely adequate to cover the prophecies of Zechariah, Simeon, Ananias, Philip's four daughters, Agabus, or Paul's assurance to the sailors, not to mention the citations from the Old Testament and the messages from angels. Surely the whole sequence of events from the conception of John to the arrival of Paul in Rome belongs within the orbit of Luke's testimony to the ways in which God is pouring out his Spirit "on all flesh." And this testimony, we must stress, is not only a fulfillment of God's preordained βουλή as revealed in the Scriptures. It is also the renewal of prophecy within the compass of contemporaneous events. Luke's work is a vast collection of testimonies to that renewal, reminding his readers that they live within the orbit of the promise, as elect heirs of the hope of Israel.[11] Such comments corroborate and amplify Schubert's thesis concerning the structural and theological links between Luke 24, Acts 28, Acts 1, and Luke 1–2.

Perhaps the most influential of the recent studies of Lucan theology is that by Hans Conzelmann. Unlike Schubert, he makes minimal use of the nativity stories. What role might the nativity stories play in modifying his portrait of Luke as a theologian? One writer, H. H. Oliver, has already answered this question.[12] Although he challenges Conzelmann's dictum that the birth stories are irrelevant to Luke's purpose (p. 202), Oliver uses those stories to support Conzelmann's conclusions with only minor qualifications. In my judgment the qualifications should take on major proportions.

If Conzelmann had taken full account of the nativity stories, I believe his position would have been changed at several major points.

He sets out with the aim of elucidating "Luke's work in its present form, . . . the whole of Luke's writings as they stand." [13] Later, however, he virtually refuses to call upon the evidence provided by the two first chapters (apart from the first four verses). Because "the authenticity of these first two chapters is questionable, we have not taken into consideration the statements that are peculiar to them" (p. 118). In effect, then he surrenders his initial aim "not to enquire into possible sources or into the historical facts which provide the material" (p. 9). On occasion he finds agreement between these and later chapters (e.g., the absence of the idea of preexistence), but so many of the features in chaps. 1–2 are either "contradicted" or "deliberately avoided in the rest of the Gospel" that they virtually cease to be usable as reflections of Lucan perspectives (p. 172). He grudgingly recognizes affinities which would be significant "if the prologue is an original component." As an example, he details several significant links between the birth and the passion stories. But these affinities point in a different direction from that suggested to Conzelmann by Luke's alterations of Mark. Since this is so, Conzelmann gives priority to his own conjectural reconstruction of Luke's editorial policy and arrives at his conclusions as if the prologue were not an original component (p. 75, n. 4; cf. also n. 1, p. 18). In effect, then, Conzelmann bases his analysis of Luke's theology not on the whole corpus, but on the chapters of the Gospel beginning with Luke 3. So when he asks, "What is the structure of the Gospel itself?" it is clear that he does not look to the birth narratives for positive clues.

I believe that it is only by thus ignoring the birth narratives that Conzelmann can appear to establish his thesis that Luke visualized the story of salvation as emerging in three quite distinct stages: the period of Israel, the period of Jesus' ministry, the period since the ascension (pp. 16-17). This will be seen most clearly if we focus attention on two pivots which Conzelmann has chosen to mark the points of transition.

The first of these pivots is defined sharply in terms of the transition between the ministry of John the Baptist and the active preaching of Jesus. "John the Baptist, according to Luke, does not proclaim the Kingdom of God and Luke 16:16 shows why: it is not yet possible for him to know anything about it. Only Jesus possesses this knowledge for it is the message of the Kingdom of God that constitutes the new element in the present epoch of salvation, in contrast to the old epoch whose last representative was John the Baptist" (p. 161). "John does not proclaim the Kingdom of God, as is made plain in 16:16 as a point of principle" (p. 20). He is not seen by Luke as "an authentic eschatological figure" (p. 101). "He does not represent the arrival of the new age, but serves to bring out the comparison between the old age and the new one which has come with Jesus" (p. 185, n. 2). These citations should make clear the contention that the turning point falls between John and Jesus. They should also make clear how much weight Conzelmann places upon Luke 16:16 in establishing the pivot. It must be said that rarely has a scholar placed so much weight on so dubious an interpretation of so difficult a logion. For him this logion determines the lines of exegesis and, in fact, the whole schematization of Luke's view of redemptive history. Strangely enough, he does not raise the question of the source for 16:16; he does not trace the *Formgeschichte* or the *Redaktionsgeschichte* of this key verse; he does not relate it to its strange setting in Luke (the controversy with the Pharisees in vss. 14-15, and the bearing upon divorce in vs. 18); he does not consider possible implications of the various syntactical problems. No—this verse achieves a quite unique status in Conzelmann's mind, invulnerable, and undebatable.

At numerous points this view of the matter contradicts the prologue, as Conzelmann admits. Let us indicate a few of those contradictions. In the prologue Luke perceives the decisive shift in God's decision to fulfill his promise and to satisfy the prayers of the patient. This decision is announced by Gabriel's message and by the powerful actions of the Holy Spirit. Gabriel and the angels are the first messengers who tell the good tidings (Conzelmann admits the Lucan character of εὐαγγελίζεσθαι but insists upon its "non-eschatological" content [pp. 23, n. 1; 40, 222-23]).

There is a genuine "typological correspondence between John the Baptist and Jesus" with John clearly cast in the role of Elijah (p. 24). Although the prologue preserves a distinction between the tasks of the two figures, at no point does it make an invidious or apologetic effort to downgrade or to deny the eschatological significance of John. (Oliver, *NTS* X, notes the distinction between "a prophet of the Most High" (1:76) and "a son of the Most High" (1:32), but this does not encourage the reader to despise the importance of the former or betray a conscious desire to stress his inferiority.) The work of both men is seen as essential to the fulfillment of the promise, as ground for the joy of redemption. Both are included within the same consolation of Israel. In fact, the mood, resonance, and thrust of the birth narratives are such as to discourage the neat assignment of John and Jesus to separate epochs. The prologue may preserve symbolic geographical distinctions between Judea (Zechariah and Elizabeth) and Galilee (Joseph and Mary) and again in the presentation scene, where Simeon may represent the south and Anna the north (the territory of Asher), but the point of the distinction is surely not to separate the old aeon from the new (Conzelmann, p. 20). The prologue does not pointedly deny John an important role in the baptism of Jesus (p. 21). In passage after passage Conzelmann interprets Luke's omissions and additions to Mark as part of a conscious intention on the redactor's part to diminish the role of John, so that he will no longer mark "the arrival of the new aeon" (p. 22-23). Oliver's observation appears to me to be entirely accurate (and far more devastating than he supposes), when he writes that Luke could make such changes in the Marcan tradition because "the relationship between the two men had *already been well established in the birth stories.*" (*NTS* X, p. 217. The italics are Oliver's.) In short, the prologue plus the bulk of the references to John the Baptist reflect a picture of Luke's thought which renders Conzelmann's interpretation of 16:16 suspect, which suggests other interpretations, and which may lead us toward viewing it as drawn from a non-Lucan collection of logia. Thereby the first of the two pivots of Conzelmann's schema is threatened.

In his location of the turning point at the opening message of Jesus, Conzelmann also places excessive weight upon the σήμερον of 4:21 as indicating a decisive shift in *Heilsgeschichte*. He is probably correct in seeing this word as typically Lucan, since it appears as often in Luke–Acts as in the rest of the New Testament combined. But he is less convincing in his contention that to Luke this *today* marks a period of time that is "now over and finished" (p. 36), thus representing a punctiliar, linear, chronological conception of events. It would be difficult to apply the same judgment to such other Lucan uses of the word as are found in 2:11; 3:22 (var.); 19:9; and 23:43 where the presence of decisive, eschatological salvation is the dominant note. This is not to say, of course, that Luke did not consider Jesus' work as more important than John's, or that the programmatic significance of 4:16 ff. is to be denied. There is much to be said for Morgenthaler's contention, however, that we should consider the whole of 1:5–4:30 as the prologue of the double-volume (Morgenthaler, pp. 155, 165).

What can be said about the relationship of the prologue to Conzelmann's second pivot, the transition from the period of Jesus' ministry to the period of the church? The passage which marks this transition is Luke 22:35-36 and especially the ἀλλὰ νῦν of vs. 36. The decisive and distinctive aspect of Luke's view of history according to Conzelmann, is the *separation* of the period of the church from the period of Jesus' ministry. To stress this separation, Conzelmann refers on no fewer than seventeen occasions to the logion of 22:36 (*ibid.*, p. 13, 16, 36, 50, 80 ff., 91-92, 103, 153, 170, 187, 199, 201, 232, 234). Again he places tremendous weight upon an uncertain interpretation of an extremely difficult verse and especially on the phrase ἀλλὰ νῦν. Before this νῦν the disciples are immune to πειρασμός; after it they are vulnerable (p. 81). He makes this interpretation a postulate, quite undebatable, which determines the interpretation of many other passages. These conclusions run counter to an analysis of this pericope by H. Schürmann, who concludes that it is highly improbable that the ἀλλὰ νῦν is due to the redactor.[14] To Conzelmann the period of the church and the Spirit begins after this (p. 150). At this point many of the teachings of Jesus are annulled and exert no further claim on the disciples (p. 13). They do not represent an ideal for the continuing present of the church (p. 14). Now the virtue of patience becomes dominant, in view of the distance from both ἀρχή and παρουσία. "The nearness of the kingdom has become a secondary factor" (p. 37). Many words and concepts lose their eschatological character: preaching (p. 221), baptism and repentance (p. 102), the victory of the disciples (p. 82), θλῖψις (p. 98), the battle against Satan (p. 156), the victory of the disciples (p. 82), John and his baptism (p. 101), the role of Jerusalem (p. 132), the mysteries (p. 103), the work of the Holy Spirit (p. 183). This last item is especially significant. Conzelmann joins Barrett in stressing the participation of the Spirit at the turning points between the epochs—at the baptism of Jesus and at the baptism of the disciples at Pentecost (p. 183). The second outpouring marks not "the start of the Eschaton but the beginning of a longer epoch, the period of the Church. . . . The Spirit Himself is no longer the eschatological gift, but the substitute in the meantime for the possession of ultimate salvation" (p. 95).

The reader will note that almost every item in this list is a matter to which the birth stories give attention. Moreover, in the prologue the accent falls on meanings other than those stressed by Conzelmann. One must conclude that Conzelmann could arrive at his understanding of Lucan theology only by ignoring or rejecting the evidence provided by the birth narratives.

It is not too much to say that three temporal phrases or words in Luke 16:16, 4:21 and 22:36 are for him much more influential than the whole of chapters 1 and 2. Let me mention two specific elements in those chapters which would point in quite a different direction.

These narratives are pervasively "eschatological" by any except a narrow, wooden definition of that term, and they even have marked affinities with the milieu represented by the Johannine Apocalypse. Yet they carry the beginning of the message of salvation back to a period before the sermon of Jesus at Nazareth (thus placing doubt upon a solely punctiliar, chronological meaning of σήμερον in 4:21). They also envisage and anticipate the whole period of Jesus' ministry and of the life of the church. The contemporaneity of the apostolic kerygma and of the eschatological events, in Conzelmann's first period as well as in his third period, is signalized by the pregnant use of the first person plural in the Canticles.[15] It is also indicated clearly by the recurrent references to all the people and to all peoples, and by the symbolic centrality of the temple, Jerusalem and Israel (1:14, 17, 33, 48, 68; 2:14; 30-32, 34-35). Whenever and wherever the church has used these stories it has celebrated its present time, its σήμερον (2:21), as a time of fulfillment. In short, those very elements which Conzelmann claims are ways of separating the three epochs are used in the prologue to suggest compresence, continuity, and contemporaneity. This is not to deny that Luke recognized that real and important changes occurred with the Nazareth sermon, with the Last Supper, with the resurrection and ascension. But it is to protest Conzelmann's exaggeration, particularization, and schematization of those moments in linear time. He has missed the subtle sense in which each prophetic message opens the way to the whole sequence of events which follows, each message a programmatic announcement of God's whole design. One finds it most difficult to read the prologue as Luke's readers must have read it, and to conclude that for Luke "the time of salvation . . . is now over and finished" (p. 36). Luke's appreciation of the Semitic "symbolism of the center" (M. Eliade) suggests a quite different stance.

III. The Consequences for Treatments of the Birth Narratives

At the outset of this essay, it was noted that many, if not most, recent studies of the birth stories view them in relative isolation from the rest of the Lucan corpus. Thomas Boslooper, for example, can devote over two hundred pages to this subject and include no more than half a dozen marginal references to other chapters in Luke–Acts.[16] This radical separation of the stories from their initial literary context is obviously based on the assumption, which often goes without explicit notice or defense, that Luke's redaction and use of the narratives is a relatively negligible factor in their interpretation. This method of analysis can be justified if the stories are demonstrably alien to the rest of Luke's work. But when we consider the cumulative evidence for homogeneity, the method becomes suspect. Various difficulties appear, to which closer scrutiny should be directed. Since Luke provides our *only access* to these particular stories, is it legitimate to view them *primarily* in terms of their Matthean parallels or in terms of correspondence to similar legends in more remote documents? Since he determined to adopt them as the most fitting introduction to his literary witness, should we not listen to them first in the context of that witness? Since his evaluation and interpretation of this material affords the earliest and most immediately accessible exegesis of them, should we so hastily pass over the clues which he provides to that evaluation and interpretation? Since there are so many marks of continuity in vocabulary, style, structure, and thematic accent, should we so quickly assume that we can treat the stories as independent sources, free from Lucan concerns and perspectives?

What, then, are some of the consequences for the treatment of the birth narratives, which stem from a recognition of the integrity of the corpus as a whole? Perhaps the best approach, within the limited space at our disposal, is to consider those features which *seem* to be of little or no interest to Luke, as judged by their absence from the later chapters.

A first example is provided by certain geographical references within the narrative. Seemingly essential to the stories are the locations of Jesus' birth at Bethlehem (2:4, 15) and John's birth in an unnamed city in the hill country of Judah (1:39). Do we not have clear evidence of an unabridged and uninterpreted source in the fact that the words Bethlehem and Judah appear only here in Luke's writings? Must we not infer that Luke had no interest in these two cities? Yet this inference is undermined when we observe that in 1:65 Judah becomes Judea, which constitutes a very important category for Luke's conception of God's plan, and when we observe that in the case of Bethlehem, the story accents the significance of this location *in Judea* as *a city of David* (2:4, 11). Quite obviously David is a strategic name in Luke's perspective. Moreover, these references appear within a bloc of material which is oriented around Jerusalem and the temple, a prominent and continuing concern of Luke. A further point—the significance of the place references in the prose narrative seems subordinate to and may be derived from the strong accents in the poetic songs on the throne of David, the house of Jacob (1:32, 33), the servant Israel (1:54; 2:32, 34), and the house of David (1:69). If one listed all the cities in which important events happened but which Luke mentions only once or twice, the list would be quite impressive (cf. Morgenthaler, *Statistik,* p. 174). It is hazardous, therefore, on the basis of place-names, to posit a source with a provenance and perspective which differ demonstrably from that of Luke–Acts.

A more impressive body of data appears when we observe the personal actors who are not mentioned later. In the order of appearance, this list would include Zechariah, Gabriel, Elizabeth, Joseph (apart from Luke 3:23, 4:22), the shepherds, Simeon, and Anna. The absence of reference in later chapters to these characters is one of the major evidences of a separate source, with separate provenance and reflecting non-Lucan motifs. This argument from silence, however, is quite precarious. We can admit, as we have, the probability of sources for Luke 1–2, but can we safely infer from the occurrence of these names the extent of those sources and the presence in them of a set of un-Lucan convictions and conceptions? We dare not overlook the multiple indications that Luke also in later chapters includes important names (e.g., the names of many disciples and even apostles, Levi, Zacchaeus, Matthias, two men called Ananias, Stephen, Philip, Apollos), and then ceases to mention them beyond the bounds of the episode in which they were involved. As Conzelmann accurately writes: "Where a question of principle is concerned, Luke refers only to Israel as such, not to individual figures in Biblical history. Where they appear, the reference is to their sayings which are more important than their existence as persons" (*The Theology of Saint Luke,* p. 173). Although Conzelmann applies this observation to Luke's picture of David, it applies even more cogently to the *dramatis personae* in chaps. 1–2. One focus of the stories, and of Luke's interest in them, is the substance of the message which is embodied in the words of the angels and the human characters. Another focus is the relation (and subordination) of each of the characters to God's plan for the redemption of Israel. A third focus is the description of each human character in such a way as to represent a type of corporate patience and expectancy, of faithful submission or doubting unbelief in the Word of God. But these foci of concern, which are implicit in the stories themselves, are precisely the traits which pervade the whole of Luke–Acts. Such accents probably constitute Luke's "exegesis" of whatever sources may have been accessible to him. If our interests in these characters diverge from his, as they often do, this exegesis stands directly in the path of our efforts to reconstruct the stories of these characters independently of his own reconstruction.

Is this equally true of the subject which has served as a magnet for virtually all later Christian treatments of chapters 1 and 2, i.e., the role of Mary as the virgin mother of Jesus? Because of its centrality in later theology, liturgy, and devotion, exegesis seem forced in dealing with this subject to press behind Luke's literary intention and his own exegetical understanding. Here, at least, many feel required to posit an ultimate source for Luke's information (Mary, herself, as the first witness) as well as intervening stages in the developing tradition[17]

The name of Mary was, of course, firmly fixed in Christian tradition long before Luke's day. Moreover, she is central to the entire collection of stories in Luke 1–2 in a way sharply in contrast to the other characters listed above. Without her the stories would lose their cohesion. (The legends concerning the birth of John and of Jesus may at one time have been quite separate, but Luke's version provides very little tangible evidence for that conjecture. I find the evidence cited by Bultmann, *History,* p. 294, far from convincing.) The frequency of reference (12 times) indicates the significance of Mary within the two chapters. It is therefore striking, indeed, that the name recurs only once later in the corpus (Acts 1:14), that Luke repeats with little modification the Marcan story of Jesus' mother trying to dissuade him from his work (Luke 8:19-20), that he is the only synoptist to record a saying which can be interpreted as a rebuke of praise given to his mother (11:27-28) and that, as Conzelmann phrases it, "Mary disappears to a greater extent in Luke than in Mark and Matthew" (*The Theology of Saint Luke,* p. 172). Moreover, many scholars have observed that nowhere later does Luke clearly refer to the virgin birth or to its attendant circumstances, a silence that is not adequately explained by 2:19.

It is not difficult to explain why exegetes, noting Luke's later silences regarding Mary and the birth of Jesus, have been impelled by theological and ecclesiastical concerns to concentrate on recovering the pre-Lucan materials and on interpreting them along lines independent of the Lucan redaction. In so doing, modern concerns usually are superimposed upon the stories in a way which locates in pre-Lucan sources the answers to post-Lucan questions. The result is thoroughly anachronistic, in part because a later attitude toward the miraculous, whether positive or negative, replaces the Lucan perspectives. The modern interpreter is tempted to view the virgin birth as the decisive element in the story, as one miraculous event set in a sequence of nonmiraculous events, an event freed from the chains of historical causation which conditioned the other events.

As they now stand in Luke, the narratives do not invite this set of attitudes. The stories unfold in such a way as to disclose a single skein of events, all of which stem from the marvelous fulfillment by God of his covenant promises to Israel. All the separate episodes participate in a single reality. If we are to introduce the dubious category of the miraculous, we should apply it first of all to the skein of events as a whole. The whole fabric is a witness to the marvelous response of God to the covenant promise and prayers of Israel, a response which is announced by angels and which releases the Holy Spirit to do its predestined work. The continuities within the sphere of earthly happenings are provided not by a network of earthly causation but by the overarching purpose of God. As Karl Barth writes: "There are no independent figures—figures who have any significance of their own apart from Christ. . . . The men of whom we hear are what they are totally through the grace of God.[18] The fabric of the story is so tightly knit, in both literary and theological terms, that it resists the tearing of one episode loose from the fabric, and the contrasting of its character as miracle to the nonmiraculous character of the rest. Nothing in the stories, for example, suggests that "the half-miracle of the birth of John is immediately surpassed by the entirely miraculous birth of Jesus" (Boslooper, *The Virgin Birth*, p. 108).

To the extent that the exegete recognizes this aspect of the language mode of the prologue, to that same extent he will recognize the pervasive priority of the pluralism of Lucan motifs enumerated above (pp. 114-18). This will lead him to recognize the degree to which the mood and motifs initiated in the prologue continue to characterize the later narratives. There are, to be sure, important contrasts between the Gospel and the Acts, and the scholar must do full justice to them. In the Acts, it is the story of Pentecost which plays an analogous thematic role. That story is dominated by the work of the Spirit, which places a sequence of marvelous episodes and speeches within a marvelous context. It sets the tone and temper of all the stories and speeches which follow, yet nowhere in those later chapters is there an explicit reference to what we might call "the virgin birth" of the church. In a similar way the first two chapters of the Gospel "set the stage" for all subsequent speeches and actions.

When this subtle homogeneity is detected, there are important consequences for the treatment of the birth narratives, many of which we have left unmentioned. It will remain, of course, an important task of the interpreter to examine them for evidence of Lucan sources (both Christian and Septuagintal), for stages in their formation, and for marks of Luke's editorial pen. But this study will be most persuasive when we accord priority to Luke's understanding and use of them. When we penetrate his theological outlook and literary craftsmanship, we will find that many of our analyses of the separate episodes have started from wrong assumptions, have raised the wrong questions, have moved in directions which can lead only to unsupported conjectures and ultimate frustration. In the end we will receive more help for our task from the editor of this two-volume work than from any other wrtier, ancient or modern, that is unless we adopt objectives which are genuinely alien to his.

NOTES

1. Paul Schubert, "The Structure and Significance of Luke 24" in *Neutestamentliche Studien für R. Bultmann* (Berlin, 1957).
2. *The Gospel According to St. Luke* (New York, 1896), pp. xli-lxx.
3. *Statistik des N. T. Wortschatzes* (Zürich, 1958), pp. 62-63, 187.
4. *Die lukanische Geschichtsschreibung als Zeugnis* (2 vols.; Zürich, 1949). Unless otherwise indicated, references are to Vol. I.
5. Cf. R. Bultmann, *History of the Synoptic Tradition*, trans. John Marsh (New York, 1963), pp. 360-61
6. Cf. H. J. Cadbury, *Beginnings of Christianity*, V, 417, 420 ff.
7. 2:29-35, A. R. C. Leaney, *St. Luke* (New York, 1958), pp. 99-100.
8. Cf. R. Laurentin, *Structure et Théologie de Luc I, II* (Paris, 1957), pp. 101-2.
9. H. J. Cadbury, *The Making of Luke–Acts*, p. 305.
10. *Theology Today*, VII (1950), 363-64.
11. Cf. C. K. Barrett, *Luke the Historian in Recent Study* (London, 1961), p. 18.
12. *NTS*, X (1964), 202-26.
13. H. Conzelmann, *The Theology of Saint Luke*, trans. G. Buswell (London, 1960), p. 9.
14. Heinz Schürmann, *Jesu Abschiedsrede* (Münster, 1957), p. 121. Cf. also my essay on this episode in *NovTest* VII (1964), pp. 128-34.
15. 1:55, 69-75, 78, 79. Cf. H. Schürmann, *Erfurter ThSt*, XII (1963), 48-73.
16. *The Virgin Birth* (Philadelphia, 1962).
17. Cf. R. Laurentin, *Structure*, p. 20.
18. *The Great Promise* (New York, 1963), pp. 1-2.

On Preaching the Word of God (Luke 8:4-21)

WILLIAM C. ROBINSON, JR.

I. The Editorial Framework

Luke 8:4 exhibits Luke's characteristic freedom in dealing with Mark's settings. The popular scene of Jesus teaching from the boat, used already at Mark 3:9, is absent in Luke's parallel at that point as well as here. Consequently at 8:22 Luke did not have this scene to fall back upon and had to create a lake setting. The mobility in Luke's setting (at 8:1 Jesus is constantly on the move) enabled him at 8:9 to avoid the awkwardness which in Mark resulted from placing a private scene (Mark 4:10 κατὰ μόνας) in the midst of a larger setting which otherwise seems fixed and uninterrupted (Mark 4:35: Jesus is still teaching from the boat as at 4:1). The reason usually given for Luke's omitting the setting of Mark 4:1 is that he had used this scene at 5:3 and so avoided using it again here.[1] Creed noted this but added: "and he feels himself at liberty to modify the details." Wellhausen left aside the whole scissors and paste approach and understood 8:4 from the present Lucan sequence: "Da Jesus sich nach Lc [8:1-3] nicht mehr in Kapernaum am See befindet, so redet er auch nicht vom Schiff aus." As at 4:31.[2] Luke here disregarded the sequence in Mark in order to fit the sequence which he himself had composed (compare οἱ κατὰ πόλιν ἐπιπορευόμενοι 8:4 and αὐτὸς διώδευεν κατὰ πόλιν 8:1). In Luke Jesus left Capernaum at 4:42, returned at 7:1, went to Nain at 7:11, and then on a wandering ministry at 8:1-3; and this last, which is not from Mark, is the general setting which Luke gave the next Marcan section, Luke 8:4–9:50. It is not as if the new setting just happened as a result of Luke's laying aside one source to resume his use of another.[3] Not only do 8:1-3 mark an important division in the Gospel,[4] but also, by being tied in closely to the structure of the whole Gospel (compare Mark 15:40-41 ||

131

Luke 23:49; 24:10),[5] they call attention to Luke's desire to periodize and thus show that his use of the setting here was intentional and may indeed be his own composition.[6]

Luke 8:4-21. After omitting Mark 3:20-30 because Mark 3:20-22 was not to his taste,[7] and because Q offered another version of the Beelzebub controversy (Mark 3:23-30), Luke changed Mark's order by putting the discussion of the parable of the sower (Luke 8:4-18) before the question of Jesus' true brethren (Luke 8:19-21). As at Luke 6:12-19 the change is pragmatic and not derived from a source other than Mark.[8]

Although in Mark this section of parables (Mark 4:1-34) already referred to the preaching of the Christian church,[9] Luke revised it to emphasize the same reference. The section in Mark could have seemed to him a discussion on parables as a mode of Jesus' teaching[10] (compare Mark 4:1-2, 10, 11*b*, 13*b*, 33-34 3:23*a*), on its esoteric aspect (Mark 4:11), and on the judgment function of Jesus' preaching (Mark 4:12*c*). In any case Luke made changes at these points. The discussion in Luke is not on parables but on the word of God.[11] The discussion of the word of God is not a discussion of Jesus' teaching about his own teaching, but rather of Jesus' teaching about the preaching of the Christian church: notice the "Christianization" or "language of the church" at 8:11-13 ("word of God," "believe and be saved," "temptation").[12] It is not merely said that the devil comes and removes the word from their hearts (Mark: which was sown in them), but a clause is added to the Marcan version: ἵνα μή πιστεύσαντες σωθῶσιν. According to von Baer, Noack, and Conzelmann,[13] Luke envisaged the period of Jesus' public ministry, between the temptation and the passion, as an ideal portrayal of the kingdom of God, a period during which, in contrast to Mark, Satan was absent (Luke 4:13; 22:3). With the passion this period came to its end, and in the subsequent epoch the church had to endure testing at Satan's hand (Luke 22:35-36; cf. Acts 26:18). Within this perspective Luke 8:12-13 is appropriate as a reference to the time of the church rather than to that of Jesus.

Luke 8:16. Influenced by the Q form of the saying (Luke 11:33) Luke here changed the Marcan transition, thereby tightening the connection with what immediately precedes.[14] Thus mention of the shining lamp follows in 8:16 directly on the statement of fruit-bearing (8:15), so that the lamp does not refer to the disciples' ability to understand Jesus' esoteric teaching, as it seems to do in Mark,[15] but refers to fruitful Christian witness;[16] ἅψας in 8:16 is then analogous to τὸν λόγον κατέχουσιν 8:15. Further reference to the missionary ministry of the church in Luke's time may be seen in the addition of ἵνα οἱ εἰσπορευόμενοι βλέπωσιν τὸ φῶς 8:16.[17]

Luke 8:19-21. It was noted earlier that 8:19-21 is a fitting conclusion to the section on the word of God, οὗτοί εἰσιν οἱ τὸν λόγον τοῦ θεοῦ ἀκούντες καὶ ποιοῦντες refers back to the interpretation of the sower: 8:14 οὗτοί εἰσιν οἱ ἀκούσαντες and 8:15 οἵτινες . . . ἀκούσαντες τὸν λόγον κατέχουσιν (cf. 6:47).[18] Although Easton said a contrast between 8:19-21 (Jesus' family) and 8:1-3 (Jesus' followers) is intended, and Conzelmann found strong anti-family polemic and election theology in 8:19-21,[19] Luke has elsewhere lessened Mark's harshness toward Jesus' family[20] and here seems to have used the section for the *positive* purpose of giving an attractive designation for those who accept the word of God.[21] Luke 8:1-3 was not intended by its author to contrast with Jesus' family but, with Luke 6:13 ff., 17, 20, to note the larger group of followers whom Jesus here instructs about Christian missions and who form the group of those who in Luke's view were qualified witnesses.[22]

In drawing attention to a parable about Christian preaching instead of to a parable about parables, Luke needed no other parables here. He could therefore easily omit the parable of the seed growing of itself (Mark 4:26-29) and that of the mustard seed (Mark 4:30-32), which he also had in Q. With these omitted, the concluding summary on parabolic teaching (Mark 4:33-34) also had to go. Luke thus broke with the topical arrangement in Mark and made one unified section.[23]

The unity of the section on Christian preaching is further defined by its full separation in Luke from the next episode.[24] Not only does the passage 8:19-21 conclude and so tend to separate from the following context,[25] but the avoidance at 8:22 of Mark's setting (Mark 4:35; cf. 4:1: Jesus teaching from the boat) and the generalization with which Luke replaced it[26] remove all indications that the events of 8:22 ff. occurred on the same day as those of 8:4 ff.

II. Some Editorial Details

Luke 8:4-21 is primarily an interpretation of the interpretation, rather than an interpretation of the parable itself. Even though one might well reach this conclusion from the preceding discussion of the framework of the section, the point is clearly discernible in the editorial details which show that the interpretation of the parable is the part of the Marcan text which was here normative for Luke. The interpretation in Luke is directly dependent on that in Mark, not upon Luke's version of the parable itself (nor on Mark's, except via the interpretation in Mark). This is most apparent at Luke 8:13, where Luke has ῥίζαν οὐκ ἔχουσιν in agreement with the interpretation of the parable in Mark, although in Luke's version of the parable the corresponding Marcan statement is replaced (Luke 8:6 διὰ τὸ μὴ ἔχειν ἰκμάδα || Mark 4:6 διὰ τὸ μὴ ἔχειν ῥίζαν).[27] Instead of Luke's version of the parable being normative for the interpretation, the interpretation may have influenced his editing of the parable. Although Luke's changes in the parable are chiefly stylistic,[28] the commentaries generally consider the addition of τὸν σπόρον αὐτοῦ (Luke 8:5) a reference to the first verse of the interpretation (Luke 8:11).[29] And while the expression τὰ πετεινὰ τοῦ οὐρανοῦ is common coin with Luke,[30] taken together with the added κατεπατήθη and with the interpretation, Luke's addition of τοῦ οὐρανοῦ may be more than an "innocent" addition having no significance.[31] Both expressions, "to be eaten by the birds of heaven" and "to be trodden under foot," are biblical terms indicating utter destruction,[32] and as such may correspond with the emphasis upon destruction which Luke has added to the interpretation by means of the clause ἵνα μὴ πιστεύσαντες σωθῶσιν (Luke 8:12). But even if these few additions should be understood as correspondences between parable and interpretation, this understanding would not reverse the opinion stated earlier, that the interpretation in Luke was not really based upon Luke's version of the parable. For whatever correspondence there may be in these cases is apparent only from the interpretation, whereas within the parable itself the additions are indeed "innocent"; furthermore there is no explicit reference to them in the interpretation.[33]

The most striking divergence from Mark in Luke's interpretation is at the point just mentioned, the insertion of ἵνα μὴ πιστεύσαντες σωθῶσιν in Luke 8:12. If this emphasis on utter destruction is not to be derived from Luke's version of the parable itself, and if it is not a "Paulinism" in Luke,[34] then what is its origin? It seems to me that it is from Mark 4:12, replacing μήποτε ἐπιστρέψωσιν καὶ ἀφεθῇ αὐτοῖς, the part of the Isa. 6 reference which Luke omitted from Luke 8:10 || Mark 4:12.[35]

III. Luke's History-of-Salvation Theology

Luke's wish to stress the serious consequences of rejecting the church's preaching of the "word of God" (8:11) is reason enough for inserting ἵνα

134

μὴ κτλ. into the interpretation of the parable (8:12), especially since the interpretation was for him the organizing center of the section on the church's preaching (Luke 8:4-21). Yet the appropriateness of the clause here is not of itself sufficient to explain why Luke omitted the similar statement two verses earlier. Nor, in view of the extended quotation of Isa. 6:9-10 in Acts 28:26-27,[36] is it very convincing when Jülicher says that μήποτε κτλ. was omitted "wohl weil Lc diese Konsequenz in ihrer furchtbaren Härte nicht aus der Feder bekam." [37] Both changes are understandable, however, when they are considered together with Luke's history-of-salvation perspective, in which the passage Luke 8:9-10 refers to the epoch of Jesus and vss. 11-15, the interpretation, refer to the epoch of the church. The latter, while distinguished from the former, is nevertheless defined by reference to it.

In Luke 8:10 the removal of Mark's μήποτε κτλ. has reduced the emphasis upon the consequences for those without insight, with the result that in Luke 8:10 the stress is now upon the gift of understanding to the disciples.[38] They are given insight into the *nature* of the kingdom of God,[39] an important theme in Luke's thought. The nature of the kingdom was the topic of the keynote address with which Jesus' public ministry began (Luke 4:16 ff.), and the substance of Peter's summation of that ministry for Cornelius (Acts 10:37-38), and of Jesus' reply to the Baptist (Luke 7:21-23, Q). For according to Luke the nature of the kingdom of God is that God's rule is gracious. Hence Christian life is marked by joy, and the final coming of the kingdom will be καιροὶ ἀναψύξεως ἀπο πορσώπου τοῦ κυρίου . . . χρόνοι ἀποκαταστάσεως πάντων (Acts 3:20-21), so that Christians need not fear its coming. Rather, when the kingdom is near (Luke 21:31), Christians are to lift up their heads, for the kingdom will be their ἀπολύτρωσις (Luke 21:28).[40]

It has already been noted that Luke conceived Jesus' earthly ministry as an ideal realization of the kingdom of God. While the ideal realization was peculiar to Jesus' epoch and thus distinguished it from the preceding epoch of the law and the prophets and from the subsequent church epoch, the preaching of the kingdom is the new history-of-salvation theme which is common to both the epoch of Jesus and that of the church (Luke 16:16), thereby connecting them. But in Luke's view the connection was not merely thematic (the common content of preaching) but also historical: the continuity of witnesses who were qualified to certify the legitimacy of the church as it was engaged in its preaching ministry. It is this history-of-salvation perspective which explains both the changes presently under discussion. The ἵνα μή clause within the interpretation emphasizes the authority of the church's preaching,[41] the distinctive history-of-salvation aspect of the church epoch. The absence of μήποτε κτλ. Luke 8:12 places emphases upon that aspect of the epoch of Jesus which was essential to the function of the church in its epoch: the qualification of the witnesses.[42]

To apply 8:4-21 strictly to the preaching of the church,—i.e., to interpret the interpretation in Mark—Luke asserted the authority of that preaching by underscoring the gravity of rejecting it (Luke 8:12), and he vindicated that authority by showing that the preaching was based upon those witnesses who were with Jesus when the nature of the kingdom of God was disclosed.

NOTES

1. H. J. Holtzmann, *Die synoptischen Evangelien. Ihr Ursprung und geschichtlicher Charakter* (Leipzig, 1863), p. 221. (B. Weiss, *Die Evangelien des Markus und Lukas* [Göttingen, 1901], p. 400, true to thoroughgoing source-critical premises, held that the absence of Mark's setting in Luke 8:4 would require any unprejudiced observer to conclude that Luke did not get the parable from Mark.)

2. At Luke 4:31 κατῆλθεν shows no concern for the sequence in Mark (from the Sea of Galilee, Mark 1:16, to Capernaum, Mark 1:21) but fits smoothly in the literary sequence which Luke has made: Luke 4:29 describes Nazareth as a city built on a hill. Cf. K. L. Schmidt, *Der Rahmen der Geschichte Jesu* (Berlin, 1919), p. 54.

3. Schmidt, *Rahmen*, p. 135 n. 1: "[dass] diese konkrete Situation von Lk konstruiert ist."

4. J. Wellhausen, *Das Evangelium Lucae* (Berlin, 1904).

5. Schmidt, *Rahmen*, p. 129: "In seinem Bestreben, die Geschichte Jesu zu periodisieren, stellt er eine Bemerkung, die bei Mk beiläufig anhangsweise vorkommt, an den Anfang der Wanderung Jesu."

6. For supporters of the Proto-Luke hypothesis and for E. Hirsch (*Frühgeschichte des Evangeliums. II. Die Vorlagen des Lukas und das Sondergut des Matthäus* [Tübingen, 1941], 205 ff.) it is important to maintain that Luke 8:1-3 is from a non-Marcan source which provides the literary matrix into which the Marcan material was inserted, but their agreement goes little beyond the common source-critical postulate.

7. See H. J. Cadbury, *The Style and Literary Method of Luke* (Cambridge, Mass., 1920), 95; on the contrast with Luke 2:46-50 see Holtzmann, *Hand-Kommentar zum Neuen Testament*, I (3rd ed., Freiburg, 1901), 136.

8. J. M. Creed, *The Gospel According to St. Luke* (London, 1942): "The parable of the sower stands well at the opening of the new section." According to Schmidt, *Rahmen*, the new arrangement is more effective: Luke "setzt die Worte Jesu über seine Familie im Zusammenhang mit der Parabel vom verschiedenartigen Acker: Jesu wahre Verwandte sind nicht seine leiblichen Angehörigen, sondern die, die Gottes Wort hören und tun, die, mit einem Worte, dem guten Acker gleichen." As these statements indicate, and as the communtaries generally imply, it is insufficient to explain the transposition as due simply to the fact that

the crowd necessary to the scene on Jesus' true relatives was removed with the omission of Mark 3:20 (F. Rehkopf, *Die lukanische Sonderquelle. Ihr Umfang und Sprachgebrauch* [Tübingen, 1959], p. 88 n. 5).

9. J. Jeremias, *Die Gleichnisse Jesu* (4th ed., 1956), pp. 65 ff.; N. A. Dahl, "The Parables of Growth," *StTh* V (1951 [1952]), 135; W. Marxsen, "Redaktionsgeschichtl. Erklärung der sog. Parabeltheorie des Mk," *ZThK* LII (1955), 267-68, 271.

10. As Matthew understood it. See W. Wrede, *Das Messiasgeheimnis in den Evangelien* (Göttingen, 1963), pp. 55 ff.; F. W. Gealy, "The Composition of Mark iv," *ExpT* XLVIII (1936-37), 40.

11. In Luke 8:11 the seed is the word of God; in 8:4 and 11 παραβολή in the singular fixes attention on the sower as a parable rather than as a parable *about* parables (so Mark; cf. Holtzmann, *Die syn. Evv.*, p. 221), as does Luke's omission of other parables and of the conclusion to the section in Mark.

12. Wellhausen; J. Weiss, *Schriften des NTs*, I, 453; Cadbury, *Style and Literary Method*, p. 122: "By giving to Christ's teachings a more definite setting Luke does not intend to limit their scope and application. The audience is neither historically reproduced nor artistically delimited, but rather taken as typical and suggestive. Luke has really in mind the Christian church of his own time. Thus, expressions in Mark and Matthew that seem to make Jesus' teaching esoteric are in Luke omitted or modified."

13. H. von Baer, *Der Heilige Geist in den Lukasschriften* (1926), p. 76-77, 103 ff.; B. Noack, "Das Gottesreich bei Lukas," *SBU* X (1948), 47; H. Conzelmann, "Zur Lukasanalyse," *ZThK* XLIX (1952), 32; and *The Theology of St. Luke* (1960). Cf. O. Cullmann, "Parusieverzögerung und Urchristentum," *ThLZ* LXXXIII (1958), 5.

14. As at Luke 8:9: παραβολή singular. Cf. Schmidt, *Rahmen*, p. 137.

15. Mark 4:9, 10, 11, 13*b*. Note omission at Luke 8:17 of Mark's "If anyone has ears to hear, let him hear." See Cadbury's remarks quoted in n. 12.

16. J. Weiss cited with approval by A. Jülicher, *Die Gleichnisreden Jesu*, II 2nd ed. (1910), 86.

17. Jeremias, *Glechnisse*, p. 40 (on Luke 11:33–8:16). Jülicher, *Gleichnisreden*, II, 86, called this interpretation a "schaler Ueberrest antiker Allegorese."

18. Holtzmann, *Hand-Comm.*, I, 1, 350; Wellhausen, *Das Evangelium Lucae*.

19. B. S. Easton, *Gospel According to St. Luke. A Critical and Exegetical Commentary* (New York, 1926), p. 117; Conzelmann, *ZThK* XLIX (1952), 21-22, n. 1; *Theology of St. Luke*, pp. 48-49.

20. Wellhausen. It should also be noted that Luke has not listed the family in the scene of the opening sermon at Nazareth (4:16-30, the only reference being "the son of Joseph" v. 22), thus perhaps consciously avoiding giving the impresson that Jesus' family took part in the rejection. Nor is Luke's statement that "no prophet is acceptable in his home town" (4:24) as pointed as its Marcan counterpart (Mark 6:4) which not only speaks of "his home town" but also has "and among his own kin, and in his own house." And in Luke 4:22 familiarity with Jesus is the cause of amazement but not, as in Mark 6:3, the cause of offense; in Luke (4:28) the rejection occurs in reaction against the universality of Jesus' sermon (4:25-27).

21. See Creed. Had such a contrast been intended Luke might better have left the pericope on Jesus' true relatives in its Marcan position and thus immediately after Luke 8:1-3.

22. See G. Klein, *Die zwölf Apostel. Ursprung und Gehalt einer Idee*, FRLANT NF LIX (Göttingen, 1961), esp. p. 202 ff.; "Lukas 1, 1-4 als theologisches Programm," *Zeit und Geschichte*, Bultmann Festschrift (Tübingen, 1964), pp. 193-216; my *Der Weg des Herrn. Studien zur Geschichte und Eschatologie im Lukas-Evangelium*, ThF XXXVI (Hamburg-Bergstedt, 1964), 37 ff.

24. Schmidt, *Rahmen*, pp. 134-35.

24. F. Schleiermacher, *Ueber die Schriften des Lukas*, I (1817), 98, 122; E. Käsemann, "Neutestamentliche Fragen von Heute," *ZThK* LIV (1957), 20-21.

25. E. Klostermann, *Das Lukas-Evangelium*, HNT (Tübingen, 2nd ed. 1929).

26. Note "one day" (Luke 8:22) instead of Mark's "on that day when evening had come" (4:35).
27. Jülicher, *Gleichnisreden*, II, 527; P. Wernle, *Die synoptische Frage* (1899), p. 24. Similar instances have been noted: ἔρχεται . . . καί Luke 8:12 || Mark, although ἦλθεν Mark 4:4 is not in the Lucan parallel (Jülicher, II, 526); εἰς τὰς ἀκάνθας Luke 8:14 || Mark, while in the parallel Luke has ἐν μέσῳ τῶν ἀκανθῶν for Mark's εἰς τὰς ἀκάνθας (P. W. Schmiedel, "Gospel," *Encyclopaedia Biblica*, II (1902), col. 1849); καλή Luke 8:15 || Mark, although in the parable itself Luke replaced Mark's καλή with αγαθή (Schmiedel); συμπνίγοντι Luke 8:14 || Mark, whereas in the parable Luke used ἀπέπνιξαν for Mark's συνέπνιξαν (Schmiedel). Exception: πέτρα Luke 8:6, 13, where Mark in both cases has substantive use of πετρώδες. The Lucan interpretation also agrees with Mark's in details which are in neither one's version of the parable, e.g., μετὰ χαρᾶς Luke 8:13 (Wernle), πορευόμενοι Luke 8:14 (Cadbury, *Style and Literary Method*, p. 98).
28. A Schlatter, *Das Evangelium des Lukas* (2nd printing 1960); W. Grundmann, *Das Evangelium nach Lukas* (Berlin, 1961).
29. Exception: B. Weiss, *Die Evangelien des Markus und Lukas*.
30. Luke's addition of τοῦ οὐρανοῦ is not an allegorical reference to Satan in the intrepretaton (Jülicher, II, 517; W. Michaelis, *ThWB*, V, 68, 25-26), even though the concept of Satan in heaven was known (H. Traub, *ThWB*, V, 533, 20 ff.).
31. Jülicher, *Gleichnisreden*, II.
32. See LXX Concordance.
33. Both M.-J. Lagrange, *Évangile selon Saint Luc* (7th ed. 1948), and W. Michaelis, *Die Gleichnisse Jesu* ([3rd ed. of *Es ging ein Sämann aus, zu säen*, 1938, and *Das hochzeitliche Kleid*, 1939], 1956), p. 23, say that the addition of κατεπατήθη has been ignored in the interpretation. Within the parable this addition—in contrast to Jülicher's view: "einer Allegorese nahe"—"will jedoch nur anschaulich unterstreichen, dass der auf den vielbegangenen Fussweg gefallene Same umkam" (Michaelis), or it is "un simple trait pittoresque" (Lagrange).
34. See E. Haenchen, *Die Apostelgeschichte* (Göttingen, 1959), p. 310 n. 3.
35. J. Schmid, *Das Evangelium nach Lukas* (Regensburg, 3rd ed. 1955). If Matt. 13:14-15 is a later interpolation into Matt. (F. Blass, *Evang. sec. lc.* [1897], LXI, cit. Jülicher, I, 128; most recently G. Strecker, *Der Weg der Gerechtigkeit. Untersuchung zur Theologie des Matthäus*, FRALNT LXXXII [Göttingen, 1962], 70 n. 3), then μήποτε κτλ. is Marcan *Sondergut*, yet even the widespread anxiety over this statement has not led to considering it a later interpolation into Mark.
36. See Haenchen, *Apostelgeschichte*, p. 647 n. 4: "reines Verwerfungsurteil Gottes."
37. Jülicher, I, 127.
38. Cf. Jülicher, I, 127-28, who offers the same formal observation tentatively—i.e., if Luke conceived 8:10 as foreword to the interpretation (8:11 ff.) and as an acknowledgment that a question such as that of 8:9 was permissible: "dann bekäme die erste Hälfte das Uebergewicht, und die zweite τοῖς δὲ λοιποῖς wäre logisch subordiniert."
39. Conzelmann, *Theology of St. Luke*, pp. 103-4, in contrast with Eduard Schweizer, "Die theologische Leistung des Markus," *EvTh* XXIV (1964), 346: "allerlei Einzelgeheimnisse."
40. Cf. my *Weg des Herrn*, pp. 64-65.
41. Luke's addition of emphasis upon the consequences of rejecting the preaching of the church does not require that Luke deemphasized the consequences of rejecting Jesus' preaching. Within Luke's portrayal of Jesus' ministry Jerusalem's fate is predicted as the paradigm of the consequences of rejecting the divine visitation.
42. On Luke's witness concept see n. 22 above.

The Story of Abraham in Luke–Acts

NILS A. DAHL

The author of the two books to Theophilus is often called the historian among New Testament authors.[1] And certainly Luke, as we may call him without prejudging his identity, was more of a historian than the other evangelists. But there were many types of historians in ancient as in modern times. To classify Luke among the historiographers, therefore, does not say very much either about his literary intentions or about his concept of history. What can be known about these matters has to be inferred from observations we can make concerning the outline of his two volumes, his style, his use of sources and traditions, etc., in comparison with other relevant literature. Important results have been achieved by modern research pioneered by men such as H. J. Cadbury and Martin Dibelius. Among their successors Paul Schubert has had the advantage of uniting in his person some of the best traditions of German and of American scholarship.[2] Yet many questions remain controversial.

Luke begins his narrative with the announcement of John the Baptist's birth and ends with Paul's imprisonment in Rome. But it seems reasonable to assume that study of his references to Old Testament narratives may throw important light on his understanding of history. Luke's account of the things which had been accomplished is told as a story of John the Baptist, Jesus, Peter, Paul, and other apostles and evangelists. In a similar way, he considers the history of Israel to be bound up with individual persons, of whom Abraham, Moses, and David are the most outstanding. The figure of Moses is closely connected with the law, and that of David with the messianic hope. For reasons of simplicity I prefer to concentrate on the story of Abraham as Luke relates it and refers to it.

In "Philo's place in Judaism," [3] Samuel Sandmel wrote: "To see what the writer makes of Abraham is often to see most clearly what the writer is trying to say." This statement may be applied to New Testament authors as well as to Jewish ones. To Paul, Abraham is the father and prototype of Christian believers. In Gal. 3 he seeks to demonstrate that God, in granting his Spirit to Gentiles who believed the apostolic message, has acted according to his promise to Abraham. In Rom. 4 the story of Abraham is adduced in order to prove the thesis that a man is justified by faith apart from works of the law. And yet, Paul insists in Rom. 9–11 that the word of God has not failed; in spite of their disobedience, the Israelites remain "beloved for the sake of the fathers." [4] Putting the accent in quite a different way, James finds that Abraham's faith was at work in his actions, and draws the conclusion that a man is justified by his deeds and not by faith in itself (2:20-24). To John, Abraham was a witness to Christ before his coming.[5] To the author of Hebrews he is an example to be imitated, as one of those who inherited the promises through faith and patience (6:11 ff.). His migration and endurance illustrate the essence of faith, as defined by the writer (11:8-19, cf. 11:1). But also the certainty of our hope and the superiority of Christ's priesthood over against that of Aaron are argued on the basis of the biblical account of Abraham (6:13–7:10).[6]

Thus, in various ways the story of Abraham is used as a vehicle for interpreting the gospel message and its significance. Paul and John, the author of Hebrews, and James, all tend to make Abraham a protagonist of the Christian faith as each of them understands it. In an opposite, yet analogous way, the rabbis visualize Abraham as a chief rabbi and Philo depicts him as a Jewish philosopher. In comparison, Luke's portrait of Abraham is more nearly one drawn by a historian. In his writings there is much less obviously Christian reinterpretation of the biblical account than in other parts of the New Testament. "Our father Abraham" in Luke–Acts remains the father of the Jews and is not said to be the father of Christian believers.[7] He is not presented as a prototype and model to be imitated. Apart from references to Abraham in the sayings of Jesus and John the Baptist, Luke is mostly content to summarize and paraphrase biblical texts. Certainly, he too uses Abraham as a part of his theological argument, but he does so by means of establishing a connection and continuity between the history of Abraham and the events of which he himself is writing.

All allusions to Abraham in Luke–Acts are found in hymns, sayings, or speeches. The material can easily be brought under a small number of headings:

a) The God of Abraham, Isaac, and Jacob, the God of the fathers: Luke 20:37; Acts 3:13; 7:32; cf. Acts 5:30; 22:14; 24:14.

b) God's covenant, oath, and promise to Abraham: Luke 1:55; 1:72-73; Acts 3:25; 7:2-8; 7:17; cf. 3:17, 32; 26:6.

c) Children of Abraham: Luke 3:8; 13:16; 19:9; Acts 13:26; 13:33 v. 1; cf. 3:25.

d) Abraham in the hereafter: Luke 13:28; 16:22-31; 20:37-38.

e) Miscellaneous: The genealogy of Jesus, Luke 3:34; the tomb which Abraham bought, Acts 7:16.

The picture transcends that of the Septuagint mainly insofar as Abraham is taken to be an eschatological as well as a historical figure. This feature is taken over from earlier Gospel tradition. Luke 20:37-38 is derived from Mark 12:26-27; Luke 13:28 is paralleled by Matt. 8:11. The story of the rich man and Lazarus must come from a special source, oral or written. Possibly it alludes to some popular tale.[8] The image of Abraham's bosom is, in any case, familiar also to the rabbis.[9] Similar ideas are also found in Old Testament pseudepigrapha. The Test. XII contain several allusions to the patriarchs as living after their death.[10] According to IV Macc. 13:17 the seven martyred brethren said: "For if we die in this way, Abraham, and Isaac, and Jacob shall receive us, and all the fathers shall praise us."

Some details indicate that Luke's rendering of the sayings of Jesus has been influenced by a phraseology used in Greek-speaking Judaism as represented by IV Macc. To the answer given to the question of the Sadducees, Luke adds "for they all live to him" (πάντες γὰρ αὐτῷ ζῶσιν), 20:38. This comes very close to two passages in IV Macc. 7:19: "Unto God they die not, as did not our patriarchs Abraham, and Isaac, and Jacob, but they live unto God" (ζῶσιν τῷ θεῷ), and 16:25: "Men dying for God, live unto God (ζῶσιν τῷ θεῷ), as live Abraham, and Isaac, and Jacob, and all the patriarchs." In Luke 13:28: "When you see Abraham, and Isaac, and Jacob, and all the prophets in the kingdom of God," καὶ πάντες τοὺς προφήτας seems to be a Lucan addition, corresponding to "all the patriarchs" (or "fathers") in IV Macc. 16:25 and 13:17. To Luke, fathers and prophets belong together.[11] Since he regards all the prophets as martyrs,[12] the affinity to the martyr-ideology of IV Macc. is rather close, although there can hardly be any question of direct literary dependence. Luke does not share the philosophical pretentions of the writer of IV Macc., who proves the thesis that reason is master of the passions by means of the noble conduct of Eleazar, the seven brethren, and their mother, who all behaved like true children of Abraham.[13] The similarities must be due to a common background, reflected in a common terminology.[14]

To Luke, Abraham is mainly the primary recipient of God's promise to the fathers. The words ἐπαγγέλειν. ἐπαγγελία, etc., are only occasionally found in the Septuagint; there is, in fact, no exact Hebrew equivalent. But the notion of God's promise to Abraham is common to the Lucan writings, the Pauline epistles, and the Epistle to the Hebrews. The terminology probably goes back to Greek-speaking Judaism.[15] The presentation of Abraham in Hebrews comes rather close to that of Luke in other respects also. The main accents are put upon God's oath and promise, and upon Abraham's migration and sojourn as a foreigner in the promised land.[16] He is placed within a succession of prophets and martyrs reaching from Abel to Christ and to the present day.[17] As each of the two writers makes the Christian adaptation in his own characteristic way, most of the common features are likely to go back to Jewish, slightly Hellenized versions of the story of Abraham.

Luke's affinity with Hellenistic Judaism is confirmed by his only comprehensive survey of Abraham's history, found in the speech of Stephen, Acts 7:2-8. This, however, does not mean that the biblical account has been fundamentally changed. There are few, if any, traces of those accretions to the story which are known from writers such as Artapanas or Eupolemus,[18] Philo, and Josephus, as well as from Palestinian midrash.[19] In his short summary Stephen—that is, the Stephen of Luke—has left out a number of tales: Abraham in Egypt, Abraham and Lot, the battle with the kings, Hagar and Ishmael, the three men and the destruction of Sodom, and, most remarkable of all, the sacrifice of Isaac. The account is concentrated upon Abraham's migration, God's promise, the covenant of circumcision, and the birth of Isaac. This means that the texts which serve as a basis are Gen. 11:27–12:9; 13:15; 15 (in part), 17, and 21:1-4. Thus the summary stresses those themes which are fundamental to the whole outline of Israel's old history, starting with God's revelation to Abraham and leading up to the conquest of the promised land; these themes are most common in biblical recapitulations and references to the fathers.[20]

Stephen's account of Abraham has definitely and, I think, consciously

142

been given a biblical flavor. At several points we find Septuagint phrases which in the Pentateuch are not related to the story of Abraham. ὁ θεὸς τῆς δόξης is taken from Ps. 28 (29):3; οὐδὲ βῆμα ποδός from Deut. 2:5; ἐν γῇ ἀλλοτρίᾳ from Exod. 2:22 or 18:3; and the end of the citation from Gen. 15:13-14 is an adaptation of Exod. 3:12. Even Μεσοποταμία, γῆ χαλδαίον, μετῴκισεν, and ἔδωκεν κληρονμίαν are Septuagint phraseology, but not used in the Genesis story of Abraham. To current, though not biblical, Jewish terminology, belong phrases like ὁ πατὴρ ἡμῶν 'Αβραάμ,' διαθήκη περιτομῆς, and οἱ (δώδεκα) πατριάρχαι.

At some points the biblical account is altered in a somewhat more substantial manner. In Acts 7:2-3 God is said to have appeared to Abraham before he settled in Haran; the vision of Gen. 12:7 and the commandment of Gen. 12:1 are both transposed to the situation of Gen. 11:31. Thus God's revelation is made the starting point of Abraham's migrations.[21] A minor point is the identification of Mesopotamia with the land of the Chaldeans; according to ancient and more usual terminology Haran is located in Mesopotamia.[22] Furthermore, Abraham is said to have left Haran after the death of his father. This is a consequence which a reader would draw from the Genesis account if he did not pay serious attention to the number of years given in Gen. 11:26, 11:32, and 12:4.[23] An unparalleled confusion is found in Acts 7:16, where Abraham's purchase of the cave at Hebron is mixed up with Jacob's purchase of a piece of land at Shechem.[24] All these are points of detail. Of theological significance is the underscoring of the facts that Abraham had neither any ground of his own nor any child when God promised to give the land to him and his posterity.[25] But unlike the author of Hebrews Luke does not spell out the religious lesson to be learned.

The most remarkable element in Acts 7:2-8, in contrast with similar summaries, is the prominent place given to a full quotation of Gen. 15:13-14, with some important variations. Usually more attention is paid to Gen. 15:6, 7-12, and 17-20, but in Stephen's speech no special importance is assigned either to Abraham's faith or to his nighttime vision. We may safely assume that the divine word about the history of Abraham's posterity has been placed intentionally in the foreground. At this point, if anywhere, the specific emphasis in Stephen's reproduction of the biblical story must be discernible. Although most commentators have not paid sufficient attention to it,[26] the specific function of the citation within the whole outline of the speech is not difficult to see. The oracle in Acts 7:6-7 predicts the succeeding events in the history of Israel, and the following parts of Stephen's speech tell about the realization of God's word to Abraham. The story of Joseph (Acts 7:9-16) reports how it came to pass that Abraham's posterity became aliens in a land belonging to others who enslaved and ill-treated them (7:18-19). The story of Moses (7:20-36) tells how they were led out, while God judged the nation by which they had been enslaved. Thus, the history of Israel is understood as a history of prophecy and fulfillment. Stephen also sets forth the way in which God kept his promise to give the land to Abraham and his posterity, although he had no offspring (7:5). Abraham became father of Isaac and, through him, of Jacob, and of the twelve patriarchs (7:8). In Egypt the people grew and multiplied (7:18). At the time of Joshua they took possession of the land, dispossessing the nations (ἐν τῇ κατασχέσει τῶν ἐθνῶν 7:45, cf. εἰς κατάσχεσιν 7:5).[27]

The importance of the scheme of prophecy and fulfilllment is confirmed by a number of references to Abraham in the speech of Stephen. The burial of the fathers at Shechem (in the tomb that Abraham had bought) serves to illustrate the fact that they were aliens (7:16, cf. 7:6). Most remarkable is the phrase, coined for this purpose, which introduces the Exodus story: "But as the time of the promise drew near, which God had granted to Abraham" (7:17). This is a direct reference to the prediction in 7:6, taken up again in 7:20: "At this time (ἐν ᾧ καιρῷ) Moses was born." Further, it is carefully pointed out that at the burning bush God revealed himself with the words: "I am the God of your fathers, the God of Abraham and of Isaac and of Jacob" (7:32). Here again, God's words—promise and commission—precede the realization which does occur (7:30-34, 35-36). But the Exodus event did not bring God's word to its final fulfillment: "This is the Moses who said to the children of Israel: God will raise up for you a prophet from your brethren as he raised me up" (7:37).

At this point it becomes clear why Stephen does not need to give, for the purpose of his sermon, any directly christological or eschatological interpretation of God's promises to Abraham. Here God's word to Abraham is seen as the beginning of a history in which partial realizations are interconnected with new promises, until the coming of the Righteous One, of whom all the prophets spoke (cf. 7:52). In Stephen's speech Moses and, to some extent, Joseph are seen as types of Christ, but the typology is subordinated to the recurring pattern of prophecy and fulfillment.

When close attention is paid to the function of the citation in Acts 7:6-7 within the whole speech, it also becomes obvious that the alteration at the end must be due to some specific reason. The Septuagint text of Gen. 15: 14*b* reads: "But afterwards they shall come out hither with much baggage." For this, Acts 7:7*b* substitutes: "And afterwards they shall come out and worship me in this place." The phrase is taken from Exod. 3:12: "And you [the Israelites] shall worship God upon this mountain," adapted to Gen. 15:14*b* and 16, "and they shall come back here." Thus, according to Stephen's quotation of Scripture, the goal of the Exodus is neither the worship of God at Mount Sinai, nor the possession of Canaan itself but, much more, worship of God in the land promised to Abraham and his posterity. This means that, just as Acts 7:6-7*b* is a prediction of Israel's coming to Egypt and the Exodus (Acts 7:9-38), so the final clause in 7:7*b* points forward to the events in the time from Joshua to Solomon and even later. The correspondence is clear; it is not so much the conquest of Canaan as the worship performed there which is the center of interest. Acts 7:44 ff.

This observation may be of considerable importance for the solution of one of the most vexing problems confronting interpreters of Stephen's speech. Often the remark in Acts 7:47 "But it was Solomon who built a house for him," followed by the remark "yet the Most High does not dwell in houses made with hands," and a citation from Isa. 66, has been taken—even by outstanding commentators—to imply a radical opposition against the temple.[28] If this interpretation were correct, there would be a sharp contrast between Stephen's point of view and that of Luke himself. But Luke is not likely to have been aware of any such contradiction, and therefore it seems reasonable to look for other possibilities of exegesis. I cannot go into detail here but may suggest an approach to the problem. The argument of Acts 7:44 ff. may be summarized in the following way: The tent of witness, made according to the heavenly model, accompanied the fathers in the wilderness and was brought into the land under Joshua. This state of affairs remained unchanged until the days of David. He found favor in the sight of God and asked leave "to find a habitation for the God (or house) [29] of Jacob." That is, he asked for the fulfillment of God's word to Abraham, "and they shall worship me in this place." With B. W. Bacon one may even say that David brought the divine promise to "the verge of fulfillment." [30] "But Solomon built a house for him." It might seem as if this brought the prediction to its definite realization, the temple of Solomon being the place for Israel's worship. But no! "The Most High does not dwell in houses made with hands."

If this paraphrase hits the main points, the argument in Acts 7:44-50 runs fairly parallel to that of Hebrews 4:3-11 or, more especially, of 4:8-9: "For if Joshua had given them rest, God would not speak later of another day. So then, there remains a sabbath rest for the people of God." By analogy we may paraphrase Acts 7:47-50 as follows: Solomon built a house for him. But had Solomon's temple been the fulfillment of David's prayer for a "dwelling-place," and its cult the worship of which God spoke to Abraham, the prophet would not have said: "Heaven is my throne and earth my footstool. What house will you build for me, says the Lord, or what is the place of my rest? Did not my hands make all these things?" One might even venture a conjecture and assume that to Luke the true answer to David's prayer in Ps. 131(132):5 was given in verse 11 of the same psalm: "The Lord swore to David a true oath (ἀλήθειαν) and shall not make it invalid: One from the fruit of thy body I will set on thy throne." We may also compare II Sam. 7: David intended to build a house for God, but through Nathan he was told that God should make him a house and raise up his offspring after him. These texts are of considerable importance for Lucan Christology and may even be in the background of Acts 7:47-48.[31] We are told that Moses and the prophets announced the coming of the "Righteous One" (7:37, 52). May we not conclude that God's word to Abraham, "they shall worship me in this place," was fulfilled not by the erection of Solomon's temple but by the reerection of the "tent of David" (15:16 = 9:9). Thus, Stephen himself would be the representative of the true worship of God in Jerusalem, the worship performed by the disciples who gathered in the name of Jesus, both in the temple and in the houses.[32]

If my proposal is not totally wrong, there is no contradiction between the speech of Stephen and the general outlook of Luke. Much more, there is another passage in Luke–Acts which strongly supports the interpretation proposed here, viz. the Benedictus, Luke 1:68-75. Here the Lord God of Israel is praised because he has redeemed his people, just as he had said through his holy prophets: "To perform the mercy promised to our fathers, and to remember his holy covenant, the oath which he swore to our father Abraham, to grant us that we, being delivered from the hand of our enemies, might serve him without fear, in holiness and righteousness before him all the days of our life." Here the messianic redemption is described in terms reminiscent of the deliverance from Egypt, and seen as the fulfillment of God's oath to Abraham.[33] The final goal is said to be worship in holiness and righteousness. According to Luke's understanding, the same true worship, made possible by the coming of Christ, must be envisaged also in the promise granted to Abraham, that "they shall worship me in this place."

When the thematic function of the quotation in Acts 7:6-7 has been recognized, it is no longer possible to hold the opinion "that the major part of the speech (7:2-34) shows no purpose whatsoever." [34] The speech contains a philosophy or, rather, "theology of history," dominated by the motif of prophecy and fulfillment. Even the opposition to the temple is subordinate to the demonstration of a continuity in history, reaching from Abraham through Moses to Jesus and on to Stephen, his suffering witness. The assumption that Luke has made use of some existing summary of Israel's history might still hold true, but there are reasons for doubt. I know of no other recapitulation of biblical history in which the idea of successive fulfillment of prophecies is so prominent, whereas this is a favorite theme of Luke's.

In Stephen's speech the Jewishness of Abraham is not concealed but emphatically pronounced. Abraham is "our father," the father of Jews (7:1). The land into which God moved him is called "this land in which you are now living" (7:4). His posterity is to worship God "in this place" (7:7). Finally it is stressed that God gave "the covenant of circumcision" to Abraham, and that Isaac, Jacob, and the twelve patriarchs were circumcised on the eighth day (7:8). But this Jewish flavor is in full harmony with good Lucan theology. Its function is to make it clear that the promise given to Abraham and now fulfilled in Jesus, first and foremost belonged to Abraham's posterity, circumcised Jews living in the land of Israel. "The promise is to you and to your children" (Acts 2:39; cf. 3:25, etc.).

Stephen confronts the Jews of Jerusalem with their own sacred history, showing that God has kept his promises. But the history has also another aspect, that of constant disobedience and opposition to God and his messengers. The Bible itself provided materials for this point of view,[35] but Stephen sharpens it, contending that by their betrayal and murder of Jesus the Jews of Jerusalem have created a solidarity between themselves and the contemporaries of Moses and the persecutors of the prophets. Over against this continuous resistance to the prophetic Holy Spirit [36] stands the succession of righteous sufferers, Joseph, Moses, the prophets, Jesus, and Stephen himself.[37] The conclusion to be drawn is, evidently, that along this line the divine promises are brought to fulfillment, while those who reject Jesus and his witnesses disinherit themselves from God's promise to the offspring of Abraham. The modern reader may doubt whether Stephen's speech conforms to the historical situation; but certainly it fits Luke's literary and theological purpose. The account of Stephen's speech and martyrdom is given as the last preaching of the early apostles and evangelists in Jerusalem. Stephen's own history is the continuation of that history which began by God's revelation to Abraham; it leads to the preaching in Samaria and beyond.

Another recapitulation of Israel's history is found in Paul's speech in Pisidian Antioch (Acts 13:16-41). Here the patriarchal story does not comprise a section in itself. But as the election of all Israelites goes back to that of Abraham, it is included in the initial phrase, "The God of this people Israel chose our fathers" (13:17).[38] The summary covers the period from the Exodus to David, from whose seed God brought a savior to Israel, as he had promised (13:17-23). Then Paul proceeds to the history of Jesus, concentrating upon the theme of the Davidic-messianic promise and its fulfillment by the passion and resurrection of Jesus.[39] But even here the election of Abraham and his descendants provides the wider context, as is made clear by the appositional expression in vs. 26: "Brethren, sons of the family of Abraham,[40] and those among you that fear God, to us has been sent the message of this salvation." What God promised to the fathers is proclaimed as fulfilled to the sons (13:32-33).[41] In the context, τὴν πρὸς τοὺς πατέρας ἐπαγγελίαν cannot exclusively refer to God's promise to the patriarchs, but must include both the promise given to David and later prophecies. However, Luke seems to think all messianic prophecies reiterate and unfold the one promise to the fathers, first given to Abraham.[42]

The speech in Acts 13, like that of Stephen in Acts 7, has been placed at a crucial point of Luke's narrative. The audience consists of Jews and proselytes gathered in a diaspora synagogue. At the end they are warned: "Beware, therefore, lest there come upon you what is said in the prophets: Behold, you scoffers, and wonder, and perish" (13:40-41, citation from Hab. 1:5). But we learn that they did not take heed. The fulfilled promise had first to be proclaimed to the "sons of the family of Abraham." When they rejected it, Paul and Barnabas turned to the Gentiles (13:44-49, with citation of Isa. 49:6).

The speeches of Stephen and Paul are preceded by those of Peter. The Abraham-theme holds a prominent place in one of them, the speech in the temple, Acts 3:12-26. Here the kerygma is condensed into the statement that "the God of Abraham and of Isaac and of Jacob, the God of our fathers, glorified his servant Jesus, whom you delivered up and denied in the presence of Pilate" (3:13). Thus, God fulfilled what he had foretold by the mouth of all the prophets from old (3:18, 21-24). At the end, Peter addresses his hearers with the words: "You are the sons of the prophets and of the covenant which God gave to your fathers, saying to Abraham, 'And in your posterity shall all the families of the earth be blessed'" (3:25). In this citation of Gen. 22:18 (12:3) Luke has replaced the τὰ ἔθνη of the Septuagint with αἱ πατριαί, thus indicating that the Jews are included among those who shall be blessed in the "posterity" of Abraham, i.e., the Christ, Jesus.[43] "God, having raised up his servant, sent him to you first" (3:26a). The blessing is taken to mean the forgiveness of sins granted to those who turn away from their wickedness (vs. 26b; cf. vs. 19). However, the Genesis citation, even in its modified form, makes Peter's speech end with a universal outlook. It also contains a warning, viz., the words of Deut. 18:19, quoted in vs. 23: "And it shall be that every soul that does not listen to that prophet shall be destroyed from the people."

Peter's speech resulted in the first arrest of the apostles (Acts 4:1 ff.). In fact, it foreshadows and prepares for the theme which is taken up and developed in Acts 7 and 13: The promise of God was given to Abraham, reiterated and spelled out by Moses and the prophets, and fulfilled through the passion and resurrection of Jesus. Apostles and evangelists bore testimony to this, first to the Jews. But their message was rejected by the majority, while Gentiles believed and became participants of what had been promised to Abraham and his posterity. The references to Abraham serve to bring this out, not only in the interrelated speeches of Peter, Stephen, and Paul, but also in the two-volume work of Luke as a whole.

The very beginning of Luke's narrative, the announcement to Zechariah, recalls the story of Abraham. In an archaizing, biblical style the birth narratives of Luke report announcements of what is going to happen and events which include new promises.[44] The whole story is full of allusions to biblical prophecies as well as to the expectations of pious Jews. Abraham is directly referred to in the hymns of Mary and Zechariah, Luke 1:54-55 and 72-73. The relevant passage from the Benedictus has already been quoted as akin to the Abraham section of Stephen's speech. In the Magnificat the text runs: "He has helped his servant Israel, in remembrance of his mercy, as he spoke to our fathers to Abraham and to his posterity for ever." As it is not possible to give any detailed exegesis, it may in this context be sufficient to point out that the phrases in the Magnificat and the Benedictus have been modeled upon the pattern of references to Abraham in hymnic and historical texts of the Old Testament.[45]

According to the prophecy of Isa. 40:3-5, John the Baptist prepared the way of the Lord, announcing the coming of One who was mightier than he (Luke 3:1-17). The saying that God is able to raise up children to Abraham from the stones (3:8) is reported as a warning to the Jews. It foreshadows the coming events, even though Luke never draws the conclusion that Gentile believers are made spiritual children of Abraham.[46] In the major sections of the Gospel there are not many references to Abraham, but some of them are peculiar to Luke and characteristic of his outlook. The argument for a sabbath healing is strengthened by the point that the woman who had for eighteen years been "bound by Satan" was a daughter of Abraham (13:16). To Zacchaeus Jesus is reported to have said: "Today salvation has come to this house, since he also is a son of Abraham" (19:9). Both stories illustrate how God's promise to Abraham was fulfilled to his children through the ministry of Jesus.

Even the idea of the patriarch's life in the hereafter has been integrated into Luke's theology of prophecy and fulfillment They live unto God forever. The God of the fathers is the God who raises the dead and who has now raised Jesus. Thus the apostolic message of Christ's resurrection is the proclamation of what was promised to the fathers and what Israel has been hoping for.[47] This theme is carried through to the end of Acts, even though the name of Abraham is not mentioned after the speeches of chaps. 3, 7, and 13 which we have analysed. To Jewish accusations Paul gives the answer: "Now I stand here on trial for hope in the promise made by God to our fathers" (26:6). Even his mission to the Gentiles is considered to be part of the continuous history which originated with God's revelation to Abraham. This is also made clear by the words of Ananias: "The God of our fathers appointed you to know his will, to see the Just One and to hear a voice from his mouth; for you will be a witness for him to all men of what you have seen and heard" (22:14-15). To Gentile audiences the apostle preaches first of all the truth of biblical monotheism (Acts 14:15-17; 17:22-31).[48]

God's promise to the fathers, from Abraham onward, is a theme which runs through the whole of Luke's two-volume work. The first volume tells the story of Jesus, by whom the salvation promised to Israel was effected. The second volume contains the story of the apostolic preaching by which this salvation was brought to the Gentiles. In a rough sketch, Luke's ideas of mission to Jews and Gentiles may be summarized in three points:

1. Salvation of Gentiles was from the beginning envisaged by God and included as part of his promises to Israel. Luke does not claim that the church has replaced Israel as the people of God, nor does he call Gentile believers Abraham's children.[49] Gentiles are saved as Gentiles. Luke takes care to adduce prophecies that really spoke of them.[50] This "proof-from-prophecy" has a double function: to prove the legitimacy of Gentile mission and Gentile churches, and to prove that Jesus is the Anointed One of whom the prophets spoke.

2. Luke wants to make it clear beyond doubt that in the course of events due respect has been paid to the priority of Israel. This is made clear by the birth stories, by the presentation of the ministry of Jesus and of the life and preaching of the earliest church, and by the stereotype picture of Paul as everywhere starting in the synagogue.[51] Luke even says that the number of believing Jews in Palestine was quite considerable (Acts 2:41; 4:4; 21:20). It would not be to the point to think that he simply assumes the mission to the Gentiles to result from the failure of the mission to the Jews.[52]

3. The priority of Israel is regarded as a matter of history; it is no longer a present reality for Luke and for churches like those of Corinth and Rome. The primary task, to proclaim the fulfillment of the promises to the Jews, *has* been carried out by the apostles; Paul's conversation with the Jews at Rome marks the end of it. (One might here compare with the concept, widespread in early Protestantism, that even the task of proclaiming the gospel to all nations had been carried out by the apostles!) The fact that so many Jews did not believe in Christ might seem to jeopardize the "proof-from-prophecy," but Luke is able to show that even the obstinacy of the covenant people had been foretold by the prophets and by Jesus. It conformed to a constant pattern of biblical history.[53] Thus the main point would seem to be that the continuity with this history had in no way been broken,

151

either by the emerging of Gentile churches, or by the exclusion of disobedient Jews.

For me, the study of Abraham in Luke–Acts has been a confirmation of Paul Schubert's thesis that "proof-from-prophecy" is a main theological and literary device of the work. It should be observed that this motif is in the foreground especially in those parts of the work at which there might seem to be some break in the historical continuity: the beginning of the gospel story, the passion and resurrection of Jesus, the transition from the ministry of Jesus to the activity of his apostles, the conversion of Cornelius, and the vocation, career, and imprisonment of Paul.[54] These are all points at which the hand of the author is easily discernible. Luke did not invent the Christian "proof-from-prophecy," but in a special way he made it a principle for the composition of a continuous historical work.

The model for his conception of sacred history as a series of predictions and events Luke found, no doubt, in the historical books of Holy Scripture. In the Pentateuch (viz., Tetrateuch or Hexateuch) God's promise to the fathers and the fulfillment of it is a main theme, *the* main theme I would think. In the deuteronomistic work of history (Deuteronomy–II Kings) the word of God, announced by prophets and accomplished in due time, is considered an active power at work in history.[55] Luke is imitating biblical historiography. To say that is not to deny his Hellenistic affiliations (an unnecessary warning were it not the case that the struggle between "Hebraists" and "Hellenists" among New Testament scholars has caused some confusion). Luke consciously imitates the language of the Septuagint, but nonetheless writes the literary Koine of his day. In a similar way he writes "biblical history," but he does so as a Gentile Christian of Hellenistic culture and in Roman times. His interest in Abraham and his archaizing tendency in general bear the stamp of an age that looked back to classical times and considered antiquity an indication of value. Luke stresses the continuity between Abraham and the church of his own time, as some generations earlier Virgil had linked Roman history with that of Aeneas. The interest in "proof-from-prophecy," oracles, portents, and predictions, was not exclusively biblical.[56] The "father of history," Herodotus, had already paid considerable attention to oracles and the way in which they turned out to hold true.

But whatever the Greek, Hellenistic, and Roman components of Luke's historiography may have been, his own conscious intention was to write history in biblical style or, rather, to write the continuation of the biblical history. This gives him a unique place even among the New Testament writers. Certainly, they all interpret the "Christ-event" within a frame of reference provided by biblical history, prophecy, and eschatology, as interpreted by contemporary Judaism.[57] The basic theme, that God's promise to Abraham was fulfilled in Christ and brought to the Gentiles by the apostolic preaching, Luke has in common with Paul and other writers after him. But Luke alone sets this forth in the form of a historical account which also includes recapitulations of the Old Testament history which is continued in the things now fulfilled. The apostolic preaching is to him not the revelation of an apocalyptic mystery, but a testimony to the most decisive events within a continuous series of predictions, occurrences, and new promises; the fulfillment of earlier prophecies is a guarantee that all that has been foretold is to be established at the proper time.[58]

In the preface to his work Luke states his purpose to be that Theophilus should know the certainty (τὴν ἀσφάλειαν) of the things of which he had been informed. This can hardly be taken to mean merely that Luke wants to give an account which is outstanding according to the standards of historical accuracy. Interpreting the preface in the light of the whole work, we must much more assume that Luke wants to show the reliability of his account by demonstrating that everything has happened according to prophecies.[59] That is part of his task as a historian, as Luke conceives it. Only with this in mind, I think, may we also say that for Luke the history of the church is its apology.[60] History, for Luke, has brought the prophecies to fulfillment, and the prophecies prove that the historical events happened according to the will of God.

Writing as a "biblical historian" Luke does not need to christianize the portrait of Abraham in any direct and obvious way. The patriarch may remain the ancestor of Israel, the starting point of that sacred history of which the Gentile church is now the legitimate continuation. Luke, if I am correct, keeps closer to the Old Testament narratives and references to Abraham than does any other Christian or Jewish writer of his time. He gives very little room to legendary accretions and refrains from daring theological interpretations. In considering God's promise to Abraham as the first link in a series of prophecy and fulfillment, he is in full harmony with the outlook of Old Testament writers. Some details in the portrait of Abraham reflect the environment of a Hellenized, yet conservative type of Judaism. It is quite possible that Luke has taken over most of his references to the patriarch from sources at his disposal, Jewish or Christian. Yet with all his biblicism and traditionalism, Luke has made the whole material subservient to his own purpose; he rephrased and adapted it, and provided proper settings within the structure of his work. His way of dealing with the story of Abraham seems likely to be typical of his literary activity in general. He keeps rather close to his sources and wants to respect what he assumes to have been the historical facts. Yet, by means of redaction, rearrangement, and some minor changes, he is able to write history in such a way that he simultaneously sets forth his theology, whether he was conscious of this or not. In that respect Luke the historian has many and even outstanding followers among modern historiographers who have dealt with the same events—no matter how greatly methods and ideas of history may have changed.

NOTES

1. Cf. e.g., C. K. Barrett, *Luke the Historian in Recent Study* (London, 1961).
2. The present study is to a considerable extent inspired by oral discussions with Paul Schubert, as well as by his essay, "The Structure and Significance of Luke 24." *Neutestamentliche Studien für Rudolf Bultmann, Bh ZNW*, XXI (2nd ed., Berlin, 1957), pp. 165-86. However, the immediate topic of my article has not been touched in our conversations, as far as I can remember.
3. *HUCA* XXV (1954), 209-37, and XXVI (1955), 151-332. The quotation is taken from vol. XXV, p. 237. For earlier literature, cf. J. Jeremias, *ThWB* I, 7-9.
4. Paul's interpretation of the Abraham story is now under discussion. Cf., e.g., U. Wilckens, "Die Rechtfertigung Abrahams in Römer 4," *Studien zur Theologie der alttestamentlichen Überlieferungen,* von Rad Festschrift (Neukirchen, 1961): G. Klein, "Römer 4 und die Idee der Heilsgeschichte." *EvTh* XXIII (1963), 424-47.—*Idem*. "Individualgeschichte und Weltgeschichte bei Paulus," *EvTh* XXIV (1964), 126-65.
5. Cf. my articles: "The Johannine Church and History." *Current Issues in New Testament Interpretation,* Piper Festschrift (New York, 1962), pp. 124-42, esp. 134; "Manndraperen og hans far." *Norsk teol. tidsskr.* LXIV (1963), 129-63, esp. 145-48; "Der Erstgeborene Satans und der Vater des Teufels." *Apophoreta,* Haenchen Festschrift *Bh ZNW* XXX (Berlin, 1964), pp. 70-84, esp. 77-78. W. A. Meeks has drawn my attention to the possibility that "Abraham's works" in John 8:39 may include his hospitality (Gen. 18). Cf. I Clement 10:7: διὰ πίστιν καὶ φιλοξενίαν.
6. Cf. H. Köster, "Die Auslegung der Abraham-Verheissung in Hebräer 6." *Studien zur Theologie der alttestamentlichen Überlieferungen,* von Rad Festschrift (Neukirchen, 1961), pp. 95-109.
7. Cf. Luke 1:73; 16:24 ff.; Acts 7:2. Only in addresses to Jews are Abraham, Isaac, and Jacob and their descendants called "our fathers," Luke 1:55, 72; Acts 3:13; 5:30; 7:32; 13: 17; 22:14; 26:6. "Our fathers" can also refer to the twelve patriarchs (Acts 7:11, 12, 15), to the Exodus generation (Acts 7:19, 38, 39, 44), or to Israelites of later epochs (Acts 7:45; 5:10). The term "your fathers" more often has negative connotations (cf. Luke

Nils A. Dahl

11:47-48; Acts 7:51-52; 28:25) as has also "their fathers" (Luke 6:23, 26). However, according to the best manuscript evidence "your fathers" is used also in Acts 7:25. There does not seem to be sufficient evidence for the sharp differentiation between two groups of fathers as suggested by A. F. J. Klijn, "Stephen's Speech—Acts VII. 2-53." NTS IV (1957/8), 25-31, on the basis of the variant reading "your fathers" in 7:39.

8. Cf. K. Grobel, "Whose Name was Neves," NTS X (1963/64) 373-82, with literature.
9. Cf. (Strack-) Billerbeck, Kommentar zum NT (München, 1924), II, 225-26; R. Meyer, ThWB III (1935/38), 825-26.—Const. Apost. VIII, 41:2 seems most likely to be influenced by Luke 16:22.
10. Test. Levi 18:14; Judah 25:1; Benj. 10:6.
11. Cf. 1:70-72; 10:24; 11:47a, 50; Acts 3:21, 25.
12. Luke 6:23; 11:47-51; 13:33-34; Acts 7:52.
13. IV Macc. 6:17, 22; 9:21; 13:12; 14:20; 15:28; 17:6; 18:1, 20, 23.
14. ὁ πατρῷος θεός, Acts 24:14, cf. IV Macc. 12:18; Josephus, Ant. IX. 256; XII. 278.—οἱ—πατριάρχαι, Acts 7:8, cf. IV Macc. 7:19; 16:25; Test. XII, inser.—θυγάτηρ 'Αβραάμ, Luke 13:16, cf. IV Macc. 15:28.
15. Cf. Schniewind/Friedrich, ThWB II (1933/35), 576-77. The term αἱ ἐπαγγελίαι τῶν πατέρων found in Test. XII, Joseph 20:1. Const. Apost. VII. 35:10; 37:1; VIII. 12:23, 24 may reflect the prayer language of the Greek-speaking synagogue.
16. Hebr. 11:11-12; cf. Acts 7:5, 8.
17. Hebr. 6:12-18; 11:2–12:11; cf. Acts 7:2-60; Luke 11:47-51. For other point of contact cf. P. M. Jones, "The Epistle to the Hebrews and the Lucan Writings," Studies in the Gospels: In Memory of R. H. Lightfoot (Oxford, 1958), pp. 113-43.
18. Eusebius, Praep. evang. IX. 17-18. The fragment attributed to "Eupolemus" must be of Samaritan origin.—A book on Abraham and the Egyptians was attributed to Hecataeus, cf. N. Walter, Der Thoraausleger Aristobulos, TU LXXXVI (Berlin, 1964), pp. 187-88 and 195 ff.
19. On these traditions cf. Sandmel, HUCA XXV-XXVI, and G. Vermes, Scripture and Tradition in Judaism, Studia Post-biblica IV (Leiden, 1961), pp. 67-126.
20. Cf. esp. Josh. 24:2-4; Ps. 104:8-11; Neh. 9:7-8; G. von Rad, Das formgeschichtliche Problem des Hexateuchs, BWANT IV (Stuttgart, 1938), 26.
21. God's initiative is also stressed in Gen. 15:7; Neh. 9:7; Heb. 11:8; Philo, De Abr., 162-67; Josephus, Ant., I, 154. But Haenchen may be right, that there is not sufficient reason to speak of a school tradition. Cf. Die Apostelgeschichte (Meyer Commentary, 3rd Abt., 13th ed. [Göttingen, 1961]), p. 229, n.
22. Cf. Judith 5:7; Josephus, Ant., I, 152.
23. Cf. Philo, De mirg. Abr., 177. The Samaritan chronology makes Terah die at the age of 145 (not 205), and thus supports the view that he was dead when Abraham left Haran. For this and similar points cf. the commentaries and H. J. Cadbury, The Book of Acts in History (London, 1955), pp. 102-4.
24. Gen. 23:16-17 and 50:13; Gen. 33:18-19 and Josh. 24:32. Possibly a Samaritan local tradition, that all the (twelve?) patriarchs were buried at Shechem, has been reinterpreted and made a proof of Abraham's lack of property in the land of the Jews.
25. Acts 7:5, cf. Heb. 11:9-13.
26. Cf., however, B. W. Bacon, "Stephen's Speech: Its Argument and Its Doctrinal Relationship," Yale Bicentennial Publications: Biblical and Semitic Studies (New York, 1902), pp. 211-76, esp. pp. 237 ff.
27. The phrase is taken from Gen. 17:8, cf. Gen. 48:4; Ezek. 33:24, etc.
28. Thus Bacon, "Stephen's Speech," p. 270, etc.; M. Simon, St. Stephen and the Hellenists (London, 1956), pp. 50-58. But cf. the critique of J. C. O'Neill, The Theology of Acts (London, 1961), 72-83.
29. τῷ οἴκῳ 'Ιακώβ is the reading of the best Egyptian uncials and of the bilingual D. It may be due to a conscious interpretation and adaptation of the Septuagint text of Ps.

131(132):5 LXX: Asking leave to find a habitation for the God of Jacob, David asked at the same time for a "dwelling place," a permanent place of worship, for the house of Jacob. For this use of σκήνωμα cf. Ps. 131 (132):7; 14 (15):1; 42 (43):3; 83 (84): 1. Cf. also II Sam. 7:10.

30. "Stephen's Speech," p. 270.
31. Cf. M. Simon, *St. Stephen*, p. 52: "It is, however, obvious that II Sam. 7, Nathan's prophecy, is also in Stephen's mind." But I doubt that Simon is correct in taking Nathan's prophecy to imply a radical opposition to the temple and in assuming that Stephen understood it that way. Cf. R. A. Carlsson, *David the Chosen King* (Stockholm, Uppsala, 1964), 106-28. As to the promise to David in the Lucan writings, cf. Luke 1:32-33; Acts 2:30; 13:23 ff., etc. E. Lövestam, *Son and Saviour*, ConNT XVIII (Lund/Copenhagen, 1961).
32. Cf. Acts 2:42, 46-47; 4:24-31; 5:12, 42; etc.
33. Luke 1:7, cf. Ps. 106:10. Already B. W. Bacon pointed out the close relations between Stephen's speech and the Benedictus, "Stephen's Speech," pp. 237-38, 244, 270.
34. M. Dibelius, *Studies in the Acts of the Apostles* (London, 1956), p. 168. Cf. p. 169: "The most striking feature of this speech is the irrelevancy of its main section." He is followed by Haenchen, *Die Apostelgeschichte*, p. 239; H. Conzelmann, *Die Apostelgeschichte*, (Tübingen, 1963), 45-51, has seen that the idea of the promise, its fulfillment, and its rejection, is a main theme of the speech. However, he does not draw the consequences, but still speaks of an underlying layer, "deren Sinn im Nachzeichnen der Geschichte als solchem (!) liegt" (p. 50).
35. Cf. I Sam. 12:6-15; Ps. 78 and 106; Jer. 2; Ezek. 20; Neh. 9. Even in Exodus through II Kings the whole history of Israel is seen by and large as a series of transgressions. Among later recapitulations, CD 2:14–6:11 is of special interest. Cf. 1QS 1:21-23. A more remote parallel is the speech in which Josephus confronted the besieged Jews with the history of their people, *Bell.* V, 375-419.
36. 7:51, cf. Ps. 106:33; Neh. 9:30; CD 5:11.
37. In Luke's portrait of Stephen (Acts 6:5, 8, 10; 7:55 ff. we find some of the same, typical features of the wise, inspired, and persecuted man of God, as in his portraits of Joseph and Moses, and of Jesus (Luke 2:40, 52; 24:19; Acts 2:22-23; 3:14; 10:38).
38. Election of the fathers: Neh. 9:7; Ps. 105:6; II Macc. 125; Ps. Sol. 9:9; IV Ezra 3:13; cf. Schrenk, *ThWB* IV (1938/42), 174.
39. Cf. Lövestam, *Son and Saviour*.
40. υἱοὶ γένους ᾿Αβραάμ. The term γένος ᾿Αβραάμ is not found in translations from the Hebrew Bible, but cf. I Macc. 12:21; Test. Napht. 1:10; Josephus, *Ant.* V, 113; *Const. Apost.* VII, 33:7.
41. The manuscript evidence supports the reading, but this hardly gives sense, in spite of Acts 2:39.
42. Cf. Luke 1:55; 1:70-74; Acts 3:13, 18, 21, 25; 26:6.
43. Cf. Gal. 3:16; Conzelmann, *Die Apostelgeschichte*, p. 35. The reader of Acts would hardly get the idea that merely the "claims of the land" are meant (against Haenchen).
44. Cf. the analysis by Schubert, "The Structure," 178-79—P. Benoit, "L'enfance de Jean-Baptiste selon Luc I," *NTS* III (1956/57), 169-94.
45. Ex. 32:13; Micah 7:20; Ps. 105:8-11, 42; I Chron. 16:5-18; Neh. 9:7-8; Ex. 2:24; 6:3-4, 8; 33:1; Lev. 26:42; Deut. 1:8; 9:5, 27, etc.; II Kings 13:23; Jer. 11:5. In Intertestamental literature this type of reference is less frequent than might possibly be expected, cf. Ben Sir. 44:21; I Macc. 4:10; II Macc. 1:2; Ps. Sol. 9:9; Ass. Mos. 3:9; Test. Levi 15:4. The general tendency is, rather, to stress the exemplary conduct, the temptations, and the apocalyptic visions of Abraham; cf. e.g., Ben Sir. 44:19-20; Judith 5:6 ff.; 8:26; IV Ezra 3:13-14; Pseudo-Philo, *Ant. bibl.* 23:4-7; 32:1-4. If the Magnificat and the Benedictus should go back to Jewish hymns, as several scholars have assumed, this would illustrate what is in any case probable: Luke has been able to find and use materials which were akin

to his own outlook while, on the other hand, his own points of view are largely traditional.

46. It is hardly fortuitous that, in contrast to Matt. 8:11-12, Luke does not directly say that many shall come from east and west and sit at table with Abraham, Isaac, and Jacob in the kingdom of God. Luke 13:27-28 brings two distinct sayings regarding a) the exclusion of Jesus' Jewish contemporaries from the communion with patriarchs and prophets, and b) the coming of men from east and west, and from north and south. Luke never speaks of a "change of peoples" in the same way as Matt. 21:43.

47. Cf. Luke 20:37-38; Acts 3:13, 25-26; 4:2; 5:30; 13:32-33; 24:14-15; 26:6-7; 26:22-23; 28:2.—Is it a mere coincidence that the Lucan emphasis on the God of the fathers as the one who raises the dead corresponds to the first two of the Eighteen Benedictions?

48. There seems to be an increasing agreement that these speeches, with their philosophical flavor, draw upon traditions of Hellenistic Judaism, cf., e.g., B. Gärtner, *The Areopagus Speech and Natural Revelation, ASNU* XXI (Uppsala, 1955). J.-C. Lebram, "Der Aufbau der Areopagusrede," *ZNW* LV (1963/4), 221-43.

49. Acts 15:14 and 18:10 do not transcend the limits of the prophecy of Zech. 2:11; cf. my article, "A People for His Name (Acts 15:14)." *NTS* IV (1957), 319-27.

50 Luke 3:6 (Isa. 40:5); Acts 2:17 (Joel 3:1 "all flesh"); 3:25 (Gen. 22:18); 13:47 (Isa. 49:6); 15:17 (Amos 9:12). Cf. biblical allusions and reminiscences in Luke 2:32; 4:24-27; Acts 1:8; 2:39; 10:34; 15:14; 26:17-18; 28:28. J. Dupont, "Le salut des Gentiles et la signification théologique du livre des Actes," *NTS* VI (1959/60), 132-55. F. Hahn, *Das Verständnis der Mission im Neuen Testament, WUANT* XIII (Neukirchen, 1963), pp. 111-19. (English translation now in *SBTh*.)

51. Cf. esp. Acts 13:46-48; 18:4-6; 28:17-31. For the pre-Pauline idea that the salvation of Gentiles would follow as a result of Israel's conversion to Jesus, the Messiah; cf. J. Munck, *Paul and the Salvation of Mankind* (London, 1959).

52. Thus Haenchen, *Die Apostelgeschichte,* 654: "Auch das letzte Kapitel gliedert sich damit vollständig in das Gesamtwerk ein, indem es das Recht zur Heidenmission im sich Versagen der Juden begründet." Cf., however, also pp. 680-82.

53. Luke 1:34; 4:24-27; 6:22-23, 26; 8:10; 11:47-51; 13:23-30; 34; 14:24; 19:27, 41-46; 20:9-18; 21:20-24; 23:28-31; Acts 3:23; 4:25-28; 7:35-53; 13:40-41; 28:25-27.

54. Cf. esp. Luke 1–2; 3:1-17; 4:16-30; 24; Acts 1:1-11; 10:1-11:18; 15:6-21. The passion of Jesus: Luke 2:35; 9:22, 31, 44, 51; 13:32-33; 17:25; 18:31-33; 19:14-17; 22:19-34. The vocation and career of Paul: Acts 9:1-18; 13:2; 16:6-8; 18:9-10; 20:23; 21:4, 11; 22:6-21; 23:11; 26:12-23; 27:9-11, 21-26, 41-34. H. H. Oliver, "The Lucan Birth Stories and the Purpose of Luke Acts." *NTS* X (1963/64), 202-26, thinks that there is some question about the motif of "proof-from-prophecy": "Against it is the consideration that it has played no part in recent *redaktionsgeschichtliche* studies of Luke–Acts" (p. 225). All the worse for recent *Redaktionsgeschichte* if that is the case! The importance of the motif was already noticed by H. J. Cadbury, *The Making of Luke–Acts* (London, 1927), pp. 303-5. Cf. also E. Lohse, "Lukas als Theologe der Heilsgeschichte," *EvTh* XIV (1954), 256-75. (See also the article by Paul Minear in this volume.—Eds.)

55. Cf. G. von Rad, "Studies in Deuteronomy," *SBTh* IX (London, 1953) pp. 74-91. *Idem. Old Testament Theology,* trans. by D. M. G. Stalker (New York, 1962), Vol. I, pp. 339 ff.

56. Luke is himself aware of this fact, Acts 16:16-18. His interests include the "popular" type of prophets, of which Agabus was an example, Acts 11:28; 21:10-11.

57. Cf. C. H. Dodd, *According to the Scriptures* (London, 1952); B. Lindars, *New Testament Apologetic* (London, 1961); N. A. Dahl, "Eschatologie und Geschichte im Lichte der Qumrantexte," *Zeit und Geschichte,* Bultmann Festschrift (Tübingen, 1964), pp. 3-18.

58. The difference between Lucan "Heilsgeschichte" and the eschatological interpretation of the "Christ-event" which, in spite of great variety, is common to Paul, Mark, Matthew, and John, has been worked out by H. Conzelmann, *The Theology of St. Luke,* trans. G. Boswell (London, 1960). However, by his emphasis on the distinction between succeeding periods Conzelmann has unduly formalized Luke's conception.

59. This is indicated already by the phrase "the things which have been accomplished among us," cf. Lohse, "Lukas als Theologe," 261 ff. The term ἀσφάλεια in itself merely refers to the accuracy of information; cf. Acts 21:34; 22:30; 25:26, but certainly Theophilus had already been informed that things had happened according to the Scriptures, and Luke feels able to prove the accuracy of this.

60. Cf. Haenchen, *Die Apostelgeschichte*, p. 656 (concluding remark).

The Christology of Acts

C. F. D. MOULE

Professor Schubert knows, far better than I, the formidable output of literature, even over the last two or three decades, relevant to the Christology
of Acts and providing evidence of an increasing awareness of the complexity
of the subject. In gratefully dedicating this small offering to him I am glad,
therefore, that it is not the only essay in this volume which is responsible for
Christology. The essay by Professor Schweizer is also relevant, not to mention the less direct light shed on the subject by others; and I am sure that
errors and deficiencies both of fact and of judgment will not go wholly un-
corrected and uncompensated, even within these two covers. What matters
most, however, is that any true insights into the meaning of Luke or of his
sources should not be left on a merely academic level, but should be made
available and applied to the church's witness at the present time. It is not
my responsibility to attempt this in this essay; but it is good that this aspect,
too, of the study of Luke–Acts does not go unmentioned in this volume.

Within the limits of a single essay, I have decided to confine my investigation to a series of comparative studies: first, between Acts and Luke's Gospel; secondly, between different parts of Acts itself; and thirdly, between
Acts and certain other New Testament documents. A great body of scholars
have done this before me: the names of some of them appear in the foot-
notes. If there is anything at all that I can add, it will only be in the arrangement and presentation and, possibly, fresh assessment of some of the facts.
In writing this essay without access to the others, I am well aware that any
such assessment, insofar as it bears not only on Christology but also upon the
methods and motives of the author of Acts, will need to be counterbalanced
—perhaps to the degree of flat contradiction—by other contributors.

I. The Christologies of Luke's Two Volumes Compared

It is a commonplace of New Testament criticism that the Gospels are theological documents and, at the very least, reflect the faith of the writers and of their communities. Some would go further and say that the Gospels do not merely reflect such faith, but have been largely created by it. In its extreme forms, this view would mean that the evangelist was making little or no attempt to reconstruct what Jesus may have seemed to his contemporaries: his only aim was to present Jesus as the Lord of the Christian confession—the Lord he was now acknowledged to be.

The Christology of Acts is exceptionally interesting, because it offers the only fully authentic test of this theory. Few critics doubt that the same person wrote both Luke's Gospel and the Acts of the Apostles. If the Christology of the two is one and the same, then the view just indicated is, to that extent, supported; but if there is a difference, it is practically conclusive proof that the view needs to be modified.

The fact is that there is a difference.[1] And the first step in defining the difference may as well be to clear away once and for all a misapprehension which sometimes appears in accounts of Luke's Christology. It is well-known that Luke, unlike the other Synoptists, sometimes refers to Jesus in his Gospel as ὁ κύριος. It is not always stated that until the resurrection this is, with very rare exceptions, confined (on the lips of men) to passages in which the evangelist is himself as the narrator alluding to Jesus.[2] Except in the vocative—and κύριε as a common form of respectful address hardly holds the same possibilities as κύριος—κύριος is not, until the resurrection, applied to Jesus in Luke's Gospel by the human performers in the drama itself, except in Elizabeth's phrase, Luke 1:43, ἡ μήτηρ τοῦ κυρίου μου,[3] possibly Zechariah's phrase, Luke 1:76, ἐνώπιον κυρίου (but only as Christianly interpreted), and Christ's own phrase, Luke 19:31 (cf. 34), ὁ κύριος αὐτοῦ χρείαν ἔχει. Angels are allowed it (Luke 2:11) but not men, with those two or, at most, three exceptions. Thus Luke is, as a rule, not anachronously (if it is anachronous) reading back into the historical situation of Jesus' ministry what seems to have been a post-resurrection title. To use it in his own capacity as a narrator is different: a Christian narrator at any period might, without incurring blame for anachronism, say, "The Lord was not styled 'Lord' while still on earth"; and that is how Luke uses the title almost exclusively up to the resurrection.[4]

But as soon as his narrative reaches the post-resurrection period, both in the

Gospel and in Acts, it is immediately different. In Luke 24:34 and from the beginning of Acts onwards, the disciples themselves are represented as doing precisely what they do not do in the Gospel before the resurrection: they freely apply the term κύριος to Jesus. Among its many occurrences there are perhaps three particularly striking phenomena. The first is the strangely absolute phrase in the preaching of Peter to Cornelius (Acts 10:36): οὗτός ἐστιν πάντων κύριος. This—the more striking when it precedes the "adoptionist" type of language in vs. 38—is capable of being equated with παντοκράτωρ; but it is more likely that πάντων is here intended to be masculine rather than neuter, and to mean that Jesus is Lord of Jews and Gentiles alike[5] (so Haenchen and Conzelmann). Comparable phrases applied to God in Jewish literature are adduced by H. J. Cadbury.[6] It is not demonstrable that such a phrase—if it has a plausible Aramaic equivalent—could not have been used by Peter himself. (See further discussion.)[7] The second phenomenon is the free interchange between κύριος meaning God, and κύριος meaning Jesus, especially in the application of Old Testament *testimonia*. It is sometimes impossible to be certain which is intended. And the third phenomenon, cohering closely with this latter, is the use of the phrase ἐπικαλεῖσθαι τὸ ὄνομα which, undoubtedly used in certain instances with reference to the name of Jesus, is irresistibly reminiscent of the Old Testament idea of invoking the name of Yahweh (cf. Acts 2:21 with 7:59; 9:14, 21; 22:16) and implies the invocation of the divine.[8]

The mainly consistent restriction of κύριος, on the lips of human observers, to the post-resurrection context is at least a hint that Luke may not have used his terms as indiscriminately as is sometimes supposed. It certainly does not prove that he avoided anachronisms or that his reconstruction was accurate: it is open to anyone, even if he concedes the use of sources, to assume that a phrase like οὗτός ἐστιν πάντων κύριος is Luke's own insertion; equally it could be argued that, since κύριος *need* mean no more than מרי, etc., there is nothing necessarily transcendental about it, and that it is perhaps mere chance that it practically never renders a pre-resurrection designation of Jesus.[9] However, as far as it goes, the use of κύριος in the Gospel and Acts suggests that Luke at least was deliberately making a distinction;[10] and that its associations in Acts are decidedly transcendental.

Are there any other features emerging from a comparative study of the Gospel and Acts which point in the same direction? The answer is "Yes." First, take the use of the term "prophet" for Jesus. This indicates a subtle but consistent contrast, as between the Gospel and Acts. With O. Cullmann[11] and others it seems correct to draw a distinction between the identification of Jesus as merely *a* prophet, and his designation as *the* prophet expected in the last days—an expectation often associated with the famous words in Deut. 18:15: "The Lord your God will raise up for you a prophet like me from among your brethren." In the original context this meant clearly that God wished to speak to his people through the living voice of a man of God like Moses and not through the pagan techniques of divination, necromancy, and so forth. But it had come to be regarded as an eschatological promise of a second Moses or even of Moses *redivivus;* and to identify Jesus with this figure ("the coming one" of Samaritan expectation[12]) was not the same as to find in him merely a prophet—one of the prophets. If so, it is significant that it is not until Acts that Deut. 18:15 is explicitly used as a *testimonium* about Jesus. In Acts 3:22-23 in a Petrine address, and in Acts 7:37 (by clear implication) in Stephen's speech, it is so applied. In the Gospel, by contrast, Jesus is spoken of as simply a prophet —and with only one exception, by those who are not yet full believers (Luke 7:16, 39; 9:8, 19; 24:19, this last being no exception since it is on tht lips of the two on the way to Emmaus *before* their disillusionment had been dispelled by the epiphany of Jesus). The only exception is in the sayings of Jesus himself in Luke 4:24, "no prophet is recognized in his own country," and 13:33, "it is unthinkable for a prophet to meet his death anywhere but in Jerusalem." These passages imply that he is styling himself a prophet; but the fact that they are in proverbial form and, in any case, on Jesus' own lips, not those of a follower, makes them scarcely exceptions.

There is, however, one further passage in Luke's Gospel to be considered in this connection. Without an express citation of Deut. 18:15, a subtle hint appears to be intended in the story of the transfiguration (in all three Synoptics). The two figures of Moses and Elijah are, no doubt, themselves significant as pointing to him who is to succeed and supersede them. But there is the further phrase (Luke 9:35 and parallels) "listen to him," which is exactly like the αὐτοῦ ἀκούσεσθε of Deut. 18:15 as quoted in Acts 3:22. If this is an intended hint in the transfiguration narrative, then it will mean: "This is the Moses-prophet, and more than a prophet—one who is a Son." But even so, it is uttered not by a man but by the divine voice.

In sum, then, Luke does maintain a subtle but precise distinction between men's recognition of Jesus during his ministry as one of the prophets, and the express claim of the post-resurrection church, together with the anticipatory hint in the divine voice at the transfiguration, that he is the fulfillment of the Deuteronomic expectation—the Moses-prophet. Whether this is historically correct or not, Luke seems to be doing it with his eyes open.

It must be added that Luke 9:8, 19 (in company with Mark 6:15; 8:28; Matt. 16:14) represents the public as speculating whether Jesus might not be Elijah. Elijah was in some traditions[13] as great an eschatological figure as the Moses-prophet, and it could be argued that, when Luke allows this speculation to have been current before the resurrection, he is giving away with the other hand what he had withheld with the hand containing the Moses-prophet. Yet, once again, there appears to be method in what he does. Like the other evangelists, Luke seems to suggest that popular speculation was mistaken in using Elijah as a term for Jesus, and represents it instead as a term used by Jesus for John the Baptist; there is never a hint anywhere of Elijah as a post-resurrection title for Jesus. Thus the Moses-prophet, excluded from pre-resurrection language, is brought in explicitly in the church's preaching; and, conversely, Elijah, speculatively offered by public rumor during the ministry, is not heard of afterwards.

Another impressive example of apparently deliberate contrast between the Gospel and Acts is furnished by the use of the term "the Son of man" in Acts 7:56. It is a familiar fact that, while in all four Gospels the Son of Man is a phrase occurring frequently and on the lips of Jesus alone (John 12:34 is hardly an exception to this latter rule), Acts 7:56 is the solitary occurrence in the New Testament outside the Gospels and on the lips of another (unless one reckons Rev. 1:13; 14:14, which are virtually direct quotations from Dan. 7,[14] and are used in a visionary context). When compared with the Gospel uses, this occurrence differs not only in being on the lips of another, but also in two further respects: first, such Gospel references as associate the Son of Man with glory are all in the future; here, by contrast, the glory is an already realized fact: he is already at God's right hand. And secondly, in Stephen's vision, the Son of Man is not seated but standing. It is natural to see the Gospel use as referring to a future vindication of the martyr-community in its central, representative figure, Jesus; at present, the Son of Man is still on earth, destined to suffer, and destined for glory only after the suffering. This solitary post-resurrection occurrence, by contrast, shows the Son of Man already in glory and standing—perhaps as in a Jewish court of law to champion the cause of the "defendant,"

Stephen, on earth.[15] The term is used to denote Christ's already achieved glory and his championship of the first martyr. It has been subtly and convincingly adapted to a distinctively post-resurrection martyr-situation.[16]

Conzelmann has familiarized us with the idea that Luke saw the era of the church as a new phase, distinct from that of the ministry.[17] It is entirely in keeping with this that Luke should be thus conscious of an explicit Christology characterizing this new phase in contrast to the veiledness of the ministry. And the same is borne out by the way in which the theme of the Spirit is handled. In the Gospel and in Acts 10:38, which is part of the deliberately retrospective and Gospel-like preaching by Peter to Cornelius, Jesus, while himself uniquely endowed with Spirit, does not yet bestow the Spirit on others, although in the Gospel he promises the Spirit's help and presence. In the Acts, however, he is explicitly spoken of as bestowing the Spirit (Acts 2:33) and working through the Spirit (Acts 16:7).

Once again, the designation of Jesus as "Saviour," although common to the Gospel and Acts, is used in a significantly different way in the two. In the Gospel it is only on superhuman lips—in the angel's announcement to the shepherds (Luke 2:11). Only two other approaches to the same sense are found within the Gospel. When Simeon, holding the child Jesus in his arms, says (Luke 2:30): "I have seen with my own eyes the deliverance (τὸ σωτήριον) which thou hast made ready" (cf. Luke 3:6), this is God's act of deliverance, but Simeon is certainly associating it with the child he is holding. The second place is at 24:21, where the disillusioned two on their way to Emmaus say that they had hoped that Jesus was going to be the one who would rescue Israel (ὁ μέλλων λυτροῦσθαι τὸν Ἰσραήλ). An angelic anticipation, a prophetic vision, and a frustrated hope—that is all in the Gospel. But after the resurrection a far more explicit phrase occurs, in Acts 4:12: "There is no salvation (σωτηρία) in anyone else at all, for there is no other name under heaven granted to men, by which we may receive salvation" (σωθῆναι); and again in Acts 5:31, where Peter before the Sanhedrin speaks of Jesus as exalted by God to be ἀρχηγὸς καὶ σωτήρ, so as to give remission of sins to Israel; and in Acts 13:23, where Paul at Pisidian Antioch again relates Jesus to Israel as Saviour. In Luke 2:11, Acts 5:31, and Acts 13:23, it looks like an allusion to the etymology of "Jesus"; and the salvation is, expressly or by implication, a moral one from sin. The term is appropriate to the Jewish contexts, but especially to the insights brought by the resurrection: Jesus now assumes the function of God as *go'el* or Champion of Israel.

Yet once more it is noteworthy that the title υἱός is given to Jesus in the Gospel only by other than human voices—divine, angelic, or satanic (Luke 1:32, 35; 3:22; 4:3, 9, 41; 8:28), or in his own monologue (Luke 10:22), until the climax of the story when, at the trial before the Sanhedrin, Jesus is asked whether he is the Son of God and gives, perhaps, a noncommittal reply (Luke 22:70). But in Acts after the resurrection Paul—though only Paul, unless the δ-text of Acts 8:37 be accepted; cf. further discussion below —explicitly affirms the title (Acts 9:20; 13:33).

One further specific piece of evidence pointing in the same direction is in Acts 18:9-10, where "the Lord" (evidently Jesus) says in a vision by night to Paul: "Have no fear: go on with your preaching and do not be silenced, for I am with you and no one shall attempt to do you harm; and there are many in this city who are my people (λαός ἐστι μοι πολὺς ἐν τῇ πόλει ταύτῃ)." Luke's Gospel shows nothing parallel to the astonishing Matt. 16:18 "οἰκοδομήσω μου τὴν ἐκκλησίαν; but in Acts in contrast to Luke's Gospel, the risen Lord is represented as speaking about a λαός belonging to him.

The common factor behind the contrasts that have been described is, of course, the consciousness of the resurrection as marking a decisive vindication of Jesus. Consistently in Acts, Jesus is recognized as the one who, though crucified, has been raised,[18]—absolutely, for like the other New Testament writers Luke clearly means that the raising is absolute.[19] There is no question of temporary resuscitation to a continued mortal life: in its own peculiar idiom, the ascension narrative[20] makes that clear. Jesus is shown in Acts as raised from death, exalted to heaven, destined ultimately to return, and meanwhile represented in the church's activities and expansion by the Holy Spirit, whose advent is the result of Christ's "withdrawal." More will be said about this conception of Jesus' withdrawal when the Christology of Acts is compared with that of Paul; but it is enough meanwhile to recognize the resurrection as the Christological watershed dividing the Gospel from the Acts.[21]

If the contrasts just reviewed are undeniable, it is the more significant that Acts evinces an unshaken awareness that the exalted Lord is identical with Jesus, the man of Nazareth. There is no trace of discontinuity: indeed, the opening words of the prologue expressly forbid it; and the emphasis upon the Galilean and Nazarene origin of the church is in keeping with this. The "two men in white" at the ascension (Acts 1:11) expressly address the disciples as "men of Galilee"; they are described at Pentecost (Acts 2:7) as "all Galileans"; and the term Ναζωραῖος is freely used of Jesus (Acts 2:22; 3:6; 4:10; 6:14; 22:8; 26:9) and once of his followers (Acts 24:5, ἡ τῶν Ναζωραίων αἵρεσις). Much discussion has been devoted to this obscure title.[22] B. Gärtner suggests its association with נצר (i.e., the holy remnant, "preserved" by God);[23] E. Schweizer offers the guess that it originally meant "the Nazirite"—not in the strict sense, but as "a holy man of God"—and that the topographical association was an afterthought;[24] O. Cullmann [25] alludes to the possibility, suggested by Lidzbarski, that it may have attached to a pre-Christian Jewish sect of "observants" (נצר) and then been transferred to the Christian sect. But H. H. Schaeder seems to have shown that the simple, topographical meaning ("of Nazareth") is, in fact, unexceptionable;[26] and it is easy to imagine that the common name "Jesus" came to be distinguished by the name of his home, and that so, in turn, the epithet passed to his followers. If this is really its origin, then its frequent use for Jesus in post-resurrection settings seems to reflect an awareness of his continuity with the Jesus of history.

If a cumulative case is thus made for Luke's recognizing continuity of person but novelty of interpretation in the post-resurrection period, this is not to say that his post-resurrection Christology is the same as that of other New Testament writers, or is even consistent with itself. These are precisely the matters which will occupy the other sections of this essay. But it can be said at once that the Acts' Christology is consistently "exalted"[27] in type. Although there are phrases which in a later context could be classed as adoptionist—Jesus is twice called ἀνήρ (2:22; 17:31; cf. Luke 24:19)—there is never any doubt that he is more than a mere prophet or rabbi of the past. Christians are commonly called "disciples"; but their Master is always an exalted, heavenly figure. This would follow from the resurrection, even if κύριος meant no more than "Master," and if its non-application before the resurrection were due to mere chance.

II. Various Christologies Within Acts

The question whether there are different levels of Christology within the Acts now requires investigation. It is difficult—perhaps impossible—to come to the inquiry without presuppositions about Luke's method. Did he freely invent words for the actors in his play, handling them, indeed, with the creative insight of a dramatist? J. C. O'Neill is typical of many when he sees the exuberance of uncommon titles of Christ in Acts 3–5 as due simply to Luke's attempt to give this part of his story an archaic, scriptural ring.[28] There are others who imagine that he made considerable use of sources, oral or written, and that, although he exercised his editorial prerogative of selecting and placing, the language is in large measure the authentic language of the period in question. On this showing, if there is a marked difference[29] between certain passages in the earlier chapters and others later in the book, it will be due not to Luke's creative imagination but to an actual difference of environment and outlook for the leading figures in the respective sections.

Nothing approaching an objective judgment will be reached without a comparative study of the phrases—though even this, of course, is at the mercy of a good deal of subjectivism.

We may start with Acts 3:19-21, for it has been claimed by J. A. T. Robinson[30] that in these verses a very primitive type of Christology seems to show through, like an outcrop of primeval rock in a contrasting landscape. The crucial words are (vss. 19*b*, 20, 21*a* in RSV, NEB, or in Nestle, 20, 21*a*): "Then the Lord may grant you a time of recovery and send you the Messiah he has already appointed (τὸν προκεχειρισμένον χριστόν), that is, Jesus. He must be received into heaven. . . ." Robinson interprets this to mean that Jesus, though indeed *designated* Christ (*de jure,* as it were), has yet to be actually *sent* as Christ (*de facto*) to the world. The disciples had seen him suffer and had seen his "private" vindication: they believe that he is God's chosen Suffering Servant. But they cannot bring themselves actually to style him Messiah until some more public vindication, which they still look for in the future. This, Robinson thinks, is an extremely primitive way of thinking about Jesus, which did not long survive, and which was soon superseded by the kind of outlook which is reflected in Acts 2, although Luke has represented that as chronologically prior to this phrase in Acts 3. Indeed in this very context, in Acts 3:18, Luke has fused with the alleged antique fragment from the earliest traditions his own summary of a much more advanced stage of thought, namely that it is the Messiah himself, startling and paradoxical though this may be, to whom suffering belongs (παθεῖν τὸν χριστόν): it is not only as the Servant, it is actually as already the Christ that he suffers.

It is probably true that παθεῖν τὸν χριστόν is Luke's own summary.[31] It (or παθητὸς ὁ χριστός) is a distinctively Lucan refrain (cf. Luke 24:46; Acts 17:3; 26:23), and the idea is rarely found explicitly stated elsewhere in the New Testament, although there are a few instances (1 Peter 2:21; 4:1, though here χριστός is anarthrous and perhaps only a proper name; and I Cor. 1:23, if χριστός is, though anarthrous, a title there). But the mere fact that παθεῖν τὸν χριστόν (or παθητὸς ὁ χριστός) is characteristically Lucan does not necessitate the conclusion that a possibly pre-Lucan phrase now fused with it must be interpreted as alien and opposite in meaning merely because pre-Lucan. And we are not compelled so to interpret this phrase as to make it mean that the suffering one is *not* (yet) the Christ "in fact," but only the Christ potentially and as "designate." If that had been the meaning, it is difficult to see why Luke placed the phrase side by side with παθεῖν τὸν χριστόν which, on this showing, is contradictory to it. Why did he not rather alter it or even reject it outright,[32] or, alternatively, retain it in its isolation as a specimen of primitive thought, without confusing the issue by juxtaposing his own summary of a later viewpoint? The "outcrop" theory, in other words, suggests an unlikely coupling of a reverence for ancient tradition with an arbitrary reversal of its meaning. It is simpler, surely, to interpret the crucial words to mean that Jesus is *already* recognized as the *previously* predestined Christ (the term προκεχειρισμένος, so interpreted, is in line with Luke's penchant for predestination), who at the end is to be sent *back again* into the world.

Admittedly, the "back again" has to be supplied from the context, and the phrase is a slightly peculiar one, as is the notoriously ambiguous ending of the sentence in vs. 21 ("the time of universal restoration . . . , of which God spoke by his holy prophets"). But the whole might not unreasonably be paraphrased as follows: "Therefore repent and turn back (to God), so that your sins may be obliterated, and so that a period of recovery (i.e., a new age of godliness) may come from the presence of the Lord (God), and so that he may send (back) the one who was long ago designated to be your Messiah, namely, Jesus. He must be received in heaven (i.e., must remain removed from mortal sight) until the time, spoken of by God through his holy prophets ever since the earliest days, when everything is to be restored to its proper position (i.e., when there is going to be a general reduction of the world's dislocation and chaos)." This makes the passage similar, in its eschatology, to Acts 1:11, although that is devoid of the problematic titles for Jesus.

In this same context vs. 26 is difficult, on any showing, to harmonize with vs. 20; for vs. 20 speaks of God's sending of Christ Jesus as a future boon, whereas in vs. 26 God's Servant (παῖς) has already been "sent with a blessing." If this latter referred to the ministry of Jesus (and the aorist, ἀπέστειλεν, is easier to translate by "sent" than by "has sent"), it would fit Robinson's theory well. But in spite of everything (aorist included), it is difficult to take ἀναστήσας . . . τὸν παῖδα αὐτοῦ ("having raised up his Servant") as an allusion, not to the resurrection but to the "raising up" (or "letting appear") of a figure upon the stage of history. The verb is so used, of course, in the original context of Deut. 18:15; but as quoted in a Christian context in Acts 3:22 and 7:37, this becomes almost inevitably an allusion to resurrection.[33]

On the whole, then, it seems that the case for finding two decidedly different Christologies side by side in chaps. 2 and 3 (not to mention in 3:18 and 20) is far from established. The matter is different with the twofold use of παῖς in Acts 3 and 4. Here, I believe, there are two recognizably distinct conceptions of Jesus. But even so they are not mutually incompatible nor incompatible with Christologies in other parts of the book. Cullmann among others has stressed the remarkable fact that παῖς is confined, in Acts, to these two chapters;[34] what is less often discussed is whether its significance is the same in both chapters. I have elsewhere[35] suggested that, whereas in 3:13 (and perhaps vs. 26) παῖς is an allusion (as most commentators agree) to the Suffering Servant of Isa. 53, in 4:27 and 30, by contrast, it is rather a parallel to the royal Davidic Servant in Jewish liturgy. In Acts 3:13, ἐδόξασεν looks like an echo of Isa. 52:13, and the context, which is essentially that of Christian apologetic and explanation, suits such a reference; but in 4:25, παῖς is expressly used of David, so that it is a natural conclusion that, when it is used of Jesus in vs. 27, it is intended in the same way. This would present a phenomenon very much like that of Did. 9, where the Jewish liturgical reference to David as the Servant of God is parallel in just the same way to its distinctively Christian adaptation in terms of Jesus as the Servant of God. This would mean that there is a clear distinction between the uses of παῖς in chaps. 3 and 4, respectively. In Acts 3, the intention is to explain how it is that glorious and daring claims are now being made for a recently crucified criminal; and the method is to identify him with the Suffering Servant who was indeed, according to Isa. 53, treated like a criminal, and whose vindication also has the authority of Scripture. In Acts 4, by contrast, the context is not explanatory and "apologetic" but exultantly adorative and liturgical; and ὁ ἅγιος παῖς σου ᾽Ιησοῦς (vs. 27) is placed in a position parallel to that of Δαυὶδ παῖς σου (vs. 25) in Jewish liturgy.[36]

Guesses about what a writer might or might not have done are always precarious; but one cannot help thinking that, if Luke had been composing freely as a dramatist, he might have used this παῖς-language again quite suitably in Pauline speeches. If he only used it as dramatically appropriate to a primitive stage of the church's development (although evidence for its "primitiveness" seems, actually, not to be forthcoming), would not "early Paul" have been as plausible a setting as "early Peter"? But in fact this use of παῖς does not recur in Acts; and the only other use of Isa. 53 in Acts— though here without παῖς—is in the story of Philip and the Ethiopian (8: 32 ff.).[37] In Luke's Gospel there is the one quotation (Luke 22:37) from Isa. 53:12. It is a standing problem why Paul in his epistles does not make more of the Servant-theme. But the fact is that he makes only slight and allusive use, and that in the whole New Testament the theme is remarkably scarce.[38] If it is right to question whether even the λύτρον-saying (Mark 10:45, Matt. 20:28) is Isaianic,[39] the Gospels contain strikingly little evidence for it; and the most notable exception, beyond the Acts passages, is I Peter 2:22 ff.

Thus in sum there is no clear evidence either that the Servant-terminology was exclusively primitive, or that Luke was inventing its application: it would appear, more likely, to belong by idiosyncratic use (perhaps Petrine) or by liturgical appropriateness on the lips on which it is, in fact, placed. The likelihood is that in Christian liturgical contexts, especially when under the influence of Jewish *berakôth*, "thy Servant Jesus" was a common usage, perhaps for a considerable period.

The examination, first of the passage Acts 3:19-21, and then of the use of παῖς in Acts 3 and 4, has led to the conclusion that in the former case we are not compelled to detect a discrepancy in sense between traditional and Lucan Christologies, and that in the latter it is not impossible that we may be witnessing the faithful representation of two different usages in two different settings—usages which, again, are Christologically not incompatible with one another or with other usages.

170

A third example of the same phenomenon—variation, though not discrepancy—may be found in the doctrines of salvation attached in Acts to the work of God in Jesus Christ. There is in Acts almost as complete an absence of any explicitly *redemptive* interpretation of the death of Christ as in Luke's Gospel. The Gospel does not even include the λύτρον-saying of Mark and Matt.; the words of institution (and then only if the longer text, 22:19-20, be accepted) are the only exception. The same is maintained in the Acts with the one exception of Acts 20:28: "the church of God (*v. l.* of the Lord), which he purchased διὰ τοῦ αἵματος τοῦ ἰδίου." Whether one reads "God" or "the Lord," and whether one renders the ambiguous words as "his own blood" or "the blood of his Own," in any case the phrase contains an allusion to the death of Christ as redemptive—blood by which a "purchase" is achieved. But in Acts this is the solitary exception. Otherwise the death of Christ is represented simply as turned into triumph or vindication by the resurrection. "Salvation" is associated with Christ clearly enough; but not explicitly salvation by his redemptive death. Is it significant, then, that the one exception should be on the lips of Paul and in an address to an already Christian community? This is Paul, not some other speaker; and he is not evangelizing but recalling an already evangelized community to its deepest insights. In other words, the situation, like the theology, is precisely that of a Pauline epistle, not of preliminary evangelism.

It is tempting to add at this point the familiar observation that the distinctive features of Stephen's speech in Acts 7 show affinities with the Epistle to the Hebrews and can be regarded as a distinguishable strain within the Acts, in character with the Hellenistic Judaism which is associated with Stephen. But, although this is probably true, it is not the Christology of Stephen's speech, strictly speaking, that is part of its distinctiveness. The allusion to the Moses-prophet (Acts 7:37) and the title "the just one" (Acts 7:52) are not peculiar to this chapter. The former has already been discussed; the latter will be considered shortly.

But the two themes that have been isolated as distinctive—the Servant, and the redemptive death—do mark their respective contexts; they appear to be in character and, though distinctive, are not mutually discrepant.

Before leaving this section of the inquiry, it will be well to add a further comment [40] on the striking phrase in 10:36, οὗτός ἐστιν πάντων κύριος. Striking in itself for its absoluteness and universality [41] the phrase is the more arresting by reason of its juxtaposition with the "adoptionist" language of vs. 38 (ἔχρισεν αὐτὸν ὁ θεὸς πνεύματι ἁγίῳ καὶ δυνάμει . . . ὁ θεὸς ἦν μετ' αὐτοῦ). Is it necessary to argue that here, too, as in the view of 3:18 ff. discussed above, two discrepant Christologies are incongruously united—a comparatively late and well-developed—perhaps Hellenistic—affirmation of Christ as world-ruler, and a primitive—perhaps Palestinian—conception of him as a man whom God had exalted to messianic status? I think it is not necessary. Given the resurrection, the two are logicaly compatible at one and the same time. Indeed, in effect they are together similar to the climax of Peter's Pentecost address in Acts 2:36: καὶ κύριον αὐτὸν καὶ χριστὸν ἐποίησεν ὁ θεός, τοῦτον τὸν Ἰησοῦν ὃν ὑμεῖς ἐσταυρώσατε. The real question is whether this kind of collocation is linguistically and psychologically conceivable in the situation depicted by Luke. What language would Peter have been speaking—Aramaic, Hebrew, Greek, or Latin? Would his language and his world of thought have compassed such terms? If Peter was speaking Aramaic (and using an interpreter) would some such phrase as is used here by the Peshitta (*hanā māryā dᵉkāl*) be conceivable? If he could speak Greek or Latin, would be he likely to use the words in the text or their Latin equivalent? Epictetus (IV.1.12) uses the phrase ὁ πάντων κύριος Καῖσαρ. Is it impossible that a phrase used of the emperor by a Hellenistic writer in about A.D. 110 should be applied (*mutatis mutandis*) by a Jew in about A.D. 30? It is extremely difficult to find any decisive evidence. One can only reiterate that the *logic* of the phrase is no more difficult than that of Acts 2:36, which in itself does not sound implausible for its ostensible setting.

To revert for a moment to Luke 1:43, where Elizabeth uses the phrase ἡ μήτηρ τοῦ κυρίου μου, it would be useful to know whether, in the type of Aramaic used by Elizabeth, "*my* Lord" would have had a distinctly different significance from "*the* Lord." One can imagine that the former might have been a more natural, and therefore less significant, honorific than the latter, which might have been more like a title of divine exaltation (מרא?).

Any decision whether Luke's words represent primitive, historical sources or spring simply from his own, perhaps Hellenistic, background must take such questions into account; but the answers to them are hard to come by.

In sum, although it cannot be proved, so far as the evidence does go Luke may be following reliable sources in the passages here examined.

III. The Christology of Acts Compared with That
of Other New Testament Writings

It is sometimes remarked [42] that what purport to be Pauline speeches or sermons in the Acts bear little resemblance to the Pauline epistles and a great deal more resemblance to the ostensibly Petrine speeches in Acts; or, in other words, that both Pauline and Petrine speeches are equally Luke's own invention. Such a statement exaggerates the uniformity within Acts, as the previous section of this essay may help to show. It also neglects certain factors essential to any significant comparison with the Pauline epistles. Not that this in itself shows that Luke did not extemporize but adhered to sources;[43] it only means that the facts are more complicated and require more sensitive formulation.[44] In particular, it needs to be remembered that it is a priori likely that there should be differences between a speaker's initial presentation of the gospel to a non-Christian audience, and the same speaker's address to those who have already become Christians; and that, with rare exceptions, the Acts speeches belong to the former, while the Pauline epistles belong to the latter class. The moment one examines the rare exceptions on either side, a striking *rapprochement* occurs. Acts 20:18 ff. represents Paul speaking to Christians; and it is precisely here, as we have already seen, that the solitary "Pauline" redemptive phrase occurs (Acts 20:28). Conversely, there are a few passages in the epistles where the writer explicitly recalls, retrospectively, the terms of his initial evangelism: I Thess. 1:10; Rom. 1:3-4 (by implication), and—most famous of all— I Cor. 15:1 ff.; and it is precisely here that we approximate to the bare κήρυγμα of the Acts— save only that in I Cor. 15:3 there is admittedly the redemptive phrase Χριστὸς ἀπέθανεν ὑπὲρ τῶν ἁμαρτιῶν ἡμῶν, which we have seen to be lacking from the initial κήρυγμα in Acts. As for the alleged uniformity of the speeches in Acts, we are not to forget that it is in Petrine contexts only that παῖς (Acts 3, 4) and the scripture of the rejected stone (Acts 4:11) are applied to Jesus (cf. I Peter 2:7 and, for the Servant-theme, I Peter 2:22 ff.);[45] that it is only by Philip the Evangelist that Isa. 53 is again applied to Jesus (Acts 8:32 ff.); and that, in the Pauline speeches alone occur not only the redemptive language just referred to, but one or two other "Paulinisms."

At the end of Paul's address at Pisidian Antioch in Acts 13:38-39 there is the celebrated passage: "You must understand, my brothers, that it is through him that forgiveness of sins is now being proclaimed to you. It is through him that everyone who has faith is acquitted of everything for which there was no acquittal under the Law of Moses." This, though not the only possible interpretation of the words,[46] seems the most natural and, if it is correct, represents a rough summary of the Pauline doctrine of faith.[47] So, too, do the words from the dialogue on the Damascus Road in the form which it takes in the hearing before Agrippa, Acts 26:18: "I send you to open their eyes and turn them from darkness to light, from the dominion of Satan to God, so that, by trust in me, they may obtain forgiveness of sins, and a place with those whom God has made his own." This is reminiscent, in particular, of Col. 1:12-13.

Once again, the use of υἱός as a title for Jesus (cf. discussion above) presents certain affinities with the usage of the Pauline epistles. Excluding the Ethiopian's baptismal confession, which occurs only in the δ-text of Acts 8:37, the title υἱός is applied in Acts twice, and both in Pauline contexts: Acts 9:20, "Soon he was proclaiming Jesus publicly in the synagogues: 'This,' he said, 'is the Son of God' "; and 13:33, where at Pisidian Antioch Paul quotes from Ps. 2:7, "You are my son; this day have I begotten you." [48] Now it is clear enough that in Christian—if not in pre-Christian—circles the use of Ps. 2 is essentially messianic; indeed, a good case may be made for recognizing that it was associated even in certain pre-Christian circles with the specifically messianic passage in II Sam. 7:12-14 (especially through the key-words σπέρμα, υἱός, ἀνάστασις.[49] Acts seems, thus, to represent Paul as using a recognized argument for the messiahship of Jesus. By contrast, there is no doubt that the most interesting and most distinctively Pauline use of υἱός, in Rom. 8 and Gal. 4, goes much deeper than mere messianism. Nevertheless, the messianic use is not in the least incompatible with the profounder use, and Ps. 2:7 may well have been in Paul's mind in Rom. 1:4, if not elsewhere.[50] It looks, then, as though Luke may have represented Paul quite correctly, although on one of the shallower of Paul's own levels of thinking. There is another New Testament writing which makes use of the *testimonium* from Ps. 2:7, namely, Hebrews (1:5; 5:5); and Hebrews also shares with Paul and John something, at least, of the deeper connotations of υἱός, while it shares with Acts the less profound, more "external" title ἀρχηγός (Acts 3:15; 5:31; Heb. 2:10; 12:2), which seems to mean something like "pioneer." The two levels are perfectly compatible within a single writer's thought.

The use of the term Χριστός in the allegedly Pauline scenes in Acts seems at first sight, in contrast to the phenomena just examined, to strike a recognizably un-Pauline note. It is a familiar fact that Χριστός in the Pauline epistles is, broadly speaking, nearer to a proper name than to a title, however much qualification and subtle nuances might be demanded for a more precise definition.[51] If one did attempt to qualify, perhaps one might say that in the Pauline epistles Jesus is characterized as one who was anointed, rather than identified as the long-expected Anointed One: that is, it is not so much that the datum is "the Christ" (unidentified) and that Jesus is then identified as that Christ; rather, the theme is simply "Jesus, called Christ." In the Acts, however, there are four verses, all associated with Paul, where the whole point is that Jesus is identified as the Christ: Acts 17:3; 18:5, 28; 26:23 (and the last presents the form which we have already recognized as a peculiarly Lucan formula—εἰ παθητὸς ὁ Χριστός). But the facts are not altogether simple; for there are three, possibly four, other ostensibly Pauline contexts where Χριστός, as in the Pauline epistles, is used more as a proper name: 16:18; 20:21, si vera lectio; 24:24; 28:31. On examination, however, the last two of these could be called editorial, for Luke is describing Paul's ministry rather than purporting to report his very words; and if 20:21 is a false or, at best, a doubtful reading, this leaves only 16:18, where Paul is using the name of Jesus in exorcism. The other instances of the same sort of use (nearly as a proper name) are all Petrine (Acts 2:38; 3:6; 4:10; 9:34; 10:48; 11:17) except for 15:26, which is in the letter from the Jerusalem council.

This looks at first as though Luke himself used Χριστός as (roughly speaking) a proper name and attributed a similar use also to Peter and the apostolic council, but, with only one exception, he gave Paul the strictly messianic use, exactly reversing the evidence of the epistles. In fact, however, the distinction attaches not to the person speaking but to the occasion. The messianic use is invariably in apologetic contexts (which happen to be Pauline), while the other use is liturgical or quasi-liturgical: it is, as one might put it, a "formula" use.[52] When once this is recognized, one may go on to recognize that, equally in the Pauline epistles, there is ample evidence that Paul did presuppose a messianic identification for Jesus, e.g., in Rom. 1:3 and 9:5. In other words, once again an apparent discrepancy between Acts and the epistles seems rather to represent the difference between two different situations which, however, could both be genuinely apostolic. In the one situation the apostle is arguing to establish his primary case for the Christian position. In the other he is building on these foundations for the benefit of those who had already accepted them.

Closely related to the theme of messianism is the question of rivalry with the emperor. This is of particular interest in any study of the Christology of Acts in comparison with that of other parts of the New Testament. It is plausible to suggest that those parts of the New Testament where a comparatively developed imperial vocabulary is applied to Christ, namely, the Pastoral Epistles and the Revelation, reflect actual conflict betwen the imperial cult and Christianity; and that, whereas before the actual clash there was a hesitancy on the part of Christians to borrow the pagan terms of adulation, once war had been declared it was better policy boldly to raid the enemy armories and use their ammunition.[53] But if so, it needs to be recognized that at least one passage in Luke and one in Acts explicitly allude to the rivalry.[54] In Luke 23:2 the charge laid by the Jews against Jesus before Pilate is the charge of treason—that Jesus had been perverting the people from loyalty to Caesar and declaring himself "an anointed king"; and in Acts 17:6-7 the Jews who are inciting the Thessalonian population against Paul and his friends describe them as those who have upset the whole world and who violate Caesar's decrees, declaring that there is another emperor (βασιλεύς), namely, Jesus. Yet on further reflection one cannot help noticing that in both cases these are represented as charges leveled against the Christians by Jewish opponents and obviously understood by the narrator himself to be false. Nowhere in the Acts are Christian evangelists themselves represented as using of Jesus such markedly imperial language as occurs in the Pastoral letters where "epiphany" and "Saviour" are used together, and where Christ is even styled (if this is the correct exegesis) "our great God and Saviour" (Titus 2:13). Thus once again Luke seems to know what he is doing. Whether he is doing it as a good dramatist, realistically reconstructing his imagined situation, or as a cool historian using traditions faithfully, is another matter. He does, it is true, once represent an official as using κύριος of the emperor (Acts 25:26). Whether this is an anachronism or not [55] is not relevant for the present purpose; but the use of κύριος as applied to Jesus (see discussion above) is not such as necessarily to imply any intended parallelism or rivalry any more than the use of Χριστός is: indeed, it is a commonplace of criticism that Luke is deliberately trying to present Christianity as a religion which the empire has no need to regard as subversive or dangerous to its peace. Is this why

Acts never uses βασιλεύς for Jesus in the apostolic preaching? (In Acts 17:7 it is, as we have just seen, part of a charge brought by opponents of Christianity.) Χριστός is just as royal but possibly not so readily intelligible. "Saviour" is applied to Jesus in two passages in Acts, 5:31 and 13:23, but, as has already been remarked, the contexts, as in Luke 2:11 also, are appropriate to an essentially Jewish, messianic connotation and are perhaps in this respect different from those of the Pastoral epistles and, for that matter, from II Peter 1:1, 11; 2:20; 3:18 where an emperor cult context seems more fitting. It is a familiar fact that the word is very seldom applied to Jesus in the recognized Pauline letters, Phil. 3:20 being the chief exception. That πολίτευμα also occurs in the same context may be significant.[56]

However, the use of λαός must still be mentioned. Although not directly Christological, Acts 18:10 has already been pointed out as indirect evidence of a distinctively post-resurrection Christology. We must now note that this use of λαός for a Christian community is not exactly paralleled in the epistles of Paul, where it occurs only in Old Testament quotations and then more often of Israel than of the church (see Rom. 9:25, 26; 11:1-2; 15:10; II Cor. 6:16). The other occurrence in Acts, apart from the direct Old Testament quotation in Stephen's speech (7:34), is on the lips of James (15:14, with which cf. I Peter 2:9-10; Titus 2:14). Does this indicate that Luke, though faithful to an early line of Christian apologetic, has this time made a mistake in attributing it to a specifically Pauline vision?

So much for possible test cases for Luke's historical precision. When we turn to the use of ὁ δίκαιος in Acts and compare it with the use elsewhere in the New Testament, the results are inconclusive. It is an extremely elusive term. Just as it has been suggested that παῖς is used in Acts 3 with reference to the Suffering Servant but in Acts 4 as a parallel to God's Servant David, so it may be that ὁ δίκαιος is capable of containing an allusion both to the Suffering Servant and to royalty.[57] Isa. 53:11 describes the innocent sufferer as "my righteous Servant"; and the *innocent* one who suffers *undeservedly* is perhaps the idea uppermost in the Petrine passage, Acts 3:14, "(you) repudiated the one who was holy and righteous when Pilate had decided to release him." (Cf. the Lucan version of the centurion's words at the cross, Luke 23:47, "Beyond all doubt . . . this man was innocent.") But to the other two occurrences something, at least, of messianic royalty may be intended to attach. The first is Acts 7:52 (Stephen's speech): "They killed those who foretold the coming of the Righteous One." Here, no doubt, the murderous attack suggests innocent suffering; but ὁ δίκαιος is explicitly connected with ἔλευσις, "coming," which lends a strong color of messianism to the term.[58] In the second passage, Acts 22:14, Ananias, the devout Jewish Christian (vs. 12) of Damascus, is represented as saying that God had predestined Paul to know his will and "to see the Righteous One and to hear his very voice." This most readily suggests a messianic vision, and it has been pointed out further that the royal associations of ὁ δίκαιος are illustrated by such passages as Zech. 9:9; I Enoch 38:2; Ps. Sol. 17:32.[59]

If one asks how far the application of the term to Jesus elsewhere in the New Testament helps to determine the meaning, the answer is obscure. In I Peter 3:18 the stress is clearly on the innocence of the sufferer, and the allusion is probably to Isa. 53. But in I John the question is harder to decide. In I John 1:9, "he is just, and may be trusted to forgive our sins," the allusion to Isa. 53 is perhaps uppermost, but this is certainly not beyond question; the same is true of I John 2:1, "one to plead our cause with the Father, Jesus Christ, and he is just." But the only other instance in I John, namely 3:7, is evidently an allusion to Jesus as being just in the sense of "moral," "upright," and therefore as making moral demands on Christians.[60] Perhaps we may tentatively conclude for the Acts uses that in the speech of Peter, as in I Peter 3:18, the allusion is to innocent suffering, while Ananias' phrase may be primarily messianic and Stephen's may combine the messianic with the suffering in a manner very suitable in a martyr's defense.

Finally we come to certain aspects of the Acts' Christology which seem definitely to mark it off from that of the more theological of the epistles. There appears to be no doctrine of the preexistence of Christ in Acts, either in the speeches or in the narrator's comments, unless conceivably in 2:25. It is at this point in Peter's Pentecost speech that Ps. 16:8 ff. is introduced. In the Hebrew this begins: שויתי יהוה לנגדי תמיד but Acts, following the LXX, reads: προορώμην τὸν κύριον ἐνώπιόν μου διὰ παντός. The προορώμην, which one would expect to mean "I foresaw" or "I had or was having a preview of," causes commentators difficulty. Either this phrase must be taken as part of the verses which follow and which in the context of Acts are clearly intended to be spoken, though *by* David, yet *in the person of* David's successor, the Messiah. In that case the προ- can hardly be pressed, and one must imagine the Messiah, speaking by anticipation through the prophetic lips of David, to be saying that he was simply *seeing* God continually before him—an expression of trust and confidence. But this surely does less than justice to the προ [61] and, still more, ignores the patent reference to *pre*vision in the προϊδών of the interpretation in vs. 31. Or else, vs. 8 might be given to David himself and προορώμην correctly translated "I foresaw" or "I had, or was having, a preview of," in which case the difficulty is that the speaker will have to be deemed to change suddenly in the subsequent verses, because the "not being left in, or to, Hades" and the "not seeing corruption" are explicitly applied in the interpretation to Christ (vs. 31). Further, the προϊδών of vs. 31 is related to the "seeing" of the resurrection of Jesus, not of his person. This is not the place for a full-length investigation into the passage.[62] The only point relevant to the present discussion is that, if one chooses to accept the second method despite the difficulty attending it, one might have a hint of a doctrine of preexistence for Christ. For it would then be possible to translate προορώμην not "I foresaw *that* the Lord," but, a more natural translation grammatically, "I had a preview of the Lord," and "the Lord," in that case, would mean the Lord Christ.

Unless one accepts such an interpretation—and it is precarious, to say the least—there is no doctrine of Christ's preexistence in Acts, though there is ample stress on foreknowledge and God's predetermined plan (see, e.g., 4:28; 9:15; 10:42; 13:27, 48; 16:14; 17:31). Neither is such a doctrine entertained in the Gospel: the Lucan allusions to the virgin birth certainly do not imply it. Thus a decided contrast is presented at this point between Luke-Acts and the Pauline and Johannine writings.

Even more clearly Acts is marked off from the Pauline writings, at any rate, by its conception of Jesus as now no longer "on earth" but "in heaven." The narrative of the ascension in Acts 1:9-11 is consistently presupposed throughout the story. In Acts 2:33 the exalted Jesus is described as having poured out the Spirit. In Acts 3:21 heaven must receive him until the proper time comes. When he appears to Paul on the Damascus Road, it is a special visitation from heaven (9:3; 22:6; 26:13). On the only other occasions when he "appears" at all it is only in a vision (9:10; 22:17-18; 23:11—by implication); otherwise it is by the Spirit (or by his Spirit) or by an angel that action is taken on earth (8:26, 29, 39; 11:28; 12:7; 13:4; 15:28; 16:6, 7; 20:23; 21:11; 27:23). More consistently than in any other New Testament writing, Acts presents Jesus as exalted and, as it were, temporarily "absent," but "represented" on earth in the meantime by the Spirit (except that, undeniably, in the vision of Acts 18:10 Jesus says ἐγώ εἰμι μετὰ σοῦ). That this is Luke's own attitude seems to follow from the fact that his narrative and his handling of whatever sources he may be using convey it, as well as explicit "preaching" on the lips of the apostles.

A smiliar "absentee Christology" does occur, indeed, in I Thess. 1:10, where the Christians are to await God's Son from heaven. But for the most part the Pauline epistles reverse this impression of temporary absence by the sense of intimate relation between Christians and Christ which pervades them. For Paul, Christ is indeed "in heaven" in the sense that he is no longer a limited individual "on earth"; but Christians are limbs of his body and are incorporated in him in such a way that all sense of remoteness is completely obliterated.[63]

Here, then, it would seem is a theological standpoint which for the reasons stated must be ascribed to Luke himself and marks a difference between his outlook and Paul's. And when one begins to ponder on its implications, it becomes clear that the conception of Jesus in the Acts is mainly an individualistic one. Despite his royal exaltation and his undoubtedly divine status, it is still as an exalted and divine individual that Jesus is viewed. But in Paul's robustly "inclusive" Christology the gap between the risen Lord and the believer is transcended and no "substitute" or *locum tenens* is needed. The Spirit is for Paul certainly the "mode" in which Christ is among his people: the Spirit is as vital in Paul's conception of daily living on earth as in the conception of Acts; but for Paul the Spirit is not the representative and substitute of an absent Christ but the mode of his very presence. And in the Gospel and Epistles of John the connection between Jesus and the Spirit, though differently expressed, is equally close.[64]

The "individualistic" Christology which is here contrasted with Paul's corporate conception has been, for the reasons stated, attributed to Luke himself. But this is not to say that he shares it with no other writer in the New Testament. Insofar as it is expressed not by Luke's narrative and handling of his material but by actual words attributed to early Christian preachers, it is represented by the phrase (Acts 3:15) ὁ ἀρχηγὸς τῆς ζωῆς, which seems to imply the kind of hero-Christology or leader-Christology which is to be found in parts of Hebrews (e.g., the ἀρχηγός passages in that epistle, Heb. 2:10; 12:2); and by the other Petrine statements, especially in Acts 2:33 and 3:21, which are not unlike another Petrine document, I Peter 1:8. It is therefore conceivably significant, that, whereas such expressions are not unrepresented in the non-Pauline epistles, the relevant Pauline statements in Acts represent, as a matter of fact, the nearest approach within Acts to the contrasting, corporate conception of Christ found in the Pauline epistles. The dialogue on the Damascus Road, in all its three versions, does identify the risen Jesus with the Christian church ("Why do you persecute me? . . . I am Jesus, whom you are persecuting"—see 9:4-5; 22:8; 26:15). Thus in the only Pauline passage that bears any relation to the matter, there is, in fact, a trace of "corporeity."

There is one other passage deserving careful examination in this connection, namely Acts 4:2, where ἐν is used in a mysterious way. In Acts 4:2, the Sadducees and others are described as pained because the apostles were teaching and proclaiming ἐν τῷ ᾽Ιησοῦ τὴν ἀνάστασιν τὴν ἐκ νεκρῶν. Is this a hint of an incorporative doctrine? On the whole, the answer is that it is less likely to mean "resurrection for those who are incorporate in Jesus" (the simple proper name, "Jesus," is in any case unlikely after an "incorporative" ἐν) than "resurrection in the case (or in the instance) of Jesus." And yet, one must admit that the ponderous phrase, ἡ ἀνάστασις ἡ ἐκ νεκρῶν, sounds uncommonly as though it were meant to mean "the (general) resurrection" (cf. Acts 24:15). We are left in uncertainty; and if—perhaps in spite of himself—Luke has after all here retained a hint of a more corporate understanding of Christ, then it is noteworthy that this time it is placed on the lips of Peter and his colleagues.

It may be appropriate to remark in this connection that there is in any case a further fact to be reckoned with, when one is trying to estimate how far an individualistic conception was normal and how far Paul's corporate sense was exceptional, in the early church. Although Luke's outlook and perhaps that of most of his sources is in the sense indicated "individualistic," the fact of baptism in the name or into the name of Jesus implies more with regard to the corporate character of Christ than Luke or the majority of early Christians may themselves have realized or made fully articulate. Paul may have been the only New Testament writer—with the possible exception of John—to make it fully articulate; but Christian practice spoke louder than words.

All in all, the evidence here displayed—unless it has been grossly misinterpreted—seems to show that the Christology of Acts is not uniform, whatever may be said to the contrary. Where Luke's own mentality can be discerned, it is different in certain respects from Paul's or that of the Johannine writings and is nearer, one may guess, to the "average" Christian mentality than to that of these giants.[65] But it is flying in the teeth of the evidence to claim that Luke has uniformly imposed this mentality of his; on the contrary, the number of seemingly undesigned coincidences and subtle nuances that have emerged suggest strongly that Luke either dramatized, thoughtfully and with considerable versatility, in an attempt to impersonate various outlooks,[66] or else used sources. If he did this, he no doubt adapted and arranged them with a free hand, but nevertheless retained their essential character.

NOTES

1. *Pace* (e.g.) H. Conzelmann's assertion of Luke's promiscuous use of titles, *The Theology of St. Luke,* trans. G. Buswell (New York, 1961), pp. 171 n. 1; 172; cf. his commentary, *Die Apostelgeschichte* (Tübingen, 1963), p. 8.
2. This seems to be overlooked, e.g., in Conzelmann's phrase, "the use of the title *kyrios* even in Jesus' lifetime" (*The Theology of St. Luke,* p. 174 n. 3).
3. See further discussion in this article.
4. The same holds good (almost) for John also; "almost" because in John 20:2 Mary Magdalene is represented as using "Lord" before she knows that he is risen; and when she does recognize him she uses 'Ραββουνεί. However, note that John 13:13 and 20:13 throw doubt on the extent to which the Johannine use of κύριος can be pressed as an index of the recognition of "Lordship" in a christological sense.
5. Cf. I Cor. 1:2.
6. In *The Beginnings of Christianity,* eds. F. J. Foakes Jackson and K. Lake (London, 1933), V, 362.
7. Incidentally, it is not to be overlooked that in a quite secular context it need carry no transcendental meaning whatever: in Gal. 4:1, κύριος πάντων only means "master of the whole estate," referring simply to the ownership of property.
8. Cf. the same use in Rom. 10:9 with 13; I Cor. 1:2.
9. What Aramaic title are we, in fact, to think that Peter might have used, in the kind of context indicated by Acts 2:36? Or is the Hebrew אדן a possibility? See F. Hahn, *Christologische Hoheitstitel,* FRLANT, LXXXIII (Göttingen, 1963), 114 against this idea. See also *ThWB* III, p. 1086.
10. See further discussion.
11. *The Christology of the New Testament,* trans. Shirley Guthrie and C. A. M. Hall (London, 1959), pp. 30 ff.
12. See, e.g., Cullmann, *The Christology,* p. 19, and literature there cited.
13. See Cullmann, *The Christology,* pp. 17 ff.
14. Cf. Justin, *Dial.* LXXVI.
15. See my paper "From Defendant to Judge—and Deliverer," Bulletin III, *NTS* (1952, repr. 1963), 47; and A. J. B. Higgins, *Jesus and the Son of Man* (London, 1964), pp. 143 ff.
16. The Revelation use is also in a martyr-context, in the sense that the whole apocalypse is a martyr book; but the question of "realization" is complicated by the proleptic character of the whole. In another martyr-context and on the lips of another than Jesus, outside the N.T., "the Son of Man" occurs in Hegesippus' account of the martyrdom of James the

Just (Euseb., *H. E.* II, 23). But here there is the more normal reference to the sitting posture and to a future manifestation: "Why do you ask me concerning Jesus the Son of Man? He is both seated in heaven on the right hand of Power, and he will come again on the clouds of heaven." H. P. Owen, "Stephen's Vision in Acts vii. 55-56," *NTS* I (1954), 224 ff., suggests that Jesus is standing on the verge of returning to earth after his exaltation; and another way of connecting the vision with the return has now been put forward by C. K. Barrett in "Stephen and the Son of Man" in *Apophoreta,* Haenchen Festschrift, ed. W. Eltester (Berlin, 1964), pp. 32 ff.: he suggests that Stephen's vision may represent "a private and personal *parousia* of the Son of man" for the individual as he dies.

17. *The Theology of St. Luke.*

18. *Sic,* not "who rose." See H. Braun, "Zur Terminologie der Acta von der Auferstehung Jesu," *ThLZ* LXXVII (1952), 533 ff. But I doubt whether the distinction is, in fact, very important, despite the conclusion that the use of the verbs in question carries a subordinationist implication. I am not denying a subordinationist strain in Luke–Acts (as judged—anachronously?—by later christological controversies); but I question how far this particular set of verbs indicates it.

19. See J. A. T. Robinson's article *"Resurrection in the New Testament,"* in *IDB* (Nashville, 1962).

20. We ought rather to say "exaltation"; there is nothing about *going* up: it is rather *being lifted* up.

21. Incidentally, it is surprising what a long career is still being enjoyed by the old suggestion that Acts 17:18 is meant to imply that the Athenians misunderstood Paul to be proclaiming a male and a female deity—'Ιησοῦς and 'Ανάστασις. How could Paul conceivably have used the abstract noun (if he used it at all) in such a way as to suggest this? Luke's summary in the last seven words of that verse would need to be isolated, in order to give rise to so absurd a misapprehension.

22. It occurs in Matt., Luke, John, Acts, not in Mark; Ναζαρηνός occurs only in Mark and Luke; Ναζαρά occurs (*si vera ll.*) in Matt. and Luke; Ναζαρέθ (or-τ) occurs in all four Gospels and Acts.

23. "Die rätselhaften Termini Nazoräer und Iskariot," *Horae Soederblomianiae,* IV (Uppsala, 1957).

24. " 'Er wird Nazoräer heissen' (zu Mc 1 24; Mt 2 23)" in *Judentum. Urchristentum. Kirche,* Festschrift für J. Jeremias, *Bh ZNW* XXVI (Berlin, 1960), p. 90.

25. E.g., in article "Nazarene" in *IDB.*

26. *ThWB* IV, 882. See, further, a bibliographical and critical note in F. Hahn, *Christologische Hoheitstitel,* p. 237, n. 4.

27. Cf. the terminology of Hahn, *Christologische Hoheitstitel,* e.g., pp. 112 ff.

28. *The Theology of Acts in its Historical Setting* (London, 1961), p. 145.

29. Cf., however, Charles E. Carlston, "The Christology of Acts" (reported in *Abstracts of Papers* at the 99th meeting of the Society of Biblical Literature [for 1963], no. 31): "Basically . . . the Christology of Acts, though resting on traditional terminology and concepts, is quite consistent with itself, with the Christology of the Third Gospel, and with the author's purpose and situation."

30. "The Most Primitive Christology of all?", *JThS* n. s. 7 (1956), 177 ff. *Twelve New Testament Studies* (London, 1962), pp. 139 ff., and *Jesus and His Coming* (London, 1957), pp. 143 ff.; cf. B. M. F. van Iersel, *"Der Sohn" in den synoptischen Jesusworten, Suppl. Nov. Test.* III (Leiden, 1961), p. 65. This theory was apparently misunderstood by R. P. Casey, "The Earliest Christologies," *JThS* n.s. 9 (1958), 253 ff. (see 261, n. 1). It is not discussed by Hahn, *Christologische Hoheitstitel,* p. 389, n. 2; or by Conzelmann, *Die Apostelgeschichte, HNT* (1963).

31. *Contra* Hahn, *Christologische Hoheitstitel,* p. 385, who takes it to be a formula taken over by Luke from elsewhere.

32. Cf. S. S. Smalley, "The Christology of Acts," *ExpT* LXXIII, 12 (1962), 358 ff.
33. See E. Lövestam, *Son and Saviour, ConNT* XVIII (Lund, 1961), pp. 9-10.
34. *Peter: Disciple-Apostle-Martyr*, trans. Floyd Filson (London, 1953), pp. 67-88; *The Christology of the New Testament*, p. 73.
35. "The Influence of Circumstances on the Use of Christological Terms," *JThS*, n.s. 10 (1959), 247 ff. (see 252); *The Birth of the New Testament* (London, 1962), pp. 20 ff.
36. Elsewhere in the New Testament, the specialized use of παῖς, as the Servant of God in Old Testament Scripture, occurs only in Matt. 12:18 (Isa. 42:1); Luke 1:54 (Israel); Luke 1:69 (David).
37. From elsewhere in the "Servant Songs" (Isa. 49:6) there is a quotation in Acts 13:47, applied not to Jesus but to the apostles.
38. See C. F. D. Moule, "From Defendant to Judge—and Deliverer," *Bulletin* III, NTS (1952, repr. 1963); M. D. Hooker, *Jesus and the Servant* (London, 1959). For a very rich bibliography on the subject, see B. M. F. van Jersel, *"Der Sohn" in den synoptischen Jesusworten*, pp. 52-53.
39. See C. K. Barrett, "The Background of Mark 10:45," in *New Testament Essays, in mem.* T. W. Manson, ed. A. J. B. Higgins (Manchester, 1959), pp. 1 ff.
40. See discussion above.
41. Note, however, as above, the purely human use of a similar phrase in Gal. 4:1.
42. See, e.g., M. Dibelius, *Studies in the Acts of the Apostles*, trans. Mary Ling (London, 1956), p. 165.
43. It is notoriously difficult to believe that James really used an argument depending on the Septuagint in contrast to the Massoretic Text (Acts 15:17)—though even this has been defended as genuine.
44. As this essay is being completed, there appears R. A. Martin's elaborate analysis, "Evidence of Aramaic Sources in Acts I-XV," *NTS* XI (1964), 38 ff.
45. Paul uses the other two "stone" *testimonia*, from Isa. 8 and 28, as does I Peter (see Rom. 9:33; I Peter 2:6, 8); but not Ps. 118.
46. For they might (though this would surely be a perverse exegesis) be made to yield an almost *anti*-Pauline sense, by substituting "is no acquittal" for "was no acquittal" (taking ἠδυνήθητε, I suppose, as a kind of gnomic aorist).
47. "Dieser letzteren Rede verleiht Lk am Schluss (13:38-39) eine leichte paulinische Färbung," Conzelmann, *Die Apostelgeschichte*, p. 8 (a little grudgingly!).
48. The earlier verses of Ps. 2 occur, in a non-Pauline context, at Acts 4:24 ff.
49. See O. Michel and O. Betz, "Von Gott gezeugt," *Bh ZNW* XXVI (1960), pp. 3 ff.; B. M. F. van Iersel, *"Der Sohn" in den synopt. Jesusworten*, esp. 78 ff.; E. Lövestam, *Son and Saviour*.
50. P. Vielhauer, "On the 'Paulinism' of Acts" in this volume, argues for a radical difference between Acts and Paul in the use of the title: in Acts 13:33 it is "adoptionist," in Paul it is metaphysical and not connected with Ps. 2:7. But, as J. Dupont observes (citing Boismard), Ps. 2:7 is, in fact, evidently in mind in Rom. 1:4 [Michel and Betz, vid. n. 49, p. 6, associate II Sam. 7:12 ff. with Rom. 1:4]; and the terms "adoptionist" and "metaphysical" both belong to a Greek philosophical context which is alien to Paul as much as to Acts. See J. Dupont, *The Sources of Acts*, Eng. trans. (London, 1964), 77, n. 3; *Rech. de Science Religieuse*, XXXV (1948), 541 ff., and M. E. Boismard, "Constitué Fils de Dieu (Rom. 1:4)," LX (1953), 5 ff.
51. Out of the large literature on this subtle problem, see, e.g., N. A. Dahl, "Die Messianität Jesu bei Paulus," *Studia Paulina*, de Zwaan Festschrift (Haarlem, 1953), pp. 83 ff.; and W. Kramer, *Christos, Kyrios, Gottessohn* (Zürich, 1963), pp. 131 ff.
52. See the careful analysis in *The Beginnings of Christianity*, I (1920), 367. R. P. Casey, "The Earliest Christologies," *JThS* n.s. 9 (1958), 253 ff., offers a discussion of the Acts usage; but his summary (261), "In Acts the usage of the title 'Christ' is uniform and cuts across all theories of source-criticism," is perplexing. J. C. O'Neill, *The Theology of Acts*, pp. 121 ff.,

argues for the comparative lateness of the "titular" use. His argument does not seem convincing to me; in any case he too ignores the differences just noted when (122) he declares "Luke's usage consistently implies that χριστός was a Jewish title with a fixed and definite meaning." See, on the other side, S. S. Smalley, "The Christology of Acts," *ExpT* LXXIII (1962), 362.

53. I myself, for instance, made this suggestion in "The Influence of Circumstances on the Use of Christological Terms," *JThS* n.s. 10 (1959), 247 ff. (see 262-63); but I am beginning to wonder whether the Pastorals are not, after all, Lucan.

54. There are also, of course, oblique hints to the same effect in the way in which the drama of the birth of Christ is staged by Luke. See K. H. Rengstorf, "Die Weihnachtserzählung des Evangelisten Lukas," in *Stat Crux dum Volvitur Orbis,* H. Lilje Festschrift (1959), pp. 15-16.

55. See Bauer's Lexicon *s.v.* 2.b, and Haenchen and Conzelmann, *in loc.* Conzelmann, on Acts 10:36, cites Epictetus IV. 1.12: ὁ πάντων κύριος Καῖσαρ (cf. the discussion of 10:36 above).

56. See J. Jeremias, "The Key to Pauline Theology," *ExpT* LXXVI (1964), 27 ff.

57. See A. Descamps, *Les Justes et la Justice dans les Évangiles et le Christianisme primitif hormis la Doctrine proprement paulinienne* (Louvain, 1950), pp. 57 ff.

58. See G. D. Kilpatrick, "Acts VII:52 ΕΛΕΥΣΙΣ," *JThS,* n.s.XLVI (1945), 136 ff.

59. See A. Descamps, *Les Justes,* p. 75, and other authors there cited.

60. It is highly improbable, although this has been suggested, that ὁ δίκαιος in Jas. 5:6 is an allusion to Jesus. Much more likely is the meaning "the just man" (in question), who suffers the injustice without retaliation.

61. Though Bauer's Lexicon, *s.v.* 3, cites Menander, inscriptions, and Philo for the sense "have before one's eyes," and assigns it this sense in Acts 2:25.

62. See the elaborate discussion in J. W. Doeve, *Jewish Hermeneutics in the Synoptic Gospels and Acts* (Assen, 1953), esp. p. 171.

63. Cf. J. Jeremias, "The Key to Pauline Theology," p. 28: "In earliest times κύριος was used as an eschatological predicate. . . . Christ was called κύριος as the coming one, as the Lord of the universe in the future consummation. Paul, however, uses the title κύριος primarily as a designation of the *Christus praesens,* the present Lord of His church."

64. For myself, I would add that even the Fourth Gospel is closer to the Lucan individualism and to the view of the Spirit as *locum tenens* than some would allow (see C. F. D. Moule, "The Individualism of the Fourth Gospel," *NovTest* V (1962), 171 ff.

65. See Campbell N. Moody, *The Mind of the Early Converts* (London, n.d., preface 1920).

66. Cf. Bo Reicke, *Glaube und Leben der Urgemeinde* (Zürich, 1957), pp. 39 ff.; J. W. Doeve, *Jewish Hermeneutics,* p. 175.

The Concept of the Davidic "Son of God" in Acts and Its Old Testament Background

EDUARD SCHWEIZER

Acts 13:33 is one of the most interesting christological statements in Acts. According to this verse, Paul states that the begetting of the Son of God, prophesied in Ps. 2:7, took place on Easter day. The purpose of this essay is to investigate the background of this idea in the Old Testament and early Christianity.

One could ask whether the statement "God raised him up" should be understood in Acts 13:33 as it is understood in 3:22; 7:37 (cf. 3:26; 13:22), namely as a reference to the first appearance of a prophet. This would indeed be the sense of the same Greek word in the Old Testament prophecy of II Sam. 7:12 (cf. Ps. Sol. 17:21, Ben Sir. 47:12). However, it is obvious that this term has been reinterpreted in Acts 13. From vs. 26 onward Paul is speaking of the death and resurrection of Jesus,[1] and vs. 34, using the same verb, speaks unambiguously of the resurrection from the dead.[2] Finally, if the author intended to use the term in the former sense, we should expect to find in our text some title of Jesus as in the parallels (Acts 3:22; 7:37; etc.), not the mere name Jesus,[3] which is typical of Luke's formulation wherever he speaks of the resurrection of Jesus. It is therefore clear that Acts 13:33 speaks of the resurrection of Jesus.

This is certainly not Pauline Christology. In Rom. 1:3-4, it is true, Paul quotes a creed[4] which contains the same concept of Jesus being installed as Son of God in power according to the Holy Spirit by the resurrection of the dead.[5] But Paul himself explicitly corrects the view of this traditional formula by introducing the title "his Son" already in vs. 3a, so that he now speaks of the Son of God (from eternity) who was installed Son of God (in power) at Easter.[6] Thus, the old formula of Rom. 1:3-4 testifies to the same pre-Pauline concept as Acts 13:33. The divine sonship of Jesus is understood as it is described in Ps. 2:7; it means the status of the one who rules as the regent and substitute of God himself. This, of course, is not adoptionism in the sense of the later dogmatic term, since it is not distinguished from another concept which emphasizes that his divine sonship is an eternal one. It is rather an unreflective expression of the Hebrew mind for which the acting, not the mere being, is the only essential thing.

The creed in Rom. 1:3-4 explicitly describes Jesus as a descendant of David. Whereas this is true for the earthly Jesus, his ruling as God's Son, which, in the mind of the congregation using this formula, seems to be strictly connected with the Davidic sonship, refers to a second stage of Jesus' existence, namely to his post-Easter lordship. Thus, a kind of two-stage Christology arises. In a similar way Acts 13:34-36 links the divine sonship of the resurrected Jesus with Old Testament quotations referring to David, and the same is true in an even higher degree for the related passage in Acts 2:24-36. Let us therefore turn to the Old Testament.

The most important passage is the prophecy of Nathan in II Sam. 7:12-16.[7] The "seed" of David shall be "raised up"; he shall be God's "son," and his "throne," "house," and "kingdom" shall last "in all eternity." He is also the "servant of God" (7:8), and God is the "Lord of hosts," the Pantokrator (7:8, 25-27). The key words of this prophecy turn up time and again whenever the Son of David is expected[8] (cf. following table). There are also new development.[9] Ps. 88 connects the idea of the "covenant" with this hope (see above) and interprets the son as the "first-born" (vs. 28; also Ps. Sol. 18:4), his power as his "exaltation" (vs. 20; cf. 18, 25) over the kings of the earth (vs. 28; also 4 Q flor. 18; cf. Ps. 2:8). The idea of "salvation" (vs. 27; also II Sam. 23:5) and the title "Messiah" appear (see table). A most interesting detail is the fact that the phrase "the true witness in heaven" (or: "in the sky"), referring to the moon, the steadfastness of which is compared with that of David's kingdom (vs. 38), is quoted in Rev. 3:14 where it refers to Christ, the true son of David. This shows how much the Davidic prophecies of the Old Testament were alive in some Christian congregations.

Nathan spoke of "my [God's] grace" toward David's son (II Sam. 7:15; cf. Ps. 89:3); this appears as "David's grace" in Isa. 55:3. It is translated in the Septuagint τὰ ὅσια Δαυίδ,[10] "the faithful blessing of David," and appears in this form in Acts 13:34, which forms the link to Ps. 16, quoted in Acts

	II Sam.	Isa.	Pss.	I Macc.	Ps. of Sol.	Ben Sir.	4 Q flor.	4 Q Bt 3⁸
the relation of "Father" (God) and "son" (Davidic king)	7:14		2:7; 88(89):27		cf. 17:27; 18:4 cf. 17:23 (21)		10	
Servant of God	7:8		88(89):4, 21, 40					
throne	7:13, 16		88(89):5, 30, 37	2:57		47	10	
seed	7:12		88(89):5, 30, 37					
kingdom of the son	7:16			2:57	cf. 17:4 of God	10	10	
in all eternity	7:13, 16 cf. 23:5	55:3	88(89):29; cf. 5	2:57	17:3 f.	cf. 47:11 f.	10	cf. iv 6 ff.
to raise up	7:12 23:1		88(89):25		17:23 (21)	47:11 f.	10, 12	iv 6 b ff.
covenant	23:5	55:3	88(89):4, 29, 40		17:15	47:11		
Messiah	23:1		2:2; 88(89):39, 52, cf. 21		17:32 18:5, 7		18	
house	7:16 23:5		cf. 88(89):5					
Gentiles			cf. 55:4 f. 2:1, 2, 8; 109 (110):6		17:3, 24, 29-31, 34		18	cf. iv 8

13:35; 2:27, 31. This verse says that God "will not let his faithful one see corruption." Even more important is the fact that Isa. 55:3-5 definitely introduces the "Gentiles" among whom the rule of the Davidic king bears witness to God's power and glory, and furthermore connects this with the "eternal covenant" of David (vs. 3).

The Gentiles are also mentioned in Ps. 2:7-8 (cf. above) as being the "inheritance" of the Davidic Son of God.[11] Ps. 2:7-8 is of particular interest, because the divine sonship is here understood as the result of God's begetting.[12] In contrast with II Sam. 7 and Ps. 89, the extension of the kingdom of God's son is spoken of in terms of space rather than time. Isa. 55:3-4 and Ps. Sol. 17 combine both views.

A most remarkable development is to be found in Ps. 110. Verse 1, with its idea of the "lordship" of the one who sits "at the right hand" of God and to whom "all enemies will be subjected," is, of course, very often quoted in the New Testament. Also, the "rod of power" (vs. 2) by which he rules the "Gentiles" (vs. 6) and the eternal priesthood according to the order of Melchizedek (vs. 4) are well known from New Testament quotations. In the Hebrew text the concept of a divine sonship is lacking; the Septuagint, however, translates vs. 3: "out of the womb, before dawn, I begot thee" which seems to presuppose the idea of a son of God born before the creation.[13]

Almost all the key terms are to be found again in Pss. Sol. 17 and 18. But the "only begotten, first-born son" of God (18:4; cf. Ps. 89:28) is now Israel (also Ps. Sol. 17:27), as it was in Jer. 3:19.[14] The Servant [15] is Israel too (Ps. Sol. 17:21). The Israelites are "the sons of the covenant" (17:15). The "seed" of David which shall last in all eternity (17:4) seems to refer to an individual king (cf. the "throne," 17:6) and the son of David who will be "raised up" (17:21) to be the "Messiah of the Lord" (cf. 17:32; 18:5, 7; Ps. 89:39, 52) is certainly the king: but the eternal kingdom is that of God (17:3). Much more important is the author's combination of several Old Testament passages. The coming king of God's "heritage," ruling over the "Gentiles" with a "rod of power," is in 17:23-24 (cf. 17:40) described with the words of Ps. 2:8-9. Isa. 11:2-4 is clearly referred to in 17:24, 35. Finally, the concept of the eschatological pilrimage to Mount Zion (Isa. 60:1-5; 66:18-20; cf. also 4 Q Bt. 3, iv 10-11) is a definite influence upon 17:31.[16] Compared with the older texts, chap. 17 shows us a view of the future which is at the same time more spiritual and more nationalistic. Israel is seen in a sharp contrast to all other nations, and the expectations are of a more and more miraculous type. I Macc. 2:57 shows for Palestinian Judaism, and Ben Sir. 47:11 for Hellenistic Judaism, how much the Jews of that time clung to the "eternal throne" promised by God himself to David.[17] The latter passage emphasizes the forgiveness of sins[18] granted to David by Nathan (II Sam. 12:13; cf. Ps. 89:32-35).

We have seen in Ps. Sol. 17-18 the firm expectation of a Davidic king; nonetheless, the promised "Son of God" is no longer understood to be an individual, but the holy part of the Israel of the latter days. The same is true for Jub. 1:24-25 and 4 Q flor. 1:10-11 (cf. lines 7-8, 11-19),[19] where the old keywords "father," "son," "throne," "kingdom," "eternity," "to raise up," [20] as well as the combination with Ps. 2 appear again. In 4 Q flor. "the Son of God" is the Messiah, but the decisive factor is again the holy people, the "tabernacle of David."

When, after this detour, we come back to Acts 13:33-37, we realize how long a history of interpretation lies in the backround of this text.[21] We find quotations of Ps. 2:7 in vs. 33; of Isa. 55:3 in vs. 34; of Ps. 16:10 in vs. 35, and of II Sam. 7:12 [22] in vs. 36. Ps. 2:7-9 had been combined with the prophecy of Nathan in II Sam. 7:12-16 as early as Ps. Sol. 17:23-24; [23] Isa. 55:3 is in and of itself a reference to the prophecy of Nathan.[24] It seems that the ambiguous keyword "to raise up" helped the first Christians to reinterpret the old prophecies of a Davidic Son of God.[25] They, of course, no longer understood this verb as referring either to his first appearance in earthly history or to his earthly enthronement as the national king, but rather in the sense in which the Christian church customarily used it for quite a time—as a reference to the resurrection. This enabled them to see the promised kingdom of David in the rule of the exalted Christ. Consequently, the day of which Ps. 2:7 spoke was the Easter day. God gave to the church on that day the fullness of his grace of which Isa. 55:3 speaks, namely the resurrection of Christ.[26] The Greek rendering of this phrase, however, led the interpreter to Ps. 16:10 where the same word designates the one who will not see corruption.[27] This, of course, was for the church a clear reference to Christ, the promised Davidic Son of God, since according to the Nathan prophecy itself, the historic David of the Old Testament did see corruption (II Sam. 7:12). The same argument is expanded at some length in Acts 2:25-26, where vs. 30 combines other phrases of II Sam. 7:12-13 and Ps. 89:4-5 with Ps. 16:10. It is worthwhile noting that in Acts 13:38 (cf. 2:38) "forgiveness of sins" reappears, as we found it in Ben Sir. 47:11 and Col. 1:12.

Finally, we may explicitly repeat that in Acts the prophecies of a coming Davidic Son of God are interpreted in the individual sense as referring to Christ, not to the holy people of the latter days, as is the case in Ps. Sol. 17-18 and partly in Qumran. However, the sharp distinction between the darkness and the light, the kingdom of Satan and that of God, that is the "lot" of the holy ones which they have gained by the forgiveness of their sins, does appear in Acts 26:18. This concept and its terminology are to be found also in Col. 1:12-14, where the divine Son is the ruler of the holy ones, not of the people as a whole. This shows that the term "Son of God" is only reluctantly applied to the church or the believer in the New Testament (cf. Rev. 2:26-28; 21:7).[28] There is but one passage in which the Nathan prophecy of the Son to whom God will be Father is explicitly referred to the church: II Cor. 6:16. This quotation is part of an interpolation,[29] and it is most illuminating that not only the Qumranian vocabulary appears here as nowhere else,[30] but that II Cor. 6:16 is the only passage in the New Testament that shares the title "Lord Pantokrator" with Revelation (cf. II Sam. 7:8, 25-27).[31]

Thus the long history of the interpretation and reinterpretation of the Davidic prophecies formed two streams. One emphasizes a Messianic figure, God's Son of Davidic descent, who rules over Israel in the latter days. In the New Testament it definitely forms the main stream and is taken up in Rom. 1:3-4; Luke 1:32-33; Acts 2:30; 13:33; Heb. 1:5-13; 5:5.[32] The other stream stresses the divine sonship of the eschatological Israel and leads to the apocalyptic or Qumranian passages of the New Testament, to Revelation, and II Cor. 6:14–7:1. This shows how much more reluctant the New Testament authors were to speak of a divine sonship of the church than was Judaism. Only the foundation of the sonship of the believer in the unique sonship of Christ himself, as we find it in Gal. 4:4-7; Rom. 8:3, 14-17, can really solve this problem. Thus, the question of the relation between the unique divine sonship of the coming Davidic king and that of the whole people of Israel, still open in postbiblical Judaism (cf. Ps. Sol. 17), is answered in the New Testament by the person of Jesus Christ, fulfilling the old Davidic prophecies and incorporating the church in his status as the Son of God.

NOTES

1. E. Haenchen, *Die Apostelgeschichte, ad loc.*
2. Cf. E. Lövestam, *Son and Saviour, ConNT* XVIII (1961), 8-10.
3. J. Dupont, "Filius meus es tu," *Rech SR* XXXV (1948), 530.
4. Non-Pauline expressions are ὁρίζειν (Acts 10:42; 17:31), πνεῦμα ἁγιωσύνης (Test. Levi 18:11; cf. Ps. 51:13; Isa. 63:10-11); non-Pauline conceptions: the birth from David's seed, the idea of the beginning of the divine sonship on Easter. The contrast of "flesh" and "Spirit" is used in a non-Pauline way: elsewhere in the Pauline letters when "according to the flesh" is connected with a verb, or when "flesh" is put in contrast to "Spirit," the former has a bad connotation. Moreover, "who" is a typical beginning of creedal formulas or hymns (cf. I Tim. 3:16; Phil. 2:6; Col. 1:15).
5. "His resurrection from the dead" (RSV) is certainly what the text means, but it is an interpretation instead of a translation. Acts 10:42; 17:31 show that "to designate" (RSV) is not strong enough to render the meaning of the Greek term. "Spirit of holiness" is a Semitism for "Holy Spirit," cf. the preceding note.
6. Therefore Paul perhaps also introduced "in power" in vs. 4 in order to distinguish this post-Easter status from the pre-Easter one.
7. Cf. G. von Rad, *Theologie des Alten Testaments* (1960) II, 58; E. Lohse, "Der König aus Davids Geschlecht," in: *Abraham unser Vater,* O. Michel Festschrift, eds. O. Betz, M. Hengel, and P. Schmidt (Leiden, 1963), pp. 337-45; and O. Betz, "Das messianische Bewusstein Jesu," *NovTest* VI (1963), 23-29.
8. E.g., M. Baillet, "Un Recueil liturgique de Qumrân, Grotte 4: 'Les Paroles des Luminaires,'" *RB* LXVIII (1961), 195-250.   This text is referred to as 4 Q Bt 3.
9. I still think that II Sam. 7 is prior to Ps. 88, although I know that some scholars reverse this order.
10. The noun is put in the plural and has exactly the same Hebrew letters as "my grace" in II Sam. 7:15.
11. Jer. 3:19 connects (a) "inheritance" from God, the "Pantokrator" of the "Gentiles," and (b) the idea of Israel being God's son; in Ps. Sol. 17:23 κληρονομία appears together with many other expressions of Ps. 2:7-9; cf. κληρονομεῖν I Macc. 2:57.
12. K. H. Rengstorf, "Old and New Testament Traces of a Formula of the Judaean Royal Ritual," *NovTest,* V (1962), 233-38 thinks that this was a model of the rite of enthronization.
13. Cf. A. George, "Le père et le fils dans les Évangiles synoptiques," *Lumière et Vie* XXIX (1956), 31.
14. Cf. n. 2 here, and Ps. 88:18 with 88:25.
15. παῖς instead of δοῦλος (II Sam. 7:8; Ps. 88:4, 21, 40).
16. In spite of 17:31c κύριος must designate "God," not the "Messiah."
17. Also Test. Jud. 22:3 (cf. 17:5-6; 24:5-6, and D. S. Russell, *Between The Testaments* [1960], p. 124-25); Pseudo-Philo, *Antiquitates Biblicae,* ed. G. Kisch (1949), 51:6; 56:2; 59:2, 4; 62:9 (cf. 51:3 and M. Philonenko "Une paraphrase du Cantique d'Anne" *RHPhR* XLII [1962] 164); II Esdras 12:32. For the transition of this expectation from David to Levi. cf. Jub. 31:13-20; for the influence of Ps. 2 on Wisd. Sol.: B. M. F. van Jersel, *"Der Sohn"* in den synoptischen Jesusworten, p. 76.
18. Cf. the motives of the "kingdom of the Son," the "heritage," and the "forgiveness of sins" in Col. 1:12-14, combined with Qumranian contrast of darkness and light, as is also the related passage Acts 26:18.
19. It is possible that "the anointed one" of Ps. 2:1 was, in line 19, interpreted as a plural, referring to the righteous ones of line 17 who severed themselves from the ungodly ones. Cf. also 4 QBT 3, III 4-6.
20. L. H. Silberman ("A Note on 4 Q Florilegium," *JBL* LXXVIII [1959], 158) sees here a midrash on II Sam. 7:11-12. For the influence of II Sam. 7 in Qumran cf. N. A. Dahl,

"Eschatologie und Geschichte im Lichte der Qumrantexte" in *Zeit und Geschichte*, Bultmann Festschrift (Tübingen, 1964), pp. 8-9.

21. Cf. T. Holtz, review of Lövestam (n. 2) in *ThLZ* LXXXVIII (1963), 203.
22. Rather than I Kings 2:10, Judg. 2:10 which is mentioned in the margin of Nestle, *Novum Testamentum Graece*.
23. The same is true for Isa. 11:4, appearing in the same combination with Ps. 2:8-9 in Ps. Sol. 17:23-24 and in Rev. 19:15; cf. the strange reinterpretation of Ps. 89:38 in Rev. 1:5 (combined with Ps. 88:28); 3:14. Isa. 66:18-20 and 60:1-5 appear also in Rom. 15:16 and Rev. 21:24.
24. Note that the word for "grace" is the same in the Hebrew but not in the Greek text.
25. Cf. Lövesam (above, n. 2) pp. 8-10.
26. J. Dupont, "TA OΣIA ΔAYIΔ TA ΠIΣTA (Acts 13:34=Isa. 55:3)," *RB* LXVIII (1961), 91-114 interprets: the good things given to the church because of the resurrection of Christ.
27. Cf. Lövestam (above, n. 2) pp. 53-55.
28. "To inherit" belongs to the tradition of the Davidic promises: cf. Foerster, "κληρονόμος," *ThWB*, III 781, 30 ff.
29. II Cor. 6:14-7:1; cf. E. Schweizer, "σάρξ," *ThWB*, VII 125, n. 219.
30. "Darkness and Light," the "lot" of the believers as over against that of the unbelievers, the strong separation of the church and the world (cf. Acts 26:18; Col. 1:12-14), "beliar," "temple of God."
31. In contrast with Revelation, here the divine sonship of the church is a present, not a future, reality.
32. Cf. Ps. 110 in Mark 12:35-37; I Cor. 15:25, 28; Heb. 1:5-13; 5:5; 7:28.

The Missionary Stance of Paul in I Corinthians 9 and in Acts

GÜNTHER BORNKAMM

The sentences in I Cor. 9:19-23 are rightly considered to be Paul's classical formulation of the maxim which characterized his whole missionary approach. But we must also recognize that the masterfully tight wording of the statements has caused them to be widely misunderstood. In a questionable way they have become part of Christian terminology, and often they are thoughtlessly misused in order to justify any form of assimilating the Christian proclamation and behavior to various ways of life. We shall, therefore, attempt more closely to define their intent and also to examine whether certain passages in Acts, as is often suggested, can serve to illustrate Paul's phrase that he became to the Jews like a Jew, to those under the law like one under the law (I Cor. 9:20).

I. Concerning the Interpretation of I Cor. 9:19-23

We shall omit a closer analysis of the larger context of chaps. 8:1–11:1. It is immediately obvious that the sentences in 9:19 ff. fit within the main theme of the whole chapter, which is the correct understanding of the freedom offered by the gospel and the practical consequences of this freedom. It is also obvious that it is not until vss. 19 ff. that Paul proceeds to statements of a fundamental and comprehensive character. Prior to this point he has spoken about his renunciation of the right to be supported by the churches. Now he turns to speak about his fundamental stance with its various expressions.

The entire passage is carefully constructed and shows rhetorical mastery. The opening and closing sentences (vs. 19; vss. 22b-23) state the whole of the fundamental theme, while in vss. 20-22a three variations on this same theme are provided:

194

a) v. 20 in relation to the Jews, in two parallel sentences, the second interpreting the first;

b) v. 21 in relation to the lawless (i.e., the Gentiles);

c) v. 22*a* in relation to the weak (a reference to the concrete problem of chaps. 8–10).

All the sentences contain:

1) a verb, emphatically placed either at the beginning or the end, describing the stance of the apostle: ἐδούλωσα v. 19; ἐγενόμην v. 20, 22*ab;* ποιῶ v. 23;

2) a concessive participial clause, defining and establishing his rights, as well as forming the background for his actual conduct: ἐλεύθερος ὤν v. 19; μὴ ὤν αὐτὸς ὑπὸ νόμον v. 20; μὴ ὤν ἄνομος θεοῦ, ἀλλ' ἔννομος Χριστοῦ v. 21;

3) an indication of the purpose (seven ἵνα-clauses!): five times ἵνα . . . κερδήσω (or κερδαίνω), once ἵνα . . . σώσω, once (concluding) ἵνα συγκοινωνὸς αὐτοῦ (sc. τοῦ εὐαγγελίου) γένωμαι.

Thus the unity of the apostle's purpose in the various expressions of his stance becomes impressively apparent through the structure, the uniformity, and the flow of the individual parts of the sentences.

However, the impressiveness of the rhetorical formulation must not blind us to the fact that with regard to content these statements pose important problems which must not be slighted. The way in which Paul characterizes the various groups immediately shows that he does not merely want to describe a missionary technique which he follows. For this reason alone it will not do to reduce the passage to the rule of Hillel: "When you come to a town, be guided by its customs" (Gen. rabba 48 to 18:8; Exod. rabba 47).[1] The problems inherent in the Pauline statements would thereby be slighted and the statements themselves seriously reduced in meaning. For being under the law and not being under the law do not denote merely natural and historical peculiarities and differentiations among people and nations. On the contrary, these expressions indicate ultimate contrasts of a religious nature. We must, therefore, assume that each of the groups mentioned could lodge a justifiable claim on the basis of its particular characteristic. This is clearly shown by the fact that Paul has to argue with various parties in his letters. For Jewish Christians and Judaists, standing under the law was obviously a requirement necessary for salvation. The same, however, is true for the "law-less," illustrated by the Corinthian enthusiasts ("all things are lawful"). For them the dismissal of every sort of legality was the proof of being a Christian. Finally, the same is true even for the "weak" who, of course, did not call themselves by that name. As Rom. 14–15 shows, they considered their own conduct to be required by the faith; and therefore they condemned the "strong." [2]

Both the context of I Cor. 9:19-23 and the content of these verses themselves show that Paul could not modify the gospel itself according to the particular characteristics of his hearers. The whole of his concern is to make clear that the changeless gospel, which lies upon him as his ἀνάγκη (9:16), empowers him to be free to change his stance. This means, however, that in the light of the gospel Paul no longer recognizes as such the religious positions of the various groups described. It would be wrong to take that as the expression of an enlightened standpoint in which he claims to rise above the prejudices of the religious views found in his environment toward a higher spiritual religion and morality. If this were the issue, the different stances which he takes in relation to Jews and Gentiles would indeed merely represent techniques of missionary adjustment. On the contrary, Paul's attitude must be understood in light of I Cor. 7:17-24. In pointed terms this means that in the light of the gospel Paul does not accept the different *standpoints* (Standpunkte) of Jews and Gentiles, but he does recognize their respective positions as the *historical places* (Standorte) where the "calling" of each man occurs through the gospel. From this perspective religious tradition and social position are relativized; at the same time they are highly significant for the realization of Christian existence. They are no longer religious qualities in themselves, i.e., conditions for the way to salvation. Nor are they ways of life which one must abandon or change in order to live as a Christian. Rather, the "place"—or "state"—of the individual becomes significant as the life-situation in which the gospel is to accomplish its purpose dialectically, liberating here and binding there. This is the reason why Paul often mentions the various religious positions and traditions in the same breath with the differences of sex, nationality, language, education, and social status.[3] Over against these, the gospel signifies liberation from all the "ways of salvation." In various religions the idea of indispensable steps and intermediate stations of an *ordo salutis* is customarily linked to the understanding of tradition. That Paul radically abandons all such preconditions is obviously closely connected with his message of justification.

Justification is not explicitly discussed in the letters to the Corinthians.

But the essential motifs of the doctrine undoubtedly play a considerable role in this correspondence, although the terminology is modified.[4] With respect to our passage the terms οἱ ὑπὸ νόμον, ἄνομος, and ἔννομος Χριστοῦ (I Cor. 9:20-21) point in the direction of this Pauline doctrine. The last of these terms is obviously formed as an analogy (to an unexpressed term), as are the related formulations νόμος τοῦ Χριστοῦ (Gal. 6:2), νόμος πίστεως (Rom. 3:27), νόμος τοῦ πνεύματος τῆς ζωῆς ἐν Χριστῷ Ἰησοῦ (Rom. 8:2). Even apart from the individual terms, however, the content of Paul's words warrants the conclusion that in line with the doctrine of justification Paul proves himself in his flexible stance toward Jews and Gentiles to be the one who does not boast of his prerogatives. So among both Jews and Gentiles he freely renounces the right which is actually his as a Christian.[5]

However, if it is true, as we said above, that it is as impossible for the individual to transcend his concrete life-situation (his "historical place") as it is to leap over one's shadow, how can Paul himself adjust to Jews and Gentiles and come into solidarity with them in the way described in I Cor. 9:19 ff.? This question still calls for a more exact answer. We have stated already that the apostle's freedom and adaptability have nothing to do with a stoic-cosmopolitan attitude which holds all men to be equal by nature, and considers all differentiations between them to be relative. Rather, his stance is rooted in the gospel and consequently—although the term is not used here—in the love which seeks not its own but the welfare of the other.[6]

This cannot be taken to mean that the apostle played different roles in different places simply for the sake of the missionary effect. To follow such a course would have concealed from his listeners the true reason for his flexible stance. True enough, his adversaries often misunderstood and denounced his stance as ambiguity, conformism, opportunism, and unprincipled vacillation. With his flexible stance Paul had to expect, therefore, not only an easier entry of his message, but also a conflicting reaction, criticism, and opposition. His approach certainly must not be seen as an easing of the σκάνδαλον-character of his message, but as an appropriate clarification of it. To speak as if Paul Judaized it in one place and paganized it in another is wholly inaccurate.

The last phrase, "that I may share in its [the gospel's] blessings" (9:23), shows conclusively how little this passage has to do with a mere art of adjustment or a successful missionary technique. The freedom of his service is not a matter of his discretion; it is a matter of his obedience to the gospel, so much so that his own eternal salvation is at stake.

II. Paul's Missionary Stance According to Acts

When one turns to compare the ideas of I Cor. 9:19-23 with corresponding motifs in Acts, it is wise to withstand the temptation immediately to discuss the above-mentioned passages often cited from Acts. Only at the end shall we ask to what extent these passages need seriously to be considered. First, we must outline briefly the leading ideas which call for a comparison. A more detailed inquiry would require us to compare the whole of the Lucan understanding of Paul and of history with that of the letters. But this would lead beyond the present essay. Moreover, it could only repeat work already done. We will, therefore, limit ourselves to an enumeration of the differences which have been, I think, correctly defined in recent research.

1. The repeated and emphatic use of the term νόμος in I Cor. 9:20-21 has already shown us how much Paul's statements are determined by his doctrine of law and grace, that is to say, his doctrine of justification.[7] It is well known that this doctrine plays no role in Acts. When occasionally it is alluded to, one finds it modified in a significant way; it is equated with the purely negatively conceived motif of the forgiveness of sin; it is not based on Jesus' atoning death; and it is understood only partially.[8] "By him everyone that believes is justified from everything from which you could not be justified by the Law of Moses" (13:38-39). For Luke, as for Paul, the law is not the way of salvation; but neither is it the way of salvation which finds its end in Christ, as it is for Paul. Thus the problem of the law, which so preoccupied Paul, simply is not existent for the Hellenist of the postapostolic age. Therefore Luke can consistently speak of the law in a positive manner. He can describe Paul as the Pharisee *par excellence* who is faithful to the law, and compared with whom the Jews are shown to be those who deny their own tradition. "Luke speaks of the insufficiency, Paul of the end of the *Nomos* which is Christ (Rom. 10:4)."[9] The consequences of this difference are far-reaching; it can scarcely be characterized as a "deficiency," however "grave."[10] Not least, the difference touches the understanding of the world as a unity which Paul himself developed, a unity rooted in the solidarity of all men, for all are lost under the law, but now all are at the same time under the solidarity of grace.

2. Closely connected with the loss of the message of justification in Acts is the surrender of Paul's eschatological understanding of history. In the apostle's preaching, theology, and mission, Jew and Gentile are seen together. To be sure, from the moment of his conversion and call Paul knows himself to be destined as apostle to the Gentiles. Nevertheless, the gospel which he is to bring to them is the message, developed face to face with the Jewish understanding of law and salvation, of one Lord over all, who bestows his riches upon all who call upon him, Jew and Greek alike (Rom. 10:11-12). As we have said already, the latter are united neither through a general conception of the world and mankind nor through a general conception of God but through the epochal event of salvation, rooted in Christ's death and resurrection and introducing a new aeon. In other words the event of salvation comes through the revelation of the righteousness of God in the gospel. The apostle often develops this in his letters by relating Jews and Gentiles to one another in turn. There is no need here to show how this dialectic dominates the epistles to the Romans and the Galatians. The fact that it plays a far smaller role in the Corinthian epistles can be satisfactorily explained on the basis of their situational character. Even in these letters, however, this characteristic feature of Paul's preaching is not lacking. It will suffice to point to (a) the confrontation between the λόγος τοῦ σταυροῦ and that which Jews and Gentiles expect from God (I Cor. 1:18 ff.); (b) the reminder of "our fathers" in the desert as a warning for Gentile Christians in Corinth who are all too sure of their salvation (I Cor. 10:1 ff.); (c) the emphasis on the unity of the church which is drawn from Jews and Gentiles (I Cor. 12:13), and not least (d) the extensive discussion of the collection which the Gentile Christian churches are assembling for Jerusalem (II Cor. 8-9; I Cor. 16:1 ff.). It is true that for the sake of the freedom of the gospel Paul found it necessary at times to risk this unity so beautifully manifested in the collection (Gal. 1-2). But it is also true that in doing battle for this unity he "worked more than all of them." For these reasons the apostle's preaching before Jews cannot be separated, either materially or historically, from his preaching before Gentiles. He certainly found himself confronted with various kinds of listeners and readers, as is shown by his letters; therefore he varied the language of his message. Nevertheless, he obviously presented himself to the Jews as a missionary to the Gentiles who had to proclaim that God's promise given to Abraham for all nations had been fulfilled. And conversely he called the Gentiles into the heritage of

Abraham, which is founded on faith, into the true "Israel of God" (Gal. 6:16).

There is therefore not the slightest reason to contest in a wholesale manner the picture, drawn by Acts (admitting that it is heavily schematized), which shows Paul (a) as a rule using the synagogues as a base of operation for his mission and (b) seeking to remain within the realm of the synagogue, until a final conflict rendered that impossible. This view has recently been challenged by W. Schmithals.[11] Calling attention to the agreement of the Apostolic Council, "that we should go to the Gentiles and they to the circumcised" (Gal. 2:9), he advanced the thesis that Paul consistently renounced any mission to the Jews. But it is historically unthinkable that Paul should have counted on a mission to the Jews to be carried out by others in the very places and towns where he was engaged in a mission to the Gentiles. As far as I can see, such an idea is not indicated in his letters. Indeed, there are some clear statements which refute it: II Cor. 11:24 shows that, although he denied the redemptive significance of the law, serving as the missionary to the Gentiles, he repeatedly experienced the sharp jurisdiction of the synagogue. Similarly, I Cor. 9:20 shows that within the limits of the freedom granted in the gospel Paul was among the Jews as a Jew in order to "win" them.[12]

The more important question is that of the fundamental conception by which Paul was guided in his mission to the Gentiles. In his book, *Paul and the Salvation of Mankind* (London: SCM, 1959), J. Munck has attempted to explain this conception on the basis of an apocalyptic idea. He suggests that the difference between Paul and the apostles in Jerusalem merely concerned the question of the chronological order of the missions to Jews and Gentiles. While—as he thinks—those in Jerusalem insisted that the gospel first had to be preached to the Jews and only then to the Gentiles, Paul, realizing the futility of their efforts among the Jews, reversed the sequence and turned to the Gentiles, intending thereby to prepare the way for the ultimate salvation of Israel. According to Munck, Paul's total effort was directed toward this goal.

This thesis must be questioned seriously at several points. To be sure, in Rom. 9–11 Paul speaks of such a sequence. He also indicates as his motivation that of making the Jews jealous by means of his mission to the Gentiles, thus evoking their faith (10:19; 11:11). But Munck obviously misinterprets the idea by giving it a place in Paul's whole thought which it does not occupy. We can hardly speak here of a fundamental motif of Paul's total mission to the Gentiles. For the basic motif is to be found in his understanding of law and grace, that is, in his message of justification. Munck attributes no significance to the fact that Rom. 1–8 precedes 9–11, and that the latter part is permeated with the central motifs of the doctrine of justification, motifs which are applied in 9–11 to the question of Israel's destiny, its hardness of heart, and its final salvation. He even goes so far as to call a sentence like Gal. 2:16 (and parallels) a Jewish-Christian statement![13] The sentences and ideas in Rom. 9–11, which Munck emphasizes, must therefore be understood differently: On the basis of scripture they interpret and, indeed, justify something which has *already occurred:* the bringing of the gospel to the Gentiles.[14] Paul himself can say that the message is directed "to the Jew first and also to the Greek." But the gospel has already come to the Greek. He then draws the *conclusion* that this surprising turn of events is a detour leading back to Israel. The interpretation of the course of history is in this way made to serve his hope even for the historical Israel. As an empirical people they are called to a life by grace alone, and God is leading them toward this realization of their destiny.

3. When we turn our attention once again to Acts, it becomes immediately clear that, while Paul views the Jewish and Gentile missions as simultaneous enterprises, Luke sees them as forming a *succession.* This view is certainly not historically incorrect in every case, but in Luke's work we see it as a basic scheme which is systematically carried through. This change means that the Pauline idea of justification has been completely replaced by the idea of Heilsgeschichte. According to Acts, the idea of Heilsgeschichte finds its origin in the resurrection and exaltation of Jesus, the outpouring of the Spirit through the exalted Lord, and the μετάνοια (repentance) granted by him. Since the Jews have not accepted it, the messengers turn to the Gentiles (13:46). In Acts we find, therefore, the principle of Heilsgeschichte and a new basis for the mission to the Gentiles;[15] these constitute a line of thought which Luke maintains consistently to the end of his book (28:28!).

4. There is a close connection between this difference and another: whereas the historical Paul declares that all are "without excuse," Luke emphasizes that the prior state of Jews and Gentiles is "ignorance." In Luke's view the Jews ignorantly delivered Jesus to the cross (3:17; 13:27) and in ignorance the Gentiles have all along worshiped the true, unknown God (17:23). God overlooked the times of this ignorance and now sends out

to all men the word of repentance (17:30). In this way the past of both Jews and Gentiles finds a graceful end, but at the same time this past is given a characteristic reevaluation: the Jews' past as prophecy, and the Gentiles' past as preparatory prelude. Thus, as it is presented in Acts, the gospel proves to be an apologia, not only proclaiming the fulfillment of the Old Testament prophecies and especially the Pharisaic hope for resurrection, but even confirming the teaching of the Greek poets concerning the natural divine origin of all men (17:28). All men are closely related to God (Acts 17:29). Every man is created to seek and experience God. Thus in the Areopagus speech the Lucan Paul guides men to the true knowledge of God. It is true that this idea appears in Acts—in the whole New Testament —only here. Its weight is nevertheless considerable. It is also true that in Acts missionary preaching is understood as proclamation and not merely as "enlightenment." Even Acts 17:30 ends with the preaching of repentance, explicitly emphasizing the "now" of Heilsgeschichte, and sharply distinguishing the epoch of ἄγνοια from that in which salvation is proclaimed.[16] Furthermore, the difference between the past and the present is not suppressed: the "unknown God" of the past is now proclaimed as the God who raised Jesus from the dead and appointed him the judge of the world. But it is precisely at this point that the contrast with Pauline theology is obvious: Instead of Paul's affirmation of the eschatological solidarity of all men under God's wrath and grace, we find here the idea that the human race is united by virtue of its kinship with God; and the motif of the turn of the ages is replaced by an immanent history of redemption, structured into periods.

From Paul's point of view, the preacher does not make a point of contact with his hearers without finding himself simultaneously confronted by opposition.[17] The same can scarcely be said of the Areopagus speech. It is composed with the intention of making a point of contact without experiencing opposition.[18] It aims to make contact with the religious presuppositions of the listeners in order to expose their actual opposition as hardness of heart.

5. But what is the specific content of Paul's maxim as formulated in I Cor. 9:19 ff.? In any case it is clear, as we have seen, that Paul intends the statements to characterize a practical stance of solidarity with various groups, rather than to describe several ways of adjusting his preaching in terms of content and language to various environments. To be sure, his letters show clearly that he took this latter task quite seriously in order to reach the

conscience of his listeners (II Cor. 4:2; 5:11).[19] Here (I Cor. 9:19 ff.) it is a matter of solidarity in practical conduct. Significantly, Paul cannot say to the "strong" that he became strong, although he could not disagree entirely with their theoretical arguments (I Cor. 8:1, 5; 10:19), and in Rom. 15:1 he places himself on their side. Nor does he defend in I Cor. 8–10 the better "theological" arguments of the weak. Rather, he calls on each to renounce for the sake of the other the use of his own ἐξουσία.

But how far did the full scope of his freedom reach? Paul does not give a casuistic answer. But some indications of the limits of the freedom granted to him and to every Christian are worth noting. They are found, for instance, in his refusal at the Apostolic Council to circumcise Titus (Gal. 2:3-5), or in his emphatically negative answer to the question whether a Christian could participate in the pagan cultic meals (I Cor. 10:14-22).

Finally, we must take up three passages in Acts—16:3; 18:18; 21:20 ff.— which are often cited as specific examples of the missionary stance Paul describes in I Cor. 9:19 ff. How are we to evaluate these passages?

a) "Paul wanted Timothy to accompany him; and he took him and circumcised him because of the Jews that were in those places [Cilicia]" Acts 16:3). It is sometimes said that Paul's consideration for the Jews living in Cilicia reflects the freedom of which he speaks in I Cor. 9:20. It is supposed that he circumcised Timothy, the half-Jew, because in this case it was not a matter of recognizing circumcision as a means of salvation; it was, rather, an act of piety.[20] Paul is said to have done it in order to clear any unnecessary obstacles for his missionary work.[21] Is this line of interpretation correct? The fact alone that Timothy was already a baptized Christian[22] (Acts 16:1) speaks against the reliability of the report. Above all, however, it must have been impossible for Paul, especially after the agreements made at the Apostolic Council, to consider circumcision as a ceremony irrelevant to faith and missionary activity. He could scarcely do such a thing for the sake of the Jews for whom circumcision meant more than that. Nor could he do it for the sake of his gospel, for it was precisely with regard to this question that there was a head-on collision between his gospel and the Jewish and Judaizing understanding of salvation.[23] We are, therefore, forced to contest the accuracy of the remark in Acts 16:3 and to explain it in terms of the well-known tendency of Luke to prove Paul's loyalty to the law, in the face of arguments to the contrary.[24] The author of Acts, however, hardly invented the report. It must have been part of a tradition. About the origin of the tradition we cannot be certain. Perhaps it stemmed from Paul's Judaistic opponents and then found its way, freed of polemical overtone, into the reports which Luke used. We may recall that in Gal. 5:11 Paul appears to protest the rumor, spread by the Judaizers, that he himself still preaches circumcision.[25]

b) We need to be critical, too, of the report that Paul took a "vow" before his departure from Corinth (Acts 18:18). Here the author of Acts can only have thought of a Nazirite vow (cf. 21:23-24), without however having an exact idea of what was involved.[26]

c) A different situation obtains with respect to Acts 21:17-26, the report about Paul's participating in the purification ceremony for four Nazirites. As is generally assumed, Luke must have had a written source for this report, but its authenticity is not thereby demonstrated. For we must ask whether the source was historically reliable or whether it was biased (e.g., in the same way as Acts 16:3). In fact, it must be admitted that important facets of the report are suspect: in explaining their motivation for exhorting Paul to participate in the vow-ceremony, the delegation from the Jerusalem church repeat both the accusations made against Paul and the need for proof that he is true to the law. These elements correspond so exactly to Luke's portrait of Paul (or the portrait of Paul given in Luke's source) that we can scarcely trust the report in its present form.[27] That does not entitle us, however, to declare the narrative wholly unhistorical. Even though the author of the source or Luke himself may have used the report for his own purposes, there are good reasons for believing that Paul did in fact respond to the request made of him, and that at this point he actually practiced his maxim to become a Jew to the Jews in the sense of I Cor. 9:20. This view becomes all the more plausible if we follow a convincing suggestion of E. Haenchen by connecting Paul's action at this point with the handing over of the collection.[28] The collection is not mentioned in Acts, but it is known to us from Rom. 15:31-32. There Paul himself speaks of the danger threatening him from the side of the Jews and, moreover, of the difficulties which might be created for him upon his arrival by members of the Jewish-Christian church. It could not be taken for granted that they would accept the collection of the Pauline churches. They knew quite well that it was intended to demonstrate the unity of the church, including both Jews and Gentiles, and that it was meant at the same time to show the legitimacy of Paul's gospel, including freedom from the law. Thus the possibility certainly existed that they might refuse such recognition for these theological reasons and because of the difficulty of their position vis-à-vis the Jews. There is every indication that in light of this situation Paul decided to participate in the cultic act for the Nazirites. He did not thereby compromise himself in the least. For participation in this private ceremony, undertaken only for his own person, certainly could not call into question the fact that the law was abolished as the way to salvation. Moreover, Paul never thought of making Jewish Christians over into Gentile Christians. He rather fought for the unity of the church including both Jews and Gentiles. The fact that he did not demand obedience to the law does not imply, therefore, that he opposed any and every observance of the law among Jews.[29]

Thus Acts 21:17-26 is one historical example showing us what Paul meant in I Cor. 9:19 ff. when he declared his readiness to become "a slave to all" while being "free from all men." As is well known, this last act by Paul in the temple was fatal for him. In other words, his faithfulness to the word of I Cor. 9:20 led him to prison and death.[30]

NOTES

1. Cf. H. J. Schoeps, *Paul* (1961), p. 231. D. Daube, "Jewish Missionary Maxims in Paul," in *The New Testament and Rabbinic Judaism* (London, 1956), pp. 336 ff.
2. In spite of the close connection between I Cor. 8-10 and Rom. 14-15, there is still the difference that the "weak" in Corinth are tempted to silence the voice of their conscience and to imitate the strong, while the vegetarians in Rome (as well as their opponents who despised them) maintained their conduct, defending it on the basis of their faith.
3. Cf. Gal. 3:28; I Cor. 7:18 ff.; 12:13; Col. 3:11.
4. This has been shown convincingly by H. Braun, "Exegetische Randglossen zum 1. Korintherbrief," in *Gesammelte Studien zum Neuen Testament und seiner Umwelt* (Tübingen, 1962), p. 178 ff.
5. Cf. H. Schlier, ἐλεύθερος, *ThWB* II 497.
6. Phil. 2:4; I Cor. 13:5; Rom. 15:2; cf. E. Käsemann, "Eine paulinische Variation des amor fati," *ZThK* LVI (1959), esp. pp. 153-54; now in *Exegetische Versuche und Besinnungen* II (Göttingen, 1964), 223 ff., esp. pp. 237 ff.
7. See above, pp. 196-97.
8. Cf. Ph. Vielhauer, "On the 'Paulinism' of Acts," in the present volume; E. Haenchen, *Die Apostelgeschichte* (13th ed., Göttingen, 1961), pp. 354, 359; H. Conzelmann, *Die Apostelgeschichte* (Tübingen, 1963), p. 77.
9. Vielhauer, "On the 'Paulinism' of Acts," p. 42.
10. As in U. Wilckens, *Die Missionsreden in der Apostelgeschichte* (WMANT V), (1961), 215 ff.
11. W. Schmithals, *Paulus und Jakobus*, FRLANT LXXXV (Göttingen, 1963) [*Paul and James*, SBT XLVI (Naperville, 1965)].
12. This is correctly stated by Vielhauer, "On the 'Paulinism' of Acts," p. 39; the agreement

in Gal. 2:9, "we to the Gentiles, they to the circumcised," can then be understood neither as a geographic division of missionary territory nor as a division between groups which are ethnically or religiously distinct. Rather, the agreement has to be understood as the release of the gospel preached by Paul and Barnabas, without the Jerusalem party recognizing that gospel as binding on them. It had to be counted as a success that the Pauline mission was accepted at all rather than being denounced by the Christian community; cf. Haenchen, *Die Apostelgeschichte*, pp. 408-9.

13. J. Munck, *Paul*, pp. 127-128.

14. This assumes that the gospel *as it was preached by Paul*, that is, the gospel of the free grace and salvation offered to the believer alone, was first proclaimed among the Jews, but rejected by them. Munck interprets Rom. 10:14 ff. incorrectly as a reference to the mission previously carried on among the Jews *by the Jerusalem party*. Because of the failure of this Jewish mission, Paul is supposed to have turned to the Gentiles, but only in order to win the Jews. Cf. *Paul*, pp. 54-55, 113, 223, 235, 256, 274, 300.

15. Cf. Conzelmann's comments on Acts 13:46 and Haenchen's correct observation: "Dass sich Paulus immer erst zu den Heiden wenden darf, wenn ihn die Juden ablehnen, macht aus der selbstverständlichen Anknüpfung in der Synagoge eine falsche Theorie."

16. Cf. Conzelmann's comment on the passage.

17. See R. Bultmann (although with some reservations), "Anknüpfung und Widerspruch," *Glauben und Verstehen* II (1952), 125 ff.

18. That is why the resurrection is introduced as "proof" (πίστιν παρέχειν).

19. But obviously without either seeking their applause (Gal. 1:10; I Thess. 2:4) or destroying the skandalon of his message.

20. Cf. most recently H. Schlier, *Der Brief an die Galater* (12th ed., 1962), p. 239.

21. Cf. what appears to me to be an exhaustive discussion in Haenchen, *Die Apostelgeschichte*, pp. 419 ff.

22. Possibly baptized by Paul himself (I Cor. 4:17).

23. Cf. esp. Gal. 5:11. According to I Cor. 7:18, Paul did not approve the cancellation of circumcision, but neither did he ask the uncircumcised to submit to it.

24. This tendentious character of Acts 16:3 is also correctly stated by W. Schmithals, *Paulus und Jakobus* (1963). However, as I said above, Schmithals drives his case too far when denies any mission by Paul in the synagogues. According to him it is Luke who made Paul into a "verhinderten Judenmissionar, der den Heiden nur predigt, weil die Juden ihn verwerfen" (p. 46). On the other hand, Schmithals surprisingly considers the report of Timothy's circumcision as authentic, relying on the vague hypothesis that Paul agreed to it because he feared that the unbelieving Jews of Jerusalem (!) would make difficulties for the church there..

25. Cf. Haenchen, *Die Apostelgeschichte*, pp. 79-80; O. Linton, "The Third Aspect, A Neglected Point of View," *StTh* III (1950/51), 79 ff. The variant reading in Gal. 2:5, which affirms the circumcision of Titus by eliminating the words οἷς οὐδὲ can hardly be original. It rather reflects the later view, documented in Acts 16:3, according to which circumcision is no longer a *casus confessionis*.

26. Cf. Haenchen, *Die Apostelgeschichte*, pp. 481-82; Conzelmann, *Die Apostelgeschichte*, p. 108; W. Schmithals, *Paulus und Jakobus*, p. 80.

27. This was correctly seen long ago by F. C. Baur, *Paulus* (1866), I 225; also Vielhauer, "On the 'Paulinism' of Acts," p. 40.

28. Cf. Haenchen, *Die Apostelgeschichte*, pp. 543 ff. and especially D. Georgi, *Die Geschichte der Kollekte für Jerusalem* (Habilitationsschrift, Heidelberg), (1965), pp. 136 ff.; also W. Schmithals, *Paulus*, pp. 70 ff. Although Conzelmann, *Die Apostelgeschichte*, pp. 122-23, questions Haenchen's reconstruction of the historical circumstances, Haenchen's suggestion is, in my view, well founded. Conzelmann finds in the report only the typical traits of Luke's (or the source's) view of history: "Das Geschick des Paulus hat sich gerade bei der Ausübung einer Gesetzesleistung erfüllt." Moreover, the intention of the story,

according to Conzelmann, is to refute in advance the accusations leveled against Paul in the subsequent court scenes. Against this we must say that Luke's finding his view of history confirmed in the report does not mean that the report is unreliable. Had this report been only a tendentious legend, the narrator probably would have chosen some other example as a climactic conclusion for proving Paul's faithfulness to the law; he would hardly have selected this eccentric ceremony of Acts 21:24 ff.

29. Cf. the appropriate remarks by W. Schmithals, *Paulus,* p. 77; "Traut man dies dem Apostel nicht zu, so lässt man ihn das Heil statt im Gesetzesgehorsam in der Gesetzesfreiheit finden, während er es doch in Christus findet, der jene Liebe zum Bruder fordert, die auch auf die christliche Freiheit verzichten kann" (I Cor. 8-10). I cannot agree, however, with his view that the Jerusalem Christians under James were not ζηλωταὶ τοῦ νόμου (Acts 21:20), and that Paul accepted the suggestion of James only for the sake of the Jews.

30. Cf. D. Georgi, *Die Geschichte,* pp. 136-41. [See also the recent article by L. E. Keck, "The Poor among the Saints in the New Testament," *ZNW* LVI (1965) 100-129 and its sequel, "The Poor among the Saints in Jewish Christianity and Qumran," *ZNW* LVII (1966).]

Concerning the Speeches in Acts[*]

EDUARD SCHWEIZER

Ever since Martin Dibelius' essay about this subject, it has been more and more widely recognized that the speeches are basically *compositions by the author of Acts* who, to be sure, utilized different kinds of material for particular passages.[1] This can be supported by *analysis of the speeches* which contain the missionary proclamation of the apostles to Jews and Gentiles.

I

First of all, the speeches of Peter and the closely related one of Paul in Antioch must be analyzed in detail.

1. The first speech of this kind is at the same time the most extensive one—the Pentecost sermon of Peter (2:14 ff.). It shows the following scheme: (a) direct address (adapted to the situation): 14*a;* (b) appeal for attention: 14*b;*[2] (c) a misunderstanding by the hearers is pointed out (underestimation of the apostles) and rejected: 15-16; (d) quotation from Scripture: 17-21; (i) new address and new appeal for attention (necessary in order to mark the transition from the quotation to the speech[3]): 22*a;* (e) christological kerygma: 22*b*-24; (f) proof from Scripture: 25-31;[4] (e') continuation of the interrupted christological kerygma: 32-33; (f') resumption of the proof from Scripture (following the scheme of vss. 25-31): 34-35; (g) reply to the problem posed by the misunderstanding 33*b*, 36; (h) call to repentance and proclamation of salvation: 38 (in response to a question from the audience, vs. 37); (i) focusing of the message upon this specific audience: 39.

[*] This essay, originally published in *ThZ* XIII (1957), 1-11, and now in E. Schweizer, *Neotestamentica, German and English Essays 1957-1963* (Zürich, 1963), grew out of a seminar conducted jointly with Hans Conzelmann; it is impossible to ascertain in detail which suggestions and insights I owe to him. The attempt of a joint seminar seemed to both of us definitely fruitful and worthy of repetition.

2. The second speech (3:12 ff.) starts out similarly: (a) direct address (more general than in 2:14): 12*a;* (b) missing; (c) a misunderstanding is pointed out (overestimation of the apostles): 12*b;* (d) quotation from Scripture (here not explicitly introduced as such): 13*a;* (e) christological kerygma: 13*b*-15; (g) reply to the problem posed by the misunderstanding: 16; (i) repetition of direct address (in a more brotherly vein) and pardon extended to the hearers: 17; (f) proof from Scripture (summarized [5]): 18, (h) call to repentance and proclamation of salvation: 19; (e′) special proclamation of the parousia[6] to be hastened by penitence, with corresponding (f′) proof from Scripture (first general, then specific): 20-24; (i) focusing of the message upon this specific audience (with reference to a passage of Scripture): 25 f.

3. The third speech (4:9 ff.) is extraordinarily short. Nevertheless it contains: (a) direct address (again adapted): 9*a;* (c) a misunderstanding or at least an open question is pointed out: 9*b;* (b) appeal for attention (as in 2:14): 10*a;* (e) christological kerygma (in terse form): 10*b;* (g) reply to the problem posed by the misunderstanding: 10*c;* (f) proof from Scripture: 11; (h) only the proclamation of salvation; but in an exclusive formulation and hence also an appeal to the hearers: 12.

4. The fourth speech (5:29 ff.) stands out from the others in that it is said to have been delivered by "Peter and the apostles." It is probably intended to be only a condensation of the content of what was said by all the apostles and therefore lacks the direct address and the appeal for attention (a, b). Its connection with the situation is formed by the repetition of the basic sentence of 4:19 (which corresponds to c), followed by the kerygma of Christ (e) which is at least reminiscent of one Old Testament phrase (d). Formally connected with it are the call to repentance and the proclamation of salvation (h), and the strong emphasis upon the apostles as witnesses.[7]

5. The fifth speech (10:34 ff.), however, is once more a regular missionary address of Peter. For the first time we here come upon a speech addressed to Gentiles, placed within the structure of Acts at a period when this problem for the first time becomes acute. Consequently, the beginning of the speech becomes a basic digression dealing with the question of whether God accepts Gentiles: 34-35. This digression replaces the link to a misunderstanding (c) which, of course, is not present here or, rather, has already been reported and corrected in vss. 25 f.[8] Verse 36 may be said to take up point (i) in a most peculiar form: the point of departure is that God sent

his message to Israel (just as in 13:26 where it can then be pointedly applied to the audience [9]); but the additional "he is Lord of all" adapts it to the situation: he who is here proclaimed is the Lord of all men.[10] The appeal for attention is here replaced by the reminder "you know" (b): 37a. It is followed by the kerygma of Christ (e) with scriptural allusion (d): 37b-42. Added to this is a summarized proof from Scripture (f): 43a. The speech closes with the proclamation of salvation which contains the challenge to come to faith (h): 43b. The focusing of the message upon this specific audience (i) at this decisive point is made by God himself by causing the Holy Spirit to fall on the hearers: 44.

6. The sixth speech (13:16 ff.) is far more complicated. It is the first speech by Paul, and it occupies an especially prominent position in the total conception of the book. Its distinguishing features evidently are that in its first half a sort of parallel is drawn to the speech of Stephen, and that afterward the Jews of the dispersion are contrasted with the Jerusalemites. The sequence of the various topics is therefore rather different from that in the other speeches; nevertheless, precisely here there are many points of agreement in details. The composition may be characterized as follows: (a) direct address (adapted to the situation): 16b; (b) appeal for attention: 16b; (c) a misunderstanding at the first contact is not present here, just as there is none in 10:34 ff.; (d) in place of the quotation from Scripture, an outline of the history-of-salvation appears [11]: 17-25; (i) repeated address (more brotherly): 26a; (i) focusing of the message upon this specific audience (conditioned by the particular situation of the speech): 26b; (e) christological kerygma (elaborated): 27-31;[12] (i?) Paul as preacher: 32; (f) proof from Scripture: 33-37; [13] (i) renewed address with appeal for attention: [14] 38a; (h) proclamation of salvation ("paulinizing"!): 38-39;[15] (i) warning against not heeding: 40 f.

II

This analytical survey of the speeches shows, with due recognition of differences in content, a *far-reaching identity of structure*. I have purposely left aside a detailed analysis of the christological kerygma. In it characteristic variations appear, and one should ask to what extent older traditions are here being used. But that is immaterial in this context, because we are only concerned with the structure of the speech as a whole.

The following *general scheme* has been discovered:

a) Direct address (in speeches 1, 2, 3, 6). It is adapted to each particular situation. Frequently it is repeated, either after a quotation in order to mark the resumption of the speech (twice in 1), or by taking up the expression "brethren" in order to indicate increased intimacy toward the audience on the part of the speaker (2, 6).

b) Appeal for attention (1, 3, 6; cf. οἴδατε, you know, in 5). The formula γνωστὸν ἔστω (be it known) occurs in 1, 3, 6 and likewise in 28:28; ἀκούσατε (listen) occurs in 6 and likewise in 7:2; 15:13; 22:1; the same idea but in solemn biblical language in 1: ἐνωτίσασθε (lend your ears). The same purpose can be achieved by giving emphasis to the proclamation of the apostle, as is evidently done in Paul's speech (6; related to it is the reference to the original apostles as eye-witnesses in 4; cf. also 5 and 6).

c) Pointing out a misunderstanding among the audience (1, 2, 3). This point is missing in 5 and 6 since nothing derogatory had been reported previously about the hearers of these speeches; they do not belong to the Jerusalemites who crucified Jesus.

d) Frequently the speech starts out with a quotation from Scripture (1, 2, 4, 5, 6). Only in 1 is the quotation expressly introduced as such; in 6 this point is elaborated into a selective sketch of the history of Israel similar to that in the speech of Stephen (which is composed differently); in all the others it is only in the Christ-kerygma that we find passages taken from the Old Testament.

e) The christological kerygma (with typical agreements in all the speeches).[16]

f) Scriptural proof proper (1, 2, 3, 5, 6). For the most part it is offered either as a specific pattern referring to David (the passage does not mean David but another—Christ, twice in 1; 6), or in a pattern summarily referring to all the prophets (2, 5, 6).[17] In 2 and 3 a specific passage is quoted.

g) For (g) the same holds as was said about (c), with the sole addition that this point is frequently treated in conjunction with the Christ-kerygma (in other words, immediately after (e)—thus in 2, 3, and in 1 at least in 2:33*b*).

h) The proclamation of salvation appears everywhere, and in 1, 2, 4 is connected with the call to repentance. It is missing, then, in the same speeches in which points (c) and (g) are missing, and for the same reason.

i) The focusing of the message upon the specific audience is found in 1, 2, 5, and 6. In 3 and 4 it cannot be present because opponents of the apostles are being addressed. In 5 and 6 it is treated with particular care since the occasion is a first missionary speech in new territory, not an address directed toward Jerusalemites. For this reason it is placed at the very beginning, preceding the Christ-kerygma, and is taken up once more toward the end by God's own intervention (5) or by a word of warning from the prophets (6, where Jews are addressed).

What has been said so far should suffice to show that *one and the same author* is decisively involved in the composition of all the speeches here investigated. By and large, any traditional material foreign to him is probably present only in the traditional themes already mentioned, especially within the actual Christ-kerygma, possibly also in the choice of the scriptural passages and in the pattern of the proof from Scripture. He is led to make certain changes within the set pattern primarily by a change of audience: when non-Jerusalemites are addressed,[18] the misunderstanding and its correction drops out, as does the call to repentance. The difference in speakers is far less important. In 13:38-39, it is true, Paul is characterized by "paulinizing" language, and the entire sixth speech is evidently treated with particular care as one which begins a new period in history (similar to Peter's Pentecost address); but basically the Paul of Acts speaks exactly like Peter.

III

Proceeding to the two *speeches of Paul before Gentiles,* we discover, besides characteristic differences, a largely parallel structure. The speech of 14:15 ff. is, of course, unusually short and in a sense fragmentary, since it is intended only to show the inhabitants of Lystra the folly of worshiping the apostles.

7. It contains the following points: (a) direct address: 15*a;* (c) a misunderstanding is pointed out (overestimation of the apostles): 15*a;* (g) correction of this misunderstanding: 15*b;* (b) reference to the proclamation of the apostles: 15*c;* (h) call to repentance: 15*c;* (d) quotation from Scripture (God the Creator): 15*d,* introducing (e) the theological kerygma: 16-17.

The appeal for attention, then, is here replaced by the reference to the εὐαγγελίζεσθαι (proclaiming) of the apostles, just as we found it in the case of 6 (likewise a Pauline speech). Otherwise only the proof from Scripture is missing which, of course, has no place here before Gentiles. Besides, this speech is about as short as the third one, so that the various points, just as there, are often interwoven in a single sentence and therefore occur in a sequence different from the customary one.

8. More interesting and more conclusive, however, is the elaborate speech before Gentiles (17:22 ff.) which stands at a deliberately chosen place in the total composition of the book. Its structure is as follows: (a) direct address (appropriately related to the situation [19]): 22a; (c) a "misunderstanding" is pointed out: 22b; 23ab; (b) reference to the proclamation of the apostles: 23c; (d) passages from Scripture (God the Creator): 24a, introducing (e) the theological kerygma: 24-27; (f) proof from "Scripture," taken from Greek poets: 28; (g) the "misunderstanding" is cleared up: 29; (h) call to repentance: 30; (i) the focusing upon the specific audience already occurs in vs. 30: πάντας πανταχοῦ (all men everywhere). In vs. 31 its urgency is emphasized by the reference to Christ as judge and to his resurrection as proof.

The differences are clear. Here before Gentiles the testimony for Christ is replaced by the proclamation of God. Consequently in both the sermons to Gentiles the Scripture quotation concerns the creator.[20] In these two speeches (in contrast with 5 and 6) a mistaken action of the hearers is reported previously (14:11-13; 17:16); hence points (c) and (g) appear again, and likewise the call to repentance (h). But precisely this speech shows that also here, as in 3:17, the way to conversion is to be made easier for the hearer. The speaker uses this "misunderstanding," then, to introduce a form of *captatio benevolentiae* (the currying of favor), by interpreting the "misunderstanding" as favorably as possible.[21] In the Pauline speeches the reference to the present proclamation of the apostle takes the place of the Old Testament prophetic appeal for attention (13:32; 14:15). *Structurally,* the proclamation of Christ is only an appendix to the speech. Here Christ appears as judge, a note otherwise struck only in 10:42 (likewise before Gentiles). The message concerning Christ is not intended to add anything basically new to the previous proclamation. It is intended to emphasize the urgency of the decision already called for, and at the same time—as the message of the resurrection—to offer the possibility of making that decision.[22] That is to say: just as elsewhere in the book of Acts, the gospel of Christ, especially the proclamation of his resurrection, serves the purpose of proving what could also be known without it and hence of making the conversion to Christian faith urgent.[23] But precisely the fact that this point projects beyond his normal speech pattern clearly shows that it is important to the author at this place. This is also expressly emphasized in vs. 32 as it had been already at the end of vs. 18, and corresponds as well to our findings for the whole book. It is the resurrection of Jesus which is again and again the parting of the ways. To be sure, it signifies nothing new in regard to knowledge already available, but it confronts the hearer with the decisive question whether he is really willing to take seriously what he already ought to know without it.

IV

We can now summarize the *results*. What is clear, first of all, is the *uniformity* of the speeches, above all in their total structure, but also in a considerable number of details. It seems clear that one and the same author has composed them, taking up traditional material only in particulars. In this light, the *variations* observed are interesting. Those due to the fact that a certain speech has been attributed to a certain apostle are relatively scant. The only instances to be discussed in this respect are 13:38-39, where Paul is made to mention justification of the believer (understood in a very un-Pauline way), and the verses which particularly stress his missionary preaching: 13:32; 14:15; 17:23. Far more significant is the change of *audience*. This shows up most clearly when the *christ*ological kerygma is replaced by the *theo*logical one wherever a typical *Gentile* congregation is listening. This can go so far that a verse from the Greek poet Aratus displaces the usual proof from Scripture. But even here the passages suggestive of the Old Testament at the beginning of the speech (17:24-25) indicate, as does the whole content of the message, that the biblical Creator is being proclaimed. Not so evident but especially interesting is another difference: the call for conversion, connected with the stating and correcting of a misunderstanding, occurs only in the speeches addressed to Judaism proper and heathendom proper. Otherwise, however, there are the speeches, one before Gentiles, one before Jews, addressed to persons about whom there is nothing derogatory to report, so that points (c) and (g) drop out. These are first the Gentiles in the household of Cornelius who is a φοβούμενος τὸν θεόν (a "God-fearer"; 10:2), and second they are the Jews of the dispersion, clearly distinguished from the Jerusalemites, who share their synagogue with the φοβούμενοι τὸν θεόν ("God-fearers"; 13:16, 26-27). Hence to a certain extent these *God-fearers in Acts* take the place of the *Galileans of the Gospel*. To them first of all is given the gospel message.[24] They are God's elect.[25]

214

NOTES

1. M. Dibelius, "The Speeches of Acts and Ancient Historiography," and "Paul on the Areopagus," both now in M. Dibelius, *Studies in the Acts of the Apostles,* trans. by M. Ling (New York, 1956). In addition, cf. W. Schmid, "Die Rede des Apostels Paulus vor den Philosophen in Athen," *Philologus* XCV (1942), 78-120; G. Schrenk, "Urchristliche Missionspredigt im 1. Jahrhundert," in *Auf dem Grunde der Apostel und Propheten* (Th. Wurm Festschrift), now included in G. Schrenk, *Studien zu Paulus* (Zürich, 1954). Schmid and Schrenk find agreement between Acts and the message of Paul. On the other hand, cf. M. Pohlenz, "Paulus und die Stoa," *ZNW* XLII (1949), 69 ff., esp. 82 ff.; M. Albertz, *Die Botschaft des Neuen Testaments,* I/2 (Zürich, 1952), pp. 102-ff.; W. Eltester, "Gott und die Natur in der Areopagrede," *Neutestamentliche Studien für Rudolf Bultmann, Bh ZNW* XXI (Berlin, 1954), 202-27. Survey of the literature in J. Dupont, *Les problèmes du livre des Actes, Anal. Lov. Bibl. et Orient.* II, 17 (1950), 88-91; and B. Gärtner, *The Areopagus Speech and Natural Revelation, ASNU* XXI (Uppsala, 1955).
2. Cf. E. Haenchen, *Die Apostelgeschichte* (Göttingen, 1956), pp. 145, 181 n. 9.
3. The ancient author, of course, has no quotation marks at his disposal (*ibid.,* p. 147 n.4).
4. Here and in vss. 34 ff. the pattern is as follows: David did not fulfill the prophecy, hence another must be meant, hence the Scripture passage witnesses to Christ. That the proofs from Scripture presuppose the Septuagint, and that the address therefore was originally drafted in Greek was demonstrated already by Argyle in *JThS* NS IV (1953), 213-14; similarly also by J. Dupont in *Anal. Lov. Bibl. et Orient.* II, 40; cf. also H. F. D. Sparks, *JThS* NS I (1950), 16 ff.
5. This summary proof from Scripture is typically Lucan: Luke 24:25, 27, 44; also 18:31 compared with Mark 10:32; furthermore Acts 26:22; 28:23; cf. also n. 17.
6. The surmise of O. Bauernfeind, *Die Apostelgeschichte," ThHK* V (Leipzig, 1939), *ad loc.;* as well as in "Tradition und Komposition in dem Apokatastasisspruch, Apg. 3, 20 f." in *Abraham unser Vater,* O. Michel Festschrift (Leiden, 1963), pp. 13-23, that an expectation of Elijah, originally Jewish but Christianized, has here been utilized, still seems to me the most plausible explanation; for it seems very unlikely to me that Luke at this point would introduce the problem of the delayed parousia—contrary to Haenchen (*Apostelgeschichte,* pp. 174-75). The author may know the expression from liturgical materials of his church and may have added it here to the catchword "repent and turn again" (3:19) with which it was already connected, in order to make the call to repentance especially urgent.
7. That this belongs to the kerygma in Acts (whether this kerygma is old or goes back only to the author) was pointed out already by T. F. Glasson in *Hibbert Journal* LI (1952-53), 129 ff., against C. H. Dodd.
8. The same misunderstanding appears also in 3:12*b* in Jewish form, in 14:15 in Gentile form. But cf. also Acts 22:8-9.
9. Cf. Haenchen, *Apostelgeschichte,* p. 304.
10. Taken by itself, a neuter interpretation would, of course, be possible: "Lord of the universe"; but that is unlikely in the context, and the parallel in 13:26 shows that something else is meant.
11. "History of salvation" only in a limited sense. The author moves from David directly to Christ (cf. scriptural proofs 2:25 ff., 34 ff.; 13:33 ff.; also 4:25 ff.); he does not, however, immediately add the Christ-kerygma, but first mentions the Baptist as the conclusion of the pre-Christian period.
12. From the very beginning the hearers are to be distinguished from the Jerusalemites who carried out the crucifixion (also in the Gospel, without Luke explicitly saying so, any uninformed reader must surely assume that the Jews, not the Romans, crucified Jesus; cf. 23:25 with Mark 15:15). The desire to facilitate the hearer's acceptance of the message is the same in 3:17 and 17:30.

13. In the same pattern as 2:25-31, 34-36; cf. n. 4.
14. The elements combined in 2:14 are here divided between vss. 16*b* and 38*a*.
15. That it is not Paul who speaks here has been observed often; cf., e.g., the article by Philipp Vielhauer in the present volume.
16. I have collected them in *Erniedrigung und Erhöhung bei Jesus und seinen Nachfolgern* (Zürich, 1962), 2nd ed., section 4*a*; cf. a short summary in my *Lordship and Discipleship*, *SBT* XXVIII (Naperville, 1960), pp. 32-33.
17. Cf. n. 5. Where he composes freely, the author apparently likes the formula "Moses and the prophets (and the Psalms)"; in our speeches only the prophets occur (besides the explicit quotation of Moses, 3:22). Furthermore, he refers to them only before Jews, except in 10:43 where the reference occurs within a christological formulation.
18. The sharp distinction between Galileans and Jerusalemites made by Conzelmann is here confirmed. *The Theology of St. Luke*, trans. by G. Buswell (New York, 1961), pp. 34, 89.
19. Ἄνδρες Ἀθηναῖοι parallel to ἄνδρες Ἰουδαῖοι in 2:14 or ἄνδρες Ἰσραηλῖται in 3:12 (cf. 13:16); the parallel speech in 14:15 has only ἄνδρες.
20. On the difficult vs. 26 and the controversy between Dibelius, Eltester, and Pohlenz one should now consult the following passages: 1QM 10:13; 1QH 1:15-17, 24.
21. For this reason, the tension between 17:16 and 23 should indeed not be overstressed; cf. Haenchen, *Apostelgeschichte*, p. 470. Stylistically both are called for: first the pointing to a wrong attitude, then its correction in the speech which aims at keeping access for the hearers wide open.
22. This holds true whether πίστιν παρασχών (17:31) is interpreted as "giving proof"— as recently Haenchen (*Apostelgeschichte*, p. 465) held, probably correctly—or as "offering the possibility of believing"—as, e.g., A. Schlatter holds in *Der Glaube im Neuen Testament* (Stuttgart, 1927), p. 267.
23. Cf. Acts 4:2 where the resurrection of Jesus is only *one* example of the general resurrection of the dead; in 23:6; 24:15, 21; 26:8 only the general belief in a resurrection of the dead is offered for discussion by Paul!
24. This is also shown by the fact that only in the two speeches addressed to the "God-fearers" is it explicitly said, even before the christological kerygma, that this message is for *them* (10:34-36, ὁ φοβούμενος αὐτόν! 13:26-27). Cf. also Luke 1:50; 23:40; Acts 10:22.
25. After the conclusion of this essay the following literature appeared: W. Nauck, "Die Tradition und Komposition der Areopagrede," *ZThK* LIII (1956), 11 ff.; H. Hommel, "Neue Forschungen zur Areopagrede, Acta 17," *ZNW* XLVI (1955), 145 ff.; W. Eltester, "Schöpfungsoffenbarung und natürliche Theologie im frühen Christentum," *NTS* III (1957), 93-114; H. Conzelmann, "Die Rede des Paulus auf dem Areopag," *Gymnasium Helveticum* XII (1958), 18-32 (now included in this vol.); W. Barclay, "Acts II, 14-40," *ExpT* LXX (1958/9), 196-99, 243-46; U. Wilckens, *Die Missionsreden der Apostelgeschichte, WMANT* V (Neukirchen, 1963), 2nd ed.; J. Dupont, "Les discours missionnaires des Actes des apôtres," *RB* LXIX (1962), 37-60.

The Address of Paul on the Areopagus

HANS CONZELMANN

I

The speech which Luke attributes to the apostle Paul during the latter's stay in Athens (Acts 17:16 ff.) is the most momentous Christian document from the beginnings of that extraordinary confrontation between Christianity and philosophy which was destined to continue through the following centuries and to determine the entire history of the Occident.

Even before the entry of Christianity into a world of antiquity, religion was involved in a far-reaching process of transformation. Philosophy exerted its own influence and also showed a new willingness to accept religious impulses (Poseidonius). Monotheistic tendencies became more and more obvious (*De Mundo,* Seneca, Epictetus). In the long run, however, another process proved to be more important: the influx of oriental cults. They not only brought foreign ideas, the dualistic belief in a heavenly world of light and salvation where the nonworldly deity resides, but they also contributed new forms of worship and a new structure of religious community. *Congregations* of a new kind arose, ignoring ethnic, social, and sex differences, and centering in the celebration of a mystery in a room set aside for cultic worship.

It is astonishing that Luke's historical work takes no notice of these new elements, even though the young Christian movement had long been involved in intense discussions with them (we note traces of them already in the letters of Paul). Twice Luke refers to the Greek gods: in the interior of Asia Minor, Paul and Barnabas are identified with Hermes and Zeus (14:11 ff.), and in Ephesus the struggle with the devotees of Artemis takes place (19:23 ff.). Significantly, however, we learn nothing specific about this goddess, who differs so markedly from her classical form. In other words, Luke draws a *classicistic* picture of Greek culture, a picture which in *his* time was approximated only in Athens, the museum of classical culture for the Hellenistic world. He thus reduces the discussion to two points, to polytheistic ideas as such (Acts 14), and to the official form of divine *worship* through images (Acts 17), simply omitting philosophy and popular piety. A similar curtailment made for the sake of polemics can be observed in the diatribes of popular philsophy. To develop his point, Luke uses the common literary means of ancient historiography, the inserted speech. Luke is the first Christian author who consciously tries to conform to the standards of Hellenistic literature (cf. the proemium of his Gospel, Luke 1:1-4). This is symptomatic: the first Christian generation had been waiting for the approaching end of the world. Now, however, the church is compelled to come to terms with a prolonged existence in this world.

Inasmuch as Luke draws upon the form of secular historiography, we must interpret the Areopagus Speech first of all as a literary speech of Luke, not a real sermon by Paul. We take this procedure for granted in our interpretation of the speeches of Thucydides, for example. It is no less relevant for the interpretation of Acts 17. Luke makes Paul say what he considers appropriate to the situation. The question whether he still had reliable reports about what Paul had actually said is only a secondary one. In my own opinion, the speech is the free creation of the author, for it does not show the specific thoughts and ideas of Paul. Besides, the framework, clearly Luke's own, purposely corresponds to the speech. Judging from a literary standpoint, this *speech* is not an extract from a missionary address, but a purely literary creation.

II

It is of paradigmatic significance within the framework of Luke's historical work that he places this speech exactly here in Athens, the center of Greek intellectual life and piety (17:16, 18, 21-23). Since both the setting and the speech are the author's work, the details related are of no value for the reconstruction of the individual historical events.[1] The value of the description rests not in the historical worth of its details as sources of information about Paul's conduct, but in the fact that it documents for us how a Christian around A.D. 100 reacts to the *pagan* milieu and meets it from the position of his faith.

If one does not begin with the question of what happened during Paul's visit but asks what results Luke draws from it, then the description of the scene, not entirely homogeneous at first glance (vs. 17 seems to disrupt it), becomes logically consistent. It follows a well-known pattern: (a) arrival in a city, (b) first missionary attempt in the synagogue, (c) turning to the Gentiles. The topic of the scenery and the topic of the ensuing address have been adjusted to each other in such a way as to affect a contrast: κατείδωλος (vs. 16, full of idols) is picked up by δεισιδαίμων (vs. 22; religious). In vs. 16 the πνεῦμα (spirit) of Paul is provoked; but in vs. 22 the tone is friendly. That is not to be interpreted psychologically as a change of mood. In vs. 22 we simply have the stylistically proper device of *captatio benevolentiae* (currying the audience's favor). The typical motif of a *periegesis,* i.e., sightseeing (vs. 16), is picked up in vs. 23. Verse 17 at first glance looks like an interpolation but actually has a firm position in the sketched pattern (starting missionary work in the synagogue[2]). In the other places, the transition from the Jews to the Gentiles happens as a consequence of a clash. Here we find nothing like it, which must mean that Luke had no concrete reports but used his pattern somewhat mechanically.

The Athenian atmosphere is suggested by describing some of the debaters as philosophers, others as typical, curious Athenians (vss. 18, 21).[3] Of the four Athenian schools, Luke mentions the two more widely known ones: Stoics and Epicureans. Here, too, he does not necessarily have any concrete reports. He takes no account whatsoever of the particular teachings of either. The memory of Socrates is, of course, evoked by the location of the discussion, the Agora (and with the catchword διαλέγεσθαι, carry on a dialogue).

The conjecture of the listeners that Paul must be ξένων δαιμονίων καταγγελεύς (a preacher of foreign divinities) contains a significant foreshadowing of the following address. Later Paul will show that he is not preaching a *foreign* god. Again one is reminded of the story of Socrates.[4] However, this does not mean, as some commentators claim, that the Areopagus, to which Paul is led, is the *court* rather than the well-known historical location, Mars' Hill; that ἐπιλαμβάνεσθαι (to take hold of) in vs. 19 means to arrest, and that the events starting with vs. 19 are to be interpreted as a court trial rather than as a philosophical discussion. The literary style of Luke rules that out: wherever he reports a trial he is absolutely unambiguous. Here, however, he barely hints at associations in order to create a stage setting, an atmosphere for the dispute. The question, therefore, is not whether Mars' Hill was a location suitable for the discussion. Luke chooses the place not from his own geographical knowledge, but because of its historical reputation. The somewhat playful shift from ξένος (foreign) to καινός (new), and from ξένος to ξενίζειν (to be strange) is also done for the sake of atmosphere. It prepares the final scene (vss. 32 ff.) and indicates in advance the impression which the content of Christian teaching is to make upon the Greeks. The entire address presses toward the focal point of its theme, formulated as: *Jesus and Anastasis.*[5]

III. The Address

The speech starts with the *captatio benevolentiae* (vs. 22). How this tactful beginning is to be understood has already been indicated in vs. 16. Of course, δεισιδαίμων here does not mean *superstitious* ('Theophrastus' character of δεισιδαιμονία!), but rather *devout*. The Christian reader of course hears the irony in it. Verse 23 brings the inner connection between the address and the setting, a firm stylistic trademark of Lucan speeches. Not historical memory but a literary device takes the inscription on an Athenian altar, *to unknown gods,* well known to travelers through travel guides, and changes it into the singular and then uses this as a point of departure for Christian ideas.[6] Surely Paul (!) cannot have spoken *this way,* nor can the Christian missionary begin his preaching in this way everywhere. It can only be the work of an author developing his paradigmatic discussion.

It is significant that Luke, in spite of his philosophical audience, does not start out from the monotheistic elements of contemporary philosophy (the Stoics), but from a subject of popular religion. And the transition from this to his own concern is not made by rational argumentation, but by an abrupt: τοῦτο ἐγὼ καταγγέλλω ὑμῖν (this I proclaim to you).

The impression of abruptness becomes even stronger when one considers how the word family of ἀγγέλλειν was used in early Christianity. At the beginning the Christians did not emerge as a new religious community within Judaism. They continued to consider themselves Jews. They did not teach a new idea about God but, within the frame of the old religion, *proclaimed a new message:* what Israel's God of old has done in these days. He has sent the promised Messiah, Jesus, whom he raised after his death. This, this only, is the new topic that is proclaimed, the εὐαγγέλιον. The situation changes when polytheists are being addressed: now the doctrine of God, which can be assumed to be known among Jews, must become the explicit content of instruction. The confession that Jesus is the Messiah is enlarged by the further article of faith: there is *one* God. But, says the author, this one God is not new or foreign even to the Greeks; he has always manifested himself and was close to them, but they did not know him.

With Luke, this point of contact does not imply a degree of compromise between the old and the new religion (such as the Stoics were prepared to make and indeed did make). On the contrary, it means that monotheistic thinking has carried through resolutely. A *new* God would only be another *relative* one, an idea with reference to the old gods. These, however, are completely ignored; they are not even mentioned polemically. By tacit implication the claim is made: you, too, had in truth always but one God, the only real one.

After these preliminaries the main body of the address unfolds. The *first part* consists of vss. 24-26.

Deliberately the nature of this God is defined not by Greek (ontological) categories but by a biblical quotation.[7] To be sure, the author takes advantage of a convergence between the Bible and Hellenism: ποιεῖν (to make) can be used by both Jew and Greek about God's creative work. *De Mundo* speaks of *Heaven and Earth,* while, on the other hand, κόσμος (vs. 24) is not a biblical expression (except when used critically in speaking of the *world* or of *this world;* however, Hellenistic Judaism, for instance Philo, had already adopted the term long ago). This confronts us with one of the most difficult problems of the address: How did the Greek ideas which echo through it reach the author? Directly from popular philosophy (diatribe), or circuitously through Hellenistic Judaism with its struggle against polytheism and idolatry? After the *biblical* coloring of vss. 24-25, Stoic color dominates vss. 26-28. But the same motifs without exception can be found within Hellenistic Judaism (including the quotation of Aratus in vs. 28!).[8]

The train of thought is this: The assertion that God is the creator is immediately given a critical turn: he needs nothing. That is a philosophical truism which was to spread widely through both Judaism and Christianity.[9] He is not the receiver but the giver, a contrasting statement that is also found elsewhere.[10] The specific deduction made from this is fundamental criticism of the building of temples, a criticism known among Stoics since Zeno (cf. Seneca).[11] However, at this point there is a clear difference: Judaism uses the idea that God needs nothing precisely in order to justify the erection of the Jewish temple.[12]

Verse 26 poses the most difficult problem of detailed interpretation. Two problems intersect:

(a) How is the following to be understood? Does ἐποίησεν . . . κατοικεῖν mean *He caused to live* (Pohlenz, Eltester),[13] or: *He made from one [Adam] every nation of men?* To prove his point, Pohlenz points to the syntactical construction: if ποιεῖν were to mean "make," "create," two infinitives of purpose would stand asyndetically side by side (κατοικεῖν and ζητεῖν, to dwell and to seek). The result would be the nonsensical statement: God has created men to live and to seek; when in reality he created them to seek, and for that reason *made them to dwell.* One must agree with Pohlenz that the construction is harsh if ποιεῖν is taken to mean "create." And yet, that is what it must mean, on account of vs. 24 and the allusion to Adam (ἐξ ἑνός).

(b). A further controversy centers around the meaning of καιροί (periods) and ὁροθεσίαι (boundaries). Pohlenz takes καιροί to be the historical epochs in which Jewish historiography divides the course of world history (Daniel). Correspondingly, ὁροθεσίαι means the boundaries of the habitations of the various peoples. ἐξ ἑνός—πᾶν ἔθνος ἀνθρώπων (from one—every nation of men) points to the differentiation of nations within originally undivided mankind (Poseidonius systematically builds upon this idea). The author, Pohlenz thinks, had in mind the familiar proof of the existence of God *e consensu gentium* in which this differentiation plays its role. Pohlenz can further point to the related verse Acts 14:16 (where in place of πᾶν ἔθος ἀνθρώπων, every nation of men, we read πάντα τὰ ἔθνη, all the nations).

But in the end the text itself revolts against such an interpretation: as if God had implanted the searching in all peoples, *in spite of* (!) their ethnic differentiation. But the text does not say that! The expression πᾶν ἔθνος ἀνθρώπων means unity, not diversity (the author therefore emphatically says: ἐξ ἑνός, alluding to the biblical story of creation).

Faced with this difficulty, Dibelius [14] suggests a different interpretation, calling it a *philosophical* one over against the *historical* one of Pohlenz. According to Dibelius periods and boundaries of peoples are no proof for the existence of God. But the *periods* and *boundaries* of *nature,* its order and rhythm, can well be considered such. καιροί, then, are the *seasons.* Indeed, *seasons* are usually ὧραι, though Philo makes no clear distinction between the two words; [15] while Pohlenz, appeals to Acts 14:16, the very next verse

(14:17) supports Dibelius. Thus linguistically, the understanding of καιροί as seasons is a possibility. The "philosophical" interpretation runs into greater difficulties, however, with the concept of *boundaries*. Dibelius understands them to be the boundaries of the inhabitable surface of the earth and has the author allude to the doctrine of the five *zones,* only two of which are inhabitable.

But here Pohlenz has, in my opinion, a decisive argument: It would indeed be a strange proof of God's universal care that he made three fifths of the earth uninhabitable. Besides, such an interpretation contradicts the text itself which states: ἐπὶ παντὸς προσώπου τῆς γῆς (on all the face of the earth), and: πᾶν ἔθνος, διδοὺς τὰ πάντα (he gives to all men . . . everything).

A new proposal comes from Eltester [16] in two articles. Substantially he agrees with the philosophy-of-nature interpretation but modifies the concept of *boundaries* in such a way as to escape the difficulties which Dibelius faced: in Jewish hymns which praise the creation, God is extolled for having shielded the habitation of men, the firm land, against the sea. *This* is the boundary which is meant.

But does this sharp alternative of natural or historical boundaries not perhaps introduce a problem of which the author was quite unaware? Eltester's interpretation has met with wide approval. But the closest contemporary documents (from the tradition of the Poseidonian view of history and from Hellenistic Judaism) do not bear it out. And the new texts from the Dead Sea show that in contemporary Judaism one could naïvely place historical and natural periods and boundaries side by side.[17] Moreover the author's concern is obviously not at all a positive development of a proof for the existence of God. His thesis is: men's destiny is to seek God; about their *finding* him he speaks somewhat skeptically:[18] vs. 27 εἰ ἄρα γε (in the hope that) with an optative (rare in the New Testament!). And this reservation concerning what men are able to achieve is not canceled by the positive statement: "Yet he is not far from each one of us," though it is brought to a certain dialectical suspension. That brings us to the second part of the address.

Dio Chrysostom [19] has a surprizing parallel to καί γε οὐ μακράν (yet not far); R. Reitzenstein even reckons with a common source. For this, however, the similarity is not great enough, especially since the term ὀυ μακράν in a similar context also occurs elsewhere. Still, the proximity to Greek popular philosophy is undeniable.[20] It becomes even closer in vs. 28, where we find statements which no longer have any parallels in the New Testament. To be sure, the triad Ζῶμεν—κινούμεθα—ἐσμέν (live—move—are) is not elsewhere documented word for word; it may be the author's own formulation. But the material has its origin in the *Weltanschauung* of philosophy.[21] We no longer hear of the *proximity* of God, but of the God-*relatedness* of man (again, cf. Dio Chrysostom) documented by a quotation—not from the Bible which contains nothing like it, but from the *Phainomena* by the Stoic Aratus.[22]

The problem of this passage is not simply that it is reminiscent of various philosophical ideas, but the fact that the author evidently took over an entire philosophical complex of ideas which *in itself* is incompatible with the biblical idea of creation. But to what extent was the author aware of the original pantheistic sense of these words, and to what extent did he simply read into them his own biblically founded monotheism? This question becomes important when we realize how the Jewish author Aristobulus long ago made use of the same Aratus quotation for the sake of belief in the biblical story of creation.[23]

But let us quickly follow the address to its conclusion. Verse 29 again draws a practical conclusion, this time against *images,* as in vss. 24-25 against *temples.* There, Jewish parallels were lacking, understandably, since the Jews themselves had a temple, at least until A.D. 70; now, understandably, in arguing against images, the parallels abound, for the rejection of idols is a fundamental commandment of Jewish religion (whence it was taken over by Christianity, where it repeatedly led to serious trouble).

But is this argument logical? We are related to God and for that reason must make no images of the Divine. Why not? Would not the opposite conclusion be at least as natural? Apparently we have two conflicting ideas: (a) the genuinely Jewish one that the Creator must not be portrayed by created things; (b) the Greek philosophical critique of images according to which living beings can be represented only by living beings. We are very close to an idea in which both reflections might be combined: man himself is the image of God. However, such a thought is not articulated.

And finally, in the third part of the address, vss. 30-31, we find a genuinely Christian statement. Its content unfolds with the same brevity as before: *Jesus and the resurrection,* judgment on the individual and the resultant warning: the need for *repentance.* The philosophical elements are gone. The world is regarded no longer with respect to its *being,* but to its *end.* The course of world history is now divided in two periods: *before* and *after* the raising of Jesus. Man is regarded solely from the viewpoint of eternal salvation, with its corollary of possible eternal damnation. And this salvation hinges upon the proclamation of *this* fact, the resurrection of Jesus. There is nothing here of the Greek idea of immortality of the soul (the address, in agreement with the entire New Testament, knows no concept of the soul in the Greek sense); rather, the dominant idea is the resurrection of the dead and the salvation of the righteous at the time of the final judgment over which this very Risen One will preside. At vss. 32-33 the scene comes to an abrupt end with the point that such teachings must sound strange to Greek ears.

IV. Conclusions?

We have observed both a Jewish and a Greek component. We have considered the possibility that the philosophical elements could have been mediated through Judaism and thereby already undergone a modification in the direction of the biblical conception of God, at least in the understanding of the author. We have further noticed the specifically Christian conclusion. How are these elements related?

The philosophical element dominates the center of the composition, which at first glance also seems to be its *content-core:* after the *nature* of God has been established (in biblical terms), the crucial point remains the relation of man to God and his religious potentialities. That is the theme of the central part. It is therefore amazing that Eduard Norden in his *Agnostos Theos*—the pioneer work of modern investigation of this address—formulated the matter: the Jewish-Christian *principal* motif—the Stoic *accompanying* motif. Should it not be turned around? Dibelius argued for doing so.

Norden's work has made it clear that the problem cannot be solved by considering the various motifs in isolation. The *structure* of the address as a whole must be regarded. Norden puts it into the category of a widespread type of religious propaganda literature found in both Jewish and pagan writings. Christianity took it over and used it not only in the book of Acts.[24] Norden proposes a further step: the address on the Areopagus is a literary imitation of a speech by Apollonius of Tyana; originating in the second century A.D., it was interpolated into the book of Acts. This hypothesis collapses because it fails to see that the address clearly shows Lucan characteristics and cannot be separated from the typically Lucan scenery. But, positively, Norden has proved its relation not only to non-Christian motifs but to entire complexes of motifs. He has *not* explained, however, the thoroughgoing reduction in which they are presented here. The typical catchwords of analogous Jewish missionary literature are missing, both the negative ones—the emphasis upon ἄγνοια as guilt, and upon the pagán gods as "nothing," μάταιοι, dead,—and the positive ones, the central formula εἷς θεός (one God), the predicates that God is the "true," the "living" God. Of course, one can point out that the intent of the speech was to find a point of contact with Greek thinking, hence the polemic is restrained. But that is not yet the whole explanation. The restraint has a chiefly theological background. Abstract Jewish monotheism is modified by the introduction of the new entity, "Jesus," in the definition of man's relation to God. From this point of view a new kind of discussion becomes systematically possible.

Comparison with other missionary literature still leaves unexplained the specific tripartite structure: (1) God and world (creation and preservation); (2) God and man (proximity); (3) God and the individual (resurrection and judgment).

To be sure, a recent article [25] did point out an analogous three-way division within Jewish literature, the scheme of *creatio–conservatio–salvatio*. Nowhere, however, do we have a passage where this pattern provides the structure. Also, the analogy breaks down at the decisive point, where the middle part deals with a twofold anthropological aspect: the man-God relationship first being determined from above, as proximity; then correspondingly from below, as being "within God," as kinship. This is a real innovation: to place this anthropological topic in the center, parenthetically between two other topics. The innovation, however, does not consist in the mere fact that the anthropological side of man's relationship to God is treated as a subject in itself. The Stoics did that much more explicitly, through detailed cosmological and psychological analyses. And, *mutatis mutandis,* so did the Jews, both Philo and Aristobulus. We have only a few fragments of Aristobulus' writings; these, however, are more closely related to the address on the Areopagus than any other Jewish text. The philosophers, too, worked out a strict pattern of precisely this two-way view from above and from below, apparently in the tradition of Poseidonius. The most important documents for it are the second book of Cicero's *De Natura Deorum;* the *Somnium Scipionis* in his *De Republica;* and the anonymous work *De*

Mundo. In this pattern a certain ontological understanding has found classical expression. It presupposes that the world is accessible to him who seeks access (a glance at Plato shows how little this presupposition was taken for granted even in Greek philosophy). Starting from this presupposition, it makes no difference whether one begins from above, with Zeus, with the whole cosmos, or from below, with man who understands it. All that matters is that both ways of viewing are oriented to each other from inner necessity: that cosmos and man correspond. Potential accessibility has become part of the *concept* "cosmos."

But now there is no way at all from this cosmoslogic-anthropologic correspondence to the three-way division of our address. The way its central part is bracketed has no analogy.

The speech's peculiar pattern of presentation emerges clearly, it seems to me, when one rids oneself of the still subconsciously present notion that we are dealing with a speech, and then analyzes the "speech" as a purely literary product. Luke is neither offering an excerpt of a real address, wherever delivered, nor does he want to sketch a model sermon for handy use by a missionary. Rather, as a historian he composes a unique situation which is of permanent importance just because of its uniqueness (cf. what Hellenistic historians say about the pedagogical value of history, e.g., Diodorus Siculus). This address was not meant to be a general pattern to be repeated everywhere. On the contrary, Luke intends to show how this unique Paul *at that one time* dealt with the philosophers in Athens in a unique discussion. If the philosophers were not even converted by a sermon of Paul, they will certainly not be converted today. Thus the Christians find their own experience substantiated: these circles do not respond to Christian missions even "today"; the truth of the faith is established in spite of its being rejected by the wise. And now we understand why Luke used as his point of departure not philosophical monotheism but popular religion.

Attention to the specifically literary pattern of presentation, then, seems to reveal one of its principles. Let us recall once more the original form of the Christian confession of faith. Here faith is not an inward mood; it has a clear-cut dogmatic content: Jesus is the Son of God, and God raised Jesus from the dead. Moreover, this one complex content is understood not as partial truth, as *one* ingredient of *faith,* but as *the* faith, *fides salvifica* (the faith which saves; cf. Rom. 10:9). We have already seen that within the Jewish sphere such a statement about Jesus suffices, since belief in the *one*

God, the Creator, can be taken for granted; but that within the polytheistic sphere an explicit statement about God becomes necessary. Consequently the basic form of the confession becomes; εἷς θεός—εἷς κύριος (one God—one Lord; I Cor. 8:6). This is the pattern which then is filled in with concrete details about the work of creation and the work of salvation. This is the confession which provides the first and the third parts of the address and constitutes the brackets around the central part which is homogeneous in itself. Every Christian reader at that time would have recognized this immediately. The central part thus becomes the place where man is called upon to meet the proclaimed message, while the first part shows him his past and present (creation, providence), and the third part unveils his future and thereby the *demand* of the present (repentance). Only the first and third parts have really didactic content, and both are related to biblical passages. It is the achievement of the author to have given the confession of faith a literary form. That he can be credited with such deliberate labor is shown by the composition of his Gospel, where he also works with a tripartite structure—in this case of the entire book. Since for his Gospel we know his sources to a large extent, we are able to follow his technique of composition and can see that it is precisely the tripartite disposition which is his own work.

By the literary application of current motifs within the framework of a given pattern of belief, the meaning of the various motifs themselves undergoes a change. Accessibility of the world in the philosophical gnostic sense is replaced by access to the relation with God through μετάνοια (repentance), knowledge of God in the sense of πίστις (faith). Luke evidently is fully aware of this change. We cannot miss the conscious harshness with which he stresses the strangeness of the doctrine of the resurrection at the end.

Above all, the change in the understanding of God and the world becomes apparent in the *understanding of history*. Ever since Poseidonius, history had been included as part of world analysis (for instance as an aspect of the theme of *origin and degeneration*). Such an analysis of history is entirely foreign to Luke. He does not say that man formerly possessed a knowledge of God and later lost it, as Stoic theory would have had it. Rather, Luke asserts that such a knowledge was always possible but was never realized.

Beside this Stoic understanding of history, the milieu of early Christianity knew an entirely different one expressed in Jewish apocalyptic: the course of the world is determined by uniqueness, by a beginning and an end (ἀρχή and τέλος). The end is not the result of a development but a direct act of God, who makes the world come to an end and creates a wondrous new world for the elect. Early Christianity took over the basic outline of this apocalyptic world view. But Luke reduced the Jewish view just as he did the Greek one: He abandoned the problem which to the apocalyptist is most important: how to divide universal history into epochs and to deduce from them the present stage in regard to the end of the world. All that remains is the sheer structure: beginning—end, and in between a single insertion which determines the situation of man in the world: the resurrection of Jesus, which introduces a historical epoch fundamentally new compared with the former one. This new epoch, however, is not characterized by factors of universal history, but exclusively through the continuing proclamation of the authenticated gospel, which offers the possibility of salvation. But that means that salvation is not gained by developing the possibilities peculiar to man. Salvation rests upon the decree of the Judge of the universe. And again: since proclaiming the gospel takes place only after the resurrection of Jesus, the hitherto existing ignorance (ἄγνοια) of man is relatively excusable—up to the present moment, the moment when Jesus is proclaimed. For *now* the possibility of faith has been irrevocably *offered,* but faith is thereby also *demanded.* Refusal means ultimate perdition. ἀκούσαντες δὲ ἀνάστασιν νεκρῶν, οἱ μὲν ἐχλεύαζον, οἱ δὲ εἶπαν, ἀκουσόμεθά σου περὶ τούτου καὶ πάλιν. (When they heard of the resurrection of the dead, some mocked; but others said, "We will hear you again about this." Acts 17:32.)[26]

NOTES

1. Whether Luke used a written source for the stage setting is a matter of dispute. Verse 18 and vss. 19-20 sound like duplicates.
2. Luke has in mind a theological conception of the relationship between the church and the people of Israel, cf. Acts 13:46.
3. Cicero, *De Fin.* V, 5: "Quamquam id quidem infinitum est in hac urbe: quacumque enim ingredimur, in aliqua historia vestigium ponimus," cf. Strabo IX, 1, 16; Pausanias I, 17, 7. Athenian piety: Josephus *contra Apionem* II, 130: τοὺς δὲ εὐσεβεστάτους τῶν Ἑλλήνων πάντες λέγουσιν. Sophocles, *Oedip. Col.* 260. Multitude of Statues: Livy XLV, 27.
4. Xenophon, *Mem.* I, 1, 1: ἀδικεῖ Σωκράτης οὓς μὲν ἡ πόλις νομίζει θεοὺς οὐ νομίζων, ἕτερα δὲ καινὰ δαιμόνια εἰσφέρων.
5. Is Luke being facetious again? Does he make the audience misunderstand Paul as if he

229

were bringing a new pair of oriental divinities, as if Anastasis were (mis)understood as a proper name?

6. Pausanias I, 1, 4: βωμοὶ θεῶν τε ὀνομαζομένων ἀγνώστων καὶ ἡρώων καὶ παίδων τῶν θησέως καὶ φαλήρου. Philostratus, *Vita Apoll.* VI, 3, 5: σωφρονέστερον γὰρ τὸ περὶ πάντων θεῶν εὖ λέγειν, καὶ ταῦτα ᾿Αθήνησι οὗ καὶ ἀγνώστων γαιμόνων βωμοὶ ὕδρυνται. Hieronymus, *Ad Titum* I, 12: "Inscriptio autem arae non ita erat, ut Paulus asseruit, 'ignoto deo,' sed, 'Diis Asiae et Europae et Africae, diis ignotis et peregrinis.' "

7. Isa. 42:5; cf. Gen. 2:7; II Macc. 7:23.

8. Aristobulus frg. 4 in Eusebius *Praep. Evang.* XIII, 12, 3 ff. II, 191 ff. Mras.).

9. Xenophon, *Mem.* I, 4, 10. Seneca, *Ep.* XCV, 47: "Non quaerit ministros deus, quidni? Ipse humano generi ministrat, ubique et omnibus praesto est." Ps-Apul. *Asclepius* XLI: "nihil enim deest ei qui ipse est omnia aut in eo sunt omnia."

10. *Corp. Herm.* II, 16: ὁ οὖν θεὸς πάντα δίδωσι καὶ οὐδὲν λαμβάνει; cf. *Corp. Herm.* V, 10.

11. Clem. Alex. *Strom.* V, 76, 1: ῎Ετι δόγμα Ζήνωνός ἐστιν ἱερὰ θεῶν μὴ οἰκοδομεῖν, ἱερὸν γὰρ μὴ πολλοῦ ἄξιον καὶ ἅγιον οὐκ ἔστιν. Seneca in *Lact. Divin. Inst.* VI. 25: "Non templa illi [Deo] congestis in altitudinem saxis extruenda sunt: in suo cuique consecrandus est pectore."

12. II Macc. 14:35: σὺ κύριε ὅλων ἀπροσδεὴς ὑπάρχων ηὐδόκησας ναὸν τῆς σῆς σκηνώσεως ἐν ἡμῖν γενέσθαι.

13. Max Pohlenz, "Paulus und die Stoa," *ZNW* XLII (1949), 69 ff.; W. Eltester, "Gott und die Natur in der Areopagrede," in *Neutestamentliche Studien für R. Bultmann* Bh *ZNW* XXI Berlin, 1954), pp. 202 ff.; idem, "Schöpfungsoffenbarung und natürliche Theologie im frühen Christentum," in *NTS* III (1957), 93 ff.

14. Martin Dibelius, "Paulus auf dem Aropag," *SBHA* (1939); also in *Studies in the Acts of the Apostles* (London, 1956).

15. Philo, *Spec-Leg.* III, 56, F.; *Opif. Mundi* LIX.

16. Cf. n. 13.

17. F. Mussner, *BZ* NF I (1957), 125 ff.

18. Cf. Philo, *Spec. Leg.* I, 36.

19. Dio Chrys. XII, 28: ἅτε γὰρ οὐ μακρὰν οὐδ᾿ ἔξω τοῦ θείου διῳκισμένοι καθ᾿ αὑτούς, ἀλλὰ ἐν αὐτῷ μέσῳ πεφυκότες, μᾶλλον δὲ συμπεφυκότες ἐκείνῳ καὶ προσεχομένοι πάντα τρόπον, οὐκ ἐδύναντο μέχρι πλείονος ἀσύνετοι μένειν.

20. Josephus, *Ant.* VIII, 108: ὅτι πάρει καὶ μακρὰν οὐκ ἀφέστηκας. Seneca, *Ep.* XLI, 1: "Prope est a te deus, tecum est, intus est."

21. Cf. the stages of existence according to Poseidonius in Cicero, *De Natura Deorum* II, 12-13, 33-34. (somatic-psychic-noetic). Already Plato, *Tim.* 37 c.

22. Similarly Cleanthes (Hymn to Zeus, *Stoic. Vet. Fragm.* I, No. 537).

23. Cf. n. 8. Aristobulus makes direct use of Aratus for his interpretation of the biblical narrative and understands the pantheistic statement as referring simply to the omnipresence and universal rule of the Creator. If Hellenistic Judaism (or Jewish Christianity) stands as a mediator between the *Stoics* and Luke, then he already found the Stoic ideas with a monotheistic modification.

24. *Odes of Solomon* 33; *Corp Herm.* I, 27-28, VII, 1-2, etc.

25. W. Nauck, "Die Tradition und Komposition der Areopagrede," *ZThK* LIII (1956), 11 ff.

26. Of more recent literature the following must be mentioned: H. Hommel, "Neue Forschungen zur Areopagrede, Acta 17," *ZNW* XLVI (1955), 145 ff. Most detailed discussion: B. Gärtner, *The Areopagus Speech and Natural Revelation*, *ASNU* XXI (Uppsala, 1955). A most important recent commentary on Acts: E. Haenchen, *Die Apostelgeschichte*, Meyer Series, 13th ed. (1961). More literature is mentioned in H. Conzelmann, *Die Apostelgeschichte*, *HNT* VII (Tübingen, 1963), pp. 102 ff.

Part III

Jewish Christianity in Acts in Light of the Qumran Scrolls*

JOSEPH A. FITZMYER, S.J.

It is by now a well-worn platitude to say that the Qumran Scrolls have shed new light on Christian origins. Yet in a volume such as this, dealing with studies in Luke-Acts and dedicated to Professor Paul Schubert, who has shown a long and sustained interest in such studies, there is room for a reassessment of the relationship between Qumran and the early church. The Qumran texts have brought to light many new details of Palestinian Judaism in the period in which Christianity emerged. They have been studied in detail by many scholars and from different points of view. It is not out of place, then, to review here the significance of these new finds for first-century Jewish Christianity as it is depicted in the Acts of the Apostles.

The Qumran literature comes from a group of Jews whose principal community center existed on the northwest shore of the Dead Sea roughly between 150 B.C. and A.D. 70. These dates are supported both archaeological and paleographical evidence.[1] The sect, whose beliefs and way of life are made known to us in this literature, is revealed to be a community that is wholly Jewish, dedicated to the study and observance of the Torah, yet living a communal, religious, and ascetic mode of life for a considerable period before the emergence of Christianity. The data from these scrolls have made the majority of the scholars who have studied them identify the Qumran sect with the Essenes, even though some of the new data is not

---

* The sigla used in designating the Manuscripts may be found in D. Barthélemy, O. P.; J. T. Milik, et al.: *Qumran Cave I; Discoveries in the Judaean Desert*, Vol. I (Oxford, 1955), pp. 46-48; or a shorter list in: F. M. Cross, *The Ancient Library of Qumran* (London, 1958), pp. xv-xvi.

always perfectly reconcilable with what was previously known about the Essenes from the classical sources of Philo, Josephus, Pliny the Elder, Hippolytus, and Dio Chrysostom.[2] For our part, this identification is acceptable, and we shall not be concerned with any further attempt to establish it. We do admit, however, especially with J. T. Milik, traces of a Pharisaic influence on the group.[3] But there seems to be little reason to connect them in any way with the Sadducees,[4] the Zealots,[5] or the Ebionites.[6] It is also necessary to distinguish at times between the Essenes of Qumran—of the "motherhouse," as it were—and those of the "camps" in the land of Damascus. For in some details the Essene mode of life differed in these two situations.

The other term of our comparison is Jewish Christianity, precisely as it is presented in the Acts of the Apostles. The influence of the Essenes on the Christian church has been detected in other writings, and a consideration of these would give a more complete picture. But we are interested only in trying to assess the extent to which the picture of Jewish Christianity as it is painted in Acts has been illumined by what we know of the Qumran sect and its literature.

If a plausible case has been made for some contact between John the Baptist and the Qumran sect,[7] the extent to which similar contact can be shown between Jesus of Nazareth and this group is far less definable. With the data available at present it is almost impossible to determine it. But in any case it is widely admitted that some influence was exerted by the Qumran Essenes on the early church, at least as it is depicted in the writings of Paul, Matthew, and John.[8] One may debate whether this contact is direct or indirect, and whether it was exerted on the early Palestinian church or only the New Testament authors. But the data in the Qumran texts provide at least an intelligible Palestinian matrix for many of the practices and tenets of the early church. Our discussion then is an attempt to assess the areas of influence and contact between the Essenes and the Jewish Christian church in Acts.

Jewish Christianity in Acts

Before attempting to compare the pertinent material, let us summarize briefly the picture of the Jewish Christian church in Acts. When we open the book of Acts, we are immediately introduced to a group of disciples of Jesus of Nazareth who are at least vaguely aware of their identity as a group. They may be addressed simply as "men of Galilee" (1:11), but they are also "chosen apostles" (1:2). Scarcely any indication is given of their previous backgrounds, but they seem to have been part of the *'am hā-'āreṣ*. This is at least suggested by the conduct of Peter and John (8:14-25; 9:43; 11:2-3) who were not concerned with Pharisaic prescriptions and distinctions. Some of the eleven bear Greek names, and yet they are Palestinian Jews who have banded together, united by a belief in Jesus, "a man certified by God with mighty works and wonders" (2:22), whom "God raised" from the dead (2:32). These disciples are his "witnesses" (1:8), and under the inspiration of God's Spirit they proclaim him and his message to "all the house of Israel": God has made this Jesus "both Lord and Messiah" (2:36). Such a christological belief sets them apart from the rest of the "house of Israel" and makes them conscious of their Jewish *Christian* character.

But from the very beginning of the story in Acts this Christian group is marked as *Jewish* in its origins and background. Before the event of Pentecost they are depicted as men looking to this Lord and Messiah as the one who would "restore the kingdom of Israel" (1:6). The "men of Galilee" go up to the temple daily (2:46; 3:1, 11); they celebrate the festival of Weeks (2:1); they observe the sabbath (1:12). One of their leaders, James, lends his support to the Jerusalem temple for a considerable time (21:8-26). The God whom they continue to worship is "the God of Abraham, and of Isaac, and of Jacob, the God of our fathers" (3:13). In time "a great number of the priests embraced the faith" (6:7), obviously a reference to members of Jewish priestly families. A nucleus of twelve—a number inspired by the twelve tribes of Israel—symbolizes the fact that the group is the New Israel.

These Jewish Christians carry their belief in Jesus of Nazareth as the Lord and Messiah from Jerusalem to Judea, Samaria, and Galilee (1:4, 8; 8:1; 9:31; cf. Luke 24:47). Gradually their numbers increase; the initial 120 members of the Pentecostal assembly in Jerusalem become three thousand (2:41), then five thousand (4:4). The number steadily grows (6:7), until a summary acknowledges, just before the message spreads to Gentile areas, that the "church throughout all Judea, Galilee and Samaria enjoyed peace and was being built up" (9:31). During all this growth the Christian group is marked off from the Jewish people as such. "None of the rest of the people dared to join them, but they held them in great esteem" (5:13). While one cannot apodictically exclude from the Palestinian church at this time converts from paganism, the picture in Acts 1–9 is certainly that of a predominantly Jewish Christian church.

Acts vaguely suggests that the Christian group looked on itself as the New Israel; this seems at least implied in the disciples' question about the restoration of the kingdom to Israel (1:6) and in the need felt to reconstitute the twelve (1:15-26). The corporate character of the Jewish Christians is formulated for the first time in the word κοινωνία (2:42).[9] It is noteworthy that before the account mentions Saul and his career, there is scarcely any attempt to depict the communiy as ἐκκλησία. The sole exception to this is the summary statement at the end of the story of Ananias and Sapphira (5:11).[10] Once the career of Saul is begun, however, then the Christian community is referred to as ἐκκλησία (8:1, 3; 9:31; 11:22 ["the church in Jerusalem"], 26; 12:1, 5; 13:1; etc.). Moreover, in none of his statements in Acts about his early persecution of the young church does Paul speak of ἐκκλησία. The persecuted "Jesus" is identified in 9:2-5 with "some belonging to the Way"; in 22:4 he says, "I persecuted this Way to the death"; and in 26:9, 15 "Jesus" is identified with "many of the saints." By the same token, it is only with the beginning of the story of Saul that we meet the expression, "the Way" (9:2; cf. 19:9, 23; 22:4; 24:14, 22), as a designation of the Christian movement. Finally, we eventually see the "the Way" referred to as a "sect" (αἵρεσις, 24:14).[11] These details seem to indicate the rather nebulous awareness which the early Jewish Christian church had at first of its corporate character.

On the other hand, it is an awareness that grows as the account in Acts advances. Even though the account was written at a later date and from a standpoint which was considerably developed, nevertheless these expressions seem to reflect an early Jewish Christian community gradually becoming consciously structured in its corporate entity. The awareness of itself as ἐκκλησία comes with persecution and missionary effort, both of which are interrelated in the account in Acts.

Though indications are given of a small nucleus in the early community which has authority and shapes the group, nevertheless they are not such as to reveal the community as a well-defined organization. There are the "chosen apostles" (1:2), the small band of the "eleven" (1:26; 2:14) or the "twelve" (6:2), which plays the important role of "witnesses to his resurrection." It is the "teaching of the apostles" (2:42) which shapes the community. Singled out as exercising authority, however, are Peter (1:15;

2:14; 15:7) and James. The latter is recognized by Peter (12:17) and greeted officially by Paul (21:18); he also settles a disputed question for the local churches (15:13). But there is also mention of "the apostles and the elders" (15:2, 4, 6, 22, 23; 16:4; cf. 21:18), whose advice and decision are sought. Eventually the community appoints seven "assistants" to care for its dole.

The picture of the life of the early Jewish Christian community is painted in idyllic colors. It is a fervent community, practicing a communal form of life; it is devoted "to the teaching of the apostles, to a community-spirit, to the breaking of bread, and to prayers" (2:42). "All who believed shared everything in common; they would sell their property and belongings and divide all according to each one's need" (2:44; cf. 2:46). "One heart and soul animated the company of those who believed, and no one would say that he possessed anything of his own" (4:32).

The first suggestion of some diversity in the Palestinian church is met in 6:1, where the "Hellenists" murmured against the "Hebrews" because their widows were neglected in the daily distribution. Ἑλληνισταί is the name for certain members of the Christian community. But 9:29 suggests that the name had already been in use among Palestinian Jews and was merely taken over by Christians to designate converts from such a distinctive group.[12] Its meaning among the Jews is a matter of debate. Since the time of John Chrysostom the "Hellenists" have been understood as "Greek-speaking Jews."[13] Their presence in the Palestinian church would be understandable in the light of Acts 2:5, 9-10. They had come from the diaspora and had taken up residence in Jerusalem. This meaning, however, has been questioned because Paul was such a diaspora Jew and calls himself Ἑβραῖος (Phil. 3:5; II Cor. 11:22); apparently he did not regard himself as a "Hellenist." Some years ago H. J. Cadbury argued that Ἑλληνιστής meant no more than Ἕλλην since it was a derivative of ἑλληνίζω, which means "to live as a Greek," not "to speak Greek." For him "Hellenist" was a title for Gentile members of the Palestinian church.[14] His explanation, however, has not been widely accepted; many commentators still prefer Chrysostom's explanation, especially since the context of Acts 6 seems to demand that the "Hellenists" were Jewish Christians of some sort. This is likewise the view of C. F. D. Moule, who recently made the attractive suggestion that Ἑλληνισταί means "Jews who spoke *only* Greek," while Ἑβραῖοι means "Jews who, while able to speak Greek, knew a Semitic language *also*."[15] This explanation seems suitable. But it should also be recalled that such a linguistic difference would also bring with it a difference in outlook and attitude. More than likely the influence of Hellenism would be greater among the "Hellenists" than among the "Hebrews." But in either case it is a question of degree, since this explanation allows the Hellenists to be Jews, as the context apparently demands.[16]

That the Hellenists were Jews of some sort is likewise recognized by O. Cullmann, who has tried to identify them in some vague way with the Qumran sectarians.[17] If this identification were correct, then the Hellenists would belong to the original Palestinian church from the beginning and would have had nothing to do with the diaspora. As Jews who differed from official Judaism and displayed more or less esoteric tendencies and an opposition to the Jerusalem temple, they would have been called "Hellenists" by the rest. From such a background would have come the "Hellenist" converts of Acts 6:1, and with them Paul disputes in 9:29. But this specific identification of the Hellenists as Jews of Essene background (or of a kind of Judaism close to it) introduces an improbability into the discussion. It is difficult to see how such strict-living Essenes, rigorously observant of the Torah and cultivating a rather exclusive way of life, even hostile to the temporizing and levitically "unclean" priesthood of Jerusalem, could give to others the impression that they were ἑλληνίζοντες, "living like Greeks." Not even their attitude toward the temple, supposing that it agreed with Stephen's, would imply their adoption of Hellenizing ways, which had become such an abomination to observant Jews since the time of Antiochus IV Epiphanes (cf. 2 Macc. 4:13-17). And their connection with Pythagoreans is more alleged than substantiated. So we see no reason to identify the Hellenists of Acts specifically with converts from Essenism or a form of Judaism close to it.

At any rate, the distinction of Hellenists and Hebrews does not introduce into the Palestinian church a non-Jewish element. This does not mean, however, that there was not a variety of Jewish converts. For there were in the early Christian community converts from the priestly families (6:7) and "believers who belonged to the party of the Pharisees" (15:5). The latter are depicted as Christians who insisted on the strict observance of the Mosaic law. And yet, they can hardly be identified simply with the "Hebrews." This latter group must have included also converts from the *'Am hā-'āres,* from the Essenes and from the Samaritans, even though none of the last three groups are mentioned as such in Acts. Possibly some Essenes were included among the priests of 6:7, but one could never restrict this notice to them alone.

The persecution which raged against the early church in Palestine was an important factor in the spread of the gospel among the Gentiles. Yet when Saul made his way to Damascus, it was to the synagogues of that town that he was heading, presumably in pursuit of Jewish Christians (9:2). And even as the missionary effort among the Gentiles got under way, the church in Jerusalem remained notably Jewish. James, the "brother of the Lord," became its leader; and though he is not called a bishop, his place of prominence there, his stability in one area, and his administrative decision for nearby local churches give him marks that resemble those of the residential bishop of later times. Be this as it may, his prominence reflects at least the predominance of Jewish Christians in the Palestinian church. Jewish practices were still admitted as part of the Christian way of life in Jerusalem as late as *ca.* A.D. 58, when Paul after a long apostolate among the Gentiles went through the rite of the Nazirite at James' request (21:23-26).

These would seem to be the main features of the picture of the early Jewish Christian church which is painted in Acts. We want to see how our understanding of such a picture has been affected by the Qumran literature. This entails a consideration of the main points of contact detected between Acts and the Scrolls.[18]

But before we look at the details it would be well to recall that the comparison of the early Jewish Christian church with the Essene communities brings out fundamental differences far more than resemblances. These differences emerge when one considers the character and the goal of the two groups. Even if we admit the difference of Qumran Essenism from that of the "camps" of Damascus, there is still a vast difference between the Essene movement and that of early Christianity. The difference is more manifest when the Jewish Christians are compared with the Qumran Essenes. The discipline there laid stress on celibacy, obligatory communal ownership of property, common meals, regulated prayer, study and esoteric interpretation of the Torah, probation for candidates, fines and a form of excommunication, and a structured organization in which monarchic and democratic elements were admitted. Such a strictly organized community the early Jewish Christian church never was. Nor did it have the exclusive character of the Essene movement; it did not retire to the desert or to the "camps." It adopted an attitude toward the law of Moses that would have been wholly inadmissible among the Essenes. It also had a backward look in that it regarded Jesus of Nazareth as the Messiah who had already come, whereas the Essene movement still shared the hope of the coming of, not a Messiah, but a prophet and two Anointed Ones.

And yet with such fundamental differences between the two groups there are a number of points of contact and influence which must be recognized. To such points we now turn our attention.

Qumran Parallels

1. Our discussion begins with those designations of the Essene and the Jewish Christian groups which are common to both Acts and the literature of the Scrolls.

The first designation is the absolute use of "the Way" referring to the mode of life lived in these communities. ἡ ὁδός is found only in Acts (9:2; 19:9, 23; 22:4; 24:14, 22) among the New Testament writings; it succinctly describes the form of Christianity practiced in Jerusalem and Palestine. E. Haenchen in his monumental commentary on Acts wrote, "We do not know where the absolute use of ὁδός for Christianity comes from." [19] He compares τὴν ὁδὸν τοῦ κυρίου (18:25) and τὴν ὁδὸν τοῦ θεοῦ (18:26), but though these expressions fill out the meaning of "the Way," they do not explain the origin of its absolute use. Acts 24:14 implies that "the Way" was a term which the Christian community used of itself in contrast to the term αἵρεσις, undoubtedly used of it by outsiders who associated it with other movements among the Jews. Haenchen rightly states that the rabbinical parallels listed in Strack-Billerbeck's *Kommentar* (2.690) are scarcely to the point.

However, the same absolute use of "the Way" occurs in the Qumran writings to designate the mode of life of the Essenes.[20] The following passages best illustrate the use of it. "Those who have chosen the Way" (1QS 9:17-18, לבורחי דרך); "These are they who turn aside from the Way" (CD 1:13, הם סרי דרך; cf. CD 2:6; 1QS 10:21). "These are the regulations of the Way for the master" (1QS 9:21, אלה תכוני הדרך למשכיל). (See further 1QS 4:22; 8:10, 18, 21; 9:5, 9; 11:11; 1QM 14:7; 1QH 1:36; 1QSa 1:28.) At Qumran "the Way" referred above all to a strict observance of the Mosaic law, especially as this was interpreted in the community. This is made clear in 1QS 8:12-15: "When these become members of the Community in Israel according to these rules, they will separate from the gathering of the men of iniquity to go to the desert to prepare the Way of HIM, as it is written, 'In the desert prepare the way of . . . . , make straight in the wilderness a highway for our God' (Is. 40:3). This is the study of the Law [which] he ordered to be done through Moses" (cf. 1QS 9:19). The absolute use of "the Way" among the Essenes may well go back to this passage in Isaiah. It should be noted too that there is a Qumran counterpart for the fuller expressions used in Acts; compare "the way of the Lord" (18:25) and "the way of God" (18:26) with דרך הואהא (1QS 8:13) and דרך אל (CD 20:18). While it might theoretically be possible that both groups (Christian and Essene) derived the use of "the Way" from Isa. 40, nevertheless the close similarity of usage suggests in this case Essene influence.

There is, however, an important difference to be noted. Among the Essenes the expression "the Way" has a dualistic connotation, for it is to be related to the doctrine of the Two Spirits (1QS 3:18 ff.), which are given to men and according to which all are to "walk." "These are their ways in the world: To illumine the heart of man and to make plain before him all the ways of uprightness <and> truth" (1QS 4:2). The word דרך is not used here absolutely; but it is impossible to divorce the absolute use of it entirely from reference to the "ways" of these spirits. Such a dualistic connotation, however, is absent from Acts.

Another designation for the Qumran community with a possible bearing on the early Jewish Christian church in Acts is יחד. According to Acts 2:42 the early Christians devoted themselves to κοινωνία. This included the communal ownership of goods (4:32b-35; 6:1), the common "breaking of bread" (2:42; 20:7), communal meals (2:46), and their contributions for the relief of the needy (11:29). But the word κοινωνία probably denoted something more than such details: the communal spirit of cooperation and fellowship existing among the early Christians. Acts 4:32a is probably a description of it: "The community of believers was of one heart and mind" (καρδία καὶ ψυχὴ μία).

Even though the precise meaning of κοινωνία is a matter of debate,[21] the term יחד in Qumran literature sheds some light on it, in providing an intelligible Palestinian background for interpreting it. It is indeed impossible to establish any direct borrowing of the term. But to prescind for the moment from specific Qumran parallels for the elements of the life designated by κοινωνία—parallels which are not perfect in all details—the sum total of them as expressed by יחד should be included in any discussion of the meaning of κοινωνία. For in the Qumran writing the word יחד often designates the "community" as such (1QS 1:1, 16; 5:1, 2, 16; 6:21; 7:20; etc. 1QSa 1:26, 27; 4QPB 5; etc.). In this usage it certainly is more specific than κοινωνία.[22] The latter may sum up the corporate spirit of the Christian group, but is not used as a name for it. But in the Qumran writings there is also a wider sense of יחד. "This is the rule for the men of the Community (אנשי היחד) who devote themselves to turning from all evil and to adhering to all that He has commanded according to His good pleasure: to separate from the congregation of the men of iniquity, to form a communal spirit with respect the Law and to wealth" (להיות ליחד). In the first case יחד seems to be the name for the group, "community," whereas in the second instance it designates rather a common participation in the study and observance of the Torah and in the use of wealth. See also 1QS 6:7 ("The Many shall watch in common," הרבים ישקודו ביחד).[23] Thus even though the word יחד often is the designation for a far more structured community than κοινωνία is, there is a nuance in the Qumran use of the word that sheds light on the Christian *koinonia*.

2. The mention of *koinonia* brings up the question of the community of goods in the early church and in the Essene sect. From Acts we learn of a communal ownership of property among the early Jewish Christians; see 2:44-45; 4:32-35. Selling what they owned, they contributed the proceeds to a common fund, administered at first by the apostles, but later by seven assistants. From it distribution was made, even daily (6:1), to all the faithful according to their needs. The main elements in this feature of common life were the surrender of private property, the deposit of it with the leaders of the community, punishment for deception, and a care of the needy from the common fund. When one reads Acts 2:44-45; 4:32-35, one gets the impression that the communal ownership was obligatory. However, 4:36–5:11 suggests that it was voluntary. "Poverty . . . [as] a religious ideal" is the term that O. Cullmann uses to describe the situation.[24] This interpretation seems to be based on 4:32*b*: "None of them ever claimed anything as his own." The motivation for this communal ownership is never described as a fulfillment of the injunctions of Jesus recorded in Mark 10:21; Matt. 19:21; Luke 18:22. It seems rather to be an ideal motivated by simplicity, detachment, and charitable sharing which springs from their corporate identity as

the Jewish Christian community. As a mode of life common to all Christians
it eventually disappears.

But an analogous situation was found among the Essenes of Qumran.
They too seem to have practiced a form of communal ownership of property
though it is not in all respects identical to that of the early church. According to the *Manual of Discipline,* anyone who would enter the "community"
has to reckon with the surrender of his wealth. "All those who dedicate
themselves freely to His truth shall bring all their knowledge, their ability,
and their wealth into God's Community in order to purify their knowledge
in the truth of God's precepts and to determine exactly their abilities according to the perfection of His ways and their wealth according to his righteous counsel" (1QS 1:11-13; cf. CD 13:11). Explicit mention is made of the
property of the whole assembly or of "the Many" (הון הרבים, 1QS 6:17).
Before the probation is over, the candidate's belongings are not to be
mingled with those of the community nor spent for common purposes.[25]
The mingling of his property with that of the community occurs only at
the end of his second year of probation, when he becomes a full-fledged
member (1QS 6:21-23). Deceit in the declaration or deposit of property
results in exclusion from the "Purity" (or sacred meal) of the community
for one year, and a reduction of the food allowance by one quarter (1QS 6:
24-25; cf. CD 14:20-21).[26] Fraud (or neglect) in the use of common property
was punished with the obligation of restitution through one's labor and/or
a fine (1QS 7:6). The emphasis on common ownership of property was
such among the Essenes of Qumran that the group was characterized by
its communal spirit with respect to the law and to wealth (להיות ליחד בתורה
ובהון, 1QS 5:2).[27]

But while entrance into the Qumran community was voluntary, the
surrender of one's property and earnings (את הונו ואת מלאכתו, 1QS 6:19)
was not. The surrender was obligatory and detailed. In this the Qumran
practice differs considerably from the early Christian communal ownership
described in Acts 4:36–5:11, which is voluntary. If the passages in Acts
2:44-45; 4:32-35 are to be understood in a more obligatory sense, then they
are closer to the Qumran practice. At any rate, there is in both groups a
willingness to surrender property and earnings as a feature of common life.
In the Essene community, however, this is but an element in a closely organized and structured community; since the early church was not thus
highly organized, the surrender of common property was of a looser sort.

As for the motivation of such a way of life, the Qumran literature itself is less explicit than the ancient sources about the Essenes. 1QS 9:22 expresses a certain contempt for riches and a salary: wealth and earnings are to be left to the men of perdition. But Josephus (*JW* 2.8, 2 #122) explicitly calls the Essenes "despisers of wealth" (καταφρονηταὶ δὲ πλούτου). And Philo too emphasizes their detachment.[28] In this respect we detect little difference between the Essenes and the early Jewish Christians.[29] Although the ultimate motivation for this poverty might be Old Testament passages such as Prov. 30:8-9; 14:20-21; etc., nevertheless this does not account for the communal aspect of it practiced in the two groups. The analogy existing between the early Jewish Christians and the Qumran community is such that one should reckon with an imitation of Qumran practices among the former, even if it is clear that modifications were introduced. In this respect we cannot agree with the radical rejection of any Qumran influence on the early Jewish Christians, such as has been proposed by H. H. Rowley, G. Graystone, and N. Adler.[30]

One last observation in this matter. Though there is provision for the needy among the Jewish Christians of Acts (2:45; 4:34-35; 6:1), it is striking that the term οἱ πτωχοί is never used there. Paul uses it in Rom. 15:26; Gal. 2:10, and one may be inclined to regard the term as a designation for the Jerusalem church. Indeed, it has often been suggested that it is the equivalent of האביונים. The latter, drawn from the Old Testament (Exod. 23:11; Esth. 9:22; Ps. 132:15), seems to have become a technical designation for the Qumran sect in use among the Essenes themselves (see 1QpHab 12:3, 6, 10; 4QpPs 37 1:9; 2:10 [עדת האביונים]; 1QM 11:9, 13; 13:14).[31]

3. Another area of contact between the early Jewish Christian church and the Essenes of Qumran which must be discussed is the organizational structure of the two groups. We have already tried to indicate the vagueness of detail that characterizes the description of the community of Christians in Acts. This vagueness must prevent us from being too absolute in any judgment about the similarity of it with the Qumran community, which was certainly much more structured than the Jewish Christian congregation.

Like the early Christians, the Essenes of Qumran considered themselves to be the Israel of the end of days. They patterned their way of life on the Israel of the desert wanderings. The original nucleus of the community seems to have been priestly, and this accounts for the title "sons of Zadok" often applied to it. But apart from the priests there were also levites and laymen (1QS 2:19-21; cf. 1:18, 21; 2:1, 11). The latter were divided into tribes and groups called "thousands, hundreds, fifties, and tens" (1QS 2:21; cf. 1QM 4:1-5, 16-17; 1QSa 1:14, 29–2:1; CD 13:1-2). This division is derived from Exod. 18:21, 25 (cf. Num. 31:48, 54); it probably designates various groups within the community with diverse status or functions. One may legitimately ask whether there were literally groups of "thousands" at Qumran. The priestly element in the community was often called "sons of Aaron," and the title probably included the Levites too. But the nonpriests were designated as "Israel." In the Damascene camps there were also proselytes (CD 14:3).

Both Aaron and Israel were accustomed to meet in a full assembly מושב הרבים) where they had fixed places and where they in common settled issues of a juridical and executive nature. Some writers have mentioned that there was also in the Qumran community a small "council" (1QS 8:1, עצת היחד), entrusted with the study of legal matters.[32] The existence of a nucleus of fifteen members is certain, but just what its function was is not clear at all. This will be discussed further below. Finally, in addition to the full assembly authority was vested in various "overseers" or "superintendents." At Qumran itself there was a "(lay)man appointed at the head of the Many" (האיש הפקיד ברואש הרבים, 1QS 6:14) and a lay "overseer of the Many" (האיש המבקר על הרבים, 1QS 6:11); the latter is probably the same as the "overseer of the work of the Many" (האיש המבקר על מלאכת הרבים, 1QS 6:20). The first was apparently a sort of superior, and the second a sort of bursar. In the Essene "camps" of Damascus there was a "priest appointed over the Many" (הכוהן אשר יפקד <בר>אש הרבים CD 14:6-7; also mentioned in 4QD) and a lay "overseer for all the camps" (המבקר אשר לכל המחנות, CD 14:8-11), as well as a lay "camp overseer" (המבקר למחנה, CD 13:7-19). The latter was entrusted with teaching, reprehension, admission of candidates, and the administration of the property of the community in the camp (CD 13:7-19). He was assisted by a group of ten judges (CD 10:4-7). Even though it is not possible to give in full detail the functions of these different authorities, this brief sketch does make it plain that the Essene communities (either at Qumran or in the Damascene camps) had a structure that was much more organized than anything which emerges from the account in Acts about the early Jewish Christian church.

And yet there are certain elements in common which call for comment. First of all, the absolute use of τὸ πλῆθος to designate the full congregation of the Jerusalem converts. It is a commonplace to point out that there are two uses of τὸ πλῆθος in Acts: [33] (a) "crowd, large number of persons" (so 2:6; etc.); (b) "the full assembly, congregation." The latter meaning is found in Acts 6:5; cf. 6:2; 4:32. It refers to the full body of Jerusalem disciples. In a more restricted sense it is used in 15:12 of the body of the apostles and elders. Again, with the spread of Christianity it is applied to the community at Antioch (15:30).[34] Since both meanings are well attested in classical and Hellenistic Greek, it may seem that these have been simply used in the account of Acts. However, given the wide use of רב, רוב and הרבים in the Essene literature there is a likelihood that the designation of the Jewish Christian community as τὸ πλῆθος was an imitation of current terminology. For in the Qumran writings the Essene assembly was often called הרבים, "the Many." Though pioneer translators sometimes sought to render it as "the Great Ones," or "the Masters," the commonly accepted explanation today refers it to the democratic assembly of the Essenes as they met in a session (מושב) to decide common matters (see 1QS 6:1, 7-9, 11-18, 21, 25; 7:16; 8:19, 26; CD 13:7; 14:7, 12; 15:8). The Greek phrase, however, is hardly the literal translation of הרבים.[35] It may reflect the Hebrew רב or רוב (1QS 5:2, 9, 22; 6:19). But it is to be noted that רב and רוב seem to designate rather the Essene assembly considered as distinct from the priests, whereas הרבים would include them.[36] For this distinction there is no equivalent in the early Christian church; it is a precision which has not been taken over. But this does not seem to invalidate the suggestion that the Essene use of רב, רוב and הרבים underlies in some way the early Christian use of τὸ πλῆθος for the full congregation of disciples.

Secondly several writers have discussed the possibility of Essene influence in the role of the twelve in the early Jewish Christian church. In Acts "the twelve" are mentioned indeed, but rarely (explicitly only in 6:2; but cf. 1:15-26; 2:14). They have been compared to 1QS 8:1: "In the council (?) of the Community [when there are? *or* there shall be?] twelve men and three priests, perfect in all that is revealed in the Law." It has been suggested that the mention of "twelve men" is "an analogue to the college of the twelve apostles of Jesus," since it is "not clear from the text whether the three priests are inside or outside the circle of twelve. Perhaps the inclusion of the three priests is to be preferred, because it enables one to see in the expression 'priest' an especial mark of honor and to avoid the rather improbable result that the other twelve were laymen."[37] But just why it is not clear that the twelve are distinct from the three is never explained; any normal reading of the line would suggest that the text mentions 15 persons. This number is confirmed, in fact, by a text from Cave IV which is unfortunately as yet unpublished.[38] Consequently, there is little reason to think that the apostolic twelve in the early Christian church was modeled on the "twelve men" mentioned in this one place in the *Manual of Discipline.* J. T. Milik and others have related the three priests mentioned there to the three priestly families descended from Levi through his sons Gershon, Kohath, and Merari (Gen. 46:11).[39] In both Essene and Christian circles the number twelve is more plausibly explained as a derivative of the twelve tribes of Israel. The element that is common to the use of this number in both circles is its appearance in an eschatological context. Jesus' saying about the twelve thrones has to do with eschatological judgment (Matt. 19:28; Luke 22:30), and the division of the Sons of Light in the eschatological war is according to twelve tribes (1QM 3:13-14; 5:1-2). The real problem in Acts—why the twelve disappear as an authoritative and administrative group within a relatively short time after the need was felt to reconstitute it by the election of Matthias—unfortunately receives no illumination from the Qumran material.

Thirdly the organization of the Essene camps in the land of Damascus was somewhat different. Here a body of ten judges functions, "four from the tribe of Levi and Aaron, and six from Israel" (CD 10:4). Again, they represent the priest and nonpriest members, but the number twelve is not operative here. It is rather ten, the number otherwise used for small groups or "cells" within the Essene community which gathered for various purposes (cf. 1QS 6:6; 1QSa 2:22; Josephus, *JW* 2.8, 9 #146). But this does not seem to have any significance for the Jewish Christian church of Acts.[40]

Fourthly, another feature of organization that has often been discussed is the relation of the ἐπίσκοπος in the early church to the Essene מבקר. Since both words etymologically mean "overseer," "superintendent," the Essene institution has often been considered as a likely model for the early Christian episcopate.[41] As far as the early Jewish Christian church is concerned, the relation seems to be negligible, for the Greek word occurs in Acts only in 20:28, in Paul's discourse to the elders (πρεσβύτεροι, 20:17) of Ephesus summoned to Miletus. He bids them, "Keep watch then over yourselves and over all the flock of which the holy Spirit has made you overseers" (ἐπισκόπους). The assimilation of the "overseer" to a shepherd is used in the instructions for the "Camp Overseer" in CD 13:7-9: "He shall bring back all those who have strayed, as a shepherd his flock" (cf. Ezek. 34:12-16; Num. 27:16; I Peter 2:25; 5:2). This would seem to make plausible the suggestion that the ἐπίσκοπος was somehow an imitation of the Essene מבקר.[42] But the leaders of the Jewish Christian church in Palestine are never called ἐπίσκοποι in Acts. And even if we find the apostles performing a role there that resembles a function of an Essene overseer as the Christians who have sold their property come and deposit the proceeds of it at the feet of the apostles (4:35, 37; 5:2; cf. CD 14:13 and possibly also 1QS 6:19-20), there is no trace of the use of such a title in the early Jewish Christian church. Nor does the passage in Acts 1:17-25 really contradict this impression. For although the word ἐπισκοπή does occur in 1:20 in connection with the office that Matthias was elected to fill, it is actually part of an Old Testament quotation Ps. 109:8: τὴν ἐπισκοπὴν αὐτοῦ λαβέτω ἕτερος. In the context ἐπισκοπή is related to both ἀποστολή and διακονία (1:17, 25). Its sense is obviously generic, and it can in no way be used to show that the "apostolate" was already an "episcopate." Even James who begins to rule the Jerusalem church in a manner that resembles the residential bishop of later date is never called ἐπίσκοπος. Indeed, his position of prominence seems to be due to the fact that he is "a brother of the Lord." In the New Testament the ἐπίσκοποι emerge in churches of Hellenistic background (see Acts 20:28; Phil. 1:1; I Tim. 3:2; Titus 1:7), as groups of "guardians" or "overseers." It is the Ephesian "elders" who are called thus by Paul in Acts 20:28. They seem to have been set up by traveling apostles (like Paul) to govern local churches, but it is only gradually that their monarchical function emerges, as in the case of Timothy in Ephesus and Titus in Crete. Granting then the common etymological meaning of ἐπίσκοπος and מבקר, and certain similar functions, it is nevertheless difficult to set up any direct connection between the Essene "overseer" and the institution of the early Jewish Christian church in Palestine.[43]

Fifthly, the early Christian church gave a special function to "elders" in addition to the apostles. The πρεσβύτεροι occur in Acts 11:30; 15:2, 4, 6, 22, 23; 16:4; 21:18. These "elders" were, however, a natural borrowing from the existing Jewish institution mentioned in Acts itself (4:5, 8, 23; 6:12; 23:14; 24:1; 25:15) and can in no way be traced to the Essene community specifically. The Essenes had such "elders" too. In the ranks of the Qumran community the priests take precedence over the elders, as they meet in full assembly (1QS 6:8). They take their place along with the priests and the

Levites in pronouncing blessings and curses after the defeat of the enemy in the eschatological war (1QM 13:1). In general, respect for them is inculcated (CD 9:4). But there is nothing to indicate that the elders of the Christian community were in any way a derivative of the Essene institution. Both communities derived the institution rather from Old Testament tradition, as Acts 2:17 and *Damascus Document* 5:4 would suggest.

Finally, by way of contrast it is remarkable how frequently one reads of the role of the "priests" and the "Levites" in the Essene communities (e.g., 1QS 1:18, 21; 2:1, 11, 19; 1QM 7:15; 13:1; 15:4; CD 3:21; etc.) and how silent Acts is about such groups in the early Christian church. "Priests" and "Levites" are mentioned in Acts only as indications of the former Jewish status of converts (6:7; 4:36). This remarkable difference between the two groups stems from their basic attitude toward the temple in Jerusalem. In both we find a kindred idea that the Jerusalem temple and its sacrificial cultus have been replaced by a community of the faithful.[44] But in the case of the Qumran Essenes this replacement was temporary; the Qumran community is the "sanctuary for Aaron, . . . the Holy of Holies" (1QS 9:5-7; cf. 8:4-6; 5:6; 11:8; 4QFlor 1:6), but only because it has considered the Jerusalem temple defiled by the worldly, temporizing priests who serve it, and hence unfit for the sacrifice to God according to the prescriptions of Mosaic law.[45] Once God's victory is won, then the pure levitical service of God will be resumed. In the early church, however, the temple and its sacrifices soon cease to have significance for Christians. Even though we read of the apostles "attending the temple together" (2:46) and "going up to the temple at the hour of prayer, the ninth hour" (3:1), yet it is not long before the opposition to the temple develops. Stephen's speech reflects this and is the beginning of the development within the early Jerusalem community (cf. Acts 6:14) that culminates in the temple symbolism found in the writings of Paul, I Peter, and Hebrews. This temple symbolism is certainly similar to that of the Essene community, but there is a difference, too. This is found chiefly in the preservation within their community of the divisions of priests and Levites who by their strict living were preparing themselves for the pure service of God in the ideal eschatological temple. As we have already remarked, there were undoubtedly some Essenes among the priests converted to Christianity (Acts 6:7), and they were most likely the bridge of contact between the two communities. However, it is important to note that they are never found continuing their function as priests even in some new way (such as blessing the bread and wine at the Christian communal meal instead of sacrificing, as did happen in the Essene community, 1QSa 2:18-19).

Such are the observations which seem pertinent to the discussion of influence of the Essene community on the structure and organization of the early Jewish Christian church.

4. When Matthias was elected to replace Judas in the number of the twelve, it is noteworthy that the other eleven are not said to have laid hands on him or "ordained" him, as is the case with the seven in Acts 6:6. Rather, once the requirements (2:21-22) are met, the commission is given to Matthias by the "Lord" himself (2:24) through the casting of the lot. The use of this means of determining the will of God is known from the Old Testament: the lot determined priestly functions in the temple (I Chr. 24:5; 26: 13-14; Neh. 10:34; etc.) and service in the army (Judg. 20:9). It is also known to have been used in rabbinical circles. It is not surprising then that the lot was also in use in the Essene community, given its place in the general Jewish cultural heritage. But several expressions in the Matthias passage are better understood against the specific background of the Essene usage. In the Qumran community the lot was used in some way to determine the candidate's admission into the community and also his rank in it. Using an expression drawn from Num. 33:54 or Josh. 16:1, the *Manual of Discipline* (6:16) prescribes apropos of the candidate's admission that the lot be used: כאשר יצא הגורל על עצת הרבים. At subsequent periods in the candidate's probation further determination is made, and finally, "if it be his lot to enter the Community then he shall be inscribed in the order of his rank among his brethren" (1QS 6:22, אם יצא לו הגורל לקרבו ליחד יכתובהו בסרך תכונו בתוך אחיו). One's rank in the community was determined by lot, too: "No man shall move down from his place nor move up from his allotted position" (1QS 2:23, ולוא ירום ממקום גורלו). (See also 1QS 1:10; 9:7; CD 13:12; 20:4.) There are elements in this Essene practice which shed light on the details of the election of Matthias. For instance, Judas is said by his vocation as an apostle to "have obtained the lot of this ministry" (Acts 1:17, ἔλαχεν τὸν κλῆρον τῆς διακονίας ταύτης). Then, the Christian community prayed that God would indicate who was to take over τὸν τόπον τῆς διακονίας ταύτης (1:25), an expression which finds its counterpart in מקום גורלו (1QS 2:23). Though these resemblances are *in se* superficial, taken in conjunction with the use of the lot to designate a man for a specific rank within the community, they do make the story of the election of Matthias a

little more intelligible.[46] We would not be able to conclude, however, that the practice was due to imitation of an Essene custom.

5. The communal meal of the early Jewish Christian church (2:46) has often been compared to the religious common meal of the Essenes described in 1QS 6:4-5; 1QSa 2:11-22.[47] The brief notice of the Christian meal in Acts, however, contains so little detail that one cannot really make a valid comparison in this case. Previous discussions of the relationship of the Essene repast to the Christian Eucharist or the Last Supper have exploited the Gospel and Pauline material, as they must; but this is outside our perspective. Even though one were to admit that the Jerusalem church were the source of the tradition about the Last Supper in Matthew and Mark, there is little reason to bring it into this discussion. The only element which should be noted is that the account of the common meal in Acts is framed merely in terms of "breaking bread," and there is no mention of "wine," the other element in the Essene meal. Though one may be inclined to admit that the meal was eaten in anticipation of the messianic banquet in the Essene community (1QSa 2:14-20), this note is not found in the account in Acts.

6. The last topic to which we shall turn our attention is the interpretation of the Old Testament found in Acts and in the Essene literature. For despite the difference in the messianic views of the two communities, which we have already noted and which certainly colored their interpretation of the Old Testament, there is a remarkable similarity in other respects which shows the early Jewish Christian community to be very close to the Essenes. For the Christians of Acts the Messiah has come (2:36), but another definitive coming of his is still awaited (1:11; 3:21). This expectation manifests a similarity with the Essene expectation of a prophet and two Anointed Ones (1QS 9:11), who are in some way related to the day of God's visitation of his people (1QS 3:18). There is the common conviction that they are living in the "end of days" (1QpHab 2:5; 9:6; 1QSa 1:1; 4QpIs^a A:8; 4QFlor 1:2, 12, 15, 19; CD 4:4; 6:11; etc.; cf. Acts 2:17: ἐν ταῖς ἐσχάταις ἡμέραις).[48] This conviction enables both groups to refer sayings of the Old Testament prophets and writings to events or tenets in their own history or beliefs. Especially pertinent is 1QpHab 7:1-5: "God told Habakkuk to write the things which were to come upon the last generation, but the consummation of the period he did not make known to him. And as for what it says, 'That he may run who reads it,' this means the Righteous Teacher, to whom God made known all the mysteries of the words of his servants the prophets" (see

also 1QpHab 7:7-8). This attitude underlies the constant actualization or modernization of the Old Testament texts being used either in the *pesharîm* or in isolated quotations in other writings. See CD 1:13 ("This is the time about which it was written," introducing Hos. 4:16); 10:16; 16:15 ("For that is what it[*or:* he] said"); 1QM 10:1; 11:11. It is this same attitude that underlies the use of the Old Testament in Peter's speech on Pentecost, as the prophet Joel is quoted (cf. Acts 3:24).

The introductory formulas often reveal this attitude more than anything else. We have elsewhere studied the similarity of these Essene formulas and their New Testament counterparts in detail.[49] We shall give here only the list of those passages which occur in Acts and are pertinent to this discussion.

Acts	Qumran Literature
1:20 "for it is written"	CD 11:20
2:16 "this is what was said through the prophet Joel"	CD 10:16; 16:15
2:25 "for David says"	CD 6:7-8 (cf. 6:13)
2:34 "he says"	CD 4:20 (?)
3:21 "God spoke through the mouth of his holy prophets of old"	CD 4:13-14
3:25 "saying to Abraham"	?
4:11 "this is the . . ."	1QpHab 12:3; 4QpIs^b 2:10
4:25 "spoke through the mouth of David his servant"	CD 4:13-14
7: 6 "So God said"	CD 6:13; 8:9
7: 7 "God said"	CD 6:13; 8:9
7:42 "As it is written in the book of the prophets"	4QFlor 1:2
7:48 "as the prophet says"	CD 6:7-8 (?)
13:33 "as it is written in the second psalm"	4QFlor 1:2; 11QMelch 9-10
13:33 "and in another place he says"	?
13:40 "Beware then lest what was said by the prophets come true [of you]"	?
15:15 "as it is written"	1QS 8:14; 5:17; CD 7:19; 4QFlor 1:2
28:25 "The holy Spirit has well said through Isaiah the prophet"	CD 4:13-14 ("God said . . .")

Two observations are pertinent. First, the Hebrew equivalents of the introductory formulas in the New Testament are found in greater abundance in the Qumran literature than in the early rabbinical compositions (such as the Mishnah).[50] Even if the formulas used show an affinity to those of the Essene writers, we cannot establish a definite borrowing of the Qumran literary practice by the early Christians. Secondly, it is not insignificant that the majority of explicit quotations introduced by such formulas in Acts are found in the early chapters which deal specifically with the early Jewish Christian church. A glance at the above list shows this. Several reasons, of course, can be suggested for the difference (e.g., that the latter part of Acts deals with Paul, his missions, his evangelization of the Greek world, etc.). But they should not be pressed to the extent of excluding all influence of Palestinian methods of Old Testament exegesis which the data would seem to suggest.

Conclusion

The features of Esssene tenets and practices which we have surveyed have often shed important light on passages of Acts that describe the early Jewish Christian church. They at least provide concrete and tangible evidence for a Palestinian matrix of the early church as it is described in Acts. The evidence varies, since it is possible at times to think in terms of a direct contact or a direct imitation of Essene usage (as in the case of "the Way"), while at other times the evidence is not so strong. Certainly, one cannot prove from such points of contact that the early Jewish Christian church developed out of an exclusively Essene framework. The most that one can say is that the early Jewish Christian church was not without some influence from the Essenes. It is not unlikely, as we have mentioned above, that among the "great number of priests" (Acts 6:7) who were converted some were Essene and provided the source of Essene influence.

In our opinion, the influence of Qumran literature on Acts is not as marked as it is in other New Testament writings (e.g., John, Paul, Matthew, Hebrews). The parallels that do exist, striking though they may be, are not numerous. In an early article on the subject, S. E. Johnson wrote, "It also appears that he [the author of Luke–Acts] is in closer touch with the Jewish sectarian background of Christianity than any other New Testament author." [51] Now that much more of the Essene literature has been published and more of its contacts with the New Testament have been studied, we can see that this judgment would have to be modified, if Johnson meant by "Jewish sectarian background" specifically the Essene background of the Qumran sect.

NOTES

1. See R. de Vaux, *L'archéologie et les manuscrits de la Mer Morte*, Schweich Lectures 1959 (London, 1961). J. T. Milik, *Ten Years of Discovery in the Wilderness of Judaea*, SBTh XXVI (Naperville, 1959), 133-36. F. M. Cross, Jr., *The Ancient Library of Qumran and Modern Biblical Studies* (Anchor, rev. ed.; Garden City, 1961), pp. 117-27. N. Avigad, "The Palaeography of the Dead Sea Scrolls and Related Documents," *Scripta hierosolymitana* 4 (1958), 56-87.

2. Philo, *Quod omnis probus liber sit*, 72-91; *Apologia pro Iudaeis*, 11.1-18 (cf. Eusebius, *Praeparatio evangelica*, 8.11,1-18); *De vita contemplativa*, 1-90. Josephus, *Jewish War*, 1.3 #78-80; 2.7 #111-13; 2.8 #119-61; 2.20 #566-68; *Antiquities*, 13.59 #171-72; 18.1,5 #18-22. C. Plinius Secundus (the Elder), *Naturalis historia*, 5.17,4. Dio Chrysostom, 3.1-4. Hippolytus, *Refutatio omnium haeresium*, 9.18-28. See A. Adam, *Antike Berichte über die Essener* (Kleine Texte 182; Berlin, 1961).

3. *Ten Years*, pp. 87-93. A. Dupont-Sommer (*The Essene Writings from Qumran* [tr. G. Vermes; Oxford, 1961], pp. 145, 408) likewise admits such Pharisaic influence on the Qumran sect, although he rightly rejects the thesis of C. Rabin (*Qumran Studies* [Oxford, 1957]) that the sect was in fact Pharisaic.

4. Despite the frequent use of the term "sons of Zadok" to designate the members of the Qumran sect (1QS 5:2,9; 1QSa I.2,24; II.2; etc.). See R. North, "The Qumran 'Saducees,' " *CBQ* 17 (1955), 44-68; J. Trinquet, *VT* 1 (1951), 287-92.

5. Thus C. Roth, *The Historical Background of the Dead Sea Scrolls* (Oxford, 1958); "New Light on the Dead Sea Scrolls," *Commentary* 37/6 (June, 1964), 27-32.

6. So J. L. Teicher in a series of articles in *JJS* II (1951), 67-99; III (1952), 53-55, 87-88, 111-18, 128-32, 139-50; IV (1953), 1-13, 49-58, 93-103, 139-53; V (1954), 38, 93-99; etc. Cf. M. A. Chevallier, *L'esprit et le messie dans le Bas-Judaïsme et le Nouveau Testament* (Paris, 1958), pp. 136-43. This view is without foundation since it utterly neglects archaeological evidence and misinterprets most of the Qumran texts that it uses. See *TSt* XVI (1955), 335-72; XX (1959), 451-55.

7. See J. A. T. Robinson, "The Baptism of John and the Qumran Community," *HThR* L (1957), 175-91; reprinted: *Twelve New Testament Studies*, SBTh XXXIV (Naperville, 1962), 11-27. W. H. Brownlee, "John the Baptist in the Light of Ancient Scrolls," *Int.* IX (1955), 71-90.

8. See P. Benoit, "Qumran et le Nouveau Testament," *NTS* VII (1960-61), 276-96.

9. The meaning of κοινωνία in this text is debated. That it refers to the specific act of a contribution during a liturgical service is not very convincing but has been proposed by J. Jeremias (*Jesus als Weltvollender*, BFTh XXXIII 4 [Gütersloh, 1930], 78; cf. E. Haenchen, *Die Apostelgeschichte* [12th ed.; Göttingen, 1959], p. 153). The communal sharing of goods, property, and food was an important part of κοινωνία, as 2:44-46 seems to make clear. But what the word immediately indicates is the corporate character of the Christian group, as it expressed itself in various ways (spiritual, material, and liturgical). See Ph.-H. Menoud, *La vie de l'Église naissante*, Cahiers théologiques XXXI (Neuchâtel, 1952), 22-34.

10. The use of the word here reflects a later awareness on the part of the author, since it forms part of a "summary." See H. J. Cadbury, *BC* V, 402.

11. Josephus never mentions the Christian movement as a αἵρεσις among the Jews. But

Acts three times (24:14; 24:5; 28:22) calls it such, using the very word that Josephus employs for the Pharisees, Sadducees, and Essenes (*Ant.* 13.5,9 #171; see also 20.9,1 #199; *Vita* 2 #10, 12; cf. Acts 15:5; 5:17; 26:5). This use of αἵρεσις for Christianity records the impression that it made on contemporary Palestinian Jews. It was regarded as another "sect" springing from the bosom of Judaism, espousing what was central to it (reverence of Yahweh, the Torah, and the temple).

12. C. F. D. Moule, whose opinion we otherwise prefer (see "Once More, Who Were the Hellenists?" ExpT LXX [1958-59], 100-102), considers the Hellenists of Acts 9:29 to be Christians. This is difficult to understand in the context. They are preferably to be regarded as Jews (so E. Haenchen, *Die Apostelgeschichte*, p. 280; M. Simon, *St. Stephen and the Hellenists in the Primitive Church* [New York, 1958], pp. 14-15).

13. *Homily 14* (in Acts 6:1); *PG* 60. 113; *Homily 21* (in Acts 9:29); *PG* 60. 164.

14. BC V 59-74; IV 64.

15. "Once More, Who Were the Hellenists?", p. 100.

16. Cf. M. Simon, *St. Stephen*, pp. 34-35. It is perhaps too strong to regard them as "paganizing" Jews, as Simon suggests.

17. "The Significance of the Qumran Texts for Research into the Beginnings of Christianity," *JBL* LXXIV (1955), 213-26; reprinted: K. Stendahl (ed.), *The Scrolls and the New Testament* (New York, 1957), pp. 18-32.

18. Most of the data for this study were amassed when H. Braun's second article ("Qumran und das Neue Testament: Ein Bericht über 10 Jahre Forschung, 1950-1959," *ThR* XXIX [1963], 142-76) arrived. Our task has been considerably lightened by this invaluable survey. Since Braun's article takes up and discusses many of the small suggestions that have been made apropos of one verse or another, we shall not repeat them here. We concentrate on the major issues on which a judgment can be based.

19. *Die Apostelgeschichte*, p. 268, n. 3. See also the comments of K. Lake and H. J. Cadbury, *BC*, IV, 100; V, 391-92.

20. For previous discussions see W. K. M. Grossouw, "The Dead Sea Scrolls and the New Testament: A Preliminary Survey," *StCath* XXVII (1952), 1-8, esp. 5-6. F. Nötscher, *Gotteswege und Menschenwege in der Bibel und Qumran, BBB* XV (Bonn, 1958), 76-96, 100-101. V. McCasland, "'The Way,'" *JBL* LXXVII (1958), 222-30.

21. See note 9 above.

22. S. Talmon ("The Sectarian יחד—A Biblical Noun," *VT* III [1953], 132-40) cites a few places in the Old Testament where יחד may even have the meaning, "congregation, community" (Deut. 33:5; Ezek. 4:3; I Chr. 12:18; Ps. 2:2). Though the first instance is plausible, the others scarcely are.

23. Recall that Philo (*Quod omnis probus liber sit*, 84 and 91) speaks of the Essene way of life as an "indescribable communal life" (τὴν παντὸς λόγου κρείττονα κοινωνίαν), using of it the very word κοινωνία. See also no. 85; *Apologia pro Iudaeis*, 11. 10-13. Josephus, however, uses τό κοινωνικόν, and this in a more restricted sense, as he refers it to the common sharing of possessions (*JW* 2.8,3 #122).

24. The Scrolls and the New Testament, p. 21.

25. The meaning of ערב in the Qumran writings has been questioned. In our opinion, the word as used in 1QS 6:17,22 describes the "mingling" of the individual's property with that of the group and does correspond to Josephus' expression (ἀναμεμιγμένων, *JW* 2.8,3 #122). The evidence of Josephus should not be written off too quickly in this regard; cf. C. Rabin, *Qumran Studies*, pp. 22-36. His reasons are not very convincing. See also M. Black, *The Scrolls and Christian Origins* (New York, 1961), pp. 32-39.

26. The text of CD is at this point fragmentary. Since it also mentions a different fine ("six days"), we might ask whether this passage is really parallel to that in 1QS 6:24-25.

27. See also CD 13:14; 14:12-16. The regulations regarding communal ownership were not the same in the "camps" of Damascus as at Qumran itself. However, there has been a tendency to exaggerate the difference. Some of the passages which have been interpreted

in terms of private ownership do not clearly state this. CD 14:12-16, for instance, does not necessarily mean that the wages are private. The שכר could well refer to the income of the "work" of the members of the "camp"; the income of two days would be put aside for the care of orphans, the poor, and the elderly. The passage seems to deal with the *community's* care of such person, a corporate duty (סרך הרבים). Likewise, in CD 13:14 the prohibition of trade or traffic with outsiders on an individual basis in any other manner than for cash is understandable in the context of communal ownership. If a member of the "camps" sold to an outsider or worked for him, his recompense was to be cash, lest he bring into the community unclean produce or products. It does not necessarily mean that the cash was his own.

28. *Quod omnis probus liber sit*, 85-86; *Apologia pro Iudaeis*, 11.11.

29. According to S. E. Johnson, "The emphasis is upon communal life and not on poverty as such" (*The Scrolls and the New Testament*, p. 133).

30. H. H. Rowley, *The Dead Sea Scrolls and the New Testament* (London, 1957), p. 13. G. Graystone, *The Dead Sea Scrolls and the Originality of Christ* (New York, 1955), pp. 33-35. N. Adler, "Die Bedeutung der Qumran-Texte für die neutestamentliche Wissenschaft," *MThZ* VI (1955), 286-301, esp. 299.

31. My earlier remarks on this subject (*ThSt* XVI [1955], 344, n. 22) need some qualification. We would, however, still reject the suggestion that these "poor" might be the Ebionites, or simply became the Ebionites later on.

32. E.g., J. T. Milik (*Ten Years*, p. 100); F. M. Cross, Jr. (*Ancient Library of Qumran*, p. 231); B. Reicke, "The Constitution of the Primitive Church in the Light of Jewish Documents," *ThZ* X (1954), 95-113, reprinted in *The Scrolls and the New Testament*, pp. 151-52.

33. See K. Lake and H. J. Cadbury, *BC* IV, 47-48.

34. In Acts 19:9 the meaning of τὸ πλῆθος is disputed. E. Haenchen (*Die Apostelgeschichte*, p. 188, n. 1) maintains that it refers to the Jewish Christian community, while K. Lake and H. J. Cadbury (*BC* IV, 48) refer it to the "congregation of the Jews."

35. *Pace* J. M. Allegro (*The Dead Sea Scrolls* [Pelican ed., Baltimore, 1957], p. 144), הרבים would correspond more exactly to the Pauline use of οἱ πολλοί (Rom. 5:15, 19) or of οἱ πλείονες (II Cor. 2:6; cf. I Cor. 9:19). Josephus uses οἱ πλεῖστοι (*Ant.* 18.1,5 #22) and οἱ πλείονες (*JW* 2.8,9 #146) of the Essene community as a whole.

36. See H. Huppenbauer, "רב, רוב, רבים in der Sektenregel (1QS)," *ThZ* XIII (1957), 136-37.

37. See B. Reicke, "The Constitution" in *The Scrolls and the New Testament*, p. 151.

38. See J. T. Milik, *Verbum Domini* XXXV (1957), 73; *Ten Years*, p. 96; *RB* LXIV (1957), 589. See also A. Dupont-Sommer, *Essene Writings*, p. 90, n. 4. Curiously enough, Milik speaks later on (*Ten Years*, p. 143) of the early church and the Essenes as both holding the "eschatological concept of the true Israel ruled by twelve leaders."

39. The connection between the "three priests" and the "pillars" of Gal. 2:9 or the mention of Peter, James, and John (Matt. 17:1) must be admitted to be extremely tenuous.

40. Gathering in groups of ten was a principle also recognized in the Pharisaic-Rabbinical tradition; cf. Mishnah, *Megillah*, 4:3. But it is debatable whether the idea of a group of ten, of whom one was a priest, had anything to do with the 120 present in the first Jewish Christian assembly in Acts (1:15): "ten members to each Apostle" (so J. T. Milik, *Ten Years*, p. 101; cf. *BC* IV, 12). The problem is that the apostles are not considered to be ἱερεῖς in Acts. See H. Braun, "Qumran und das Neue Testament," p. 147.

41. Josephus speaks of the Essene ἐπιμεληταί (*JW* 2.8,6 #134; 2.8,3 #123); this seems to be his equivalent for the Hebrew מבקר or פקיד. This Greek word is not used in the New Testament nor in the LXX. Although ἐπίσκοπος is used in extrabiblical Greek for a civic, financial, and religious "overseer," it is also found in the LXX (Num. 4:16; 31:14; Judg. 9:28; II Kings 11:15,18; etc.). In most cases it translates some form of the root פקד, as does the verb ἐπισκέπτειν. Only rarely does the latter translate the Hebrew בקר (Lev. 13:36; II Esdras 4:15,19; 5:17; 6:1; 7:14; Ps. 26/27:4; Ezek. 34:11,12). For further dis-

cussions of this problem see J. Jeremias, *Jerusalem zur Zeit Jesu* (Göttingen: 2nd ed.; 1958), II, 1, pp. 132-33; K. G. Goetz, "Ist der מבקר der Genizafragmente wirklich das Vorbild des christlichen Episkopats?" *ZNW* XXX (1931), 89-93; H. W. Beyer, ἐπίσκοπος, *ThWB* II, 614-15; B. Reicke, "The Jewish 'Damascus Documents' and the New Testament," *SBU* VI (1946), 16; W. Nauck, "Probleme des frühchristlichen Amstsverständnisses (I Peter 5:2-3)," *ZNW* XLVIII (1957), 200-220; A. Adam, "Die Entstehung des Bischofsamtes," *Wort und Dienst* NF V (1957), 103-13; W. Eiss, "Das Amt des Gemeindeleiters bei den Essenern und der christlichen Episkopat," *Welt des Orients* II (1959), 514-19; F. Nötscher, "Vorchristliche Typen urchristlicher Ämter: Episkopos und Mebaqqer," *Die Kirche und ihre Ämter und Stände* (Festgabe J. Kardinal Frings; Köln, 1960), 315-38.

42. Cf. J. Dupont, *Le discours de Milet: Testament pastoral de saint Paul (Acts 20:18-36)* (Paris, 1962), p. 149, n. 1. This is not the place for a more detailed comparison, but CD 13:5-13 would lend itself to further discussion in this matter of the Christian "overseer."

43. We do not exclude the possibility of Essene influence on the early church in non-Palestinian areas. If, as seems likely, some Essene influence reached Damascus in the "camps" and even further into the hinterlands of Asia Minor (see P. Benoit, *NTS* VII [1961], 287), then possibly the connection of the Essene מבקר with the Christian ἐπίσκοπος should be sought in such areas.

44. See B. Gärtner, *The Temple and the Community in Qumran and the New Testament*, *SNTS*, Monograph series I (Cambridge, 1965), 99-101.

45. See 1QpHab 9:4-7; 10:9-13; 11:4-12; 4QpIs^b 2:7,10; 4QpIs^e 10-11; CD 11:17-20; 4QpNah.

46. Cf. W. Nauck, "Probleme des frühchristlichen Amtsverständnisses," pp. 209-14. E. Stauffer, "Jüdisches Erbe im urchristlichen Kirchenrecht," *ThLZ* LXXVII (1952), 203-4.

47. E.g., F. M. Cross, Jr., *Ancient Library*, pp. 235-37. M. Black, *The Scrolls and Christian Origins*, pp. 102-15. K. H. Kuhn, "The Lord's Supper and the Communal Meal at Qumran," *The Scrolls and the New Testament*, pp. 65-93. J. van der Ploeg, "The Meals of the Essenes," *JSS* II (1957), 163-75. E. F. Sutcliffe, "Sacred Meals at Qumran?" *Heythrop Journal* I (1960), 48-65. J. Gnilka, "Das Gemeinschaftsmahl der Essener," *BZ* V (1961), 39-55.

48. The phrase is derived from Isa. 2:2; cf. Mic. 4:1 Dan. 2:28. There is, however, a textual difficulty here: Vaticanus reads simply μετὰ ταῦτα; we have used what seems to be the better reading, based on Sinaiticus, Alexandrinus, and the Codex Bezae.

49. "The Use of Explicit Old Testament Quotations in Qumran Literature and in the New Testament," *NTS* VII (1960-61), 297-333.

50. *Ibid.*, pp. 304-5.

51. "The Dead Sea Manual of Discipline and the Jerusalem Church of Acts," *The Scrolls and the New Testament*, p. 129.

The Book of Acts as Source Material for the History of Early Christianity

ERNST HAENCHEN

I. Introduction

It is not easy to deduce facts and lines of historical development from an ancient author. For in his decisions about selection, combination, and presentation of facts, he will have been influenced by his own view of the history about which he writes. Besides, authors like Sallustus or Tacitus were moralists, concerned with the moral education of their readers. The case of Luke—the commonly used name of the author of Acts—is more difficult still. Luke was no professional historian and was not interested in writing a history of early Christianity, aside from the fact that in his time the modern concepts *history and early Christianity* were still nonexistent. According to his preface for the Third Gospel, he wanted to pass on a certain church tradition which he considered authentic. For the period of Jesus' ministry this tradition was a plentiful stream. But for the time between Easter and the death of Paul, the time with which the book of Acts deals, it was just a trickle. Moreover, the tradition was passed on and collected only insofar as it was edifying, that is, as far as it inspired and strengthened faith. This was primarily true of the Gospels: they told of Jesus' deeds and words. The message was passed on by the apostles and other disciples. Beyond this, whatever they themselves said and whatever wonders they performed did not weigh heavily in comparison. Therefore no one before Luke had thought of giving a connected account of the events after Easter. Here, then, Luke did pioneer work. He had no predecessor, nor any real successor, for the later Acts of the Apostles, for instance those of Peter, Thomas, and John, are almost completely legend and fiction, and to a considerable extent they are propaganda for Gnostic ideas.

258

II. Structure and Method of Acts

The book of Acts was not a "bestseller." Only slowly in the wake of the Third Gospel, did it gain recognition in the church. At the time of John Chrysostom it had been so nearly forgotten that he devoted a whole series of homilies to it. Yet Luke had done everything possible to make this book appealing to the Christian community. He writes history by telling stories: short, impressive, and dramatic scenes in relatively independent succession. He likes to use words and phrases of the Septuagint; in other words, he writes in "biblical style."

The work is skillfully *arranged*. The first of its four parts, chaps. 1–8:3, begins with a conversation between the disciples and the Risen One who answers their most important question; that is, most important to the readers. Thereupon the author describes the real beginning of the first congregation through the sending of the Spirit at Pentecost, and the congregation's preaching which falls entirely to Peter. To be sure, several other apostles, like John and Matthias, are occasionally mentioned also. But they remain shadows. Luke does not care to portray individual personalities, nor would the tradition have helped him to do so. The history of the early congregation makes up this first part, a quarter of the whole book.

The large second section begins at chap. 8:4. The entire early congregation, with the exception of the apostles, is driven from Jerusalem. This part ends in chap. 15 with the ultimate recognition of the Gentile mission free of the Torah. In this part events within and outside Jerusalem alternate. The local history of the early church and the beginning of worldwide mission to the Gentiles are thus integrated.

The third part starts at chap. 15:36. From here on Luke turns all his attention toward the Pauline mission which commands the stage until chap. 21:26. Luke tells the story of this mission as that of a single great journey (the form of the travelogue was a very popular one at that time, especially in novels).

With the arrest of Paul in chap. 21:27 ff. the fourth and last part of the book of Acts begins. The motto of this section is apology, the defense of Christianity against accusations raised especially by the Jews. In a certain sense, Luke here becomes the forerunner of the apologists. He very skilfully succeeds in giving Paul again and again a chance of pleading his defense, thereby making even the imprisoned Paul the center of action. When he takes the Christian message to Rome, capital of the world, the book has reached its internal goal along with its external conclusion.

What *method* does Luke use for this development? In the very first verses —as was then customary with multivolume works—he refers back to the content and conclusion of the first book: the story of the ascension. But he modifies it: whereas in the Third Gospel it takes place on Easter Day itself, it now happens forty days later. The fact that Luke can present the same event so completely differently shows the astonishing liberty this author takes. This is most evident in the three reports of the call of Paul (chaps. 9; 22; 26). Depending upon the requirements of the context, the very same event each time is thrown into a new light. That is important for the question of the historical value of the book of Acts. The author is not so much a historian in our sense of the word as he is a fascinating narrator. He writes not for a learned public which would keep track of all his references and critically compare them, but rather for a more or less nonliterary congregation which he wants to captivate and edify. For this purpose he uses a peculiar technique: he joins short, compact, picturesque scenes together like the stones of a mosaic.

III. An Example of Lucan Style

In Acts 1:3-8 we have the first of these small narrative units. For forty days the Risen One talks with his disciples about the kingdom of God. These forty days are not Luke's invention; he follows a recent and—in my judgment—secondary tradition. It did not agree with the end of his Gospel. And yet Luke took it up, for it permitted him to begin the book of Acts not with the apostles remaining alone, but with the Lord giving directives for the future. In vs. 8 he gives them a promise and a commission at the same time, and indirectly indicates the content and structure of Acts. At this point we notice how thoughtfully Luke works. Even though he is a popularizing narrator, he does not write at random but according to a well-considered plan. To be sure, this strategy has its limitations. The reference to the reign of God in 1:3 is only a literary device to prepare the readers for the question of the disciples about it in 1:6. If anyone takes the words of 1:3 seriously as history—that Jesus talked about the kingdom of God with his disciples for forty days—he either makes Jesus a preposterously poor teacher who cannot clarify what he means in ever so long a period, or he makes the disciples appear incredibly foolish. Luke intended neither the one nor the other. So we are left with the explanation that already in 1:3 the author wanted to suggest the theme of 1:6. He did not reflect upon the consequence which vs. 3 would have if understood historically, because he did not mean this verse historically. Luke is done an injustice if every detail in the book of Acts is taken as material for historical reconstruction, reconstruction of the history of the early church (Urgemeinde).

Acts 1:8 contains the missionary command to the church—although the concept *church* is still strange to Luke; only in 9:31 does he use the word to mean several local congregations. Here we see clearly how Luke conceived of missionary development: it begins in Jerusalem among Jews only; this limitation drops out as the mission spreads to Samaria (Samaritans were no longer Jews but not yet Gentiles either); and finally the world mission "to the end of the earth" develops, presumably to Rome. Thus the links of the chain between 1:8 and chap. 28 are joined. Paul appears as almost the sole representative of the mission to the Gentiles. His crossing back and forth on his journeys gives the reader little opportunity to surmise that the history of early Christian missions was much more colorful and diverse than Luke paints it. And yet, perhaps he was quite aware of the diversity —he does mention Barnabas, Apollos, Aquila, and Priscilla—and deliberately simplified the picture. Thereby he makes the historical path of the "Word of God" from Jerusalem to Rome intelligible and clear.

Luke certainly was not the first to tell the story of the ascension (1:9-11). New and peculiar to him, however, is the commentary which the doubled *angelus interpres* (1:10-11) gives: Assured of the return of the Lord, the Christians are to turn to their task here on earth. Luke does not yet express this openly. Only as the book of Acts unfolds does he make it clear: the great task is the Christian world mission. The word of the angels, then, carefully prepares for an entirely new position of the Christians toward the world. Luke himself lives exactly at the time of transition when the old hope and the new realization of the situation still live side by side, at the dawn of a new day in history. To him who knows how to read between the lines and to hear what is left unsaid, the book of Acts gives rich information about what is commonly called "the postapostolic age."

IV. The Historical Gain from the First Part of Acts

Traditional materials are few in the first part. That becomes clear when we disregard the great Lucan speech-compositions. We then are left with the following: the story of the miracle of Pentecost (chap. 2; using Jewish tradition), the story of the healing of a lame man (chap. 3), the judgment of God upon Ananias and Sapphira (chap. 5), and the dispute between "Hellenists" and "Hebrews" (chap. 6:1). With the exception of a comment like 4:36 and a few names, that is all there is to be found of concrete tradition. It is amazing, however, how much Luke has made of so little! He has constantly steered the plot toward a climax: the church, represented by the apostles, gets involved in deeper and deeper conflict with the High Council. The Council does not react to the first address of Peter (chap. 2); after the second (chap. 3), it has Peter and John arrested, threatens them and forbids them to preach (chap. 4). In chap. 5, all the apostles are arrested and sentenced to the harsh punishment of thirty-nine lashes (see also II Cor. 11:24). This conflict reaches its climax in the stoning of Stephen and the flight of the entire congregation (8:1).

In spite of this outward pressure the church seems to thrive inwardly: all believers have everything in common (2:44); they sell their homes and possessions and distribute the proceeds as needed (2:45; it escaped Luke that the two reports do not quite agree). All believers were of one heart and soul (4:32). But then we learn of the embezzlement of holy property (5:1-11), and chap. 6:1 gives proof that the congregation was by no means unanimous.

In both cases, in the presentation of external and the internal situation, the creative imagination of Luke had to fill out and connect the individual traditions into a new unit. In doing so he, of course, injected foreign elements into the sparse material. The first hearing before the Sanhedrin (chap. 4) is artificially joined to a story of a healing which did not call for such a consequence. The climax in the dispute with the High Council is given in 4:19 and 5:29 in the words of Socrates borrowed from Plato's *Apology* (29 D): "I shall, then, obey God rather than you." A plausible motive exists neither for the first nor for the second arrest, and the focal point of the entire line of action—the persecution and flight of the whole congregation following the murder of Stephen (8:1 in disagreement with 8:3)— is a mistaken interpretation of remnants of tradition. In reality only the Hellenistic part of the congregation led by the seven and headed by Stephen was persecuted. The Hebrew part, which according to Luke was led by the apostles, remained unmolested.

The church at that time, then, was by no means of one heart and soul but was split into two independent groups. Luke did not find it easy to make this split appear to be harmless. He does not mention the cause of the distinction between Hellenists and Hebrews which suddenly appears in 6:1. Presumably (see the names of the "seven" in 6:6) the Hellenists were Greek-speaking Jews of the dispersion who had settled in Jerusalem (cf. also 6:9 and 9:29), and the Hebrews were Aramaic-speaking Jews of Palestine. But if in the daily distribution of food the Hellenistic widows were repeatedly neglected (the imperfect tense in 6:1 expresses continuation or repetition) and the Hellenists therefore murmured against the Hebrews, the distributors must have been Hebrews. And they must have had a grievance against the Hellenists, or they would not have slighted their widows. The mere distinction between Jews of the dispersion and Jews of Palestine is not enough to explain the separation of the two groups. To be sure, Luke smoothed over the difference as far as possible; to do so he had to have the whole congregation persecuted and driven out. But although according to 9:31 the churches in Judaea, Galilee, and Samaria were enjoying peace again, 11:19 says that those who were scattered because of the persecution of Stephen were still fugitives, wandering as far as Phoenicia, Cyprus, and Antioch. Here it becomes clear that only one group—the Hellenists—was persecuted, the group which then initiated the Gentile mission, characterized by freedom from the law. But even before that, this group must have differed noticeably in its life and doctrine from the Hebrews, otherwise it would not have been singled out for persecution. Some scholars, however, consider the Hellenists to have been Greeks, in other words uncircumcised Gentiles whom the earliest church had admitted nevertheless. Three objections are fatal to this hypothesis: (1) In that period of nationalistic and growing religious rigidity, the Jews of Jerusalem would have expelled the whole church immediately if it had accepted any uncircumcised Gentiles. (2) James, the Lord's brother, was able to preach Jesus as the Messiah in Jerusalem up to the early sixties because he rigidly adhered to the law. (3) The difficult negotiations between Antioch and Jerusalem concerning the Gentile mission which was free of the law (cf. Gal. 2 and Acts 15:1-2) would never have come about if the earliest church had admitted uncircumcised Gentiles before that time. The Hellenists must have taken a freer stand toward the law than the Hebrews, possibly appealing to Jesus' own attitude.

Did Luke still possess exact information about these circumstances, or did his ignorance of them mislead him to blunt the contrast between Hellenists and Hebrews? That he did know somewhat more than he says can be deduced from 6:1. Besides, his presentation remains full of contradictions. To all appearances a new office was created in order to do away with the abuses. But Luke does not say that the seven become the newly inducted deacons (although he repeatedly uses the concept διακονία in 6:1-6), nor does he present the occupation of two of the seven, Stephen and Philip, as that of deacons, but rather as that of independent missionaries. The split between the two groups, then, must have happened through some provocation, perhaps negligible in itself—the first confessional schism in church history. Perhaps the Hebrews did not even regret that they were no longer burdened by the membership of the Hellenists in their congregation. Luke, edifying writer that he was, was happy about the chance to settle the misunderstandings through the creation of a new office. None but a very alert reader notices the ticklish undercurrent in the way this episode is told. One of the seven, Nicolaus, is called a proselyte of Antioch, a detail that anticipates the fact that some of the fugitive Hellenists, among them probably Barnabas, went to Antioch.

In chaps. 6–8:3 two accounts are clearly mingled: the stoning of Stephen by an unruly crowd and his execution by the High Council. This second item was probably introduced by Luke himself; in his eyes the Sanhedrin was always the real enemy of the Christians and at the same time this detail furnishes him the needed audience for the extended speech of Stephen. It goes without saying that this speech does not consist of old tradition. Rather, Luke cleverly combined a synagogue sermon about the destiny of Israel with passionate complaints against Israel which he drew from his own circle.

To introduce Paul at this point presented a real difficulty for Luke. At first Paul only looks on and consents as Stephen is executed (8:1). Two verses later he himself is already "the" persecutor. In 9:1 and especially in 22:4 ff. and 26:9 ff. this is further intensified: Paul has always voted for capital punishment at the trials of the Christians, hence with his conversion the persecution of Christians is immediately over. Luke's desire to make Paul a Jerusalemite zealous for the Torah generated this theme. As a matter of fact it was not within the jurisdiction of the high priest and Council to bring about a persecution of Christians in Damascus. Probably Paul then lived in Damascus and persecuted the local Hellenistic Christian community through the means at his disposal in the local synagogue. Here, too, Luke had to make his own combinations with the limited reports from the time of the apostles and to bridge over the gaps in the traditions by his own assumptions. The book of Acts may be read properly as source material for early Christianity only if the reader frees himself from the charm of its simplified presentation and does not overlook the thread of what is edifying in the Lucan fabric.

V. The Historical Substance of the Second Part of Acts

Here it is only in chaps. 11:1-18; 12; and 15 that the events take place in Jerusalem, after the account had already shifted to the Mediterranean coast (Azotus—Caesarea) and to Samaria. From Antioch it takes a big jump (chap. 13-14) to Cyprus and Asia Minor. The author no longer had a realistic picture of the events, but had to combine, as best he could, single pieces of tradition into a comprehensive view which was as harmonious as possible. The proof of this is furnished by the stories about Philip in chap. 8, for 8:13 suddenly interrupts the activities of Philip in Samaria and replaces him with Peter and John, the messengers of the early church. According to 8:40 Philip settled in Caesarea where we still find him in 21:8. But according to chap. 10 it was Peter who founded the Christian community in Caesarea! Perhaps this congregation later claimed to have been founded as a Gentile-Christian church by Peter himself through his baptizing a Roman centurion. For Luke, this secondary tradition grew to incomparable importance, for it described the decisive turning point in the history of early Christianity. With it the story about a Jewish sect which believed in Christ became the history of a new world religion.

If one is to understand correctly Luke's attitude at this point, one must consider the fact that Luke was no longer able to grasp theologically, as Paul had, the legitimacy of the mission to the Gentiles free of the Torah. To him there was no question about mission to the Gentiles; that God had willed it was beyond all doubt. But how could it be shown graphically that God had willed it? In the thinking of that generation there was just one way of doing so: through miracles. That is why heavenly interventions here become more frequent (and are now and again retold): in bright daylight Cornelius is visited by an angel—it was not the night vision of a dream—who announces that God has heard his prayers and considered his alms, and commands him to send for Peter, whose exact address is given—fortunately Luke already had moved him into nearby Joppa. What Peter is to do, the wise narrator does not report just yet: Peter himself does not know it yet! In the meantime he has, however, a vision of clean and unclean creatures (10:10-16); vs. 28 explains how Peter or Luke understood it: "God has shown me that I should not call any man common or unclean." But that is not all. When the messengers from Cornelius knock at his gate, the Spirit tells Peter to accompany them without hesitation, for he himself had sent them. About the relationship God-Spirit-Angel Luke did not stop to speculate, assuming that his readers knew that they belonged together. In the meantime in Caesarea, Cornelius was expecting them with his kinsmen and close friends. When the distinguished guest arrives and asks why Cornelius has sent for him, the reader gets to hear the story of the angelic message once more, this time from the mouth of Cornelius. In 11:1 ff. he will hear it for the third time, as the eyewitness report of Peter to the congregation of Jerusalem. This repetition duly impresses upon the reader the participation of heaven in the first baptism of a Gentile. Now Peter understands that God shows no prejudice, no partiality, "but in every nation any one who fears him and does what is right is acceptable to him" (10:35). Whoever can say that cancels out the preeminence of Israel, whether he knows it or not: if God preferred one people such as Israel he would be partial! Luke has no inkling of the extent to which he thereby eliminates the continuity of the story of salvation between Jews and Christians. It certainly is not Pauline theology that appears here, nor is it anything ever thought of by Peter. It is, rather, the theology of Gentile Christianity toward the end of the first century in which Luke lived not only outwardly but theologically; it no longer sees any sense or any truth in Israel's election. What Paul foresaw with apprehension (Rom. 11:18 ff.)—that the Gentiles would no longer acknowledge Israel's preeminence—has here become fact. Even if in the following chapters the church of Jerusalem intermittently plays an important role, it is already apparent that in reality it has lost its position of leadership. It cannot resist the wondrous power of God who sends his Holy Spirit to the Gentiles even before baptism; this is irrevocable proof that he desires that Gentiles be baptized, without circumcision. The fact that the Gentiles speak in tongues like the apostolic community at Pentecost definitely makes it clear: Gentile Christians and Jewish Christians are of equal rank. To be sure, the earliest church did not immediately comprehend. How could it? The church, and the reader too, must be informed again, though in a shortened version, and acknowledge in amazement: "Then to the Gentiles also God has granted repentance unto life" (11:18)! Luke is careful here not to credit Peter openly with the founding of a Gentile-Christian congregation although in truth it should have come to that (cf. 10:24 and 44). But he must not lay his colors on too thickly. It remains hard enough to understand that in the course of a few years the early church will have forgotten again what in 11:18 it had learned and confessed.

Luke had still another reason to be grateful for the tradition of a baptism of Gentiles by Peter: in this weightiest decision in the apostolic period, human structures, in spite of all that was extraordinary, must not be ignored: Peter and the earliest church also had a role to play. The very church of Jerusalem, guardian of orthodoxy, acknowledged the shocking claim of equal rights of the Gentile Christians! Jerusalem has spoken, as in the later formulation: *Roma locuta, causa finita* (Rome has spoken, the case is closed). The normative human authority has approved the mission to the Gentiles which did not require the law: to the Gentiles also God has granted repentance unto life!

One point has puzzled many people: clearly Paul was the favorite hero of Luke. Why then did he withdraw the title "the apostle to the Gentiles" from him and present it to Peter? Did Luke's imagination here run away with him, or did he coolly and purposefully calculate what his own time required? In my opinion neither alternative is correct. Here again Luke supported his picture of "church history" with certain traditions circulating at that time. Indeed, there must have been rumors to this effect even in Paul's own time. Why else did he in his letter to the Galatians so desperately insist upon his being an apostle not from men or through a man? Why did he affirm by oath (Gal. 1:20) that he had made contact with Jerusalem only late and casually? Evidently even then it was said in some circles that Paul was not really a true apostle: all that he taught correctly he owed to the apostles in Jerusalem. Such a version of the early history of Paul apparently also found its way to Luke, who accepted it in all innocence. It sounded so plausible since clearly Paul was not one of the twelve apostles. Only by their approval could he pursue his course and follow the example of Peter.

But the tradition which Luke followed not only cast a false light upon Paul but was also fragmentary, and the combination of these two factors could bring damaging results. That can be demonstrated by one important case.

According to Acts 9:19-20 Paul, a few days after his baptism, started his missionary work among the Jews of Damascus. Before long, however, they tried to do away with him. Since they guarded the gates by day and by night, he could escape only by way of a basket lowered over the wall. He went to Jerusalem where Barnabas introduced him to the initially suspicious congregation. Having been accepted by the apostles into their community, he began his mission work with the Jewish Hellenists, the Jews of the dispersion. Again a murder plot threatened and again he was saved by Christians who sent him back to Tarsus by way of Caesarea.

At first glance this story seems complete and convincing enough. But it is wrong. Following his call—neither he himself nor the book of Acts calls it "conversion"—he went not to Jerusalem, as apparently claimed by some, but to "Arabia." We must not suppose this to mean that he visited Israel's holy places on the Sinai peninsula and there in meditation tried to come to terms with his past. He went, rather, into the land of the Nabatean Arabs whose border was not far from the gates of Damascus. Why he did not remain in Damascus where he had separated himself from the Jewish community and had persecuted the Christian one is perhaps quite understandable. It seems that Paul then attempted to work as a missionary among the Jews and Nabateans in the latters' territory.

In this connection it has occasionally been pointed out how different the course of the history of the church, and not of it only, would have been if Paul had been successful in the East, anticipating by centuries the triumphal progress of the later Nestorian missionaries. But such perspectives must not obscure the fact that Christian missions in the West already before and without Paul had produced great results. "Unknown soldiers" of Christ had founded the congregations of Damascus, Antioch, Ephesus, and Rome. Even success in the East would not have hindered the progress of the Word of God in the West. But Paul simply was not very successful in the East, although he worked there for more than two years as a missionary. Rather, his preaching of Jesus as the coming Messiah seems to have roused the suspicion and enmity of King Aretas IV. Paul had to return to Damascus, his second home. But here, too, the situation was unbearable in the long run, especially since the ethnarch, Aretas, who probably resided in the Arabian suburb, had the gates of the "City of the Damascenes" guarded —from the outside, of course. It has been surmised that the ethnarch was the commander in charge of the city at that time and that Rome had made a present of Damascus to Aretas (the reason for this conjecture being that no Roman coins from certain years have been found in Damascus). But if that were true the commander of the city, who could have relied upon Jewish spies, would have ordered a police raid to arrest Paul and send him to Petra. As a matter of fact, the ethnarch was not in the "City of the Damascenes" but lay in ambush outside it. Here II Cor. 11:32-33 becomes important. The Christians lowered Paul in a basket over the wall by night. And now, three years after he had become a Christian, he decided to seek out Peter in Jerusalem. James, the brother of the Lord, who was probably already influential at that time, also came into contact with the former persecutor of the Christians. The other apostles Paul did not meet, as he himself assures us. What the topic of his conversations with Peter was, we do not know. Only one thing is certain: Paul did not, at that time in Jerusalem, introduce himself as *the* apostle to the Gentiles, who preached Christianity without the Torah to the Gentiles and who claimed equality with Peter. They would most likely only have shaken their heads at such claims. In any case, if all this had then been discussed and agreed upon, the later negotiations between Antioch and Jerusalem would have been altogether unnecessary. Probably the only thing that Paul was able to achieve at that time was to convince them that the Lord had appeared also to him. But let us not forget that more than five hundred other Christians could boast of such an appearance as well! Presumably the result of these discussions was that Paul was acknowledged as a Christian and a missionary who was now going or being sent to try to work in his home province of Cilicia. For Paul could not yet point to any corroborating missionary success, nor is it likely that he then looked upon himself as he did later when he wrote to the Galatians and Romans.

Another example of insufficient information with false conclusions on the part of the author is disclosed by chap. 11:27-30. At that time prophets from Jerusalem are reported to have walked to Antioch, a distance of 180 miles. One of them, named Agabus, is said to have foretold a great famine over all the world, which then occurred under Claudius. The congregation of Antioch immediately takes up a collection for Jerusalem and sends it by Paul and Barnabas. Here, I believe, three different recollections are combined: (1) the journey of Barnabas and Paul to the so-called Apostolic Council; (2) the collection from the Pauline congregations which Paul toward the end of his missionary activity in the East of the Mediterranean world took to Jerusalem, a fact not mentioned in Acts; and (3) the report of a terrible famine under Claudius which afflicted, though not all the world, Palestine and Jerusalem. That Paul did not travel to Jerusalem at the time given in Acts 11:30 can be inferred with certainty from the enumeration of his journeys in Gal. 1 and 2.

On the other hand Luke does give many an important and indisputable report. In 11:26, for instance, we read that it was in Antioch where the disciples were first called Christians. Luke himself makes no use of this name. He calls the Christians either disciples—probably already in his time an archaic term—or brethren. The name Christian, especially since the persecution by Nero, did not have favorable overtones. Tacitus with his usual sarcasm says (*Ann.* XV, 44) that the crowds called these people, who were hated for their wickedness, the "Good Ones" (*Chrestianos; chrestiani* at that time was pronounced just like *christiani*). Tacitus himself, being an educated historian, of course knew that *auctor huius nominis Christus* (Christ, the author of this name) had been executed by the procurator Pontius Pilate in the reign of Tiberius. Luke mentions the infamous name in passing only, perhaps indicating that the notorious fellows called by that name in reality were those peaceful "brethren" described in his book. We have no reason to doubt the truth of the statement that this name arose in Antioch.

The space allotted does not permit the discussion of all the short narrative units. The example of a few must show how they can be tested for potential historical worth, for instance in chap. 15. Luke starts out by saying that some men from Judea, that is to say, Jewish Christians from Jerusalem, came to Antioch and taught that circumcision was necessary for salvation. Barnabas and Paul opposed them, and the congregation finally sent the two of them to Jerusalem to negotiate. There in the congregational meeting certain Pharisees who had been converted to Christ had likewise required circumcision and the observance of the entire law. Here now we see plainly how artificial Luke's reconstruction of the events in chaps. 10 and 15 really is. For Peter now claims that it was he whom God "in the early days" had chosen to convert the Gentiles. That seems to have been forgotten in the course of the years by the church of Jerusalem, and it is enough for Peter to remind the forgetful people of that bit of recent history. James adds a scriptural proof, but insists that the Gentile Christians, too, abstain from meat offered to idols, from blood, from what is strangled, and from unchastity (15:29). Luke reports that this was communicated to the congregation of

Antioch by letter and by delegation. Again Luke confuses two things. Paul offers a report in Gal. 2 concerning the negotiations in Jerusalem which he and Barnabas had conducted chiefly with the three "pillars," Peter, James, the brother of the Lord, and John. And he expressly emphasizes in Gal. 2:6 and 10: "Those, I say, who were of repute added nothing to me," and, "Only they would have us remember the poor, which very thing I was eager to do." Consequently, those four demands were not raised and agreed upon until a later occasion in which Paul was not involved.

Already chaps. 13 and 14 of Acts contain a travelogue. It gives, however, surprisingly few concrete details: a tangled story about the Jewish magician Elymas, also called Bar-Jesus, who was temporarily blinded by Paul; a report of the premature return trip of John Mark; and finally the stoning of Paul in Lystra. The story of the adoration of Barnabas and Paul as the gods Zeus and Hermes incarnate, told before the story of the stoning, follows a tradition which transfers a legendary motif, already used by Ovid, to the two "apostles" (as they are called for once). Due to the lack of concrete material, some critics have taken this whole journey to be a Lucan invention. However, we must remember that this earliest of Paul's journeys naturally was the least well known. We therefore cannot expect Luke to furnish us with a detailed description of it. In the account of this first journey in which Paul works beside Barnabas, the "we" of the later accounts does not yet appear. This circumstance, too, probably means that Luke did not yet have any eyewitness reports at his disposal, as he did for later sections where he indicates this to the reader by using "we." The difficult chronological problems cannot be dealt with here.

VI. Historical Problems in the Third Part of Acts

According to 15:36 ff., Barnabas and Paul fell out over John Mark, who on their former trip had turned back prematurely. In contrast, critical scholars have referred to Gal. 2:13 where even Barnabas under Jewish-Christian pressure gave up communion fellowship with the Gentile Christians in Antioch. Presumably this argument in Antioch was the reason why Paul now set out on his missionary task independent of that congregation, accompanied only by Silas and Timothy. That Paul belatedly had Timothy circumcised is one of those slanderous rumors which were spread abroad about Paul; perhaps it is this very rumor he refers to in Gal. 5:11. Luke was quick to believe it because Paul thereby more closely corresponded to his ideal of a law-abiding Jew.

The famous "we" appears for the first time in 16:10 and disappears in 16:17. Usually it means Paul and his companions, and sometimes only the latter. On the strength of Philem. 24, Col. 4:14, and especially II Tim. 4:11, it has been surmised that Luke the Physician wrote the book of Acts, that he had joined the little group of Christian missionaries in Troas. Since the "we" disappears in 16:17 at Philippi, only to emerge again (in 20:5) years later at that same place, the conclusion has been drawn that Luke remained in Philippi and practiced his profession. But that would have been a strange way to act for a man who had just joined a group of Christian missionaries, all the more amazing since 16:10 reads: "And when he had seen the vision, immediately we sought to go on into Macedonia, concluding that God had called us to preach the gospel to them." For this reason Luke has been thought by some to have been the leader of the newly founded congregation of Philippi. However, at that time a monarchic episcopacy was still unheard of, nor does the Letter to the Philippians warrant any such assumption. This indicates again how dangerous it is for scholarship to interpret a New Testament writing in the light of a second century tradition instead of starting with the writing itself. Granted that no scholar is immune against wishful thinking, whether positive or negative, and that therefore self-criticism is constantly necessary—when all indications converge as they do in the book of Acts, and when they all speak against the author's having been an eyewitness, we must not blindfold ourselves.

But how can we get around the fact that the "we" does not reoccur until 20:5? What does it mean that it continues up to 21:18—skipping the inserted account of Paul's speech to the elders of Ephesus at Miletus—only to reappear at the time of the journey to Rome? Martin Dibelius, to whom we are so greatly indebted for a new understanding of Acts, probably saw the matter correctly: Luke's "we" is a literary form! But what does that mean? Dibelius offers two possibilities: the "we" may suggest that the narrator himself took part in the journey; or it may mean that for some of the trips he was able to depend upon reports from an eyewitness. I consider the latter possibility the correct explanation. How in each case Luke succeeded in procuring his material we do not know. Harnack, by his linguistic comparison of the "we" sections with the other sections of Acts, showed—reluctantly—that Luke revised even these we-sections. This assumption seems most plausible.

In this part of Acts, also, the individual small units are of decidedly varying historical value. For instance, vss. 11-15 in chap. 16 are precise and graphic, and there is no reason to question their historical reliability. But the very next story about the demoniac slave girl clearly is a narrative unit not logically tied to the context in which it now stands. Nobody can be indicted for driving out an evil spirit; people would be careful not to arrest so powerful an exorcist who might greatly harm them by means of the evil eye or otherwise. But the author was interested in playing down as much as possible the discord which Paul and Silas had with the leaders of this Roman colony. Most likely the missionaries had overlooked the law which forbade Jewish propaganda among Roman citizens—who in those days was capable of recognizing that the Christian preaching about Jesus as the Messiah was non-Jewish? Also, the report of the events in prison immediately takes a legendary turn: an earthquake able to shake off a prisoner's chains has never yet occurred. On the other hand, the quaking of a house as a divine response to prayer had been told frequently in pagan Hellenism. Probably only the conclusion is historical: having been released from jail, Paul and Silas were immediately told to leave the city.

In 17:6 the situation betrays a much later time, a time in which Christian missionaries were preaching throughout the whole Roman Empire, the author's own lifetime.

Chapter 17:13-16 presents us with the rare opportunity of comparing the report of Paul himself and the Lucan presentation with regard to its historical value. According to Luke, certain Jews from Thessalonica stirred up the Beroean mob against Paul, whereupon the Christians immediately sent the endangered apostle off to the sea, some of them bringing him as far as Athens. Silas and Timothy remained in Beroea, however. As his companions took leave of Paul in Athens, he entreated them to send him Silas and Timothy as soon as possible. But from I Thess. 3:2 we learn that Timothy did go to Athens with Paul. Paul sent him back from there to Thessalonica because he was anxious about that young church. Von Dobschütz, in his well-known commentary on the Letters to the Thessalonians, tried to harmonize the Pauline passage with the Lucan one (pp. 130-31) by having Paul send Timothy from Beroea not to Athens but to Thessalonica. But even in this apologetic effort the account of Acts had to be corrected. Of course one can say that this divergence is unimportant, and so it is. But even this divergence, so slight in itself, shows that we can by no means be certain that a Lucan report corresponds to the facts, even if such a report is in itself consistent and seems to offer a precise report.

Probably here, too, it must be assumed that Luke had received only fragmentary reports about this part of the Pauline mission and tried to utilize them as well as he could. The words of I Thess. 2:2, προπαθόντες καὶ ὑβρισθέντες . . . ἐν Φιλίπποις, assure us that Paul was in great trouble in Philippi. In Acts 16:22-24 and 16:33 Luke also speaks of this. In the Lucan report the impression of Paul's suffering is treated far too lightly and to a certain degree canceled by the miracle of divine liberation which changes even the jailer into a believer. If such a miracle really followed upon the whipping and jailing in Philippi, Paul's own words in I Thess. 2:2 do not make sense: "Though we had already suffered and been shamefully treated at Philippi, we had courage in our God to declare to you the gospel of God in the face of great opposition." This statement incontestably confirms what has already been deduced: the miracle story of Acts 16:25-34 is an inserted legend from later times.

I Thess. 2:14 also enables us to supplement the Lucan account. Luke only reports that Jason, Paul's host, had to furnish a bond for Paul. But what Paul says makes it clear that the Christians in Thessalonica were quite literally persecuted by their own countrymen. Basically, Luke's thoughts dwell only upon Paul. Only those who come close to Paul momentarily take on life in Luke's narrative. Paul here mentions persecutions to which the churches of Judaea were exposed. We are not, of course, to think of the persecution which Paul supposedly started in Jerusalem, nor of the one in Damascus in which Paul really did take part. Of these Judaean persecutions Luke apparently knew nothing. This passage also indicates how fragmentary our knowledge of early Christian history is. And yet, without the book of Acts our situation would be incomparably worse.

One more passage in this third section gives us a chance of bringing texts of Acts and Paul himself face to face. Luke tells of Paul's sojourn in Athens in a strangely vague manner. We hear a great deal about Athens, but we do not learn with whom Paul lived, how long he stayed, and what the results were of his sabbath sermons in the synagogue. Instead, Luke devotes his whole artistry and space to a description of Athens and the Areopagus scene. Luke may have had an older story about an Areopagite named Dionysius who showed interest in Paul, and from this may have inferred an Areopagus sermon. But he makes no mention of the regular founding of a church, nor could he have, for according to I Cor. 16:15 the household of Stephanas in Corinth constituted the "first converts in Achaia," and Athens belonged to this province. Also, I Cor. 2:3 points to a failure in Athens. Here Paul writes that he came to Corinth ἐν ἀσθενείᾳ, which can mean either sickness or weakness. In spite of that, his preaching here was ultimately a great success. That he went to Corinth "in much fear and trembling" would be quite conceivable if an attempt at founding a church in Athens had failed. What is lacking in Luke's portrait of Paul here is any mention of the hours of despondency (cf. II Cor. 11:28), of fear and trembling. The Lucan Paul is always in good spirit: never is he at a loss for words; he performs great miracles just as readily as Peter (Acts 19:11 ff.; cf. 5:15). Precisely because the Lucan Paul is so strong it is not his weakness that can bring the power of Christ to perfection (II Cor. 12:9). That shows better than many another detail the inadequacy of the Lucan presentation of Paul where deeper understanding is involved.

VII. The Problem of the Fourth Section of Acts

With the arrest of Paul, the author of Acts gets himself into a desperate situation. What does a dramatist do when his hero is put out of action before the last act? To be sure, Shakespeare in *Julius Caesar* knew how to solve this problem. But Luke had no Christian Mark Antony at his disposal, nor could he conjure up the ghost of Paul. Samuel Becket in his play *Happy Days* actually succeeds in making his heroine, who in the course of the drama is being buried, incapable of action from the very beginning. The heroine-author achieves a semblance of action through a constant recalling of the past. Luke incidentally made use of this device in the apologies of this fourth section. But it does not offer him a real solution. He does not represent a generation of despair or catastrophe, but one of hope and salvation. And it is a literary masterstroke of his to have succeeded in presenting the imprisoned Paul as such a savior.

Again and again Paul speaks in Acts of his past; he never tires of demonstrating how faithful to the law he is as a Jew, and how irreproachably he has lived. But such apologies are not a retreat into memories of happy days now past. Rather, they step up the dramatic action to higher and higher levels. First Paul, bound in chains, speaks to Lysias, the Roman tribune and commander of Jerusalem, then to the people of Jerusalem themselves. Then follows the scene before the Sanhedrin; next Paul defends himself—against Tertullus and the Sanhedrin—before Felix, the governor. Finally he even gets permission to defend himself and prove his innocence before Governor

Festus and King Agrippa. In 27:24 a still further hearing before an even more august judge is discreetly intimated: Paul will appear before Caesar! In short, the seemingly hopeless plight of an author prematurely deprived of his hero has been brilliantly overcome by Luke. The arrest permits him to give Paul an entirely new line of activity, a new field of action.

From a historical point of view, has integrity always been maintained? Scholars and critics, at any rate, agree that Luke himself in his report of the journey to Rome (chap. 27) inserted the verses which glorify Paul. For these, there was no support in tradition. In spite of that, it can be shown, I believe, how Luke composed these scenes from some traditional material at his disposal. The source which somehow went back to the report of a traveling companion, perhaps Aristarchus (cf. "we"), in vs. 12 mentioned that while taking council in Fair Havens the majority decided to sail on, since the beautifully named harbor was only a stopping-place, "not suitable to winter in." It turned out later that the continuation of the trip was disastrous. The minority, then, had been right in voting against it. For Luke the question now was: who had had the foresight to advise against proceeding? Naturally he thought of Paul—not, of course, on account of the latter's wide travel experience, something in which the shipowner, the captain, and presumably many of the ship's personnel were his superiors. But Paul always had God on his side, of course. Thus his "I perceive" (27:10) in his advice against proceeding was of prophetic nature. Luke on his part reports all this not as a mere surmise with great inner probability but as reality itself. The opposing party consisted of the experts who had judged on the basis of their experience with the weather—in other words, with mere worldly wisdom. That Luke gives the centurion the deciding voice does not quite fit in with his mention of the majority. But later in 27:3, following his source, Luke would need the centurion, Rome's representative, as Paul's friend and helper, which he already has shown himself to be.

Since Paul had announced the disaster which later did not turn out to be quite so bad after all, a certain difficulty arose for the author. He could not very well let Paul say: "Go ahead and sail, your ship will be doomed but you yourselves will get through." His warning could be taken seriously only if he predicted the loss of ship, cargo, personnel, and passengers. Since the last part of this warning was not to be fulfilled, God must have informed Paul ahead of time. For this reason Luke inserted Paul's speech of 27:21-26. It relates that during that very night an angel had told him that God had given into Paul's hands the lives of all those who sailed with him. Since Paul himself had to appear before Caesar, the ship could not simply go down with all aboard, rather, all had to be saved for Paul's sake. In a sense, then, Paul is the savior of them all. In formulating this speech, Luke was not quite successful. He does not let Paul start with the angel story immediately, but begins the account with the motif of ἀσιτία, the fasting of the wind-tossed people. However, the speech does not end, as one might expect with his urging them to eat now that they know they will be saved. Luke reserves this for later; he lets Paul end with the prediction that the ship will run aground upon an island. Of course this, too, is part of his prophetic foreknowledge. Thereby Luke has connected the prophetic discourse of Paul with one further detail from his source material, to the effect that the sailors sensed that they were approaching land and dropped anchor. The anchors were lowered from the stern so as to prevent a dangerous 180 degree turn of the ship. But to be entirely safe, they lowered the boat into the sea—probably by order of the captain—by means of a block-and-tackle attached to the foremast. The soldiers, uncomprehending and suspicious landlubbers, cut away the ropes in order to prevent the sailors from their suspected flight and the boat drifted off. Luke did not realize that this was a chief contributing factor in causing the shipwreck on the following day. If they had still been in possession of the lifeboat, they would not have had to try to beach the ship but could have anchored in the bay and landed everyone with the lifeboat. Luke here saw his opportunity of again presenting Paul as their savior: it was he who had instigated the soldiers' action which eventually got them to land. That means, however, that Paul himself was in fact a cause of the shipwreck.

After all this, Luke sees fit to continue Paul's speech of 27:23-26. Now Paul indeed admonishes them to eat having gone ἄσιτοι, without food, for so long: they all take heart and eat and so does Paul (cf. 27:36 with 27:22).

Having lightened the ship by throwing overboard the grain cargo, they try to land on a sandy beach in what today is called the Bay of St. Paul. But the ship strikes a shoal and breaks up. Here Luke intervenes again: "The soldiers' plan was to kill the prisoners, lest any should swim away and escape" (vs. 42). But the centurion who wants to rescue Paul—now it is Rome that rescues Paul!—gives orders how they are all to reach shore. As a matter of fact, it would probably be the captain who would give such orders in a situation of this kind.

In what follows, the author seems to forget altogether that Paul is a prisoner (especially apparent in 28:14a). Of course, he has not really forgotten (cf. 28:16), but the reader is not to feel it.

In 28:17-31 Luke accomplishes a literary masterstroke. In order to let Paul, the chosen instrument of the mission to the Gentiles, introduce Christainity into Rome, the author hides the Roman congregation from view. Instead of getting in touch with it, Paul makes contact with the Jews who allegedly know nothing of the Christians except that they are defamed everywhere (28:22). The Jews invite Paul to expound his teachings to them. When they remain unconvinced, Paul announces to them (as already in 13:46 and 18:6): "This salvation of God has been sent to the Gentiles; they will listen." Luke has written the Jews off.

Considering all this, what was the meaning of the apologies starting with chap. 22? In them Luke has shown that Christianity in its doctrine of the resurrection agrees with the strictest sect within Judaism, that of the Pharisees. The difference between Christianity and Judaism is an internal Jewish matter, incomprehensible even to a benevolent Roman like Festus. Rome, then, should not get embroiled against the Christians and their mission in which there is nothing subversive. Let the government take again the attitude which it had taken in Paul's last two years in Rome, when he was allowed to preach "quite openly and unhindered" (28:31).

With that, the goal of the book has been reached: the story of the Christian mission has arrived at Rome, and the author recommends to Rome a course of action for the future in line with her actual practice—up to Nero's senseless reversal of it—, namely, to let Christian preaching be unimpeded. Not only does the book of Acts point out the triumphal procession of the Word of God from Jerusalem to Rome, but it is also concerned about peaceful coexistence between the pagan state and the Christian church. It was, in fact, to take two and a half centuries more before a Roman emperor decided upon such a course.

The question of the historical reliability of the book of Acts does not touch the central concern of the book. By telling the history of apostolic times through many individual stories, the book primarily intends to edify the churches and thereby contribute its part in spreading the Word of God farther and farther, even to the ends of the earth.

Acts and the Pauline Letter Corpus

JOHN KNOX

When I first knew Paul Schubert we were both students at the University of Chicago. He was near to finishing his work there, having already written his brilliant essay on the Pauline thanksgivings, and I was only beginning my own graduate study; but he was one of several whose achievements both challenged and encouraged me in the way only gifted fellow students can. The professors in our field were Edgar Johnson Goodspeed and Shirley Jackson Case; Harold R. Willoughby and Donald W. Riddle, associated with them, were well launched in their distinguished careers as teachers and scholars, and Ernest Cadman Colwell was just beginning his. For me to think of Paul Schubert is also to think of these five men and of the "joy of study" they both exemplified and inspired.[1]

Probably the most exciting theme of discussion among us at that particular time was Dr. Goodspeed's hypothesis concerning the collecting, editing, and publishing of the Pauline letters and the relation of the Epistle to the Ephesians to this corpus. He had partially adumbrated his theory in *The Formation of the New Testament,* published in 1926,[2] and had more fully stated it in *New Solutions of New Testament Problems* (1927). In *The Meaning of Ephesians,* which was being written during the period of our residence at the University of Chicago and was published in 1933, he believed he was presenting virtual proof of his hypothesis. He was literally full of his idea, convinced both of its validity and of its great importance for the understanding of how early Christian literature developed. The publication of the Pauline letter corpus was, as he put it, the watershed in that development; and the distinctive structure of his *Introduction to the New Testament* (1937) was determined by that conviction. He was quite sure at the time that he had made a significant discovery, and that New Testament

279

studies would thenceforth be different because of it. It belongs to the pathos of life and history that in actual fact this idea of his has apparently had little continuing influence. Perhaps in some future generation the idea will be rediscovered and will play its proper role.[3] For I am persuaded that on the main lines Dr. Goodspeed was right—that the assembling and publishing of the Pauline letters was the definite and highly significant event in the history of New Testament literature which he found it to be, and that Ephesians was the Catholic epistle designed to open the corpus.[4]

It is not the purpose of this essay to review or discuss Dr. Goodspeed's hypothesis as a whole, but rather to consider critically the place the book of Acts had in it. It was his view that the appearance of this book suggested to the collector the idea of the letter corpus. The ground for this conception lay chiefly in two considerations. The first of these was that the author of Acts makes no use of the letters. How, Goodspeed asked, can this fact be explained if the letters were as widely known as they apparently were at the end of the first century and the beginning of the second (that is, *ex hypothesi,* after the formation of the corpus)? Would not the author of Acts, of all people, have used the letters of Paul if he had known them? On the other hand—and here is the second consideration—where shall we find a more adequate occasion for the making of the collection than the appearance of this striking portrait of Paul as the greatest of the early missionaries? Dr. Goodspeed confirmed his opinion that Acts suggested the collection by noting that if the collector, already having in his possession Philemon and Colossians, had gone to the churches mentioned in Acts as having been established or visited by Paul, he would have found just the letters we have, Philippians, Thessalonians, Romans, and the rest. As will be seen, I have never found Dr. Goodspeed's argument for this opinion convincing; but the question he is seeking to answer is not an uninteresting or unimportant one and provides the subject of this essay: namely, in what historical relation do Acts and the Pauline letter collection stand to each other? Did the appearance of Acts suggest the letter collection, as Dr. Goodspeed supposed, or is it possible that the letter collection had some part in providing the occasion of Acts? Or should we conclude that there is probably no connection at all between these two literary events?

This question, or series of questions, about the letter corpus and its original publication is to be distinguished from the more general query as to whether letters of Paul were known at all to the author of Acts; but our way of dealing with the latter issue has so obvious and important a bearing on any answer we may give to the other question that we must begin by considering it. Professor Goodspeed assumed a negative answer: the source materials to which the author refers in his preface (Luke 1:1-3) did not include letters by the apostle—a conclusion in which contemporary scholars generally concur. This consensus has not always existed, however, as Morton Enslin reminds us in a significant article.[5] The Tübingen school assumed not only that the author of Acts knew the letters but also that one of his strongest motives was to contradict and neutralize them wherever they did not confirm his own conception of early Christian solidarity and order. Thus could be explained the author's failure to pay much attention to them when this issue of conflict versus order was *not* involved, and everywhere else to consider them only to correct them. Professor Enslin finds that, in reaction to the Tübingen position, criticism swung, in this regard as in so many others, to the opposite pole, and that its present categorical denial of Luke's use of the letters is as doctrinaire as the Tübingen school's assertion of it. He believes—or did when this article was written—that the denial was, to say the least, premature. And he proceeds to reopen the question, first by appealing to the a priori improbability that Luke, writing at the end of the century, would not have known letters of Paul and, secondly, by citing a number of passages in Acts which may plausibly be taken as pointing to the author's dependence on one or another of them.

Considering these two arguments in reverse order, I should say that the effort to demonstrate Luke's use of Paul with actual evidence fails, as all efforts to do this have previously failed, because every instance of his alleged dependence on the letters can be explained almost, if not quite, as plausibly by the hypothesis of his access to some independent tradition. Enslin explicitly acknowledges this at one point where the Didache happens also to agree with Luke and the letters as against other ancient witnesses. But it is obviously only an accident that at this point we have this check; in all the other cases we conceivably might have. And if a tradition independent of Paul can be appealed to in this instance, why not in the others also? To take an example which Professor Enslin does not cite: When Luke has Paul say before leaving Ephesus (Acts 19:21) that after visits to Macedonia and Achaia, he plans to go to Jerusalem and then to Rome, is he showing his knowledge of Corinthians and Romans, or is he depending upon some other source? This would seem to me one of the most likely instances of dependence upon the letters. But it cannot be claimed as certain. And the same must be said about all the other alleged instances. Nor is their cumulative force impressive. They can all be explained by independent traditions. As a matter of fact, in the absence of adequate evidence of *verbal* dependence (and this, it will be agreed, we do not have in the case of Acts), can there ever be, in a situation like this, any certainty of dependence at all? Indeed, the lack of verbal conformity may have the effect of reversing the argument. Can it be supposed that Luke used the letters of Paul as sources for *facts* or *data* but succeeded in avoiding (or would even have tried to avoid!) any trace of their actual language? In a word, so important is verbal reminiscence that one is almost justified in saying that *in the absence of it* every possible piece of evidence of Luke's having used the letters increases the probability that he did not use them. The citing of evidence, therefore, tends to defeat itself and to point more and more to the conclusion that Luke got his data on Paul's life and teaching from other sources.

That independent traditions of Paul were in fact current in Luke's time is obviously true. Luke demonstrably had other sources for his account of the apostle's career, whether he knew and used the letters or not. Of this there is no need to speak further. But it may be pertinent to observe that some of the *Tendenz* to be found in his work almost certainly belonged in the first instance to the sources he employed. If, for example, we regard Acts 15 as a report of the same event described by Paul in Gal. 2:1-10, we are not necessarily to suppose that Acts is correcting Galatians. Actually, it would be more accurate to say that Galatians is correcting Acts—not Acts itself, of course, but that understanding of Paul's relation to the Jerusalem apostolate which happens to reach us in Acts but which was obviously prevalent in Paul's own time (since he is concerned in Galatians to deny its truth) and which undoubtedly left its traces in records to which Luke a generation or so later had access.

So far as the actual evidence goes, then, I should say that no convincing case can be made for Luke's reliance on the letters of Paul or for his knowledge of them at all.

When we turn, however, from actual evidence to the other side of Professor Enslin's argument, to the a priori case for Luke's knowledge of the letters, we find ourselves in a quite different position. For this case is strong, indeed almost unanswerable. One can hardly reflect at all on what Luke's situation would have been as he began to write Acts without deciding that he must have known letters of Paul. How could he have escaped knowing them? Goodspeed replies, in effect: "Because they had not yet been collected and published. They lay neglected, often in scrappy form, in the archives of the several churches." But this answer is hard to take. I agree with Enslin that it is all but incredible that such a man as Luke, writing in any one of the later decades of the first century about Paul and his career, should have been "totally unaware that this hero of his had ever written letters" and quite as hard to believe that he would have found it impossible, or even difficult, to get access to these letters if he had wanted to. Paul had been too central and too controversial a figure in his own time to have been forgotten so soon. Too many important churches owed their existence to him for his name not to have been held in reverence in many areas and his work remembered.

The reply has been: "Yes, he was remembered as a great missionary leader and founder of churches, but not as a writer. He first became known in that capacity when his letters were collected and published." It is difficult to suppose, however, that Paul's letter-writing activity was not a more important element than this explanation allows, both in his own *modus operandi* among his churches and in the image these churches would have had of him from the beginning and would have continued to have after his death. One may say this, not only because of the intrinsic impressiveness of the letters—how could such letters have been entirely ignored later and even the fact that Paul wrote them forgotten?—but also because Paul himself lets us know that in his own time he was recognized, conspicuously and favorably, as a letter writer. He quotes his opponents as saying: "His letters are weighty and strong, but his bodily presence is weak and his speech is of no account" (II Cor. 10:10). Can we believe that such letters, thus noted and appreciated even among his critics, should have dropped entirely from sight a generation after his time, especially in view of the fact that the letters themselves were actually in existence and were available to the collector of them? And is it really credible that a biographer of Paul, as intelligent as Luke, could have been entirely unaware of them?

The argument thus arrives at what appears to be a stalemate: scholars on the one side, observing that Luke made little or no use of the letters and nowhere refers to Paul as writing them, conclude that he could not have known them; scholars on the other side, sure that Luke could not have failed to know them, conclude that despite the meagerness of actual evidence he must have used them. This impasse should lead us to examine the hidden major premise of both sides, namely: If Luke knew the letters of Paul, he must have used them. I believe we are forced by the literary evidence (or, rather, by the lack of it), on the one hand, and by the a priori probabilities, on the other, to question this premise and to consider seriously the possibility that Luke knew, or at least knew of, letters of Paul—even *the* (collected) letters of Paul—and quite consciously and deliberately made little or no use of them.

That the author of Luke–Acts should have felt an aversion to the letters, or bias against them, is entirely understandable, although certainly from a disinterested historian's point of view (which he was not), his neglect of them would be indefensible. The letters of Paul were in considerable part polemical documents and, insofar as they were known and used in the decades immediately following his career, were no doubt often—perhaps more often than not—employed in controversy or at least in partisan ways. I would understand one of the major purposes of both the collector of the letters and the writer of Ephesians to be the saving of the letters of Paul from such factional use. That this effort did not fully succeed is proved by the Marcionite movement's adoption, and near-appropriation, of this very corpus for its own purposes. Not until the time of Irenaeus, after the Pastoral Epistles had also been added, is it clear that the letters of Paul are finally freed from their schismatic associations and made fully at home within the Catholic Church.[6] We cannot reject the possibility that Luke, writing before this full "catholicizing" of Paul's letters had taken place (when, possibly, they were most conspicuously identified with heretical groups), *chose* to ignore both the letters and Paul's character and role as a letter writer. Indeed, I see no other way of reconciling his actual nonuse of, and silence about, the letters with the knowledge of their existence which we are almost bound to ascribe to him.

In this connection the silence is more important than the nonuse. For one thing, we can be absolutely sure of it, whereas (as Professor Enslin's article reminds us) one cannot be of the other. It can be argued that Luke did make *some* use of the letters. I have said that I do not believe one can demonstrate that he did; but, so long as only a meager use is claimed, one cannot demonstrate that he did not. I would point out, however, that any evidence that Luke may actually have used the letters makes more striking and significant the fact that he is completely silent about Paul's having written them. It would obviously be false to suppose that, for a contemporary or a near-contemporary of Paul, his letter-writing was as conspicuous a feature of his career as it is for us, or even as it became almost at once with the collection and publication of his letters; but, as we have already had occasion to note, there can be no doubt that the writing of letters to churches was a very important and distinguished part of his activity as an apostle and that it was recognized to be such at the time. It Luke not only knew of Paul's letters (as he must have) but also actually made some use of them, it becomes harder to account for his omission of any mention of this aspect of Paul's career—unless he *wished* to be silent about it. He includes a letter from the apostles and elders at Jerusalem which Paul is to read in the churches of the Gentile mission, but does not so much as mention a letter of Paul himself. The fact that this apostolic letter deals, irenically and compromisingly, with the same issue discussed by Paul in some of the most polemical passages in his letters—passages, moreover, regarded as normative by Marcion, his followers, and no doubt his precursors—this fact increases the likelihood that a conscious minimizing of the latter is involved in Luke's silence.

I urge, then, that consideration be given to the possibility that, far from providing the original suggestion for the collecting of Paul's letters, Acts was itself prompted, at least in part, by what its author regards as a schismatic use of them among pre-Marcionite, perhaps even Marcionite, Christians. Of the two works, the collected letters and the book of Acts, there can be no question that the former is related more deeply and intimately to what we may call the authentic Pauline tradition. Not only is it true that the letters are for the most part Paul's own letters, almost certainly treasured, insofar as copies of the several letters might be available, in the Pauline churches, but also it may be said that Ephesians, the work of the collector or of some collaborator, is profoundly Pauline—that is, it represents an authentic expression of Paulinism in a way Acts does not. That the appearance of a secondhand account like Acts should have been necessary to inspire the devoted work of the collector or the author of Ephesians seems hardly likely.[7] On the other hand, Marcionism's appropriation of Paul's letters and its threat to take exclusive possession of Paul himself as "the Apostle" on the basis of its interpretation of them might quite plausibly have provided the occasion for a portrait based definitely and consciously on different traditions.

The fact that the book of Acts, in which this portrait is set (which, indeed, could be thought of as being little more than this portrait with its setting), is the second volume of a two-part work, the first volume of which is a form of the very Gospel which Marcion adopted and associated with Paul's letters to make what was in effect the Scripture for his churches—this fact, it still seems to me,[8] rather strikingly confirms this understanding. Is it merely coincidence that the Gospel-Apostle format appears only in these two instances? Admittedly it may be so. But can it also be merely fortuitous that in both of these cases the "Apostle" section is concerned predominantly with Paul—in one case with Paul as "the Apostle" and in the other with him as related and subject to a more Catholic apostolate? If the answer again is "yes," can we dispose in the same way of the further fact that in both cases the Gospel section is a form of the same Gospel, the Gospel of Luke? Can *all* of this be coincidence?

If one understands Luke–Acts as representing in some degree a reaction to Marcionism's use of Luke and Paul, one is not forced to ascribe to that work an inordinately late date, since we do not know how early Marcion's career and influence began, although it is easier and more natural in that case to think of the work in its final form as belonging to the second century than to the first. The primitive gospel, which Marcion had already adopted, as well as much of the source material in Acts, would, needless to say, have been earlier. Only the finished work, Luke–Acts, would have to be dated as late as, say, A.D. 125. I see no decisive, or even important, evidence of an earlier date.

NOTES

1. The quoted phrase was made the title of a book of essays in honor of Professor Frederick C. Grant. This book was edited by Sherman Johnson, who was also one of "the several" fellow students at the University of Chicago whom I have mentioned. Dr. Grant himself was at that time not far from the University and has been close to it in spirit ever since.

2. This book and also the three others referred to in this paragraph were published by the University of Chicago Press.

3. It can be argued, and has been, that Dr. Goodspeed himself was not so much a discoverer as a rediscoverer. He in effect says this on pp. 74 ff. of *The Meaning of Ephesians,* mentioning Jülicher and Johannes Weiss. (See esp. the latter's *Das Urchristentum* [Göttingen, 1917], pp. 533 ff.; Eng. tr. by F. C. Grant and others, *The History of Primitive Christianity* [New York, 1937], II, 683 ff.). I seem to recall Dr. Goodspeed's telling, with a kind of wry amusement, of a conversation he had with Adolf von Harnack (this must have been at the very end of Harnack's life) about either the manuscript of *New Solutions of New Testament Problems* or the book itself. Harnack had said—certainly with no excess of kindness—that the "solutions" were neither new nor solutions! As to whether Dr.

Goodspeed's "solution" of the problem of Ephesians was a true solution or not is a matter on which opinions may differ. But I should say that he was not mistaken in calling it "new." He took earlier hints and made something firm and coherent out of them, noting possible bearings and connections which had not been seen before. Perhaps, in such a matter as this, one should not ask for greater originality.

4. It would obviously be mistaken to deny any continuing influence to Goodspeed's idea about the collection and Ephesians, although I must confess that outside the number of some of his pupils I know of very few who have shared both his conviction of its truth and his sense of its significance. Of these, C. L. Mitton is most notable. See his *The Epistle to the Ephesians* (Oxford, 1951) and *The Formation of the Pauline Corpus of Letters* (London, 1955). A quite positive attitude is taken also by P. N. Harrison in *Paulines and Pastorals* (London, 1964), *passim,* and in *Polycarp's Two Epistles to the Philippians* (Cambridge, 1936), pp. 236 ff., *et passim;* B. H. Streeter, whose book *The Primitive Church* appeared only a year or two after Dr. Goodspeed's *New Solutions,* accepted some of the latter's suggestions, and the same can be said of C. F. D. Moule. See his *The Epistles of Paul the Apostle to the Colossians and to Philemon.* Mention should also be made of articles by C. R. Bowen ("Ephesians Among the Letters of Paul" in the *AThR* [1933], 299 ff.) and Lucetta Mowry ("The Early Circulation of Paul's Letters" in *JBL,* LXIII, 73 ff.). Those scholars who have made passing references to Goodspeed's views on this theme are too numerous to mention. My point is simply that very few except from among the number of his pupils have found them both true and important. Recent work on Ephesians has paid little, if any, attention to the idea which, as Goodspeed believed, is the key to the understanding of its occasion and purpose.

5. " 'Luke' and Paul," *JAOS* LVIII (1938), 81 ff. For convenience in this essay I shall use the term "Luke" without quotation marks to designate the author of Luke–Acts.

6. See Walter Bauer, *Rechtgläubigkeit und Ketzerei im ältesten Christentum* (Tübingen, 1934), pp. 228-30.

7. This has always seemed to me the weakest point of any importance in Dr. Goodspeed's hypothesis. In his last work on this theme (*The Key to Ephesians* [Chicago, 1956]) Dr. Goodspeed does me the great honor of adopting a suggestion of my own about the possibly close relation of the one-time slave and later bishop of Ephesus, Onesimus, with the collection of Paul's letters. I cannot believe that, if Dr. Goodspeed had held from the beginning such a view of the original auspices of the collection, it would have occurred to him to attribute the idea of it to the appearance of Acts. Surely, in that case, he would have found the roots of the conception in the continuing devoted memory of a disciple and, presumably, of the community of the Pauline tradition in which the disciple lived and worked.

8. I am referring here to the central thesis of a book long out of print, *Marcion and the New Testament* (Chicago, 1942). I am not infrequently asked whether I would significantly alter that book if it were being issued again. There is no doubt that I should want to make some revisions. In particular, the part of the chapter on "The Gospel of Luke" which deals with the *text* of Marcion's "Gospel," I should want to do again from the beginning because of the statistical errors I have found in it; but only a subordinate point is involved in such a rechecking. The general thesis of the book is in my judgment still defensible and I am persuaded of its truth: that Marcion appropriated and revised as "the first Christian Scripture" the collected letters of Paul and a primitive Gospel substantially equivalent to what later became the first volume of Luke's work, and that this action stimulated, and determined the definitive form of, both Luke–Acts and the ecclesiastical canon of the New Testament.

Ephesians and Acts

ERNST KÄSEMANN

The more important the Lucan theology becomes for our understanding of early Christian history, the more we must investigate the presuppositions behind its origin. Theological patterns are never the work of a single man, no matter how much he may have given them his imprint. We cannot overestimate the creative power which put together the Acts of the Apostles and gave it a coherent theme. To be sure, the traditions and tendencies of a particular church piety in the Pauline mission area can be regarded as its actual support. This justifies a comparison with Ephesians. So far as I can see, such a comparison has not yet been undertaken; [1] indeed, the necessity and usefulness of such an undertaking have scarcely been recognized. The following remarks may move toward a frontier not yet explored; in this way they are more a sketch of a task than a solution.

I

In the New Testament it is Ephesians that most clearly marks the transition from the Pauline tradition to the perspectives of the early Catholic era. This is indicated even by the method which structures this letter. In scarcely any other writing does the train of ideas appropriate so extensively earlier motifs and formulas. The entire letter appears to be a mosaic composed of extensive as well as tiny elements of tradition, and the author's skill lies chiefly in the selection and ordering of the material available to him. One cannot overestimate the craftsmanship which united innumerable pieces of thoroughly disparate origin into a thematic goal which had been worked out carefully. The distinctiveness of the conception leads us very close to Paul, who here found a worthy disciple. Paul also, as form criticism shows, frequently relied on extant tradition. Yet he did not do it in order to help express his own ideas but to strengthen their validity, just as he did with

288

scriptural proof. For Paul, the tradition is not the basis and limit of his assertions. On the contrary, time and again he breaks away from the beaten path toward new conceptual horizons, and it is not uncommon for him to use critically and dialectically the very ideas and slogans of his environment against those who advance them. This critical dialectic is precisely what characterizes his relation to tradition, which for him is not the substance of proclamation but a mode of presenting it. In this way, the relation between the discussion partners is indicated but the argument itself is not prejudiced.

In this light, the freshness and vitality of the Pauline language stands in contrast with Ephesians which, like the Fourth Gospel, has a remarkable hieratic style which often sounds turgid in our ears. It is shot through with edifying expressions which come from an early Christian "language of Canaan." The parallels which one derives from Paul's letters usually point to a hymnic-liturgical heritage which he himself cites. True, he does not disdain rhetorical means and is in control of an effective pathos. Still, he develops it more in dialogue than in the meditative-doxological style of Ephesians. If one views Acts in this light, he cannot expect that its narrative use the same style as a letter or even the emphasis of Ephesians. Similarities emerge at the point where also Acts uses earlier tradition, especially of the hymnic-liturgical kind. On the other hand, it would be worthwhile to investigate precisely the language of edifying piety used by Acts, perhaps by comparing it with I Clem., and to mark it off from early Christian missionary terminology. This would show that Luke presupposes a church that has expanded across the world as well as a church that is consolidating itself internally, a church which separates itself from its environment sociologically as well as with respect to a certain ideological terminology.

Above all, we must nevertheless note that Acts and Ephesians have the same relation to tradition as such. A history of a Christianity that is penetrating the empire can be written only if one is interested in collecting and structuring the church's tradition to begin with, and if this can be made into the foundation of a process of development inferred from such material. The presentation must couple exemplary episodes and form, out of the many scattered individual traditions, a controlling image of tradition which is characteristic for the whole. This concept of the tradition must then be able to serve as the locus of developing Christianity, its mission, and its theology. Because we have grown accustomed to this controlling image, we usually no longer appreciate the difficulty involved and the greatness of this undertaking. Yet only such a procedure makes it possible to view the emerging of the church as a coherent process, and in its own way it helped also to consolidate the history-determining factor called "Christianity."

The gospel never existed without tradition. Already Jesus set his message in agreement and in contradiction to the Old Testament and to Jewish tradition. But it is still something new for Christianity to create its own traditions and to become coextensive with them. For now, these traditions which grew out of the gospel can, in a particular historical moment, be reduced to the controlling images which represent their nucleus and be themselves regarded as gospel. Thereby, one takes a step away from early Christianity which understands itself eschatologically and moves toward the early Catholicism which regards itself as a force in history. Ephesians as well as Acts marks the moment of this transition. Both still know the gospel only in the form of tradition, nourish their proclamation either meditatively (Eph.) or narratively (Acts) out of the material of the tradition, and conversely by means of this same tradition make their message normative. Actually, then, the church creates the controlling image of its message, with variations, to be sure, which are conditioned by the respective times and places in which they are rooted. The catchword propounded by the Pastorals, "sound doctrine," characterizes this fact very clearly and is something like the common denominator which can be found in most of the New Testament writings of the postapostolic period.

Closely realted to this is the fact that the church itself more and more becomes the content of theology. For Ephesians as for Acts, it is the "center of time," [2] i.e., the exclusive place and means of salvation—in this regard the eschatological phenomenon per se. Obviously it is true that the exalted Christ rules it through his Spirit. Still, to say it pointedly, this is not its proper and total essence as in Paul, but its most important attribute. Whatever may be the good reasons why Ephesians and Colossians set Christ as the head over against his body instead of having him penetrate the body pneumatically as in Paul, nevertheless the earthly body of the exalted Lord thereby achieves an unmistakable independence which it did not have with Paul. Now it becomes possible for Acts to narrate the history of its development and for Ephesians to reflect on the *notae ecclesiae*. The two are not mutually exclusive but belong inseparably together, as each of the writings scrutinized here shows in its own way.

The interest of Ephesians in the redemptive-historical anchorage of the church clearly provides a bridge to Acts. It is expressed by the very fact that, for the sake of this theme, the letter writer has taken up the hymn in Eph. 1:5-12a and, having provided it with an introduction and a postscript, has placed it at the beginning. The community of believers is as much the content of the pretemporal election as the will of God which manifests itself eschatologically so that the cosmic peace may once again be produced out of the chaos, a peace consisting in the universal reconciliation of the new world (cf. 2:14 ff.). That in this process christological expressions are modified in an ecclesiological direction is simple enough to understand. Nevertheless, they receive their real thrust by the fact that the author of this message gives them a pointedness in 1:12b; 2:1-3, 11-13, 19-22; 3:6 which actually does not belong to them and is rather imposed on them. Parallel to the heavenly event there runs an earthly one which also illuminates it, namely, the incorporation of the Gentile Christians into the people of God, which is represented by Jewish Christianity as the holy remnant of Israel. If anywhere, the letter betrays its historical setting precisely here. What Paul mentioned hypothetically in Rom. 11:17 ff. has happened here: Jewish Christianity is pushed aside and despised by the steadily growing Gentile Christianity. The author of Ephesians, doubtless a Jewish Christian, reminds the Gentile Christians of their roots and of the origin of the gospel. It is the indelible character of the church to be constituted out of Jews and Gentiles; by this means, spiritually understood, the Gentile Christians are proselytes. As in Acts the historical development characterizes the indispensable nature of the church, because God's guidance is reflected in this development. The church remains the *una sancta* only by overcoming this religious antagonism.

Along the same lines we observe that Eph. 3, in agreement with almost the entire New Testament except John, points out the theological significance of the apostolate. A close relationship to Pauline thoughts and formulas is not to be overlooked, but neither should one obscure the discrepancies. The fact that in vs. 5 the holy apostles and prophets are mentioned points to a past period whose representatives are, in a redemptive-historical perspective, separated not only from earlier generations but are also, as recipients of revelation, set apart from the rest of mankind in general. The Spirit, illumination, and divine plan of salvation were imparted to them in a special way; in fact, according to 3:10 this occurred so that through the church and in it the manifold wisdom of God will be made known to the spirit-powers just as it is to the Gentile Christians who, according to vs. 6, learn of their share in the inheritance of the people of God. According to 2:20 the apostles function as the foundation of a unified Christianity, whose truth and rightness in turn are demonstrated by referring to these witnesses. The whole portrait of Acts is nothing less than the visualization of such theologoumena in narrative form. It rests, surely, on the conviction that the plan of salvation is to be discerned in history, and that continuity with the holy origins legitimates the church. For Acts, these origins are also determined by the actions of the apostles and prophets, whereby Paul, set in a context of the tradition of the Jerusalem apostolate, is included as the founder of Gentile Christianity in Asia and Europe.

In view of the time in which Acts and Ephesians were written, the silence about heresy in both writings is striking. Luke naturally did not want to burden the sacred past with such somber features. Therefore, as in the case of Simon Magus in 8:9 ff. or Bar-Jesus in 13:6 ff., he shows only an encounter with magicians and reserves for the future the intramural heresies suggested in 20:29-30, a *vaticinium ex eventu*. Eph. 4:14-15 likewise hints of threatening dangers, and the threefold pronouncement of 4:5, doubtless derived from a baptismal rite, is obviously directed against heretical groups. Nevertheless, in keeping with the developing orthodoxy, one no longer attacks the opponent directly, as Paul did, but opposes him with the fascinating phenomenon of the *una sancta apostolica* as in the Pastorals or in John 17. While this theme of ecclesiastical unity and its characteristics does not lack edifying intent, it nevertheless grows primarily out of the conflicts already present. In the same way, in both writings church order is developed beyond that which existed in the lifetime of the apostles. Just as Acts no longer limits its circle of readers, so Ephesians is unquestionably a "catholic" tract in the sense of addressing itself to Christianity in the widest sense. The episcopal office, in contrast with the Pastorals, does not yet move into the foreground. Nevertheless, on the basis of Acts 20:17, 28, 35 it is clear that its function is in firm hands and that the title "bishop" has been found, although it still alternates with that of elder. Luke, who deliberately characterizes the beginnings as charismatic—namely by direct leading of the Spirit—is also here in a transitional situation. But the situation is no different in Ephesians. The time of the apostles and of early Christian prophets is, for his circle, apparently past. The process by which traditions are transmitted is characterized, according to 4:11, as moving from pastors to teachers to evangelists, whereby the charismatic church order is still dominant. On the other hand, the training of the congregation is entrusted to this fixed circle, and the pastors certainly exercise the administrative functions which will soon fall to the bishops. That in Acts the Christian family appears, as in the *Haustafel* of Ephesians, completes the picture; it mirrors the congregation in its smallest unit.

The differences between Ephesians and Acts should not be leveled for the sake of a concordance. That the atmosphere in these writings is different cannot be denied. One can determine that Ephesians belongs more to the eastern, Acts more to the western part of the Pauline mission field. Ephesians is rooted in the world of Hellenistic mystery-religion piety; in contrast, Luke represents, despite all miracles and various traditional elements, the enlightened—or better, rationalizing—religiosity of Hellenism, without which he could not have written the history of Christianity. He relates this backward to the history of Jesus and to the Old Testament—matters in which Ephesians, despite several Old Testament reminiscences, is scarcely interested. On the other hand, Luke has kept surprisingly little of the specifically Pauline message, and Paul himself, as an evangelist in the Gentile world, is merely an extension of the twelve. At the same time, as one can say pointedly, he knows Paul's letters no longer and not yet. By contrast, for Ephesians Paul is the apostle per se, for whom the others are merely the foil. Just as literary dependence on Paul, the teacher, is scarcely deniable, so the Pauline tradition forms the heart of the tradition into which other materials have been fused. As far as substance is concerned Ephesians is older, while Acts shows the direction the development takes as the Pauline mission field incorporates itself more and more into the whole church. While we have seen the differences we also should recognize in both writings the single trend which marks the Pauline mission field after the apostle's death, and which allows one to place Acts more precisely in the overall historical and theological development.

II

Finally, our approach will be confirmed and exemplified in connection with a particular passage. Eph. 1:12*b*-14 contains in concentrated form the themes which are painted broadly by Acts in the Cornelius story. These themes provide the basis of the Gentile mission. To be sure, one can see this only if he sees the relationship of these verses to what has been said already and grasps their scope and their details on this basis.

In this passage, exalted language continues to be used. Nevertheless, we are not dealing now with the style of a hymn but with an accumulation of themes and formulas of the early Christian baptism message which were taken over into the language of edification. This is shown most clearly when one speaks of the sealing with the Spirit, as in II Cor. 1:22 where the Spirit is portrayed as the down-payment of future glory. If the Spirit generally is regarded as a baptismal gift, then according to the oldest baptismal terminology, "sealing" occurs when one receives the Spirit. According to Rev. 7:3 this designates the property which belongs to the coming world and preserves it against earthly annihilation. From the same complex of themes comes the idea of the Spirit as a down-payment. It is the guarantee of future glorification. By the time of the author of Ephesians, such apocalyptic ways of looking at the matter and such expressions have long since been left behind. The phrase is transmitted as a respected item of the baptism message. In the same way, the formula "to hear the word of truth," when used with the absolute πιστεύειν, designates the acceptance of the Christian message. In the intention of the author of Ephesians, however, the phrase actually describes Christian doctrine. Here we must pay attention to the fact that the verses abandon the first person plural, as the hymnic speech originally required, and move toward the form of address. Closely following the conclusion of the hymn is the *applicatio,* as occurs in reverse order at the transition of 2:1-3 to 2:4-7. This same shift elsewhere also characterizes the shift from hymnic material to paraenesis (e.g., 2:8, 14, 19). Such a shift from remembering the basic sermon to admonition to perseverance belongs to the fixed style of those writings which intend to stabilize young congregations in the Christian life. True, here this pattern is modified. Not exhortation but remembrance dominates our verses; by this means they also continue the hymn. This can only mean that the author causes the concrete application to follow the general expressions of the hymn. For him, the miracle of the church manifests itself most strongly in the miracle of the Gentile Christian who has been accepted into the church. In order to make this idea clear it is spelled out in a whole series of wondrous events: the Gentiles have heard the word of truth, subsequently became believers, were sealed with the Spirit, and in this way have won a share in salvation. The amazement over these events, in which both human readiness and divine guidance and confirmation are reflected, is undeniable. It occasions the exalted language with its abundance of set formulas. These developments are especially astonishing from the Jewish-Christian standpoint. In these events it becomes evident that God himself eschatologically broke through the limits of the old people of God and fulfilled his promises in a new reality. The prophecy that those who were "far off" would become "near" (2:13) and that the Gentiles should be added has been actualized.

On this basis also the details of the text must be interpreted. The greatest difficulty is provided by the phrase ἀπολύτρωσις τῆς περιποιήσεως. One can hardly interpret the genetive as epexegetical and translate "redemption which makes property." An object would then be indispensable. Equally problematic is the translation "redemption that allows one to claim the heavenly inheritance." The relation to the foregong κληρονομία remains obscure if it is not specified by a pronoun. The simplest and most obvious solution is to remember that in the Old Testament Israel is called God's own people (*Eigentumsvolk*). On this basis, the genetive has a qualitative meaning and speaks of a redemption which comes to God's own people. Thus the verses climax in the claim that the Gentiles participate in this redemption which properly belongs to Israel or to a holy remnant in Jewish Christianity. Precisely the same point is made by the expression πνεῦμα τῆς ἐπαγγελίας, which is known in reverse form ἐπαγγελία τοῦ πνεύματος in Acts 2:33; Gal. 3:14. Naturally, one can understand it in purely formal terms as a worn-out phrase, so that it speaks merely of the promised Spirit. Nevertheless, 2:12; 3:3; 6:2 show that in Ephesians ἐπαγγελία always means the promise made to Israel. This must be taken into consideration here. The Gentiles have been sealed with the Spirit, which was the actual content of the divine promise to the old people of God; to this extent, as the down-payment of the heavenly inheritance, it surpasses the Old Testament possession of the land. Finally, the controversial sentence in 12*b* fits into this interpretation. It goes beyond the formula "to the praise of his glory" which is used in 6*a* and 14*c,* and yet it is also a transition to vss. 13-14. By praising Gentile Christianity, an antithesis to what follows is created rather forcibly. This is done by making the hymn refer to Jewish Christianity. As Jews who believe in the Messiah they are already προηλπικότες and are now set into the doxology of the salvation-event. If this interpretation is correct, the true wonder of Gentile Christianity is seen in the fact that the Gentiles are included in the elect people and its holy remnant. This corresponds exactly to what is said in 2:1-3, 11-13, 19-22; 3:6, and it also characterizes a concern of the author which runs through the entire work. He used the formulas from the missionary and baptism message to emphasize this concern also here at the very beginning of the letter; in this way he gave concreteness to the previously cited hymn. His tradition, his method of working, and his theology come into view at the same time.

The proximity of the formulas used here to the Pauline message is clear. In exactly the same way also Acts availed itself of an abundance of beautiful formulas from the tradition of the sacred past. The substantive distance from Paul can be recognized when one sees that here the theme of the people of God, the holy remnant and its proselytes, obscures the theme of the body of Christ and modifies it. Paul, likewise, speaks of a new people of God. But he does so polemically, in order to insist that the church, in contrast with Judaism, is the true Israel. The idea of a holy remnant is used only in Rom. 9:27 ff.; 11:4, 13 ff., and again polemically. For Paul, the church is basically the New World, as is clear from the perspective of his ecumenical mission. Therefore the church is to be called a "people" only in a secondary sense. At first we are surprised that Paul's pupil does not respect this critically developed intention of his teacher and therefore lapses behind it: he does so when he emphatically juxtaposes the expression the body of Christ with that of the people of God, the holy remnant, and thereby in effect modifies the Pauline ecclesiology. Still, there are weighty reasons for doing this. The author of Ephesians stands in a new situation and is accountable to it. The concern of the world mission, which doubtless continued, allows him to retain the idea of the body of Christ. But a shift in emphasis is disclosed by the very fact that for him the body of Christ grows not only into the open world but also, and perhaps even more importantly, into the heights of heaven. The theme of the church dominates him to such an extent that the church is no longer mentioned as part of a continuing contrast to the world. The church has become an independent theme vis-à-vis cosmology, just as it became one with respect to Christology. Intra-church problems press to the fore and cause, at the same time, the idea of mission to recede. In this way it is still possible and meaningful for the theme of the people of God to gain a positive significance, and for the theme of the body of Christ to be, in a certain sense, supplemented or even corrected. By this means the redemptive-historical aspect can be presented more sharply in an ecclesiological way. The Gentile Christians, who understand themselves as members of the body of Christ and boast of having received the Spirit, are in danger of absolutizing their true and present situation, and beyond this, of forgetting the history of the gospel and of the promise. It is a chief concern of Ephesians to bring this history to remembrance and to make the acknowledgment of it obligatory for the sake of the unity of the church. In this regard also it coincides with the intention of Acts. Just as the astonishment over the acceptance of the Gentiles in Eph. 1:13-14 has its closest parallel in the conclusion of the Cornelius pericope, so the redemptive-historical aspect dominates the work of Luke as a whole and also its ecclesiology. To both of them the "center of time" [3] is inconceivable without the holy beginnings and without a backward look toward the promise and the anticipation of the saving event given in the Old Testament. The church stands in continuity with the people of the old covenant; this continuity is demonstrated by Jewish Christianity.

NOTES

1. The comparison of Acts and Ephesians made by C. L. Mitton is of a different order inasmuch as it is concerned primarily with particular phrases. Cf. *The Epistle to the Ephesians* (Oxford, 1951).
2. This phrase alludes to the title of Conzelmann's book, *Die Mitte der Zeit*, whose English title does not translate the German but replaces it with the colorless *The Theology of St. Luke*, trans. Geoffrey Buswell (New York, 1960).
3. "Die Mitte der Zeit"; cf. n. 2.

Luke's Place in the Development of Early Christianity

HANS CONZELMANN

I. The Problem

It would be easy to determine the place of the Lucan writings in early Christianity if we knew the author, especially if we could be sure that the Third Gospel and the book of Acts were written by Luke, the physician and companion of Paul (Col. 4:14). Then the time of composition could be limited to the years A.D. 60-80. The work would then be the most prominent document of the second generation, written in immediate contact with firsthand tradition. Actually, Luke's authorship is still maintained today,[1] but it is also strongly contested.[2]

Although Luke–Acts is now being studied vigorously, with regard to the date we are not yet beyond the summary given by H. J. Cadbury:[3] the possible limits of the composition are about A.D. 60 (the imprisonment of Paul) and A.D. 150 (Marcion). Both limits are still defended.[4]

Recent research has partly turned away from the question of authorship and has concentrated on the literary style and theology of the two-volume work.[5] What this means for the task of determining Luke's place in early Christian history will be discussed below. For the moment we shall remain with the external data. Some limits can be drawn with confidence: (a) The work was written after the destruction of Jerusalem in A.D. 70. This is evident from Luke 21:20-24, although the view that this passage refers to the fall of Jerusalem is contested again and again. It is said that this is actually a prophecy and that, besides Mark 13, Luke used a second prophetic source.[6] But, compared with Mark, the style of this passage is historicizing and not apocalyptic. Moreover, the passage fits into a typically Lucan thought complex: the fate of Jerusalem and the *eschaton* are to be separated from each other.[7] Also, the way in which Luke connects the idea of the church with

Jerusalem presupposes that the city no longer stands, as we shall show later. (b) Paul's death is presupposed.[8] This eliminates the thesis that Acts is an apology for Paul in prison (in Rome or Caesarea). This hypothesis is impossible for internal reasons as well, for it explains neither the range nor the ordering of the material nor the way in which it is presented.[9] (c) More difficult is the later time limit. The main problem still remains: How is one to explain the fact that Acts shows no trace of using Paul's letters? Closely related questions are, When and how did the *Corpus Paulinum* enter public circulation, as a gradual process of collection,[10] or as a complete edition,[11] and when? [12]

Basically, four theses are possible: (1) Luke did not yet know the *Corpus Paulinum* for he wrote before its publication, i.e., around A.D. 70-90. This assumption seems to be the simplest, but it has its difficulties as emphasized especially by John Knox.[13] (2) Luke knows the *Corpus,* but he deliberately ignores it.[14] But what would be the reason for doing so? (3) Luke writes after the publication of the *Corpus* but does not know of it.[15] But is this probable? (4) Luke knows the *Corpus* and uses it too, but he does not give this impression to the reader.[16] This assumption will find little assent.

The result thus far is not very satisfactory. We can exclude an extremely early time of composition. All other questions remain open for the time being. What criteria do we have for making progress with this question?

II. The External Evidence for Luke–Acts [17]

If Luke were dependent on Josephus, we would have a definite *terminus ante quem non*. But dependence cannot be shown.[18] What do we have in terms of indirect evidence, i.e., traces of use by other writings? The Pastoral letters probably do not know Acts.[19] The same can be said of the letters of Ignatius.[20] Positive contacts seem to exist with the Kerygma of Peter,[21] the Gospel of Peter,[22] the Epistula Apostolorum,[23] the Gospel of Thomas,[24] and the "Unknown Gospel." [25] But none of these provides us with any certainty. The relations to Justin are contested (see below).[26]

We possess definite evidence only from the second half of the second century. The martyrdom of the men of Lugdunum (A.D. 177-78) cites Acts 7:60 (Eusebius, *Hist. Eccl.* V 2, 5). The Acts of Paul (before A.D. 197) know the book of Acts.[27] Explicit evidence is further found in the "Canon Muratori" and in the falsely called "Anti-Marcionite Prologue" of the Third Gospel.[28]

The chronological indications within the Lucan work [29] do not enable us to fix the date. They do not lead us beyond the era described in Acts, the time of Nero.[30]

III. Source Analysis as a Criterion?

The analysis of Luke's Gospel at least results in a *terminus post quem:* after Mark and Q. But neither of these sources can be dated precisely. We would arrive at a relatively early date if the "Proto-Luke Hypothesis" could be sustained. Unfortunately, this is not the case.[31] The source analysis of Acts is completely problematical and is as unresolved today as it was many decades ago. We are no longer so confident with respect to the previously widespread assumption that the first part of Acts is based on a Jerusalem source. There have been repeated attempts to reconstruct the "Antioch Source," but they are not convincing. The main controversy still focuses on the "we-sections" of the second part of Acts. Do they demonstrate that the author of the book writes as an eyewitness? Or does he use the report of an eyewitness? A third possibility is offered by Dibelius: the first person plural represents a literary device and proves neither that the author was an eyewitness nor the use of a source. Dibelius substitutes the hypothesis of the "Itinerary" for the "we-report," but this is even less probable than a "we-source."[32] Again we are faced with a *non liquet.*

IV. Internal Evidence: Luke as Historian

Since external criteria fail, we are thrown back on the effort to determine the historical place of Luke's writings by means of internal evidence. Here it is important to distinguish between the general place in the ancient history of ideas and the particular place in church history, for Luke's significance consists, among other things, in his claim to be the first Christian to write "literature."

To be sure, opinions about Luke as a historian conflict sharply.[33] That elements of ancient historiography can be found in his work is undeniable.[34] But they are too weak to prove him to be a historian in the sense of ancient literature.[35] On the one hand, one finds elements of the style of Hellenistic historiography and the Hellenistic novel.[36] On the other hand, the Lucan prose is not literary prose.[37] All the observations concerning his style merely lead up to a general characterization and not to a classification within the history of Hellenistic style.

The same is true for the question of the Lucan view of the *Imperium*

Romanum. Luke does not discuss it for its own sake. He does not pursue any political interests.[38] He views the *Imperium* only from the perspective of the expansion of Christianity. He assumes that Christianity is known to the public as an entity *sui generis.*[39] This is the case since Nero, according to Tacitus.[40] But is Luke's image reality or a program? Furthermore, two aspects—the theological and the historical—are mixed. On the one hand, Luke shares the apocalyptic judgment of the worldly power: it is in Satan's hands (Luke 4:6). On the other hand, he does not convert this view into a political program of "intellectual resistance against Rome." [41] He maintains neutrality in reporting about state affairs and state officials.

The Lucan Paul is proud of being a Roman citizen.[42] Luke consciously creates the impression that Christianity can spread without trouble.[43] That this image does not correspond to reality can be seen from the persecution logia in the Third Gospel as well as from his efforts to prove Christianity to be politically loyal. Obviously, Luke has actual cause for such apologetics. There is a certain contradiction between theory and praxis which cannot remain hidden from the reader. Of course, Luke takes care to eliminate it by presenting the Jews as the initiators of the persecution.[44] In this he is a precursor of the apologists (Justin!).[45]

The Jews, like the *Imperium,* are viewed in a double perspective, theologically and empirically: Israel is the precursor of the church and the "Jews" are the persecutors.

What is the result of these considerations? They do not lead us to a precise classification either. All we can say is that Luke sees the events which he describes from a certain distance: Augustus, the *oikoumene* (civilized world), the census, events during the reign of Claudius, developments in Palestine (Judas the Galilean and Theudas, the "Egyptian," Gamaliel). Legendary traits are already blended into the presentation, e.g., the story of Agrippa's death (which has a parallel in Josephus). Legends permeate also the history of the Christian mission in Philippi and Ephesus. Therefore we can speak of a distance—but how great is it?

V. The Image of the Expansion of Christianity

We do not investigate this image in order to reconstruct early missionary history,[46] but in order to find out, perchance, the geographical location of the author. One conclusion is certain: he does not write in Palestine.[47] Two further observations can be interpreted in different ways. The "way" [48] in

Acts is significant geographically as well as theologically and leads to Rome as the final goal.[49] Is the book, therefore, written in Rome? This would correspond to the missionary program in Acts 1:8 as well as to the image of the *Imperium* and to the reduction of the geographical horizon to the *orbis Romanus*.[50] But there are other indications. The author seems to see the church from the perspective of the Aegean region.[51] Apart from the prelude to the so-called first missionary journey, Paul's work is limited to this realm. Of course, this largely corresponds to the facts as shown by our primary sources, the Pauline letters. But for Luke, this limitation constitutes a theological program indicated in Acts 16:6-16: God's way logically leads to Europe. At this point the narrative becomes more precise and intimate. Still, Ephesus—actually the most important center of Paul's activity—appears in a twilight.[52] The Aegean region and Rome need not be mutually exclusive, for the author could have grown up in the former and then moved to the latter.[53]

The geographical horizon becomes even clearer when we realize which regions are omitted or mentioned only in passing.[54] Galatia is scarcely mentioned (Acts 16:6; 18:23). The important mission undertaken by Paul's aides in Asia is passed over. The congregations in the Lycos valley are missing,[55] and the same is true of places mentioned in the Pastorals, Crete and Dalmatia.[56] From such a concentration a specific picture emerges. The two focal points of the realm of the church are Jerusalem and Rome. The *actual* border is Antioch, which disappears from the record after Paul's puzzling journey in Acts 18:21 ff. Luke's image is an ideal. It is disturbed only at one point, in Ephesus (Acts 20:17 ff.). What does this mean? It probably reflects disturbances after Paul's time, but we cannot be sure that they occurred in Luke's time.

VI. New Directions? (O'Neill)

Recent scholarship has discovered the theology of Luke in its essential forms and content. This theology not only manifests a developed stage in eschatology which contradicts an early date of composition, but it also indicates the practical application of eschatology and a theory of redemptive history to the life of the church in the world—further proof that Luke looks back over an extended development. The church has adjusted itself to an extended existence in the world. It is developing a "Christian bourgeoisie" (M. Dibelius) which is related to the Pastoral letters. The world becomes a place where the church is at home, a notion which Paul sharply rejected (Phil. 3:20). How is this understanding of church and world related to other early Christian documents?

One point of reference is represented by Mark's Gospel. Here the reflection on redemptive history is still much more primitive than in Luke. O'Neill[56a] wants to advance toward Luke from the opposite point. He shares the widespread conviction that the Lucan theology is "early Catholic."[57] He then seeks to date it. "The attempt will be made in this chapter to date Acts by discovering positive theological parallels between Luke and other early Christian writers" (p. 5). His method is correct in that he does not look for contacts between individual ideas but between whole lines of thought, especially of writers who certainly are not dependent on Luke. This procedure can lead to the discovery of a theological milieu. If the dates of one of the respective writers are known, conclusions can be drawn also for Luke. O'Neill passes quickly over Hebrews and Barnabas, and rightly so.[58] He correctly points to I Clem. 5. However, he does not analyze more closely the relationship between Luke and I Clem.[59] This is unfortunate for he touches on the right points. He sees that also I Clem. describes Rome as Paul's goal.[60] The Pastoral letters also are too summarily dismissed. But O'Neill states correctly that they do not know the Lucan work.[61] This makes all the more important the similarity in the understanding of tradition and the attitude toward the world ("Christian bourgeoisie," see above).

But O'Neill obviously considers these points of contact as secondary. He purposely aims for another comparison—with Justin Martyr. His fundamental thesis is that the latter, contrary to current opinion, does *not* know Luke. By an analysis of individual passages,[62] he seeks to support the argument by dating Justin early (p. 17-18). This, however, is not convincing. But the other point is more important: What is the material relationship between Luke and Justin, according to O'Neill?

There is similarity regarding the christological kerygma and the christological titles (e.g., the titular use of Χριστός; cf. *Apol.* 40:6; 31:7, etc.). In similar fashion, both connect the work of Jesus with the work of the apostles. The understanding of the apostolate is also alike, for the apostles appear as a unit and both writers exclude Paul from the apostolic circle. Between resurrection and ascension the risen Lord charges "the apostles" with the world mission beginning in Jerusalem.[63] There is also similarity regarding the theology of the resurrection [64] and the attitude toward Jews and Gentiles: Justin writes an apology for the Romans and a dialogue with a Jew.[65] There is a corresponding reproach of the Jews: they killed the Lord [66] and they do not understand the promise.[67] Like Luke, Justin looks back to the ἐρήμωσις (devastation) of Palestine.[68]

To O'Neill these agreements appear to be so striking that he places Luke in the same generation as Justin and argues that Luke did not write before A.D. 115.[69] This date creates difficulties because of Paul's letters. Since O'Neill does not assume that Luke knew them and yet ignored them, he has to find another explanation. He thinks that Goodspeed has placed the publication of the *Corpus Paulinum* too early and that Justin did not know the letters either, arguing that this was still possible even in A.D. 130.

We may begin our critique by observing that there is no doubt that Justin is early Catholic. But this is true already of Ignatius and I Clem.[70] In this case, however, dating the Lucan work by comparing it with Justin is questionable. A further question must be raised: Is Luke himself early Catholic? The following, among other considerations, are definite marks of early Catholicism: the understanding of the church as an institution of salvation, an institutional definition of the ecclesiastical office (priesthood) and the sacraments, tying the Spirit to the institution and making the tradition secure through apostolic succession. All these features are lacking in Luke or can be found only as initial traces.[71] Above all, the idea of succession is totally absent. One cannot be a successor to the apostles in the sense of continuing their office because their office is uniquely limited to the primitive times of the church. Their heritage cannot be administered in any other way than through faithful preservation of their legacy, the doctrine.[72] In this point Luke differs not only from Justin but also from I Clem. He must be dated accordingly.[73] Despite the many similarities between Luke and Justin, there are also pervasive differences which point to a chronological distance: Luke shows apologetic tendencies, but he does not yet write an "apology." Moreover the style of the debate with the Jews is different. Luke argues by summarizing and in terms of redemptive history; Justin proceeds to describe precise details.[74] The proof from Scripture is developed far beyond the Lucan stage. Justin looks back to the "Memoirs of the Apostles" and quotes them. Luke uses and elaborates them by writing his Gospel and by attempting to provide the final version. Finally, the reception and appropriation of Greek philosophy is completely different.[75]

VII. An Attempt to Place Luke Historically

In comparison with Mark, Luke appears advanced;[76] compared with Justin he appears relatively primitive.[77] This provides us with two opposite points of departure. But Luke himself furnished a more precise indication. He understands himself to be the steward of the tradition. He does not limit himself to handing it on, but he reflects on the *nature* of the tradition by defining his own standpoint in the chain of tradition. He does so explicitly in the prologue, Luke 1:1-4, but implicitly throughout his entire work. He places himself within the third generation.[78] This gives us a decisive criterion. One can give a simple explanation for this determination of his own standpoint—that this merely corresponds to the facts: Luke has received the tradition from the apostles via Paul and therefore stands in the third generation. But this explanation is not sufficient. The synoptic tradition could not have been mediated by Paul, and the school of Paul tends to place its master at the beginning of the chain of tradition.[79] Moreover, it does not explain the peculiar pathos of the Lucan prologue;[80] here Luke not only looks back to earlier generations but he systematizes this retrospect. He makes qualitative distinctions between the three stages of the tradition: eyewitnesses, collectors, and his own final composition. He does not merely want to complement but to replace his predecessors. He offers not a contribution to the tradition but *the* tradition. Only when we realize this can we understand the unity of the two-volume work: the Lord and his apostles, and Paul as the link to the present.

Luke believes that once the tradition is formed it can no longer be developed.[81] This also excludes the idea of an inner development of the church. There is only the one transition from the primitive church to the present Gentile Christian church free from the law.

The idea of the third generation was not invented by Luke. It was widespread in many variations. It is presupposed in the Pastoral letters[82] and developed in I Clem. 42.[83] It is so powerful that it dominates whole generations which historically can no longer be counted among the third generation; that is, it is maintained by Polycarp, Papias, Quadratus, Irenaeus;[84] and later Eusebius made it the principle for his understanding of church history as a whole.[85] Luke's basic concept has determined the image of church and church history until today. The following characteristic holds more or less for all the representatives of the idea of a "third generation": the time of the apostles is seen as an epoch *sui generis*. But between them and us stretches another epoch with a value of its own, the time of the disciples of the apostles. It must be noted that the idea of the "apostolic age," which is sketched here, is in fact the idea of the "apostolic and the postapostolic" age. Here a specific understanding of the tradition is expressed. It is the assumption behind the idea of the apostolic canon and the apostolic rule of faith, both of which dominate the old Catholic theology. Here, in this concept of the third generation, the "twelve apostles" assume their function in church history.[86] It is Luke who translates the idea of the twelve apostles into a structural principle of church history.[87] It has long been recognized that the Lucan representation and connection of events does not simply correspond to reality (period of the apostolic, Jewish-Christian primitive church, then the first conversion of Gentiles by Peter,[88] then the model mission of Paul in the so-called first missionary journey, and the following apostolic Council as the pivotal point). A definite principle underlies this picture, namely, that Luke is separating the original time (*Urzeit*) of the church from the present. But that is not all. The original period is divided into two parts: the period of the *Urgemeinde* (original Jewish-Christian community), and the foundation of the Gentile Christian church. In Luke's account this is the transition from the apostles to Paul. Withholding the apostolic title from Paul does not mean degrading him but necessarily follows from the principle: only as one outside the apostolic circle can Paul be the (only!) link between the initial time and the present.

The exclusive interest in this delineation of the epochs explains Luke's style of presentation. For one thing it explains the consistent lack of reference to the time of the author. Furthermore, it clarifies a fact which has puzzled many: that one actor after another—except Paul and the strange figure represented by the "we"—disappears from the scene: John, Peter, and, following Paul's imprisonment, James, and the Jerusalem church. In the end the only ones left are he who mediates this past to the present, Paul, and the one who represents those who have received the tradition from Paul, "we." The way leads to Rome.

Glancing back once more we recognize that Luke, from the vantage point of the third generation, designs his image of the early church as one which observes the law and thereby maintains the continuity with Israel in terms of redemptive history. The law is a fundamental mark of the primitive period and Luke has to accept the tension this creates: his Paul remains in this continuity until the end of his life. Once more historical facts have been structured by Luke according to his principle of redemptive history. The church appears as a unity precisely through the structuring of its history into two epochs. The church of the present, i.e., the author's own time, is exclusively the Pauline church which lives in the tradition of "the apostles," the received doctrine and the received power of the Spirit; externally, it lives under the conditions of the Roman world. The Jews, however, are dispersed until the consummation of the times of the nations (Luke 21:24). This comprehensive synthesis becomes visible—in retrospect—from the first chapter of Acts onward, beginning with the commission of the apostles (1:8). It also appears when the primitive church recognizes that the way of the gospel leads to the Gentiles, and finally when the Jerusalem church itself disappears from the account.[89] If we now read once more I Clem. 42 [90] the historical place of Luke becomes more or less clear. Still, this leaves us with the puzzle that Paul's letters have not been used.

VIII. Luke, Paul, and the *Corpus Paulinum*

Not only is the historical distance between Luke and the history of Paul considerable, but also the theological difference between the two is great. In Luke the specifically Pauline ideas are missing, such as the theology of the cross,[91] the doctrine of justification,[92] etc. A psychological explanation of these differences does not suffice.[93] They must be understood *historically*. Therefore, it is necessary to include also the theology of Paul's disciples in the comparison. This, in turn, presupposes a tradition-critical analysis of the *Corpus Paulinum* in two respects: (1) the appropriation of Paul's theology by a "school," (2) the function of the formulas of confessions of faith as criteria for theology, for distinguishing between orthodoxy and heresy.[94] Concerning (1) we can understand the existence of deutero-Pauline literature only if we assume that Paul founded an actual school.[95] Traces of the academic work of the school can be found already in the authentic letters.[96] They are also recognizable in the works of the disciples and are especially clear in Col. and Eph.[97] In spite of all the differences within the school there are certain similarities which cannot be explained on the basis of common dependence on Paul, but which reflect a historically conditioned development. With Paul's death not only his teaching but also the image of his work becomes the content of the tradition.[98] Through both, teaching and image, Paul becomes the paradigm of the transmission of the tradition. Equally symptomatic is the view of Israel from the perspective of a church for which Judaism is no longer primarily a practical but a theoretical problem (except for the fact of persecution). The issue is no longer Israel's conversion but the understanding of the theoretical basis of the church: redemptive history, Scripture, the law. The formation of a theoretical literature about these issues is a symptom of the new situation.[99]

Luke participates in this development through his historical writing as a whole [100] and through a twofold specific contribution: the speech by Stephen in Acts 7 and the corresponding speech by Paul in Acts 13:15 ff. In part, therefore, he conforms to the development in the school of Paul.

But he also sets himself off from it by placing the tradition concerning Jesus at the beginning and then (logically) making the twelve apostles the primary bearers of the tradition. This means that he not only *stands alone* within the Pauline tradition, but also that he *chooses to stand off by himself*. This is the price he has to pay for his synthesis.[101]

Did Luke, therefore, consciously ignore the *Corpus Paulinum?* This question arises because neither Paul's letters nor those of his disciples agree with the view of history which Luke desires to convey.[102]

Concerning (2), the question arises why Luke nevertheless holds to Paul. We do not know the biographical and psychological reasons. In any case, Luke needs Paul precisely for his purpose of documenting the unity of the church. His synthesis is possible because factors making for unity exist. The most significant factor, from a literary viewpoint, is the common confession of faith.[103] Already for Paul this is the decisive criterion for theological statements.[104] Of course, it also functions in his school; [105] indeed, it is even further developed there.[106] Luke, too, participates in this development. He uses the received kerygma, in his own version, as a major point in the missionary speeches. He presents the unity of the tradition by showing that in this point Peter and Paul agree.[107]

Vielhauer characterizes Luke's Christology as pre-Pauline. This is correct. But we must add that Paul is working with pre-Pauline formulas and transmits them to his disciples. But perhaps we can be still more precise. Although the formulas do not include the idea of preexistence, we find the idea in Paul.[108] With the exception of Luke, his disciples follow him. Luke stays with the Christology of the synoptic tradition which does not know preexistence. Yet it is hard to imagine that *Luke* did not know the idea. Hence he must have omitted it deliberately. Furthermore, the type of Christology which he represents has also a post-Lucan history, for to it belongs the so-called "Roman" confession of faith, the earlier form of the Apostolic Creed.[109] How closely is this Christology to be linked to the church in Rome? [110]

IX. New Ways of Interpretation?

Until now, exegesis has been accustomed to explaining the famous speeches in Acts primarily as self-contained units. Luke himself invites this interpretation since he uses a specific scheme at least for Peter's missionary speeches to the Jews.[111] But recently O'Neill has called for recognition of the connection between the speeches. He contends that they are interrelated and that the ideas are not repeated but progress in the context of the narrated events.[112] Indeed, cross-references are undeniable; they are especially clear in the analysis of Israel's history in Acts 7 and 13:15 ff.[113] In this sense O'Neill consistently interprets Stephen's speech in its Lucan context; [114] that is, this critique of temple worship presupposes the destruction of the temple in Jerusalem. Luke could outline his picture of earliest Christianity only in the situation after A.D. 70, a Christianity that is faithful to the law, yet is driven out of the temple practically by God himself.[115] This estimate of Stephen's speech is related to the estimate of Justin.[116]

It must be acknowledged that O'Neill's consistent interpretation in terms of redaction-criticism (*Redaktionsgeschichte*) represents important progress. But we must object to the attempt to prove from Stephen's speech that Luke belongs to the time of Justin.[117] The relationship to Israel is not the same in both writings. It is correct to say that for Justin the historical connection between the church and Israel is no longer crucial, and that he reduces the issue between the church and Judaism to the existence of the common Book.[118] But this is not the case with Luke.[119] For him the Old Testament is not only the inspired book to be used for proof from Scripture but also the historical source of the first epoch of redemptive history, the time of the law and the prophets. Precisely because we agree that Stephen's speech belongs in the time after A.D. 70, we cannot put it very long after the destruction of Jerusalem and the temple. Thus here, too, we arrive at the same period and at the same historical situation toward which earlier indications pointed—the time when the "third generation" conceived of the idea of the apostolic age or, roughly speaking, the transition from the first to the second century.

NOTES

1. See the review of J. C. O'Neill's book, *The Theology of Acts* (London, 1961), by H. F. D. Sparks, *JThS* NS XIV (1963), 457 ff.
2. O'Neill; see note 4. Today the attempt to prove that the author was a physician has ended. In this article we shall call the author of Luke–Acts "Luke" irrespective of the actual authorship.
3. In the monumental contribution of America to research in Acts, *The Beginnings of Christianity* I (London, 1922 ff.), Vol. II pp. 358-59.
4. An example of early dating is C. S. C. Williams, *ExpT* LXIV (1953), 283-84, who claims Acts was written A.D. 66-70, *after* Proto-Luke but before the present form of the Third Gospel. On this point, see Paul Schubert's comments in *Neutestamentliche Studien für Rudolf Bultmann, Bh ZNW* XXI (2nd ed. Berlin, 1957), p. 173 n. 19.
5. H. J. Cadbury, *The Making of Luke–Acts* (London, 1927; reprint 1958); *The Book of Acts in History* (London, 1955); M. Dibelius, *Aufsätze zur Apostelgeschichte* (Göttingen, 1951, E. trans.: *Studies in the Acts of the Apostles*, trans. by Mary Ling (New York, 1956). Regarding Luke's theology, see Philipp Vielhauer's article in *EvTh* X (1950-51), 1 ff. (This article appears in the present volume as "On the 'Paulinism' of Acts.") Regarding the summaries, see Ernst Haenchen, *Die Apostelgeschichte* (Göttingen, 1961).
6. C. H. Dodd, *JRomSt* XXXVII (1947) 47 ff.; Paul Winter, *StTh* VIII (1954) 138 ff.; L. Gaston, *ThZ* XVI (1960), 161 ff.
7. Luke 19:11 ff., 39-44; 23:27-31.
8. This is proved not only by Acts 20:17. With regard to the most important moment of Paul's last years there is a notable agreement among the three chief sources: Acts, the Pastorals, and I Clem., as we shall show later.
9. C. K. Barrett, *Luke the Historian in Recent Study* (London, 1961), p. 63.
10. Harnack, Lietzmann, as well as Feine-Behm-Kümmel, *Einleitung in das Neue Testament* 13th ed. Heidelberg, 1963, p. 353; E. trans. by A. J. Mattill as *Introduction to the New Testament* (Nashville, 1966), pp. 338 ff.
11. Edgar J. Goodspeed and John Knox.
12. Goodspeed: around A.D. 90.
13. John Knox, *Marcion and the New Testament* (Chicago, 1942), p. 132: The nonuse of Paul's letters by Luke creates difficulties for *each* hypothesis. If Luke, for instance, wrote around A.D. 60 in Rome, he should at least be expected to know the letter to the Romans. The corresponding problem exists for Corinth, Macedonia, etc. (Knox returns to these problems in his contribution to the present volume, "Acts and the Pauline Letter Corpus.")
14. Günter Klein, *Die zwölf Apostel, FRLANT* NF LIX (Göttingen, 1961), 189-90.
15. O'Neill.
16. W. L. Knox, *The Acts of the Apostles* (Cambridge, 1948), p. 28 n. 1.
17. The main data are collected by Haenchen, *Die Apostelgeschichte*, pp. 1 ff.; H. Conzelmann, *Die Apostelgeschichte* (Tübingen, 1963), pp. 1-2.
18. The following passages are relevant: Acts 5:36 (Josephus, *Ant.* 20:97 ff.); Acts 12:21 (*Ant.* 19:343 ff.); Acts 21:38 (*Ant.* 20:169 ff.; *Bell.* 2:261 ff.). All the other points of contact are vague. Against Luke's dependence from Josephus see *Beginnings of Christianity* II, 355 ff.; Dibelius, *Studies in Acts.* Differently, Knox, *Marcion*, p. 137.
19. This is evident from II Tim. 1:5; 3:11; cf. O'Neill, *The Theology of Acts*, p. 9.
20. Acts 20:17 ff. does not fit with Ignatius, *Eph.* 9:1. Ignatius does not know the crisis which Luke sees approaching the city (actually, saw); cf. Walter Bauer, *Rechtgläubigkeit und Ketzerei im ältesten Christentum* (2nd ed. Tübingen, 1964), pp. 86-87.
21. First part of the first century. Wilhelm Schneemelcher characterizes this writing as a link between the missionary preaching in Acts and the apologetic period. There are traces of the use of Luke–Acts. Hennecke-Schneemelcher, *Neutestamentliche Apokryphen* II (3rd ed, Tübingen, 1964) 59-60.

22. See C. Maurer in Hennecke-Schneemelcher, *Neutestamentliche Apokryphen* I (3rd ed. Tübingen, 1959), 118-19; E. trans. by R. McL. Wilson, *New Testament Apocrypha* (Philadelphia, 1963), I, 180. The document is probably from around the middle of the second century.

23. H. Duensing tends toward a date in the first part of the second century; see Hennecke-Schneemelcher I, 126 ff.; E. trans. 189 ff.

24. Of course the complicated and still confused situation with respect to the history of the tradition must be taken into account; see W. Schrage, *Das Verhältnis des Thomas-Evangeliums zur synoptischen Tradition und zu den koptischen Evangelienübersetzungen* (Berlin, 1964).

25. P. Egerton 2, around A.D. 150; so Joachim Jeremias in Hennecke-Schneemelcher I, 58 ff. (E. trans. 94 ff.).

26. Concerning Marcion, see John Knox, *Marcion*.

27. W. Schneemelcher is skeptical but admits knowledge of Acts by the *Acta Pauli; Apophoreta,* Haenchen Festschrift (Berlin, 1964), pp. 236 ff.

28. The confused statements of the Muratori Fragment are without any historical value. The "Anti-Marcionite" Prologue usually is placed in the time before Irenaeus. But this date has been questioned by Haenchen (*Apostelgeschichte,* pp. 8 ff.), for good reasons. The tradition that Luke is from Antioch originates from this prologue. It is defended by A. Strobel, *ZNW* XLIX (1958) 131 ff.

29. Jack Finegan, *Handbook of Biblical Theology* (Princeton, 1965), pp. 259 ff., 302 ff., 316 ff.

30. An expression such as βασιλεῖς καὶ ἡγεμόνες does not provide guidance either; moreover, it seems to be traditional. Cf. Nicolas of Damascus, *FGrHist* XC, Fr. 137,2.

31. Kümmel, *Introduction,* pp. 92 ff., G. D. Kilpatrick, *JThS* XLIII (1942), 36; MacLean Gilmour, *JThS* XLVII (1948), 143 ff.

32. Regarding "We" and the "Itinerary," cf. A. D. Nock, *Gnomon* XXV (1953), 499; E. Haenchen, *ZThK* LVIII (1961), 329 ff.; *Apostelgeschichte* (see index: Reisetagebuch); Conzelmann, *Apostelgeschichte,* pp. 5-6.

33. See the excellent report by Barrett.

34. They are described excellently by Cadbury, *The Book of Acts in History;* see also E. Trocmé, *Le "Livre des Actes" et l'histoire* (Paris, 1957). In addition to style and content the formal characteristics are to be noted—the dedication and the introduction (cf. Cadbury, *Beginnings of Christianity* II, 489 ff.).

35. It was Eduard Meyer who described Luke as a historian of the common ancient type. He is largely followed by A. Ehrhardt, *StTh* XII (1958), 45 ff., but with a stronger emphasis on the Jewish historiography; cf. Barrett, *Luke the Historian,* pp. 32 ff. For a summary, see Bertil Gärtner, *The Areopagus Speech and Natural Revelation* (Uppsala, 1955), pp. 26 ff. Concerning the ancient theory of historiography, see Lucian's treatise on the subject; cf. G. Avenarius, *Lukians Schrift zur Geschichtsschreibung* (Meisenheim, 1956).

36. Haenchen aptly characterizes the style as "dramatic episode"; good examples are Curtius Rufus (historiography) and Achilles Tatius (novel).

37. Of course, Luke is far superior to the later apocryphal literature about the apostles. The latter uses motifs of the popular novel: travel adventure, intensification of miracles, erotic motifs.

38. Had this been the case, he could easily have taken up the tendencies of contemporary literature where tyranny and royal cult are opposed. Nero and Domitian could have served as paradigms; neither is mentioned.

39. Acts 11:26; cf. the programmatic declaration, "This was not done in a corner," Acts 26:26, before the trip to Rome.

40. Tacitus knows the name "Christ" and also knows that his followers are erroneously called Chrestiani by the people (*Ann.* XV 44).

41. H. Fuchs, *Der geistige Widerstand gegen Rom* (2nd ed. Berlin, 1964).

42. A Roman proconsul becomes a Christian; another, Gallio, exhibits exemplary behavior as a

judge. When Luke criticizes an official, it is not because he serves the state but because he serves it badly: cf. Felix and Festus.

43. This is the impression which he wants to leave with the reader: Paul is preaching in Rome ἀκωλύτως, although as a prisoner. Moreover Luke seems to presuppose a flourishing Roman congregation in his own time. This corresponds to the evidence in I Clem. (in spite of occasional persecution!).

44. W. Richardson, *Studia Evangelica* II, *TU* LXXXVII (Berlin, 1964), 629, thinks that one can hardly imagine this picture for the time after Nero and Domitian. But this is not the case. The Jewish war did not infringe upon the status of the Jews in the empire. They merely had to pay the temple tax to the state. Although Suetonius reports that Domitian fought "Jewish custom" and extracted an especially harsh collection of the *fiscus Judaicus*, this does not mean a general deprivation of rights and has no consequences, especially after the *damnatio* of Domitian. Cf. the complaints about Jewish agitation against Christainity by Justin and in the Martyrdom of Polycarp, etc.

45. Aristides, *Apol.* 15:2. The view that even Jesus was killed by the Jews is found for the first time in Luke 23:25-26; later in Justin, *Dial.* 17; cf. 108, 117.

46. Harnack, *Mission und Ausbreitung des Christentums* (2 vols.; 2nd ed. Leipzig, 1924).

47. This eliminates one definite hypothesis—that "Luke" has collected "proto-Lucan" material when he was a companion of Paul in Caesarea (during Paul's two-year imprisonment).

48. For this term, see William C. Robinson, Jr., *Der Weg des Herrn, Studien zur Geschichte v. Eschatologie im Lukas-Evangelium, ThF* XXXVI, trans. by Gisela and Georg Strecker (Hamburg, 1964). (Privately published as *The Way of the Lord*.)

49. Concerning this "orientation" of the presentation, see esp. O'Neill.

50. Only *once* does Luke go beyond this realm: in the list of nations in Acts 2:9-11. But this wide horizon is not elaborated subsequently in terms of a Gentile mission among those nations. Luke omits the whole expansion in the East (even east of the Jordan!).

51. See Trocmé, *Le "Livre des Actes,"* p. 74.

52. Acts 20, but already Acts 19. Concerning the local color in the account about Ephesus, see Cadbury, *The Book of Acts in History*, pp. 41-42.

53. Cf. the close relations between the two centers, shown by I Clem.; these are also presupposed in the Pastoral letters. Concerning the synthesis, cf. I Clem. 5.

54. For a survey of the actual expansion, see Harnack, *Mission und Ausbreitung* II, 529 ff.; 621 ff.

55. This is especially striking. Luke is mentioned in the (Deutero-Pauline) letter to the Colossians (Col. 4:14), actually addressed to the churches in the Lycos valley.

56. Cf. Illyricum, Rom. 15:19. Moreover, why is there no mention of Titus in Acts?

56a. J. C. O'Neill, *The Theology of Acts* (London, 1961).

57. Vielhauer, Käsemann, Günther Klein.

58. Similarities between the Lucan writings and Hebrews are collected by C. P. M. Jones, *Studies in the Gospels*, R. H. Lightfoot Festschrift (Oxford, 1955), pp. 113 ff.

59. Evidently already under the impression of his hypothesis about Justin.

60. Rome, not Spain, as is often contended! Following P. N. Harrison, *The Problem of the Pastoral Epistles* (Oxford, 1921), pp. 107-8 (". . . goal in the West as opposed to its starting-point in the East"). O'Neill, interprets the expression τὸ τέρμα τῆς δύσεως in terms of Rome. We may add that even if τὸ τέρμα τῆς δύσεως is to be interpreted in terms of Spain (so Karl Holl), the goal which is emphasized is Rome; see Karl Holl, *Gesammelte Aufsätze* II (Tübingen, 1928), 65, n. 2. It must also be noted that I Clem., as well as Acts and the Pastorals, knows only one imprisonment of Paul. Regarding the important passage, I Clem. 42, see below.

61. See above.

62. O'Neill, *The Theology of Acts*, pp. 28 ff. He examines the "synoptic citations" in Justin and concludes that contacts with Luke are not due to his use of Luke's writings but

to the use of a source common to both. Cf. H. Köster, *Synoptische Überlieferung bei den apostolischen Vätern, TU* LXV (Berlin, 1957) 87 ff., who thinks that Justin used a Gospel harmony (the test case for Köster is *Apol.* 16:9-12). On the other side, H. F. D. Sparks, in his instructive review of O'Neill *JThS* NS XIV (1963), 457 ff. seeks to show that Justin does know Luke, especially on the basis of *Apol.* 15:9 (Luke 6:28); 15:12 (Luke 9:25; cf. Mark 8:36); *Dial.* 81:4 (Luke 20:36; cf. Mark 12:25). We may point to the interesting passage about the unknown God, *Apol.* II, 10:6.

63. *Apol.* 31:7; 39:3; 49:5; 50:12.

64. But with Justin the ideas are developed farther. He explicitly distinguishes the resurrection from the Greek doctrine of the soul, *Dial.* 80:4.

65. Cf. Acts 2:25 ff. (*Apol.* 35:5); Acts 4:13 (*Apol.* 39:3); Acts 5:29 and 4:19 (*Dial.* 80:3); Acts 10:41 (*Dial.* 51:2).

66. Luke 23:25-26 (*Apol.* 35:5).

67. Acts 13:27 (*Apol.* 49:4; *Dial.* 110:2).

68. Luke 21:20 ff. (*Apol.* 53:3,9).

69. Is this date suggested by Cadbury, *Beginnings of Christianity* II, 358? It does not naturally follow from the comparison.

70. Barrett, *Luke the Historian,* pp. 68 ff.

71. There is no structured hierarchy. Occasionally, the Spirit is linked to the person of the apostles or to Paul. The first church officials are installed by Paul and Barnabas, who on this occasion are for once called apostles (Acts 14:23; cf. vss. 4, 14). But this is not used to develop a principle of church order. Luke says nothing about the origin of the college of elders in Jerusalem.

72. Well stated by Barrett, *Luke the Historian,* pp. 68, 75. E. Käsemann, *ZThK* LIV (1957), 20-21, puts the evidence in Luke this way: The word is no longer the only criterion for the church, but the church legitimates the word. The apostolic origin of the church office guarantees the legitimacy of the proclamation. But this is a misrepresentation, since Luke does not know a "church office" in Käsemann's sense. The apostles are—as eyewitnesses —guarantors for the faithful transmission of Jesus' teaching and of the image of his work. Barrett correctly states that they are primarily witnesses and not administrators (*op. cit.,* p. 71). Cf. also Schneemelcher (in Hennecke-Schneemelcher II, 7) who says that Luke is still oriented toward the person of the apostles, not toward an abstract "apostolicity."

73. Again we arrive at the period between A.D. 70-90.

74. Luke reduces the images of Judaism to the opposition between the two groups. Justin goes into details. This corresponds to the style of polemics against the heretics as it evolves from the Pastoral letters to Justin. The Pastorals polemicize wholesale, but later one begins to describe the heretics and to develop arguments against them.

75. Luke could have referred to the example of Hellenistic Judaism. In the Areopagus speech he borrows some of its motifs; but he develops them in a more primitive way, quite differently from Justin, and retains more of their original character.

76. Mark understands the time of the church as the time of mourning over the absence of the "bridegroom" and as the time of world mission. He does not yet interpret it positively by means of a thoroughgoing Christology and concept of the church.

77. "Primitive" is, of course, not a value judgment.

78. W. Michaelis, *Einleitung in das Neue Testament* (3rd ed. Bern, 1961), pp. 14 ff.

79. So esp. the Pastorals, see note 101.

80. Cadbury, *Beginnings of Christianity* II, 489 ff.; Günter Klein, "Lukas 1, 1-4 als theologisches Programm," *Zeit und Geschichte,* Bultmann Festschrift (Tübingen, 1964), pp. 193 ff.

81. Luke does not know a *traditio viva* in the sense of Catholic theology.

82. It is already expressed in the fact that these are put forward as letters from the apostle to his disciples. Thereby the author places himself in the ranks of the disciples.

83. I Clem. 42:1-4: Ὁι ἀπόστολοι ἡμῖν εὐαγγελίσθησαν ἀπὸ τοῦ κυρίου Ἰησοῦ, Ἰησοῦς ὁ Χριστὸς ἀπὸ τοῦ θεοῦ ἐξεπέμφθη. Ὁ Χριστὸς οὖν ἀπὸ τοῦ θεοῦ καὶ οἱ

ἀπόστολοι ἀπὸ τοῦ Χριστοῦ· ἐγένοντο οὖν ἀμφότερα εὐτάκως ἐκ θελήματος θεοῦ. Παραγγελίας οὖν λάβοντες καὶ πληροφορηθέντες διὰ τῆς ἀναστάσεως τοῦ κυρίου ἡμῶν Ἰησοῦ Χριστοῦ καὶ πιστωθέντες ἐν τῷ λόγῳ τοῦ θεοῦ, μετὰ πληροφορίας πνεύματος ἁγίου ἐξῆλθον εὐαγγελιζόμενοι, τὴν βασιλείαν τοῦ θεοῦ μέλλειν ἔρχεσθαι. Κατα χώρας οὖν καὶ πόλεις κηρύσσοντες καθίστανον τὰς ἀπαρχὰς αὐτῶν, δοκιμάσαντες τῷ πνεύματι, εἰς ἐπισκόπους καὶ διακόνους τῶν μελλόντων πιστεύειν.

84. Only artificially and by a tour de force can Irenaeus count himself with the third generation: as a child he saw the aging Polycarp who, as a child, saw the aging apostle John.

85. Eusebius, *Hist. Eccl.* III, 32:7-8, reports about Hegesippus: "The same man, relating the events of the times, says that the church continued until then as a pure and uncorrupt virgin. If there were any who tried to corrupt the sound doctrine of the preaching of salvation, they still hid in a dark hiding-place. But when the sacred chorus of the apostles in various ways departed from life, as well as the generation of those who were deemed worthy to hear their inspired wisdom, then also the faction of godless error arose by deceit of teachers of another doctrine. These, since none of the apostles (sic!) survived, henceforth attempted shamelessly to preach their 'knowledge falsely called' against the preaching of the truth." (Quoted from R. M. Grant, *Second-Century Christianity* [London, 1957], p. 61) This report does not give Hegesippus' view of the past but that of Eusebius. This is evident from a comparison with Hegesippus' original text, *Hist. Eccl.* IV, 22:4-5. For Hegesippus, only James and his succession is significant, not "the apostles." For an analysis, see the Göttingen dissertation by H. Kemmler, *Hegesipp, ein judenchristlicher Apologet* (1965).

86. G. Klein, *Die zwölf Apostel,* maintains that the term and the idea of the "twelve apostles" as such was Luke's own creation. But while it is correct that historically the twelve and the apostles were not identified, they were identified already before Luke, in Mark (Mark 6:7,30; cf. 3:14) as well as in Q (Matt. 19:28); cf. also Matt. 10:2; Rev. 21:14.

87. The comparison with Ignatius of Antioch is instructive. *Magn.* 6:1; 13:1 (cf. I Clem. 46:6); *Trall.* 3:1; 7:1; 12:2; *Rom.* 4:3. In Ignatius the time dimension is missing. He develops the view of unity onesidedly.

88. Occasional remarks disclose that the events took a different course; cf. esp. Acts 11:20.

89. It is significant that Acts ends with a dispute between Paul and the *Jews* in Rome. Nothing is said about Jewish *Christians* in Rome, although Luke is aware of their existence. O'Neill wants to explain this by arguing that the main point of the Lucan account (since Paul's inauguration of the mission) is not the expansion of Christianity but the separation of the church from the synagogue, the establishing of the church as an independent entity. There is truth to this view. But precisely for an independent church it is important to remain in continuity with Israel in terms of redemptive history. Until the last chapter Paul remains a Jew faithful to the law.

90. See note 83.

91. Properly emphasized by C. H. Dodd and others.

92. Of course Luke is familiar with justification by faith, but not in its Pauline profile. This can be seen when he alludes to Pauline phrases in Acts 13:38-39. Here Pauline terminology is mixed with the un-Pauline idea of forgiveness of sins. In Acts 15:11 it is Peter who speaks in "Pauline" terms.

93. This is attempted by Walter Eltester, "Lukas und Paulus," *Eranion,* H. Hommel Festschrift (Tübingen, 1961), pp. 1 ff., who says that being Greek, Luke did not understand the Jewish motifs in Paul's theology. This raises the question, however, why Paul should have been successful as a missionary among the Greeks. Furthermore, Luke well understood other Jewish ideas, e.g., the doctrine of the resurrection of the dead. He emphasizes that it is maintained by the Pharisees and is "strange" to the Greeks (Acts 17:18-20, 31-32).

94. H. Köster, "Häretiker im Urchistentum als theologisches Problem," *Zeit und Geschichte,* Bultmann Festschrift (Tübingen, 1965), pp. 61 ff.

95. Moreover, this assumption is indispensable also for the reconstruction of his mission. Paul was not a lonely herald wandering from town to town. He organized centers of the mission (cf. the expansion of Christianity in Asia). This required training collaborators, who received their own tasks. If Paul, when faced with a critical situation, dispatches Timothy and Titus to Corinth, they must have possessed a large measure of theological education. We must think also of the collaboration over several years between Paul and Apollos, both trained in Hellenistic Jewish theology. This means *eo ipso* the foundation of a "theological faculty" (of course in terms of those times). Most likely we should think of Ephesus as the place of this academic activity (cf. the note about the school of Tyrannus, Acts 19:9).

96. Sometimes "blocks" emerge which are only loosely connected with their contexts. They partly spell out ideas which go far beyond the topic that surrounds them. In these passages we find ideas of the Hellenistic Jewish theology, esp. its "wisdom," cf., e.g., I Cor. 2:6 ff.; 10:1 ff.; 11:2 ff., 13; II Cor. 3:7 ff.

97. Eph. meditatively expands the ideas of Col.

98. The combination of doctrine and image is found in Acts and the Pastorals, nor is I Clem. 5 to be overlooked. Here an essential element is martyrdom. Luke, however, cannot speak of it because of his apologetic purpose, but he gives clear enough pointers to the Christian reader.

99. The oldest document of this type stems from Paul himself, Rom. 9–11. But the difference is evident. For Paul the dispute is still acute, while the post-Pauline writings view it from a distance; cf. esp. Eph. and Heb.

100. Cf. the well-known scheme according to which Paul always begins his mission in the synagogue. That this is a theological program for Luke is evident from Acts 13:46; 18:4-6 and esp. 28:26-28.

101. We must compare him with the Pastorals in which Paul is the first link in the chain of tradition. Indeed, the Pastorals do not know a general apostolic tradition. For them "apostolic" means "Pauline." In Luke, however, Paul by necessity moves into the second link in the chain.

102. Of course he could still have used the letters as sources. But we have no knowledge of his needs and methods. The allusions in Luke 1:1-4 do not allow us to make a definite judgment. Goodspeed thinks that the publication of Acts inspired the editing of the *Corpus Paulinum*. To this, John Knox correctly answered that the Paul of Acts does not write any letters (*Marcion*, pp. 134-35). [The reader may want to compare this view with that of Ernst Käsemann's essay in this volume.]

103. The exact text is not yet authoritatively fixed. Nevertheless, fixed patterns, contents, and phrases are in existence. A guideline is provided in Rom. 10:9.

104. This could be shown also through an analysis of Romans where the train of thought is purposely attached to the traditional credo; cf. 3:21 ff.; 4:25 ff. (together with the end of chap. 8); 6:1 ff.; 14:7 ff.; see also I Cor. 15:3 ff.; I Thess. 4:13 ff., etc.

105. Especially clear in Col. 2:6 ff., where we can see not only the impact of Rom. 6 and the christological formula hidden in it, but where the formula itself continues to function directly. The same is true of Eph. 2:5 ff. Extensive use of formulas is made in the Pastorals.

106. Especially in the "scheme of revelation" (see N. A. Dahl, *Neutestamentliche Studien für R. Bultmann* [Berlin, 1954], pp. 4 ff.)! It seems to have been sketched in the Deutero-Pauline writings following I Cor. 2:6 ff.; see Col. 1:26-27; Eph. 3:4 ff.; II Tim. 1:9 ff.; Titus 1:2-3; Rom. 16:25-26 (post-Pauline!); I Peter 1:18 ff.

107. Besides Peter's speeches, see those of Paul in Acts 13:15 ff.

108. Preexistence is not found in any christological formula except in the cosmologically oriented passage of I Cor. 8:6. It is expressed in hymns, which have a wholly different *Sitz im Leben* and, correspondingly, have a different theological function.

109. Karl Holl, *Gesammelte Aufsätze* II, 115 ff.

110. Incidentally, how does the so-called *Testimonium Flavianum*, with its explicitly Lucan christological formulation, get into the text of Josephus (*Ant.* 18:63 ff.)?

111. Dibelius, *Aufsätze zur Apostelgeschichte* (E. trans., *Studies in the Acts of the Apostles*); Ulrich Wilckens, *Die Missionsreden der Apostelgeschichte* (Neukirchen, 1961); C. F. Evans, *JThS* NS VII (1956), 25 ff.; E. Schweizer, *ThZ* XIII (1957), 1 ff. [Schweizer's article is included in the present volume.]

112. The author recalls with pleasure the guest lecture in Göttingen by Paul Schubert in which he argued for a similar program and demonstrated it on the basis of Paul's Areopagus speech.

113. J. T. Townsend, "The Speeches in Acts," *AThR* XLII (1960), 150 ff.

114. O'Neill, *The Theology of Acts*, pp. 71 ff.

115. According to O'Neill, the degree of the church's emancipation from Judaism corresponds exactly to the external relations between the two as presented in the account in Acts 6–8.

116. *Dial.* 117; cf. *Orac. Sib.* IV 8 ff.

117. Occasionally, O'Neill himself seems to sense the distance; cf. p. 112.

118. O'Neill, *The Theology of Acts*, p. 92.

119. Against O'Neill, p. 90, who says, "Acts presents a theology in which the church has abandoned the people and appropriated the book." Rather, it is typical for Luke that the historical break between the church and the Jews allows for the continuity to emerge between Israel and the church in terms of redemptive history.